EFFICIENT AUDITING
OF PRIVATE COMPANIES

A guide to audit planning,
implementation and control under the ISAs

EFFICIENT AUDITING
OF PRIVATE COMPANIES

A guide to audit planning,
implementation and control under the ISAs

SWAT UK Limited

Third Edition

Wolters Kluwer (UK) Limited
145 London Road
Kingston upon Thames
Surrey KT2 6SR
Tel: 0844 561 8166
Fax: 020 8247 1184
E-mail: customerservices@cch.co.uk
www.cch.co.uk

This publication is sold with the understanding that neither the publisher nor the authors, with regard to this publication, are engaged in rendering legal or professional services. The material contained in this publication neither purports, nor is intended to be, advice on any particular matter.

Although this publication incorporates a considerable degree of standardisation, subjective judgment by the user, based on individual circumstances, is indispensable. This publication is an 'aid' and cannot be expected to replace such judgment.

Neither the publisher nor the authors can accept any responsibility or liability to any person, whether a purchaser of this publication or not, in respect of anything done or omitted to be done by any such person in reliance, whether sole or partial, upon the whole or any part of the contents of this publication.

Views expressed in this publication are the author's and are not necessarily those of his firm or of the publisher.

British Library Cataloguing-in-Publication Data

A catalogue record for this book is available from the British Library.

Typeset by YHT Ltd, London.
Printed and bound in the UK by Hobbs the Printers.

Contents

Contents

Preface

The aim of this book is to provide the reader with a guide on how to deal effectively with the audit of private companies. The book is intended to give practical guidance based on SWATUK's experience of dealing with a wide range of firms from sole practitioners to large multi-partner practices. This is not just another textbook on how to apply International Standards on Auditing (UK & Ireland) (the ISAs).

The third edition of *Efficient Auditing of Private Companies* has been extensively rewritten to meet the requirements of the ISAs and reflects the wide experience SWATUK has in how the ISAs should be applied to private companies. When the ISAs were first implemented the focus of many firms was on compliance; however, we are now a few years down the line and most firms are now looking to improve efficiency whilst maintaining compliance. The practical guidance and examples in this book are intended to help firms with that process.

The International Audit & Assurance Standards Board's clarity project is now complete and it is expected that the Auditing Practices Board in the UK will adopt the clarified ISAs for accounting periods commencing 15 December 2009. However, this means that they will not apply until December 2010 year ends and that audit work on these audits in most cases will not start until 2011. There is therefore plenty of life left in the existing ISAs and it is vital that firms are not only complying with the current ISAs but doing so cost-effectively before the new clarity versions come into force.

We continue to hope that this book will enable practices to comply with the requirements of Audit Regulation and the ISAs whilst making a profit at the same time.

Andrew Holton
Divisional Director – Publications
SWATUK Limited

Part I   Planning

Chapter 1 Introduction

1.1 The purpose of this book

As the title of this book suggests, its objective is to enable auditors to carry out audits in an efficient manner. To be efficient an audit needs to be effective both in terms of cost and in achieving the audit objectives. The process of performing an efficient and effective audit can be divided into the following three parts:

I) planning;

II) implementation; and

III) completion.

This book has been divided into three sections with these headings to assist reference during the course of an audit. The guidance in each section is based on the experience gained by SWATUK from working with a wide range of firms and does not purport to represent the views of the Financial Reporting Council or the Auditing Practices Board.

Part I of this book considers the steps that should be taken to enable the auditor to plan an efficient and effective audit. Paragraph 2 of International Standard on Auditing (UK and Ireland) ('ISA') 300 *Planning an audit of financial statements* states: 'The auditor should plan the audit work so that the engagement will be performed in an effective manner'. The important point to note here is that the audit must be performed 'in an effective manner'. Inadequate attention paid to the planning of the audit may result in a lot of wasted time and effort, and very often means that some risk areas that should be addressed are missed. Worse than this, the firm may not comply fully with Auditing Standards. These are mandatory and obviously there would be implications for the firm's audit registration should the firm receive a compliance visit from either the QAD, AIU or ACCA Monitoring Unit. It is therefore absolutely essential that adequate time and effort is put into the planning of each job.

Under the old Statements of Auditing Standards ('SASs'), many practices considered planning to be a necessary evil, undertaken as a cursory task at the beginning of the job or, even worse, as a form-filling exercise at the end. Things have improved a little since the introduction of ISAs but, even now, this view still prevails in some firms. It is important that everyone is committed to the planning process and understands the benefits to be gained from effective planning. These many benefits include the ability to:

- identify and concentrate on the problem and high risk areas;

- help the auditor decide on ways of auditing particular areas;

- help the auditor assign work to the appropriate level of staff, with the relevant experience;

- enable the auditor to communicate to staff what work they have to do and which working papers are expected;

- avoid, or at least predict, the possible overruns on budgeted fees and ensure that the audit is carried out efficiently and effectively;

- facilitate the control and review of work; and

- ensure that the auditor is able to reach an appropriate audit opinion.

In many respects, it is the last two points that are the most important. Many people do not invest the necessary time and effort in planning because they believe that they have insufficient time. This is particularly true in the current economic environment, where many clients are putting their accountants under increasing pressure to reduce or maintain fee levels. Many people are tempted to just wade in and only appreciate later that this will usually result in more work being undertaken. In addition, it is important to note that a job that has been properly planned is much easier and quicker to review.

Since the changeover – towards the end of 2004 – from Statements of Auditing Standards to International Standards on Auditing (UK and Ireland), there has been much greater emphasis on documenting the auditor's knowledge of the client and the potential risks arising therefrom. Much of this work feeds directly into the audit planning, and so this area is more important than ever in achieving a compliant yet efficient audit.

1.2 Auditing standards and scope of this book

When undertaking an audit, the auditor must comply with Auditing and Ethical Standards and take account of a good deal of guidance material. These consist mainly of:

- International Standards on Auditing (UK and Ireland);
- APB Ethical Standards;
- APB Practice Notes;
- APB Bulletins;
- Statements of Standards for Reporting Accountants;
- Audit Regulations; and
- various other publications.

1.2.1 International Standards on Auditing (UK and Ireland) ('ISAs')

ISAs and the International Standard on Quality Control (ISQC) (UK and Ireland) 1 contain basic principles and essential procedures, together with related guidance in the form of explanatory and other material, including appendices. ISAs apply to all audits of financial statements for periods commencing on or after 15 December 2004.

The focus of ISQC 1 is directed more towards general firm-wide procedures rather than those in respect of individual audits. Therefore, whilst this book refers to ISQC 1 where appropriate, it does not purport to cover all of its requirements.

1.2.2 APB Ethical Standards

Ethical Standards ('ESs') contain basic principles and essential procedures (identified in bold type), together with related guidance in the form of explanatory and other material. The standards cover the integrity, objectivity and independence of auditors and apply in the audit of financial statements.

The original ESs applied to audits of financial statements for periods commencing on or after 15 December 2004. Revised ESs issued in April 2008 become effective for audits of financial statements for periods commencing on or after 6 April 2008.

1.2.3 APB Practice Notes

Practice Notes are intended to assist auditors in applying Auditing Standards of general application to particular circumstances and industries. Practice Notes are persuasive rather than prescriptive. However, they are indicative of good practice, even though they may be developed without the full process of consultation and exposure used for APB Standards.

This book deals with the general principles of auditing, and accordingly does not cover the specific requirements of auditing any particular type of entity or industry. However, auditors of specialised entities should still find much that this book has to say useful. Practice Notes dealing solely with issues pertaining to audits in the Republic of Ireland are outside the scope of this book.

1.2.4 APB Bulletins

Bulletins are issued to provide auditors with timely guidance on new or emerging issues. Like Practice Notes, Bulletins are also persuasive rather than prescriptive, and indicative of good practice.

Many Bulletins cover matters pertaining to specialist audit reports such as those relating to interim statements, public sector and listed entities, etc, revised and other specific reports. These are outside the scope of this book, as are Bulletins solely pertaining to audits in the Republic of Ireland.

1.2.5 Statements of Standards for Reporting Accountants

These are also issued by the APB and are outside the scope of this book.

1.2.6 Audit Regulations

The Audit Regulations are published by the ICAEW on behalf of the ICAEW, ICAS and ICAI and must be complied with. Provisions relating to firms as a whole rather than to individual audit principals are outside the scope of this book.

1.2.7 Other publications

The various Institutes, the ACCA and the CCAB also publish a number of useful newsletters and guidance for auditors.

There are also various Acts of Parliament and Statutory Instruments which contain general rules for the appointment, function and removal of auditors, and rules governing which entities require an audit, such as the Companies Act and Charities Act. Some entities are governed by their own special legislation, which may also state whether they are required to be audited. This book assumes that the auditor has checked the relevant legislative and other requirements and has determined that the entity in question does, indeed, require an audit.

Independent examinations, assurance engagements, interim statements, abbreviated audit reports and audit reports not on financial statements are all outside the scope of this book.

1.3 Getting started

Not only must auditors not wade straight into the audit, but they must also not rush into the planning process without adequate preparation. Obviously, the first step is to consider independence and acceptance procedures so as to ensure that the practice can actually undertake the assignment. This issue will be addressed in more detail in Chapter 2. The second step is to ensure that there is sufficient background information on the client and that sufficient time is spent updating and reviewing this information.

The stages of audit planning have been set out below and will then be dealt with in more detail within Part I. Each stage must be properly documented:

a) assessing client acceptance and auditor independence;

b) reviewing correspondence with the client;

c) updating and reviewing the permanent file;

d) recording or updating the systems notes, and assessing the design and implementation of controls;

e) undertaking preliminary analytical procedures;

f) assessing risk at the financial statement and assertion levels and determining suitable responses to those risks;

g) considering the audit approach that should be taken on each individual section of the audit;

h) assessing materiality;

i)   determining which staff should undertake which tasks and for how long they will be needed;

j)   documenting the overall audit strategy and plan; and

k)   review and authorisation of the planning by the partner.

There are several points during the audit where added input is required from the client in order to complete the planning process. This means in practice that audit planning cannot usually be completed in a single step and may require at least three stages. As the planning should be completed before the core audit work is carried out, this means starting the audit planning early, ideally before the client's year end.

Whilst there is plenty of flexibility in the order in which the elements of audit planning may be completed, the following flowchart gives a suggested order of attack.

1.3.1 The planning process

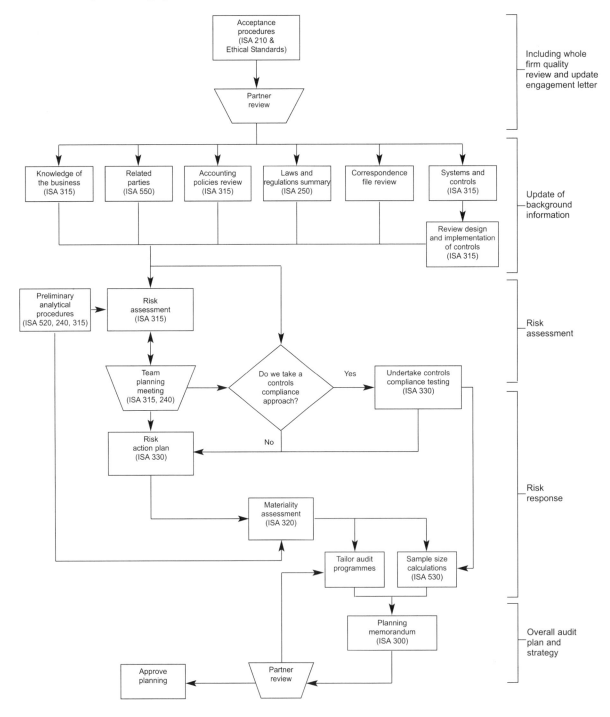

Chapter 2 Acceptance procedures

2.1 Introduction

Paragraph 14 of ISA 220 *Quality control for audits of historical financial information* requires the engagement partner to ensure – before commencing any audit engagement – that appropriate procedures regarding the acceptance and continuance of the audit have been followed and that the conclusions reached are appropriate and have been documented. ISA 300 *Planning an audit of financial statements* notes that for continuing engagements, these procedures often occur shortly after or in connection with the completion of the previous audit.

ISA 300 goes on to state that the auditor's consideration of client continuance and ethical requirements, including independence, occurs throughout the audit as conditions and circumstances occur. It is therefore clear that such work should not be 'set in stone', and should be monitored and reassessed throughout the audit as required.

ISA 220.16 notes that such procedures include the consideration of:

- the integrity of the owners, key management and those charged with governance (for example, directors or trustees);

- whether the audit team is competent to perform the engagement, and whether its members have sufficient time and resources. This is particularly important where the practice is dealing with either a large entity or an entity working in a specialist area; and

- whether the firm and the audit team can comply with ethical requirements.

One of the main reasons for such preliminary procedures is to ensure that the engagement partner and the firm as a whole are independent. Auditors must, if they are to undertake a proper audit, be able to demonstrate that they have been objective. This objectivity can only be assured if a firm is, and is seen to be, independent.

Objectivity is the state of mind which has regard to all considerations relevant to the task in hand, but no other considerations. Both objectivity and independence are key concepts in the revised APB Ethical Standards (ES).

ES1 (Revised) *Integrity, objectivity and independence* requires firms with more than three partners to designate one of them as ethics partner with responsibility for:

- the adequacy of the firm's ethical policies and procedures;

- compliance with Ethical Standards;

- communication to partners and staff within the firm; and

- the provision of related guidance to individual partners.

ES1 expects firms with only two or three partners to regularly discuss ethical issues amongst themselves to ensure that a consistent approach is adopted and that the ESs are followed. Sole practitioners are expected to take advice on difficult or judgmental matters either from their professional body's ethics helpline or through discussion with a practitioner from another firm. In all cases, it is important that such discussions are documented.

In order for both the practice and the individual to demonstrate independence, ESs identify a number of specific issues that need to be addressed. A firm's independence and objectivity can best be assessed by completion of a questionnaire at the start of each assignment. An example form is shown below.

Client:		Ref:
Year end:		**C1.1**
File no:		

ACCEPTANCE PROCEDURES

Regulations state that 'a Registered Auditor shall not accept appointment or continue as auditor if the firm has any interest likely to conflict with carrying out the audit properly' and ISA 200.4.1 requires compliance with APB Ethical Standards.

This questionnaire assumes a knowledge of APB ethical standards. It must be completed annually for all clients to ensure that the standards have been complied with.

Note whether advantage is being taken of ES – Provisions Available for Small Entities. YES / NO (delete as appropriate)

		Yes	**No**

1   ***Undue dependence on an audit client***

    a)   Do the total fees for this client/group of clients exceed:

        i)   10% of the annual fee income of the audit firm or the part of the firm by reference to which the audit engagement partner's profit share is calculated?   ☐   ☐

        ii)   15% of the annual fee income of the audit firm or the part of the firm by reference to which the audit engagement partner's profit share is calculated?   ☐   ☐

    b)   Is this client/group of clients highly prestigious?   ☐   ☐

    c)   Is this client/group a public interest client or group?   ☐   ☐

    Notes
1. APB Ethical Standards require an external independent quality control review where the regular annual fee income will regularly exceed 10%.
2. Where fees will regularly exceed 15%, this is an insurmountable threat and the firm must resign.
3. The above figures become 5% and 10% respectively for listed or public interest entities.
4. A public interest client is one that would attract national attention if a problem were publicised.

2   ***Loans to or from a client; guarantees; overdue fees***

    a)   Do you or any of your staff have any loan or guarantees to or from the client?   ☐   ☐

    b)   Are there any overdue fees for any services?   ☐   ☐

3   ***Goods and services: hospitality***

    Have you or any of your staff accepted any material goods or services on favourable terms or received undue hospitality from the company?   ☐   ☐

4   ***Litigation***

    Is there any actual or threatened litigation between yourself and the client in relation to fees, audit work, or other work?   ☐   ☐

5   *Family or other personal relationships*

Do you or any of your staff have any personal or family connections with the company and its officers?   ☐   ☐

6   *Ex-partners or senior employees*

a)   Has any officer of the company been a partner or senior employee in the practice?   ☐   ☐

b)   Is the partner or any senior employee on the audit joining or involved in substantive negotiations with the client?   ☐   ☐

7   *Mutual business interest*

Do you or any of your partners or staff have any mutual business interests with the client or with an officer or employee of the client?   ☐   ☐

8   *Beneficial interests and trusteeships*

Do you or any of your staff have any financial involvement in the company in respect of the following:

i)   any beneficial interest in shares or other investments?   ☐   ☐

ii)   any beneficial interest in trusts?   ☐   ☐

iii)   any trustee investments, nominee shareholdings or 'bare trustee' shareholdings?   ☐   ☐

iv)   any trusteeships in a trust that holds shares in an audit client?   ☐   ☐

9   *Associated firms*

Are you or your staff associated with any other practice or organisation which has any dealings with the company?   ☐   ☐

10   *Provision of other services, specialist valuations and advocacy by the firm or a network firm*

Note
A network firm is any entity that is:
(i) controlled by the audit firm; or
(ii) under common control, ownership or management; or
(iii) otherwise affiliated or associated with the audit firm through the use of a common name or through the sharing of significant common professional resources.

a)   Are any services in relation to the management of the company performed by the firm or a network firm?   ☐   ☐

b)   Are any accounting services performed for the company, such as preparation of the statutory accounts from trial balance, bookkeeping or payroll services?   ☐   ☐

c)   Do the accounts include any specialist valuations carried out by the firm or a network firm?   ☐   ☐

d)   Is either the firm or a network firm currently acting for the client as an advocate in any adversarial proceeding or situation, such as a hearing before the Commissioners?   ☐   ☐

e)   Has the firm or a network firm been involved in the design, provision or implementation of any IT systems?   ☐   ☐

f)   Does the firm or a network firm provide advice on taxation matters or undertake tax compliance work for the client?   ☐   ☐

g)   Have any other services been provided to the client that may cause a threat to the firm's objectivity or independence?   ☐   ☐

11   **Rotation of audit engagement partner**

Have you been acting as the audit engagement partner for more than ten years?   ☐   ☐

Note

There are specific requirements in ES3: Long association with the audit engagement *that apply to listed companies. See paragraphs 12 to 18 of ES3.*

12   **Adequate resources**

a)   Are there any indications that the engagement team is not competent or does not have the necessary time and resources?   ☐   ☐

b)   Are there any indications that the firm or engagement team will not be able to demonstrate compliance with ethical requirements?   ☐   ☐

13   **Proper performance**

a)   Are there any aspects of the client, or other factors, that will adversely affect the firm's ability to perform the audit properly?   ☐   ☐

b)   Are there any issues concerning the integrity of the principal owners, key management or those charged with governance of the entity?   ☐   ☐

Safeguards

Where any of the above questions have been answered 'yes', specify what safeguards are proposed to maintain integrity and independence, and to ensure the availability of resources and the ability to perform the audit properly.

_____

_____

_____

_____

_____

_____

_____

_____

_____

Conclusion

Having regard to any safeguards identified above, I am satisfied that appropriate procedures regarding the acceptance and continuance of this client relationship and audit engagement have been followed, and that the conclusions reached in this regard are appropriate and have been properly documented. In arriving at this conclusion, I confirm that I have:

a)   obtained all relevant information from the firm (and, where applicable, network firms) to identify and evaluate circumstances and relationships that may create a threat to independence;

b)   evaluated information on identified breaches, if any, of the firm's independence policies and procedures to determine whether they create a threat to independence for this audit engagement;

c)   taken appropriate action to eliminate such threats or reduce them to an acceptable level by applying safeguards;

d)   documented the conclusion on independence and any relevant discussions within the firm that support this view; and

e)   informed the client of all significant facts and matters that bear upon the firm's objectivity and independence.

Partner _____   Date _____

Consultation (to be completed where appropriate)

In my opinion the steps proposed are sufficient to maintain independence and to ensure the availability of resources and the ability to perform the audit properly.

Second Partner _____   Date _____

The remainder of this chapter considers independence issues in the same order as the subjects appear on the questionnaire.

2.2 Undue dependence on an audit client

ES4 (Revised) *Fees, remuneration and evaluation policies, litigation, gifts and hospitality* suggests that there is a potential independence problem due to a self-interest threat where the total fee income either to the practice as a whole, or to the profit pool of the partner concerned, from one client or group of connected clients exceeds 15 per cent of the gross practice income. For listed or other public interest companies the equivalent figure is 10 per cent. Where it is expected that this level will be regularly breached (that is, ignoring one-off extras), the firm should resign as auditor.

The Standard goes on to say that independence should be considered at levels of five per cent below these – that is, at 10 per cent and 5 per cent respectively. In these instances, the partner should inform the firm's ethics partner, and consider whether appropriate safeguards need to be applied to maintain objectivity and independence. For unlisted entities that fall into the 10-15 per cent bracket, an external independent quality control review of the audit must be undertaken before the audit report is finalised.

The practice must also consider its position where the client is highly prestigious or has a high profile, even though the fee may not be particularly high, as there is a greater threat in this instance that the auditor will not wish to 'upset' the client.

From an audit point of view, the first thing that should be done is to obtain details of all of connected clients. This will not only be clients within a group but also those clients that are in the same sphere of influence. In some cases, the clients may not even have common ownership (note that the 15 per cent rule does not apply in such scenarios) but may just be connected via, for example, a trade association that has a tendency to recommend a particular auditor to its members. In this situation, the risk would be that if one audit client were to be upset, he or she could influence the others. This type of information, once obtained, should be placed on the permanent file and reviewed on an annual basis.

Having completed this list, the auditor needs to establish the level of the relevant fees, remembering that this will be the total fees for the client, not just the audit fee. It will also include any associated fees that might be obtained – for example, from the provision of financial services. The audit partner should then consider whether there is a potential problem. If there is, the practice should arrange an external independent quality control review by an organisation such as SWATuk Limited.

2.3 Loans to or from an audit client; guarantees; overdue fees

The existence of any financial relationships – be they loans, guarantees or overdue fees – will obviously have an impact on the independence of the practice as a whole and also on the partners and staff. ES2 (Revised) *Financial, business, employment and personal relationships* addresses these matters and contains a number of outright prohibitions.

2.3.1 Overdue fees

The issue that occurs most often is that of overdue fees. The particular concern with overdue fees is that where a significant part is not paid before the auditor's report on the financial statements for the following year is due to be issued, a self-interest threat to the auditor's objectivity and independence is created, because worries about recoverability of the fees could, for example, cause the practice to back down on a contentious issue when otherwise it would not have done.

The auditor should review the firm's own debtors' ledger to ensure that there are no amounts outstanding from a client when their audit commences. If there are overdue amounts that cannot be regarded as trivial, the audit engagement partner, in consultation with the ethics partner, should consider whether the firm can continue as auditor or whether it is necessary to resign. Where the outstanding fees are in dispute and the amount involved is significant, the threats to the auditor's objectivity and independence may be such that no safeguards can eliminate them or reduce them to an acceptable level. If the firm does not resign from the audit engagement, appropriate safeguards should be applied – for example, independent second partner review and the ethics partner should be informed.

2.3.2 Financial interest in an audit client or affiliate thereof

Apart from a limited number of specific exceptions, the audit firm, or any partner in the audit firm, or a person in a position to influence the audit or an immediate family member of such a person may hold:

a) any direct financial interest in an audit client or affiliate thereof;

b) any indirect financial interest in an audit client or affiliate thereof, where the investment is material to the audit firm or the individual, or to the intermediary; or

c) any indirect financial interest in an audit client or affiliate thereof, where the person holding it has both:

   i)   the ability to influence the investment decisions of the intermediary; and

   ii) actual knowledge of the existence of the underlying investment in the audited entity.

In this context, 'immediate family' means a spouse or equivalent (that is, a partner) or a dependent. 'Indirect financial interests' include holdings held by a partner in the audit firm who is not in a position to influence the conduct and outcome of the audit, or an immediate family member of such a partner, in an authorised unit or investment trust, an open-ended investment company or an equivalent investment vehicle that the firm audits. Such interests can therefore be held as long as they are not material to the individual, and the individual has no influence over the investment decisions of the audit client.

The specific exceptions to this prohibition are detailed in (a) to (d) below.

a) Where an immediate family member of a partner, who is not in a position to influence the conduct and outcome of the audit, holds a financial interest in an audited entity or affiliate thereof due to its compensation arrangements (for example, a share option scheme, where the shares have not vested), or an interest in a decision made, or a transaction undertaken, by an entity with whom they have a contractual business or employment arrangement (for example, a partnership agreement). However, where such interests are significant or the relevant partner has close working contacts with the engagement team, the ethics partner must consider whether any safeguards need to be put in place.

b) Where any of those persons listed above are members or shareholders of an audited entity as a result of membership requirements, or equivalent. In this case, the audit firm must ensure that only the minimum number of shares needed are held, and that this shareholding is not material to either the audited entity or the individual. Such a shareholding must be disclosed to the audit client.

c) Where a direct or indirect financial interest is held in a trustee capacity by a person in a position to influence the conduct and outcome of the audit, or by an immediate family member of such a person, provided that:

   i)   the person is are not an identified potential beneficiary of the trust; and

   ii) the financial interest held by the trust in the audited entity is not material to the trust; and

   iii) the trust is not able to exercise significant influence over the audited entity or an affiliate of the audited entity; and

   iv) the relevant person does not have significant influence over the investment decisions made by the trust, in so far as these decisions relate to the financial interest in the audited entity.

d) A direct or an indirect financial interest is held in a trustee capacity by the audit firm or by a partner in the audit firm (other than a partner in a position to influence the conduct and outcome of the audit), or an immediate family member of such a person, provided the person is not an identified potential beneficiary of the trust.

2.3.3 Loans and guarantees

Generally speaking, loans and guarantees of borrowings to or from audit clients, or their affiliates, are not permitted by the audit firm, by anyone in a position to influence the conduct and outcome of the audit or by immediate family members thereof. The exceptions are:

- loans to, or guarantees of the borrowings of, an audit client or its affiliates where this represents a deposit made with a bank or similar institution in the ordinary course of business, on normal business terms; and

- loans to, or guarantees of the borrowings of, those in a position to influence the conduct and outcome of the audit and immediate family members thereof by an audit client that is a bank or similar institution, in the ordinary course of business, on normal business terms, which are immaterial to the audit client. In the case of such loans or guarantees to the firm, these must be immaterial both to the audit client and to the firm.

2.4 Goods and services: hospitality

This issue is applicable not only to partners, but also to audit staff and to their immediate families of both. The issue is that if goods, services or hospitality have been obtained, then the client may feel that it has a 'hold' over the auditor. Alternatively, the auditor may not wish to put the relationship with the client at risk and, as a result, may be disinclined to take a hard line in respect of any contentious issues.

There is not a problem where the auditor has received goods on normal commercial terms or has occasionally been taken out for a pub lunch. However, a problem would arise if the auditor had received material hospitality (such as a holiday abroad) or goods at a favourable rate (for example, a substantial discount on a car purchase) from an audit client.

ES4 (Revised) makes clear that any gifts other than those that are clearly trivial should not be accepted, and hospitality should only be accepted if it is reasonable in terms of its frequency, nature and cost. The Standard also requires firms to establish policies on such matters and to issue guidance to assist partners and staff to comply with those policies. The firm should impress upon the partners and staff the need to make the audit compliance principal aware of any hospitality offered (except for an invitation to lunch) before it is accepted.

2.5 Litigation

Where litigation is threatened or already in progress between the practice and the client in relation to the fees, audit work or other work, then this would constitute a major threat to the objectivity of the practice. This is a slightly strange situation as one would expect that if a client were suing a practice for negligence in respect of work undertaken earlier, it would be unlikely to want the practice to act for them again. However, this situation might arise if that action was, for example, taken against an audit practice that had subsequently been absorbed into a new practice. The problem in this situation is not only that the auditor may not be objective, but also that the management may be less willing to disclose relevant information to the auditor. Therefore, the firm should not continue with the audit unless such litigation is insignificant.

2.6 Family or other personal relationships

Again this issue is relevant not only to the audit partner, but also to the staff involved on the audit. Where there is such a connection, this will result in a self-interest threat, which may affect the objectivity of both the partners and staff.

Before looking at the rules more closely, we need to appreciate that ES2 differentiates between various family members depending on their perceived closeness to the individual concerned. 'Immediate family' means a spouse or equivalent (that is, a partner) or a dependent, whereas 'close family' means a non-dependent parent, child or sibling. It is assumed in the Standard that an individual is aware of, and can influence the behaviour of, an immediate family member, but that this is not normally the case with close family members.

It is important that partners and professional staff report to the firm any immediate family, close family and other personal relationships involving an audit client that they consider might create a threat to the auditor's objectivity or a perceived loss of independence, so that an assessment of the issue can be made and any safeguards deemed necessary can be put in place.

In the case of an immediate family member of a person in a position to influence the conduct and outcome of the audit, that person must cease to hold a position in which he or she exerts such influence on the audit.

In the case of a close family member of a person in a position to influence the conduct and outcome of the audit, or any family member of a partner in the firm, the issue should be reported to the audit engagement partner, who should take appropriate action – if necessary in consultation with the firm's ethics partner. This might involve 'Chinese walls' to ensure that the individual does not become involved in any way. In many respects, the bigger the practice, the easier this will be. However, this may not be sufficient, and it may be decided that either the person must cease to hold a position to influence the conduct and outcome of the audit, or the firm should resign as auditor.

2.7 Ex-partners or senior employees

There is also a potential risk of independence being compromised where a partner or member of staff within the practice becomes involved in the management of the audit client, either on a permanent basis or a temporary basis (such as secondment). This will be a particular problem where that involvement is at a senior level – for example, as finance director.

2.7.1 Permanent positions with an audit client

There are various safeguards that should be implemented to ensure that this does not become an insurmountable threat. For example, the firm should ensure that no significant connections remain between the firm and the individual leaving the practice. This means all capital balances and similar financial interests (including retirement benefits) should be fully settled – unless these are made in accordance with predetermined arrangements that cannot be influenced by any remaining connections between the officer and the firm. In addition, the individual should not participate or appear to participate in the firm's business or professional activities. Such situations are more likely to be an issue where the individual was a principal within the practice rather than a senior employee.

All staff and principals involved in audit work must be aware of their duty to inform the practice if they enter into negotiations to join a client entity. At such a point their involvement in the audit must cease. If this occurs during the course of an audit, it is important to ensure that any significant audit decisions made by the partner or member of staff concerned are reviewed, to ensure that objectivity has not been compromised. If the person joining the client is an audit partner, the review should be performed by an audit partner who is not involved in the audit engagement. Where the audit firm, due to its size, does not have a partner who was not involved in the audit engagement, such a review should be performed by an external reviewer, such as SWAT∪κ Limited.

The firm must resign as auditor in the following circumstance: where the individual joining an audit client is a partner who has been involved in the audit of that client at any time in the previous two years in any of the following capacities:

- as audit engagement partner;
- as engagement quality control reviewer;
- as key partner involved in the audit; or
- as a partner in the chain of command.

and is appointed as a director or to a key management position with the client. If the person joining the client in such a role is anyone else from the audit team, the partner needs to consider the composition of the team and whether it needs to be strengthened to guard against any self-interest, familiarity or threats of intimidation.

2.7.2 Temporary positions and secondments with an audit client

The provision of partners or staff to an audit client either on secondment or some other temporary basis is only allowed where:

a) it is for a short period of time and does not involve the performance of non-audit services that are not permitted under ES5; and

b) the client agrees that the individual will not hold a management position, and will be responsible for directing and supervising the individual's work, which must not include such matters as:

  - making management decisions; or

  - exercising discretionary authority to commit the client to a particular position or accounting treatment.

The potential management threat posed by secondments and other temporary positions means that, for example, interim management arrangements involving participation in the financial reporting function are not allowed.

A self-review threat can also arise if, on return to the firm, the seconded individual is assigned a role that requires him or her to review the work undertaken whilst working for the client. Accordingly, the individual should not be given such a role on the audit team. The length of time such a restriction is needed will depend on the length of the assignment and the seniority of the individual within the audit team. As a minimum, this restriction should apply, at the least, to the first audit following the completion of the loan assignment.

2.7.3 Client staff joining the audit firm

Under ES2 (Revised), anyone who was in a position to exert significant influence over the preparation of the financial statements of a client who then joins the audit firm, may not be assigned to a position in which he or she is able to influence the conduct and outcome of the audit of that client or its affiliates for two years following the individual's departure from the client.

There are also statutory prohibitions within both the Companies Act 2006 and other relevant legislation, such as the Friendly and Industrial and Provident Societies Act 1968, which place restrictions on who can be appointed as auditor. Obviously, the practice should consider whether any of these provisions have been breached whenever there is some connection with the client. This is particularly important for Friendly and Industrial and Provident Societies where the Act prohibits a firm from acting if it employs in any capacity an individual who is an officer or a servant of the society. This provision is more restrictive than the provisions within the Companies Act.

2.8 Mutual business interests

The practice should consider whether there are any mutual business interests between itself and the client that could impact on its objectivity. This could be by way of some form of joint venture, or even a personal joint venture between a senior member of staff or partner within the practice and the audit client or senior individuals within the audit client.

Audit firms, persons in a position to influence the conduct and outcome of the audit, and immediate family members of such persons should not enter into a business relationship with an audit client, its management or its affiliates, except where it:

  - involves the purchase of goods and services from the audit firm or the client in the ordinary course of business and on an arm's length basis, and which goods and services are not material to either party; or

  - is clearly inconsequential to either party.

Where such a relationship has been entered into by the firm, either the relationship should be terminated or the firm should not accept appointment as auditor.

Where such a relationship has been entered into by a person in a position to influence the conduct and outcome of the audit, or an immediate family member thereof, either the relationship should be terminated or the person should surrender the position in which they exert such influence on the audit engagement.

2.9 Beneficial interests and trusteeships

There are certain circumstances where a practice will be precluded from acting as auditor for the client. This issue of various beneficial interests is considered below.

2.9.1 Beneficial interests in shares and other investments

ES2 (Revised) notes that none of the following:

- the audit firm;
- any partner in the audit firm;
- a person in a position to influence the conduct and outcome of the audit; nor
- an immediate family member of such a person;

may hold:

a) any direct financial interest in an audit client or its affiliates;

b) any indirect financial interest in an audit client or its affiliates where the interest is material to the audit firm or the individual, or to the intermediary; or

c) any indirect financial interest in an audit client or its affiliates where the person holding it has both

   i)   the ability to influence the investment decisions of the intermediary; and

   ii) actual knowledge of the existence of the underlying investment in the audited entity.

Such circumstances constitute an insurmountable threat of self-interest and the firm will be precluded from acting for that client in an audit capacity. The firm should only act if the interests are disposed of.

2.9.2 Beneficial interest in trusts

Where a direct or an indirect financial interest in the audit client or its affiliates is held in a trustee capacity by a person in a position to influence the conduct and outcome of the audit, or an immediate family member of such a person, a self-interest threat may be created – either because the existence of the trustee interest may influence the conduct of the audit, or because the trust may influence the actions of the audited entity. Accordingly, such a trustee interest may only be held when:

- the relevant person is not an identified potential beneficiary of the trust; and
- the financial interest held by the trust in the audit client is not material to the trust; and
- the trust is not able to exercise significant influence over the audit client or its affiliates; and
- the relevant person does not have significant influence over the investment decisions made by the trust, in so far as they relate to the financial interest in the audit client.

Any of these possibilities, particularly the last three, could cause problems. The issue revolves around whether the trustee is 'a person in a position to influence the conduct and outcome of the audit'.

A direct or an indirect financial interest in the audited client or its affiliates held in a trustee capacity by the audit firm, or by a partner in the audit firm or their immediate families, can only be held when that person is not an identified potential beneficiary of the trust.

Where the audit firm acts as trustee, and the trust holds in aggregate one per cent or more of the issued capital of the company, details of the trust investment must be disclosed in the directors' report or the auditors' report.

2.10 Associated firms

When considering the issue of independence, the practice should also consider whether there is any involvement with any other practice or organisation that has dealings with the client. There are two common possibilities: network firms and outside sources.

2.10.1 Network firms

A network firm is defined by the glossary to the Ethical Standards as any entity which is part of a larger structure that is aimed at cooperation, and which is:

- controlled by the audit firm; or
- under common control, ownership or management; or
- clearly aimed at profit or cost sharing; or
- otherwise affiliated or associated with the audit firm through common quality control policies and procedures, common business strategy, the use of a common name or through the sharing of significant common professional resources.

It should also be noted that for the purpose of the Ethical Standards, the definition of an audit firm also includes network firms in the UK and Ireland which are controlled by the audit firm or its partners.

Any receipt of gifts or hospitality, or provision of non-audit services by another member firm of a network should be considered.

2.10.2 Outside sources

Alternatively, threats to the auditor's independence could arise through pressures exerted upon the practice by an outside source that introduces business – for example, bankers, solicitors or government. Consider the situation where the auditor has a good relationship with the local bank and the bank is keen to see the financial statements of a mutual client reflecting a certain position. If the auditor does not 'play the game', then not only will this impact on the current audit but also on a number of other audit clients who were introduced to the practice by the bankers. It may also affect any future referrals.

The auditor should ensure that any potential threat is identified at the planning stage and that, where necessary, protection – possibly in the form of a second partner review – is put into place.

2.11 Provision of non-audit services

The provision of non-audit services to an audit client is probably the most common potential threat to independence. ES5 (Revised) *Non-audit services provided to audited entities* requires a range of actions to be undertaken before providing such services. In order to understand the implications of a threat, it is important to consider the nature of the threat. There are threats posed by self-interest, self-review, management, advocacy, familiarity and intimidation.

Self-interest threat

The main self-interest threat arises from economic dependence on fees (see section 2.2)

Self-review threat

This arises where the results of a non-audit assignment are reflected in the financial statements, on which the auditor then gives an opinion. In assessing the significance of such a threat, the firm needs to consider the extent to which the non-audit service will involve a significant degree of subjective judgment, and so have a material effect on the financial statements.

Management threat

This arises where the firm undertakes work that involves making judgments and taking decisions that, properly, are the responsibility of management. As auditors, a firm may become closely aligned with the views and interests of management and this, in turn, may impair or call into question the firm's ability to apply a proper degree of professional scepticism during the audit.

Advocacy threat

In order to act in an advocacy role, the firm has to adopt a position closely aligned to that of management – for example, assisting an audit client with an HMRC investigation. This may create both actual and perceived threats to the firm's objectivity and independence. If the advocacy role is in respect of a material item in the financial statements, then it is unlikely that safeguards can eliminate or reduce the threat to an acceptable level.

Familiarity (or trust) threat

This is when the auditor is predisposed to accept or is insufficiently questioning of the client's point of view. This can arise, for example, where close personal relationships are developed with the client's staff through long association with the client (see section 2.12).

Intimidation threat

This arises when the auditor's conduct is influenced by fear or threats – for example, where the auditor encounters an aggressive and dominating individual.

2.11.1 Safeguards

Where safeguards can eliminate or reduce the threat to an acceptable level, the non-audit service may be provided to the client. Of course, the converse is also true. Examples of possible safeguards include:

- performance of non-audit services by a member of staff outside the audit team;
- review of non-audit work performed by audit staff by a member of staff outside the audit team;
- second principal review of the file, that principal being unconnected with the engagement;
- rotation of the engagement principal and/or senior staff on the audit; and
- review by an external qualified source such as SWATUK Limited.

The responsible individual on the audit should decide on the appropriate action taking into consideration the individual circumstances of the client and the requirements of the APB Ethical Standards (Revised). This decision should be reviewed by another audit principal not involved in the audit prior to the audit work commencing. At this stage, the second principal is merely confirming whether or not the suggested action is appropriate, given the potential independence problem highlighted.

Where the audit engagement partner concludes that no appropriate safeguards are available to eliminate or reduce to an acceptable level the threats to the auditors' objectivity, including any perceived loss of independence, related to a proposed engagement to provide a non-audit service to an audit client, he or she should inform the others within the audit firm who are concerned of that conclusion. Then, the firm should either

- not undertake the non-audit service engagement; or
- not accept or withdraw from the audit engagement.

Paragraph 27 of ES5 (Revised) notes that in deciding whether a management threat exists, the firm should consider whether:

- the non-audit service results in recommendations by the audit firm justified by objective and transparent analyses or in the client being given the opportunity to decide between reasonable alternatives;
- the auditors are satisfied that a member of management (or a senior employee of the audit client) has been designated by the audit client to receive the results of the non-audit service and make any judgments and decisions that are needed; and

- this member of management has the capability to make independent management judgments and decisions on the basis of the information provided – that is, can be considered to be 'informed management'.

If there is no one in the client's management team that has the authority and the capability to make a particular decision, then any such decision must have been taken by someone. The question is who? A reasonable and informed third party might conclude that the only other candidate is someone from the audit team. Since the auditors are required to be independent of management, there is a clear conflict when they also act as management. Therefore, in the absence of informed management, it is unlikely that any safeguards can eliminate the management threat or reduce it to an acceptable level.

It is important that common sense is applied when considering whether a client has informed management. Informed management is not a fixed standard that applies in the same way to all clients. It will apply to different clients and even to the same client in different ways, depending on their backgrounds and the services provided. For example, a straightforward accounting service does not require a significant degree of technical knowledge. If the service is explained in layman's terms, most clients – who after all are running a business – are likely to understand the service sufficiently to be classified as informed. However, this would not be the case with, say, complex tax planning.

The audit engagement partner should also ensure that the directors are appropriately informed on a timely basis of the following:

- all significant facts and matters that bear upon the auditors' objectivity and independence in the provision of non-audit services, including the safeguards put in place; and

- for listed companies, any inconsistencies between APB Ethical Standards (Revised) and the company's policy for the supply of non-audit services by the audit firm, and any apparent breach of that policy.

2.11.2 Documentation

The audit engagement partner should ensure that the reasoning for a decision to undertake an engagement to provide non-audit services to an audit client, and any safeguards adopted, is appropriately documented. Any significant judgments concerning the threats identified, the safeguards implemented and communication with the directors should be documented.

2.12 Rotation of audit engagement partner

Under ES3 (Revised) *Long association with the audit engagement*, an audit engagement partner is generally not permitted to remain in charge of the audit of a listed company for a period of more than five consecutive years. In addition, someone who ceases to act under this provision must not return to the role in relation to that audit until a minimum of five years has passed.

In respect of all audits, the Standard requires that where audit partners and staff in senior positions have a long association with the audit, the firm should assess the threats to its objectivity and independence as auditors and, where the threats are other than clearly insignificant, the firm should apply safeguards to reduce the threats to an acceptable level. Where appropriate safeguards cannot be applied, the firm must either resign as auditor or not stand for reappointment, as appropriate.

Appropriate safeguards may include:

- removing ('rotating') the audit engagement partner and the other senior members of the engagement team after a predetermined number of years in that role;

- involving an additional partner, who is not and has not recently been a member of the engagement team, to review the work done by the audit partner and the other senior members of the engagement team, and to advise as necessary; and

- applying independent internal or external quality reviews to the engagement in question, such as those performed by SWATuk Limited.

Once a partner has been the audit partner continuously for ten or more years, the Standards require careful consideration as to whether a reasonable and informed third party would consider the firm's objectivity and independence to be impaired. If the audit partner is not rotated, then either alternative safeguards such as those outlined above must be applied, or the firm must document the reasons and communicate them to the directors.

2.13 Adequate resources

The audit engagement partner should also consider whether the firm has adequate resources, and that the staff have the necessary skills to perform the audit properly. This is especially relevant if the client operates in an unusual or niche industry sector, or where there are specific legislative requirements – for example, charities, pension schemes, financial services, trade unions, etc. It is not uncommon for firms to accept a new client in such a field without having the specialist skills and knowledge to adequately perform the audit.

2.14 Proper performance

Finally, it is also worth considering whether there are any other aspects of the client, or any other factors, that will adversely affect the firm's ability to perform the audit properly. For example, there may be questions as to the integrity of the client's management, and these may raise doubts over the reliability of explanations and information provided by management. Such doubts may cause the auditor not to accept the audit assignment.

2.15 Smaller entities

As well as the five Ethical Standards, the APB has also published ES *Provisions available for small entities (Revised)* (PASE). As the title suggests, this Standard applies to small entities only. A small entity is defined as follows:

a)   any company, which is not a UK listed company or an affiliate thereof, that qualifies as a small company under section 382 of the Companies Act 2006;

b)   where group accounts are produced, any group that qualifies as small under section 383 of the Companies Act 2006;

c)   any charity with an income of less than the turnover threshold applicable to small companies as identified in section 382 of the Companies Act 2006;

d)   any pension fund with less than 1,000 members (including active, deferred and pensioner members)*;

e)   any firm regulated by the FSA, which is not required to appoint an auditor in accordance with chapter 3 of the FSA Supervision Manual, which forms a part of the FSA Handbook†;

f)   any credit union which is a mutually owned financial cooperative established under the Credit Unions Act 1979 and the Industrial and Provident Societies Act 1965 (or equivalent legislation), which meets the criteria set out in (a) above;

g)   any entity registered under the Industrial and Provident Societies Act 1965, incorporated under the Friendly Societies Act 1992 or registered under the Friendly Societies Act 1974 (or equivalent legislation), which meets the criteria set out in (a) above;

h)   any registered social landlord with fewer than 250 units; and

i)   any other entity, such as a club, which would be a small entity if it were a company.

Notes

* In cases where a scheme with more than 1,000 members has been in wind-up over a number of years, such a scheme does not qualify as a small entity, even where the remaining number of members falls below 1,000.

† This relates to those firms that are not required to appoint an auditor under rule 3.3.2 of the FSA Supervision Manual.

ES PASE includes both alternative provisions that small entities may apply instead of the requirements of the full Standards and exemptions from parts of those Standards. These are described below.

2.15.1 Alternative provisions

The audit firm is not required to have an external independent quality control review where it is expected that the total audit and non-audit fees for the client will regularly exceed 10 per cent (but not regularly exceed 15 per cent) of the annual fee income of the audit firm or the part of the firm by reference to which the audit engagement partner's profit share is calculated (normally required by ES4). However, the audit engagement partner must disclose the expectation that fees will amount to between 10 per cent and 15 per cent of the firm's annual fee income to the ethics partner and to the client.

When undertaking non-audit services for an audit client, the firm is not required to apply safeguards to address a self-review threat (normally required by ES5), provided that the client has 'informed management' (see section 2.11.1) and the firm extends the cyclical inspection of completed engagements that is performed for quality control purposes.

2.15.2 Exemptions

When undertaking non-audit services for an audit client, the firm is not required to adhere to the prohibitions in ES5 relating to providing non-audit services that involve the audit firm undertaking part of the role of management, provided that:

- it discusses objectivity and independence issues related to the provision of non-audit services with those charged with governance, confirming that management accepts responsibility for any decisions taken; and
- it discloses the fact that it has taken advantage of this exemption in the audit report, and either the financial statements or the audit report discloses the type of non-audit services provided.

The firm may undertake an engagement to provide tax services to an audited entity where this would involve acting as an advocate for the audited entity, before an appeals tribunal or court, in the resolution of an issue that is material to the financial statements, or where the outcome of the tax issue is dependent on a future or contemporary audit judgment (normally prohibited under ES5). Again, the firm must disclose the fact that it has taken advantage of this exemption in the audit report, and either the financial statements or the audit report discloses the type of non-audit services provided that give rise to the advocacy threat.

Where a former partner is appointed as a director or to a key management position at an audit client, having acted – at any time in the two years prior to this appointment – as audit engagement partner (or as an engagement quality control reviewer, key partner involved in the audit or a partner in the chain of command), the firm is not required to resign as auditor (normally required by ES2) provided that:

- it takes appropriate steps to determine that there has been no significant threat to the audit team's integrity, objectivity and independence; and
- it discloses the fact that it has taken advantage of this exemption in the audit report, and either the financial statements or the audit report discloses the fact that a former audit engagement partner has joined the audited entity.

These alternative provisions and exemptions may be of real practical value to many smaller audit practices, where numerous non-audit services are typically provided to the firm's audit clients, and where there may be practical difficulties in having non-audit staff perform or review such work. The exemptions should, however, be used with caution due to the disclosures required in the financial statements when using them.

If advantage is to be taken of these provisions, the auditor's documentation of acceptance procedures should clearly indicate that this is the case.

2.16 Review procedures

The audit regulations require that, on an annual basis, each principal, member of staff, subcontractor and consultant who is involved in audit work must complete an independence form. This form will, *inter alia*, record details of any audit clients with which that individual has an involvement. The audit compliance principal should review all the forms and ensure that the relevant audit files are appropriately updated. Such procedures should help ensure that an individual does not become involved in an audit when it is not appropriate to do so.

All individuals involved in audit work must keep the audit compliance principal fully informed of any changes to the circumstances recorded on their annual statement, so that these can also be fed through to the relevant audit file.

All of the points raised above must be considered both as the first step on each audit file and on an ongoing basis throughout the audit.

This book is concerned with the audit file itself, rather than whole-firm procedures. The *Audit Compliance Manual* (also published by Wolters Kluwer) contains extensive guidance on whole-firm audit procedures and includes an example 'fit and proper' form.

Chapter 3 The correspondence and permanent files

3.1 The correspondence file

A useful part of the planning process is the review of the correspondence file. This serves to remind the auditor of issues which have arisen during the course of the year that could have an impact on the audit. It can also provide useful information that the partner may have forgotten to pass on to the audit staff!

The auditor should carefully review the correspondence within the file, making a more detailed note on any issue that would have a significant bearing on the audit approach. Many firms summarise every piece of client correspondence, when much of it comprises routine covering letters and has little or no impact on the audit. The auditor is looking for matters which significantly affect the audit – for example:

- correspondence confirming the amount of corporation tax payments on account during the year should help the auditor to check the accuracy of the corporation tax control account entries;

- discussions with the client prior to the year end regarding bonuses might influence the auditor's expectations of wages and salaries expense and accruals when undertaking preliminary analytical procedures; and

- indications that the owners are considering selling the business would affect the audit risk assessment.

In firms where separate correspondence files are maintained in each department, it is important that the auditor reviews them all.

3.2 The permanent file

A permanent audit file is essential, but it is even more important that it is kept up to date and maintained as a workable file. This is especially true under ISAs, as a lot of the background information which drives the planning and risk assessment is maintained here.

Many firms do not allow sufficient, or indeed any, time in the budget for updating the permanent audit file, which often then becomes merely a receptacle for old, out-of-date documents and information that staff are unsure where to file. Furthermore, people often do not spend adequate time updating the permanent file on the grounds that they have been dealing with the client for a number of years and therefore know all there is to know. A problem may then arise when, for some reason, a key partner or member of staff is no longer involved in the assignment. This can result in difficulties for the person taking over the assignment, particularly if that person no longer has access to the original partner or staff member involved.

The contents of the file should be reviewed at the start of each assignment, and any necessary amendments made. The permanent file should be organised into sections, including the following:

- client-specific background information and knowledge;
- industry or sector information;
- a register of significant laws and regulations;
- details of all related parties;
- review of accounting policies;
- accounting systems and controls;
- statutory information;

- taxation;
- assets;
- contracts, leases and agreements;
- information of continuing interest; and
- the accounts for previous years.

Each of these areas is considered separately below, with examples given of the sorts of information that may be relevant and the possible risks arising from such information.

Whether gathering, preparing, updating or reviewing information for the permanent file, it is important to remember that the main objective of audit planning is to identify any risks that could have a material impact on the financial statements. In order to identify such risks, the auditor needs to understand the entity being audited and its environment. The information recorded on the permanent file should therefore be focused on this objective, and highlight any associated risks.

3.3 Client-specific background information and knowledge

As a starting point, the standing data that a practice has on its database should be incorporated within this section. This should include details of the client's name, VAT registration number, etc., together with details of the client's key members of staff and other professional advisers. In addition, in order to comply with the money-laundering regulations the file should record the steps taken by the practice to confirm that the client is a bona fide business operation.

In order to understand the classes of transactions, account balances, and disclosures to be expected in the financial statements, and to identify potential risk areas, ISA 315 *Understanding the entity and its environment and assessing the risks of material misstatement* also specifically requires the auditor to have knowledge of the following aspects of the client's business.

- Operations

    This might include information about customers, suppliers and any other relevant information. For example, an entity that is largely dependent on one main customer or supplier may be at risk if that entity moves its business elsewhere or ceases trading.

- Ownership and governance

    An understanding of the ownership and relations between owners and other people or entities is also important in determining whether related party transactions have been identified and accounted for appropriately. See section 3.6 for further details.

- Investments

    Some clients – typically, charities – are dependent on investments to provide an income stream. A stockmarket downturn can put the going concern of such entities at risk. There may be a significant risk of accounting errors arising where entities are investing in complex financial instruments which need to be valued.

- Group structure

    A client may have a complex structure with subsidiaries, etc., in multiple locations. In addition to consolidation difficulties, other issues may arise, such as whether investments are joint ventures, subsidiaries, or associates.

- Financing arrangements

    The financial statements of highly geared entities may, for example, be at risk of manipulation in order to meet banking covenants, or be at risk of being unable to continue as a going concern if interest rates rise substantially or credit is withdrawn.

3.3.1 Entities which do business electronically

Increasing numbers of entities are undertaking elements of their operations electronically. This might include such things as purchases and sales made via websites, online or internet banking, etc. It is important that the auditor obtains an understanding of such activities sufficient to identify any potential risks arising from those activities. This may involve consideration of the client's use of service organisations (see section 10.4.2) and looking at the IT aspects of the client's systems in more depth (see Chapter 4).

3.3.2 Objectives, strategies and related business risks

ISA 315 goes on to require that the auditor obtains an understanding of the client's objectives and strategies, and the related business risks that may result in material misstatement of the financial statements. Business risks result from significant conditions, events, circumstances, actions or inactions that could adversely affect the entity's ability to achieve its objectives and execute its strategies, or through the setting of inappropriate objectives and strategies.

This is an area that many auditors struggle with. Some clients, especially smaller ones, may not have a formal business plan or written plans and objectives for the business, which absence often results in the auditor not considering this issue. However, the absence of any sort of strategy or plan for the business may in itself be a risk, particularly in certain industries which, for example, depend heavily on fashions, trends or the latest technology, or are highly competitive. Such issues can have a significant impact on the going concern of an entity if not adequately addressed by the directors.

As well as affecting going concern directly, the objectives and strategies of the client can lead to other risk factors. For example, consider a manufacturing client moving production abroad to save costs. This might give rise to following situations.

- There will be a foreign exchange risk when the overseas costs are translated back into Sterling.
- Inadequate local knowledge of the country in question may result in an increased risk of falling foul of local laws and regulations, giving rise to fines and penalties, etc.
- New staff with no experience of the company or particular product(s) may result in production problems and give rise to quality control issues, with adverse knock-on effects on the company's reputation and customer goodwill.
- Overseas tax may need to be considered, possibly including transfer-pricing regulations.

This area is one of the most important to consider when planning an audit, due to the wide-ranging impact that strategic decisions can have on a business. It is vital that such issues are discussed with the directors, especially where there is no formal business plan.

3.3.3 Measurement and review of the entity's financial performance

The ISA also requires the auditor to understand the measurement and review of the entity's financial performance. This is not the equivalent of simply printing out some figures and ratios and putting them on the permanent file! It requires the auditor to consider what specific performance measures are important to the entity, and whether any risks arise from these measures – risks such as those exemplified below.

- In a business where turnover growth is the most important factor, sales staff may be pressurised into doing business with uncreditworthy customers, or even to generate fictitious sales, especially if their remuneration is based – at least in part – on reaching sales targets.
- Key measures for many charities include the amount of administrative expenses and/or fundraising costs compared to the income generated, as funding bodies often look at these ratios when making decisions about funding. This might result in pressure to manipulate income recognition or to not account for all expense invoices.

3.4 Industry or sector information

This should give some background detail on the type of trade, major products of the client, technological developments and competition in the market. In addition to the above the auditor might want to include details of any other factors that could affect the business. Where clients have some form of brochure, it is useful to place a copy on file and to highlight the important areas. But simply placing a copy of the brochure on file and doing nothing with it is not sufficient!

Where the business does not have a brochure, auditors should seek, through enquiry and their own knowledge of the business, to make some useful comments on the file on the nature of the trade and industry sector. The internet is always a good place to start, as a wealth of information can be found there – for example, the client's own website and those of its competitors, and the sites of trade and professional bodies. There are also companies that provide sector information for a fee, although *www.keynote.co.uk*, for example, provides a short executive summary of many of its industry reports for free. Trade magazines and publications are also a good source of knowledge.

This type of information is useful in identifying external risks affecting the client, and often these will impact in some way on going concern risk. For example, clients in industries where technology advances rapidly must run effective research and development programmes to avoid being 'left behind' by their competitors.

3.5 Register of significant laws and regulations

The permanent file should include details of significant laws and regulations applicable to the client. ISA 250 *Consideration of laws and regulations in an audit of financial statements* requires the auditor to obtain a general understanding of the legal and regulatory framework applicable to the client and its industry sector, and how the entity is complying with that framework, including the procedures followed by the client to ensure compliance.

Again, the objective here is to identify those laws or regulations that may give rise to business risks that have a fundamental effect on the client's operations, and to consider their impact. For example, non-compliance with certain laws and regulations may cause the client to cease operations or call into question the client's continuance as a going concern.

Laws and regulations can be divided into:

- laws and regulations governing accounts;
- general business laws and regulations; and
- other specific laws and regulations.

3.5.1 Laws and regulations governing accounts

Relevant laws may include such things as the Companies Act or Charities Act, while relevant regulations would include the choice of GAAP used (for example, the FRSSE, full UK GAAP or IFRS). All members of the audit team should ensure that they are familiar with the relevant requirements.

3.5.2 General business laws and regulations

This might include things such as health and safety, employment legislation and planning regulations. The extent to which these may present significant risks may depend on the type of sector the client is in, as instanced below.

- Health and safety might be a minor issue in an office, but a significant risk in a factory where heavy machinery is operated or toxic chemicals are used. A serious breach of health and safety legislation can lead to large fines for the entity, possible legal action and a loss of reputation.

- Employment legislation has become increasingly complex in recent years, and a failure to comply can have a significant effect on entities of all sizes – for example, unfair dismissal claims in employment tribunals. Certain industry sectors are also more at risk from the working time or minimum wage regulations, where non-compliance can result in heavy fines.

- Obtaining planning permission is a critical issue for many businesses such as housebuilders, supermarkets, etc.

3.5.3 Other specific laws and regulations

The auditor should also ascertain details of specific laws and regulations which could have an impact on the business, for example:

- Financial Services and Markets Act for financial services business;
- food hygiene regulations and licensing laws for restaurants and pubs; and
- child protection legislation for schools, charities, etc.

It is not sufficient to just list the relevant acts or regulations. The auditor should then consider whether, as a result of non-compliance with any laws or regulations, there are any potential contingent liabilities (for example, warranty claims, legal action, fines or penalties, etc) or any issues that would have a material impact on the financial statements, in particular the client's ability to continue as a going concern – for example, bad publicity leading to a critical loss of customer and/or supplier goodwill.

Many small entities are only governed by general business regulations, which would not have a significant impact on their ability to continue as a going concern, nor would they result in material contingent liabilities should they not comply. However, a significant minority of such entities will be governed by additional laws and regulations, which could have a significant impact on the entity's operations. Where this is the case, it is essential that the auditor has an understanding of such laws and regulations. The auditor does not need to become a legal expert, but some understanding is necessary to ascertain the nature of the relevant laws and regulations and to determine, through investigation and discussion with the client, the types of situation that could result in significant risks.

When seeking to determine whether there are any specific laws and regulations which could have a significant impact on the client, the auditor should consider the following questions:

- Does the entity make payments or returns to a separate licensing agency?
- Is the entity subject to regular or potential reviews of its operations by an external agency?
- Does the entity deal with hazardous material or dangerous machinery?

An affirmative answer to one or more of the questions above is an indicator that there could be laws or regulations that could have a significant impact on the client if they are not complied with.

3.6 Register of related parties

The permanent file should contain details of all known related parties, plus details of any regular or past transactions with them. ISA 550 *Related parties* notes that due to their nature, related parties and transactions may not always be easy to identify, and lists the following nine audit procedures to be performed in respect of the completeness of the register and any such information provided by the client.

a) Review previous year's working papers for names of known related parties.

b) Review the client's procedures for identifying related parties.

c) Inquire into the affiliation of directors and officers with other entities.

d) Review shareholder records to determine the names of principal shareholders or, if appropriate, obtain a listing of principal shareholders from the share register.

e) Review minutes of the meetings of shareholders and directors and other relevant statutory records, such as the register of directors' interests.

f) Ask other auditors currently involved in the audit, or predecessor auditors, about their knowledge of additional related parties.

g) Review the client's tax returns and other information supplied to regulatory agencies.

h) Examine invoices and correspondence from lawyers for indications of the existence of related parties or related party transactions.

i) Ascertain the names of all pension and other trusts established for the benefit of employees and the names of their management.

The disclosure of related party transactions is important, and the risk of incomplete disclosure may be high for certain clients. However, the register of related parties is often incomplete or out of date. It is important that the above procedures are performed to keep the register relevant and up to date, and that the risk of undisclosed related party transactions existing is carefully considered.

3.6.1 Pension schemes

Pension schemes are worthy of a specific mention at this stage, for two reasons. Firstly, it is often the case with entities that have schemes such as Small Self Administered Schemes ('SSASs'), that there will also be loans and other transactions between the entity and the scheme which will need disclosure in the financial statements.

Secondly, entities with defined benefit pension schemes will fall under the accounting requirements of FRS 17 (there are similar rules in the FRSSE for small entities). Obtaining the figures for the accounts will generally require the input of an actuary, and the process will necessitate careful planning and organisation by both the entity's management and the auditor, and should therefore be considered at as early a stage as possible. The reliance on the work of the actuary as an expert will need to be considered (see section 10.4.5).

The auditor should obtain a copy of the scheme's trust deed and rules, to identify obligations to pay retirement benefits. However, there might also be benefits payable that are not recorded in the rules. For example, there might be:

- legal obligations to pay retirement benefits, which arise from informal agreements rather than from a formal contract;
- constructive obligations (for example, where pension benefits are regularly enhanced beyond the minimum required by statute); or
- statutory requirements that override the original provisions of a scheme.

A thorough understanding of the scheme is therefore needed to be able to identify any such risk factors.

3.7 Review of accounting policies

Again, the aim here is to identify risks that arise from the accounting policies applied by the client. This involves more than simply photocopying the accounting policies note from the financial statements and placing it on the permanent file. ISA 315 notes that the review needs to consider the client's accounting policies for appropriateness and consistency with:

- the business;
- the applicable financial reporting framework (for example, the FRSSE, UK GAAP or IFRS); and
- the client's industry. Certain industries have industry-specific policies which, generally, should be followed unless there is a good reason not to do so. One way to check this is to compare the client's accounting policies with those of a competitor or other entity in the same industry sector. These can be obtained either from Companies House or, in the case of a listed company, for free from its website.

The ISA requirement also encompasses the methods the client uses to account for significant and unusual transactions and the effect of significant accounting policies in controversial or emerging areas for which there is a lack of authoritative guidance or consensus.

Consideration should also be given to any new Accounting Standards which are relevant to the client, and consider when and how the client will adopt such requirements. Where the client has changed its selection of, or method of applying, a significant accounting policy, the auditor should consider the reasons for the change and whether it is appropriate and consistent with the applicable financial reporting framework.

Examples of potential risks arising from accounting policies include:

● those arising from whether research and development costs should be capitalised or expensed, and if the former, from what point and over what period should they be amortised?

● Non-depreciation of buildings on the grounds that the depreciation charge and accumulated depreciation are immaterial. This is in accordance with FRS15, but many clients forget to consider the accumulated depreciation, and this can become material over time.

3.7.1 Revenue recognition

ISA 240 notes that material misstatements due to fraudulent financial reporting often result from an overstatement of revenue (for example, premature revenue recognition or recording fictitious revenues) or from an understatement of revenue (for example, improperly shifting revenues to a later period). Therefore, the auditor ordinarily presumes that there are risks of fraud in revenue recognition and considers which types of revenue, revenue transactions or assertions may give rise to such risks. If the auditor has not identified, in a particular circumstance, revenue recognition as a risk of material misstatement due to fraud, the reasons for arriving at this conclusion should be documented.

3.8 Accounting systems and controls

The permanent file should contain a record of the client systems and controls, including the key business processes. This is considered in more detail in Chapter 4.

Irrespective of whether or not the auditor wishes to try to place reliance on the client's systems and controls, these must be documented in accordance with the requirements of ISA 315, and the design and implementation of controls must be checked. Further guidance on this can be found in Chapter 4. The adequacy of the books and records should also be assessed as the basis for preparing the accounts and, where appropriate, the compliance of the books and records with the requirements of the Companies Act for maintaining *proper* (for periods commencing before 6 April 2008) or *adequate* (for periods commencing after 6 April 2008) accounting records.

3.9 Statutory information

The permanent file should contain some basic statutory information about the client. This should include such things as a list of shareholders, details of any current mortgages and charges, directors' interests in the shares and debentures, as well as a copy of the latest annual return and any elective resolutions. A copy of the memorandum and articles of association or other governing document, such as a trust deed, should also be placed on the file. The auditor should highlight any issues relating to these items that are of particular interest, particularly if they are different to the norm (that is, standard Table A provisions) – for example, restricted borrowing powers or the treatment of gains and losses on the disposal of investment properties.

The permanent file should be a workable file containing information relevant to the audit. It should not be treated as an archive. It is very common for audit practices to incorporate too much information in this section. For example, it is not unusual to see three or four years' worth of annual returns on the file. The more superfluous information that is kept on the file, the less likely it is that the file will be used properly. Information that is not of immediate relevance to the audit should be placed on a separate file or archived.

The permanent file should also contain a copy of the most recent letter of engagement. Whilst some firms do not issue engagement letters for other services, they are mandatory under paragraph 2 of ISA 210 *Terms of audit engagements*. The letter should be reviewed annually, not only to ensure that it is the most up-to-date version from a technical viewpoint, but also that it reflects all of the work to be undertaken for the client. The letter of engagement is a contract between the auditor and client, and if it does not reflect the actual work being undertaken, it will not be valid in the event of any dispute. Products such as the *Engagement Letters Toolkit*, also published by Wolters Kluwer, ensure that the auditor always has the latest wording.

It is essential that the terms of engagement are reviewed at the beginning of the assignment, as well as at the end. If they are reviewed on starting the audit, then at least there is an opportunity to issue an updated letter to the client and to ensure that this is signed and returned before the audit is completed.

All firms should ensure that a copy of the letter of engagement is actually retained. Many firms do not have a system for following up letters once they have been despatched to the client. In addition, they often print only two copies, both of which are sent to the client, one for the client to keep and one to return. With the frequent changes that occur to engagement letters, it is essential that the auditor maintains a record of what has been sent to the client.

3.10 Taxation

Most firms keep separate tax files so only information of direct relevance to the audit (such as copies of any PAYE dispensations) should be on the permanent file.

3.11 Assets

Details of any major assets, properties, etc. should be maintained on the permanent file. Where the practice maintains the client's fixed asset register, a copy is usually kept on the permanent file. However, the filing of numerous copies or scanned images of purchase invoices should be avoided.

3.12 Contracts, leases and agreements

There should be a section in the permanent file containing copies of any contracts, leases and agreements that could have an impact on the audit. This may include details of bank overdrafts and loan facilities, securities, covenants, finance and operating leases, etc. It is not sufficient to simply place copies of the contracts or agreements on file. The auditor should review each document and note or highlight any key points that could be of relevance to the audit – for example:

- the banking facility letter may contain details of banking covenants, which if broken may result in withdrawal of funding, giving rise to a going-concern risk;

- covenants and guarantees may need to be disclosed in the financial statements; and

- lease agreements should contain details of the amounts to be paid and the period of the lease, including any break clauses, options to purchase, etc. These will materially affect the accounting for and disclosure of leases.

3.13 Information of continuing interest

Copies of selected correspondence and other information of continuing interest that the auditor may wish to refer to during the course of the audit should be placed on file. This will include, for example, copies of any letters of comment sent to the client and details of the client's responses. It is not necessary to copy or scan every audit-related letter sent to the client!

3.14 Previous years' accounts

The auditor may wish to maintain copies of the signed accounts within the permanent file. However, on the basis that most firms will incorporate a copy of the previous year's accounts on the current file, it is probably more appropriate to retain signed accounts on a separate dedicated file. Retaining these on the permanent file will very quickly make it an unwieldy tool. Obviously, it is important for the auditor to retain a signed copy of the accounts; the issue is simply where these should be kept.

3.15 Access to information by successor auditors

If the firm is undertaking the audit of a new client, one of the most time-consuming activities is the gathering of background information for the permanent file, as this usually has to be done from scratch. It was perceived that this may be a barrier to entities changing auditors.

Schedule 10 of the Companies Act 2006 permits a successor auditor access to relevant information held by the predecessor auditor. The Audit Regulations (regulation 3.09) have now been amended to give effect to this requirement. Therefore, whilst the requirement to provide information to a successor auditor originates in the Companies Act, it now applies to all audits carried out under the audit regulations, whether for companies or not, in respect of appointments for the audits of financial years starting on or after 6 April 2008. Auditors of new clients should therefore give due consideration to requesting access to the predecessor auditor's working papers.

Technical Release AAF 01/08 *Access to Information by Successor Auditors* repeats the requirements and gives further practical guidance to both successor and predecessor auditors. The main points to note are set out below.

- Information is for the purposes of the successor's audit and must not be disclosed to a third party, unless the successor is required to do so by a legal or professional obligation. The term 'third party' includes the client, although the successor may discuss the information with the client where to do so is a necessary part of the audit work. Because the auditor is complying with a mandatory requirement, providing access to relevant information will not breach professional confidentiality or data protection laws. However, because of the danger of tipping off, any money-laundering report and papers recording the predecessor's related consideration of apparently suspicious activities should not be provided by the predecessor to any person (including the successor) unless the predecessor has clear advice that to do so would be lawful.

- The new right does not alter the existing liability of each auditor in relation to its respective audit.

- The request can only be made after formal appointment of the successor auditor. The provision of information should be on a timely basis.

- The request must be in writing and should not include unnecessary information. It should be as specific as possible and should avoid, wherever possible, a request for 'all relevant information'. It does not matter whether those working papers are filed on the current audit file, a permanent file or a systems file.

- The predecessor should be prepared to assist the successor by providing oral or written explanations on a timely basis.

- The period for which information is requested would normally be the period in respect of the last audit report signed by the predecessor and would include any subsequent interim review. If the successor considers that it needs information relating to an earlier period, then the successor should be prepared to list precisely what information is required and give reasons that demonstrate why such additional information is 'relevant' in accordance with the regulations.

- It would be usual for the basis on which the information is to be provided to be documented in writing by an exchange of letters between the two auditors, copied to the audited entity. Guidance on suitable wording, including example letters, is provided in the Technical Release.

3.15.1 Practicalities of access

Where working papers are held electronically, the predecessor will need to consider how to provide access to the relevant audit documentation without putting at risk the confidentiality of the firm's audit methodologies or confidential information of other clients.

It is reasonable for the successor to make notes of the review but there is no obligation to allow copying of audit working papers. The Technical Release states that it would be reasonable to allow, as a minimum, the copying of extracts of the books and records of the client. It would also be reasonable and helpful to allow copying of papers such as breakdown of analyses of financial statement figures and documentation of the client's systems and processes.

If the successor does ask to copy documents, it would be sensible to check them and to keep a record of which items were copied.

The Technical Release also suggests that it would be reasonable for the predecessor auditor to seek to recover costs, but without any element of profit. However, there is no obligation on the successor to make any payment and therefore the predecessor may wish to look to the client for recovery of costs.

3.16 Conclusion

A properly maintained permanent file is essential in performing an effective audit under ISAs, and it is important that it is treated as such. Some audit systems use checklists to help the auditor consider relevant issues. An example of such a checklist is shown below.

Client:	Prepared by:	Date:	Ref:
Year end:	Reviewed by:	Date:	
File no:			

KNOW YOUR CLIENT CHECKLIST

Y, N,
N/A   ***PAF Ref***

This checklist is intended as an aide memoire for issues that should be addressed on the permanent file. Where a matter is relevant, it should be addressed in sufficient detail on the file so as to provide a basis for further review as part of the risk assessment or evaluation of systems. The checklist should not be regarded as exhaustive.

1. The sector in which the client operates

1.1   The market and competition, including demand, capacity, and price competition.

1.2   Cyclical or seasonal activity.

1.3   Product technology relating to the client's products.

1.4   Energy supply and cost.

2. The regulatory environment in which the client operates

2.1   Accounting principles and industry-specific practices.

2.2   Regulatory framework for a regulated industry.

2.3   Legislation and regulation that significantly affect the client's operations

- Regulatory requirements.

- Direct supervisory activities.

2.4   Taxation (corporate and other).

2.5   Government policies currently affecting the conduct of the client's business:

- Monetary, including foreign exchange controls.

- Fiscal.

- Financial incentives (for example, government aid programs).

- Tariffs, trade restrictions.

2.6   Environmental requirements affecting the industry and the client's business.

3. Other external factors currently affecting the client's business

3.1   General level of economic activity (for example, recession, growth).

3.2   Interest rates and availability of financing.

3.3   Inflation, currency revaluation.

4. The nature of the client's operations

Business operations

4.1   The nature of revenue sources (for example, manufacturer, wholesaler, banking, insurance or other financial services, import/export trading, utility, transportation, and technology products and services).

4.2   Products or services and markets (for example, major customers and contracts, terms of payment, profit margins, market share, competitors, exports, pricing policies, reputation of products, warranties, order book, trends, marketing strategy and objectives, manufacturing processes).

4.3   Conduct of operations (for example, stages and methods of production, business segments, delivery or products and services, details of declining or expanding operations).

4.4   Alliances, joint ventures, and outsourcing activities.

4.5   Involvement in electronic commerce, including Internet sales and marketing activities.

4.6   Geographic dispersion and industry segmentation.

4.7   Location of production facilities, warehouses, and offices.

4.8   Key customers.

4.9   Important suppliers of goods and services (for example, long-term contracts, stability of supply, terms of payment, imports, methods of delivery such as 'just-in-time').

4.10   Employment (for example, by location, supply, wage levels, union contracts, pension and other post-employment benefits, stock option or incentive bonus arrangements, and government regulation related to employment matters).

4.11   Research and development activities and expenditures.

4.12   Transactions with related parties.

Investments

4.13   Acquisitions, mergers or disposals of business activities (planned or recently executed).

4.14   Investments and dispositions of securities and loans.

4.15   Capital investment activities, including investments in plant and equipment and technology, and any recent or planned changes.

4.16   Investments in non-consolidated entities, including partnerships, joint ventures and special-purpose entities.

Financing

4.17   Group structure – major subsidiaries and associated entities, including consolidated and non-consolidated structures.

4.18   Debt structure, including covenants, restrictions, guarantees, and off-balance-sheet financing arrangements.

4.19   Leasing of property, plant or equipment for use in the business.

4.20   Beneficial owners (local, foreign, business reputation and experience).

4.21   Related parties.

4.22   Use of derivative financial instruments.

Financial reporting

4.23   Accounting policies and industry-specific practices.

4.24   Revenue-recognition practices.

4.25   Accounting for fair values.

4.26   Stocks/inventories (for example, locations, quantities).

4.27   Foreign currency assets, liabilities and transactions.

4.28   Industry-specific significant categories (for example, loans and investments for banks, accounts receivable and inventory for manufacturers, research and development for pharmaceuticals).

4.29   Accounting for unusual or complex transactions, including those in controversial or emerging areas (for example, accounting for share-based payments)

4.30   Financial statement presentation and disclosure.

5. Objectives, strategies and related business risks

How does the client address industry, regulatory and other risk factors relating to the following:

5.1   Industry developments (a potential related business risk might be that the client does not have the personnel or expertise to deal with the changes in the industry).

5.2   New products and services (a potential related business risk might be that there is increased product liability).

5.3   Expansion of the business (a potential related business risk might be that the demand has not been accurately estimated).

5.4   New accounting requirements (potential related business risks might be incomplete or improper implementation, or increased costs).

5.5   Regulatory requirements (a potential related business risk might be that there is increased legal exposure).

5.6   Current and prospective financing requirements (a potential related business risk might be the loss of financing due to the client's inability to meet requirements).

5.7   Use of IT (a potential related business risk might be that systems and processes are incompatible).

5.8   Effects of implementing a strategy, particularly any effects that will lead to new accounting requirements (a potential related business risk might be incomplete or improper implementation).

6. Measurement and review of the client's financial performance

6.1   Key ratios and operating statistics.

6.2   Key performance indicators.

6.3   Employee performance measures and incentive compensation policies.

6.4   Trends.

6.5   Use of forecasts, budgets and variance analysis.

6.6   Analyst reports and credit rating reports.

6.7   Competitor analysis.

6.8   Period-on-period financial performance (revenue growth, profitability, leverage).

7. Accounting systems

The client's systems should be documented to include the following areas:

7.1   The classes of transactions in the client's operations that are significant to the financial statements.

7.2   The procedures, within both IT and manual systems, by which those transactions are initiated, recorded, processed and reported in the financial statements.

7.3   The related accounting records, whether electronic or manual, supporting information, and specific accounts in the financial statements, in respect of initiating, recording, processing and reporting transactions.

7.4   How the information system captures events and conditions, other than classes of transactions, that are significant to the financial statements.

7.5   The financial reporting process used to prepare the client's financial statements, including significant accounting estimates and disclosures.

7.6   Roles and responsibilities in relation to financial reporting.

8.   Control environment?

Do we have notes on the attitude of the company to the following matters?

8.1   Communication and enforcement of integrity and ethical values.

8.2   Commitment to competence

8.3   Participation by those charged with governance

8.4   Management's philosophy and operating style

8.5   Assignment of authority and responsibility

8.6   Human resource policies and practices

9.   Risk of fraud

Do we have notes on the following matters?

9.1   Management's assessment of the risk that the financial statements may be materially misstated due to fraud.

9.2   Management's process for identifying and responding to the risks of fraud, including any specific risks of fraud that management has identified or any account balances, classes of transactions or disclosures for which a risk of fraud is likely to exist.

9.3   Management's communication, if any, with those charged with governance regarding its processes for identifying and responding to the risks of fraud in the entity.

9.4   Management's communication, if any, with employees regarding its views on business practices and ethical behaviour.

9.5   How those charged with governance exercise oversight of management's processes for identifying and responding to the risks of fraud in the entity, and the internal control that management has established to mitigate these risks.

10.   Control activities

10.1   For areas where there is a risk of material misstatement, do we have notes on relevant control activities?

Control activities include:
- *Authorisation/Performance reviews*
- *Information processing*
- *Physical controls*
- *Segregation of duties*

10.2   Are there any particular issues arising from the use of IT that require documenting?

11.   Monitoring controls

11.1   For areas where there is a risk of material misstatement, do we have notes on how the client monitors the operation of controls and control activities in those areas?

For example, monitoring by management or a separate internal audit function.

It is important to note that such checklists, however comprehensive, are simply a guide to the information that should be recorded. Completion of the checklist does not, in itself, provide compliance with ISAs.

Having reviewed and updated the permanent file where necessary, the auditor is ready to move on to the next stage of the audit planning.

Chapter 4 Accounting systems, processes and controls

4.1 Why document the system?

The auditor needs to be able to conclude as to whether the client has maintained books and records deemed 'proper' (for periods commencing before 6 April 2006) or 'adequate' (for periods commencing on or after 6 April 2008), in accordance with the Companies Act 1985 or the Companies Act 2006 respectively. This will necessitate the auditor obtaining an understanding of the client's accounting and internal control systems.

Moreover, ISA 315 *Understanding the entity and its environment and assessing the risks of material misstatement* requires auditors to obtain '...an understanding of internal control relevant to the audit', with a view to identifying types of potential misstatements, considering factors that affect the risks of material misstatement, and designing the nature, timing, and extent of further audit procedures. This applies even if the auditor is not going to rely on the accounting system.

Internal control as discussed in ISA 315 consists of the following components:

- the control environment;
- the entity's risk assessment process;
- the information system, including the related business processes, relevant to financial reporting, and communication;
- control activities; and
- monitoring of controls.

The auditor should therefore document the client's systems, paying particular attention to control aspects.

4.1.1 Other benefits

Documenting how a client's systems work will give the auditor a basic understanding of the client's business. This will enable the auditor to provide the client with useful commercial feedback on the way the business is run, thus providing the client with recommendations that can be utilised to ensure that the client remains effective in the market place.

By reviewing the client's systems, weaknesses can be identified and commercial points can be included in the management letter or management report, highlighting to the client where it could be losing money, or could make more money if the controls were put in place.

It is also possible that a full systems review may be requested by the client, which will lead to further work for the practice.

4.1.2 Controls testing or compliance-based approach

Testing controls, where possible, can lead to a more effective audit with reduced levels of substantive audit work. As the auditor is already required to document the systems and check the design and implementation of controls to comply with ISA 315, it may require only a little more time to go one stage further and test the operational effectiveness of the controls. Combining this with analytical review can reduce the level of substantive testing undertaken by at least a half.

Understanding the client's business and how the systems work is far more exciting than testing numerous invoices for a substantive test, and can provide the audit team with a more interesting and stimulating approach.

4.2 What is an information system?

Information systems produce reports containing information that make it possible for management to operate, control and report on a business. This information can relate to operational, financial or compliance matters or a combination of these – for example:

- **Operational matters**– production statistics, sales by customer, market share, warranty claims, stock movement reports;
- **Financial matters** – management accounts, budgets, cash-flow forecasts, trial balance, debtors' listings, bank reconciliations; and
- **Compliance matters** – personnel data, tax information, trading statistics.

Auditors are interested in the information systems that help management produce reliable financial statements. These are primarily the accounting systems. There may be an overlap between the purposes for which the information is used. For example, auditors will review the sales system to identify how despatches of sales are recorded and processed for the purposes of the financial statements; while the client may review the reports produced from the sales system to look at sales by customer for production purposes.

4.3 Types of system

An information system can be characterised by the following terms:

- **formal** – for example, IT-based accounting systems processing data;
- **informal** – for example, conversations with suppliers, regulators and customers (credit control);
- **routine** – for example, sales and purchases recording; or
- **one-off** – for example, market research initiatives, estimating provisions at the year end.

Whatever the nature of the system, auditors need to understand and evaluate its likely effectiveness in communicating information to management as part of the overall control of the business.

4.4 Which business processes should auditors document?

In order to identify the key business processes to be documented, the following steps should be considered:

- identify the significant account balances displayed in the financial statements (using your prior knowledge of the business);
- consider the underlying nature of the transactions (routine, non-routine or accounting estimates); and
- identify the client's procedures that process these transactions.

It is important when deciding what to document that the auditor considers what is important for the business rather than just simply focusing on large numbers in the accounts. For example, if the client was a consultancy business, a key business process would be wages and salaries. Not only is this a large expense in the accounts but a key factor in controlling the business and productivity, as such a business is a service-based industry.

Key business processes will often include those for recording sales, purchases, fixed assets, stock, wages and salaries.

It should also be noted that it does not matter whether the client's information system is manual or computerised; it should still be documented and understood.

Many clients will operate processes that are not relevant to the audit and therefore – in accordance with ISA 315 – need not be considered. The ISA gives the example of a commercial airline's automated procedures to maintain flight schedules, which while clearly important to the company, would not ordinarily be relevant to the audit.

4.4.1 Other areas requiring special attention

The client's procedures for consolidation and obtaining appropriate information in respect of FRS 17 *Retirement benefits* should also be documented, where relevant.

4.5 Understanding key business processes

Whatever documentation method auditors use, the same information should be recorded to confirm their understanding of the information they have been given. This includes the following elements:

- initiation of the transaction;
- processing;
- accounting records; and
- entities that do business electronically.

4.5.1 Initiation of the transaction

A transaction is any event (sale, purchase, cash receipt), between the client and a third party, which needs to be included in the financial statements. Each party to the transaction receives something from the transaction – for example, purchase of some goods for the customer and cash receipt for the client.

At the initiation stage, the information needed will include date, party, quantity and sometimes price. This will be the minimum information used to record the transaction in the system. This stage of the process can be split into the following three parts:

data capture – no transaction has occurred but information has been processed (for example, a purchase order);

initiation – for example, goods are received and checked and a goods received note is completed; and

data entry – for example, the goods received note details are entered onto the system to be matched with the invoice when sent from the supplier.

4.5.2 Processing

Processing considers how the system gathers together all the information about individual transactions and combines this information into accounting records. It is particularly important that this area is considered and recorded, but it is an area that is often ignored with computerised accounting packages, and the processing function is left as a 'black hole'. The auditor must understand how the processing function works in order to be able to audit it efficiently.

4.5.3 Accounting records

The auditor should review the information produced and consider whether or not it is sufficient to produce the accounting records.

4.5.4 Entities which do business electronically

The nature of the e-business strategy adopted by the entity will affect the special skills and knowledge that the auditor requires, which may include IT-related issues. The auditor should consider whether the firm has such knowledge, and whether the use of an expert is required (see section 10.4.5).

4.6 Controls over key business processes

A common weakness on many audit files is that the systems notes document the client's key business processes but do not adequately address controls. Having considered key business processes, ISA 315 also looks at controls from a further four aspects – namely, the control environment, the client's risk assessment process, control activities and the monitoring of controls. Each of these is looked at below, and needs to be documented as part of the auditor's systems notes.

4.6.1 The control environment

The control environment includes the attitudes, awareness, and actions of management of internal control and its importance within the business. The control environment also includes the governance and management of the entity and sets the tone of an organisation, providing discipline and structure and influencing staff. Having a strong control environment therefore forms the foundation of good internal controls.

ISA 315 notes that the control environment includes the following seven elements:

a) **Communication and enforcement of integrity and ethical values**

   Controls can only be effective where those who create, administer, and monitor them are people of integrity with ethical values. The integrity and ethical behaviour of client staff are those of the organisation as a whole. Hence interest in how they are communicated (for example, by policy statements or codes of conduct) and how they are reinforced in practice (for example, action taken by management to remove or reduce incentives and temptations that might prompt staff to engage in dishonest activities).

b) **Commitment to competence**

   This includes management's consideration of the competence levels for particular jobs, the related skills and knowledge needed and how they can be acquired by staff.

c) **Participation by the directors or trustees**

   The level of involvement of the directors or trustees is critical to a strong control environment. Apart from being responsible for the overall oversight of the organisation and its control, other relevant activities undertaken by them include scrutiny of staff's activities, raising and pursuing difficult questions with management and staff and taking suitable action.

d) **Management's philosophy and operating style**

   This includes matters such as management's attitude to risk, the aggressiveness of the accounting policies chosen by them and their manner in dealing with accounts staff.

e) **Organisational structure**

   This provides framework for the organisation, and takes into account authority, responsibility and reporting lines. Organisational structures vary widely, but to be effective should suit the needs of the particular organisation, taking into account its size, industry sector and operations, amongst other things.

f) **Assignment of authority and responsibility**

   This links into the organisational structure, by covering how authority and responsibilities are assigned and how reporting lines are established. It also includes the entity's policies on the conduct of business and the entity's objectives, and how they are communicated within the organisation.

g) **Human resources ('HR') policies and practices**

These relate to the recruitment, orientation, training, evaluation, counselling, promotion, compensation, and discipline of staff. ISA 315 includes the example of standards for recruiting the most qualified individuals with an emphasis on educational background, prior work experience, past accomplishments, and evidence of integrity and ethical behaviour. Such standards demonstrate the client's commitment to competent and trustworthy people.

It is clear that the size of the entity will affect its implementation of the above elements. For example, in small companies there may not be many, if any, layers of management between the staff and directors, and detailed codes of conduct and staff manuals may not exist. The control environment may be more informal in such entities, but its characteristics still set the tone and ethos of the organisation and have an important bearing on control risk.

Obtaining relevant information about the control environment can be done in several ways, including:

- inquiry of management and staff;
- observation of the actions and decisions of management and staff; and
- inspection of documents such as organisation diagrams, job descriptions, staff handbooks, firm-wide policies and communications to staff.

The information obtained by the second of these methods is likely to increase the longer the client is with the firm. Care therefore needs to be taken when auditing a new client for the first time, where the auditor's experience of the client is very limited.

Despite the importance of the control environment, this is an aspect of controls that many firms ignore, instead focusing their documentation on control activities. Much of the relevant information will be in the heads of the partner and manager, who may have worked on the client for the longest time and thus built up detailed knowledge and experience. It is important to document such matters on the file so that they can be fully taken into account when considering risk.

4.6.2 The client's risk assessment process

The client's risk assessment process is how it identifies and responds to business risks and their consequences. The auditor will be interested in how management identifies risks relevant to the preparation of financial statements, estimates their significance, assesses the likelihood of their occurrence, and decides how to manage them. An example might be the risk of material misstatement due to a significant estimate. Relevant risks may also include both internal and external events and circumstances which adversely affect the entity's ability to initiate, record, process, and report financial data.

Risks can arise or change due to circumstances, examples of which include:

- changes in the regulatory or operating environment;
- new members of staff;
- new IT systems;
- rapid growth of the business, particularly if the expansion is into new products, activities, markets or countries; and
- restructurings, including staff redundancies and changes in organisational structure.

Although smaller clients may not have formal, structured risk assessment processes, the above issues are still relevant to all organisations. Management may be aware of risks related to these objectives not through a formal process, but through direct personal involvement with employees and outside parties.

4.6.3 Control activities

Control activities are the policies and procedures that help ensure that management's wishes are carried out. Control activities, whether IT-related or manual can be used by both management and staff at various stages in the process.

Control activities relevant to the audit can be categorised as policies and procedures relating to the following elements:

- performance reviews;
- information processing;
- physical controls; and
- segregation of duties.

Performance reviews

These include activities such as reviewing of actual financial performance versus budgets, forecasts and prior years, comparing internal and external data and reviewing functional or activity performance.

Information processing

There are many types of control used to check the accuracy, completeness, and authorisation of transactions. These can be split into broadly two categories, namely application controls and general IT controls.

Application controls apply to the processing of individual applications, and help ensure that transactions occur, are authorised, and are completely and accurately recorded and processed. Examples include checking the arithmetical accuracy of records, numerical sequence checks, and manual follow-up of exception reports.

General IT controls are policies and procedures that relate to many applications and support the effectiveness of application controls. These commonly include controls over networks, software acquisition, development and maintenance, and access security. Specific examples include preventing users from making changes to software and password controls.

Physical controls

These activities encompass the physical security of assets. Examples include limiting access to assets, records, computer programs and data files, and periodic counting of cash or stock. The extent to which physical controls intended to prevent theft of assets are relevant to the audit will depend on the susceptibility of those to misappropriation, as well as their materiality.

Segregation of duties

This should reduce the opportunities for any one person to be in a position to both perpetrate and conceal errors or fraud in the normal course of his or her duties. Examples include reviewing bank reconciliations and approving purchase orders. Achieving appropriate segregation of duties can be difficult in small clients, but with the audit threshold increasing all the time, this is becoming less of a problem than it used to be.

4.6.4 Monitoring of controls

The monitoring of controls is a process to assess the quality of internal control performance over time to ensure that controls continue to operate effectively, and it requires corrective action to be taken where necessary.

Ongoing monitoring activities should be built into the normal recurring activities of management. For example, if the timeliness and accuracy of bank reconciliations are not monitored regularly, staff are likely to stop preparing them. Monitoring activities may also include using information from external third parties – for example, customers implicitly corroborate invoices by querying any that appear to be incorrect.

In many larger organisations, the work of internal auditors may contribute to the monitoring of controls. However, the monitoring activities of small entities are more likely to be informal and, typically, will be performed as a part of the overall management of the organisation. A key monitoring control in a smaller client is the review of management information against budget or forecast. Management's close involvement in the business often means that managers can identify significant variances from expectations and financial reporting inaccuracies.

4.7 Application of controls

This section gives examples of controls grouped by relevant assertion and by financial statement area. The lists are not exhaustive, but they may give the auditor an idea as to what type of controls to expect.

4.7.1 By assertion

Completeness

- Sequential numbering of goods despatched notes (GDNs) and goods received notes (GRNs).
- Sequentially numbered till rolls and cash banked daily.
- Exception reports of missing numbers.
- Numbered stock sheets at a stocktake.
- Matching of invoices to GDNs and GRNs.
- Fixed asset numbers.
- Numbered job cards followed through the manufacturing process.
- Numbers assigned to employees for personnel and payroll purposes.
- Pre-listing and comparison – for example, 12 cheques listed compared to 12 cheques entered onto the computer (batch totals).

Existence

- Signed proof of despatch by the customer on receipt of goods.
- Sales credits are authorised before despatch.
- Goods checked on receipt and a GRN completed and matched to the supplier invoice.
- Exception reports of despatch notes producing more than one invoice.
- Signed contracts for all employees, including P45 and references where relevant.
- Regular physical inspection of assets owned by the company.
- Stock checks carried out on a regular basis.
- Purchase invoices are authorised by an appropriate person.
- Checking data to master files (for example, stock prices).
- Authorisation – for example, purchase orders authorised before an order is placed.
- Cancellation of spoilt cheques.

Accuracy

- Batch totals of information entered onto the computer.
- Add list kept and checked to the totals entered onto the computer.
- Regular review of the customer database to ensure that customer names and addresses are correct.
- Price list updated and regularly reviewed for changes.
- Grid stamp signed by the staff checking the date, quantity and price on the supplier invoice to the GRN.
- Payments made are checked against the supporting documentation and authorised.
- Employee payroll records are only updated from signed contracts each year following director approval.
- Validity checks are undertaken to ensure, for example, that sales discounts are always within a specific range.

4.7.2 By financial statement area

Sales

Where the client operates credit control procedures for debtors, this should effectively control the existence and accuracy of debtors, and the completeness and accuracy of cash receipts provided that the following occur:

- new customers are asked for suitable credit references and a search is completed;

- credit limits are set, regularly reviewed and adhered to;

- remittance advices are sent to customers on a monthly basis;

- overdue debtors are regularly reviewed by an authorised person and agreed action taken to recover the money;

- overdue debtors are put on stop until money is received;

- the detailed debtors' ledger is regularly reconciled to the sales ledger control account; and

- any differences identified are reviewed and written off as appropriate.

Purchases

If the client regularly reconciles all suppliers' accounts to supplier statements and an independent person reviews the statements, making adjustments where necessary, this should cover the completeness, existence and accuracy objectives. Nil balances on the client's ledger should also be reconciled.

Bank and cash

Reconciliations should be performed on a regular basis between the cash book, bank statements and the nominal ledger, to ensure completeness, existence and accuracy. A person of an appropriate level should review the reconciliations, looking particularly at reconciling differences and making any necessary adjustments to correct the client books if appropriate.

Tangible fixed assets

- A budget detailing the capital commitment should be drawn up at the beginning of the year, and agreed by the relevant owners of the business or the directors.

- Any addition during the year should only be made after the relevant authorisation form has been completed. If the addition has already been agreed as part of the capital budget at the start of the year, the department manager's signature should be required.

- If the capital purchase had not been agreed at the start of the year in the capital budget, a director's signature should also be required.

- The authorisation forms should be sequentially numbered and filed.

- The management should undertake regular existence checks of the fixed assets, with the results being reconciled to the fixed assets register. Larger capital items should have unique numbers assigned to them from the fixed asset register.

- No capital items should be scrapped or sold without the prior approval of the directors. Levels of authority can be set for this purpose. For example, allowing disposals of up to a set amount to be dealt with by a manager.

- A regular review of depreciation rates should be undertaken to ensure that the rates are adequate and not excessive.

Stock

- Regular stock checks should be undertaken by the management. Any discrepancies between book stock and physical stock should be fully investigated to identify pilfering, damaged, or misrecorded items. The book values should be corrected.

- Variances highlighted between standard cost and actual cost should be investigated over and above an agreed limit, to ensure that management has adequate control over pricing and quantity purchased.

- Stock movements should be reviewed within the above exercise to identify slow-moving or obsolete items.

4.8 Documenting key business processes and controls

The easiest way to do this is to start from the final figures included within the accounts, and work back to the initiating transaction. This approach ensures that the auditor does not document any unnecessary information. For example, if the auditor started from a despatch note, in a company with basic procedures, there may be four copies that are sent to different places. The auditor is interested in the copy sent to the accounts department to raise the invoice. By working from the sales account and tracking back to the despatch note the auditor has immediately identified the documents needed, and has not wasted time recording information that may not be used for the accounting records (for example, a copy kept on the customer file).

There are numerous documentation methods, the most common of which involve the use of narrative notes, flowcharts or questionnaires. These can either be used individually or in conjunction with each other, depending on the size and complexity of the client and the preferences of the auditor.

4.8.1 Narrative notes

Narrative notes are usually sufficient for smaller, more straightforward clients. When completing a manual record of the accounting system, the auditor's notes will need to include:

- a brief description of the key business processes;
- a description of the controls at each stage of the process; and
- a walk-through test to confirm the auditor's understanding.

The notes should:

- be clear and concise;
- be easy to review; and
- lay out the controls in a logical manner.

A two-column approach can work well, with the systems notes in the left-hand column and details of the controls operating at each stage in the right-hand column. Some firms use a four-column approach, with additional columns for risks identified and points for the letter of comment, which ties in the systems notes directly with the risk assessment. Alternatively, narrative notes can benefit from the use of a highlighter to pick out the key controls from the text.

An example of effective narrative notes is shown below.

Example Company Limited   *AW 3/08*   **3.4**

Systems Notes

Purchase ordering

	Weakness (Ref A6)	Control (Ref C5.1)
A1 Purchase order completed by Terence Ipplepen (TI).		
A2 Orders above £ 1,500 are authorised by Raymond Chard (RC).		Y (16)
A3 Orders with new suppliers are authorised by Raymond Chard (RC).		Y (17)
A4 Orders are three part documents and are pre-numbered:		
1. Copy to supplier		
2. Copy retained by TI		
3. Copy to accounts.		
A5 TI copy filed by supplier.		
A6 Accounts copy placed in an order outstanding file in numerical order.		
A7 The outstanding orders file is periodically reviewed by RC.		Y (18)
A8 Any acknowledgements of orders from suppliers are filed by TI by supplier.		

Goods received – factory

	Weakness	Control
B1 All deliveries are recorded in a goods received book. This lists the date, supplier, goods received note number and purchase order number.		
B2 Goods received are checked against the goods received note (GRN).		Y (3)
B3 Any missing items are reported to the supplier and noted on the (GRN).		Y (3)
B4 The GRN is signed by the stores manager.		Y (3)
B5 Stock records are updated from the GRN. This is also noted on the GRN.		
B6 The GRN is passed to accounts.		
B7 The GRN is matched with the outstanding purchase order		
B8 If any items on the order are still outstanding, a copy of the order is taken and placed on the outstanding orders file, which is amended to show what is still outstanding.		
B9 The order with the GRN attached is placed on a fulfilled orders file in purchase number order.		
B10 There is a separate lockable store for the more valuable components, to which only the directors, the store manager and the factory manager have a key.		Y (4)

Purchase invoices (all)

	Weakness	Control
C1 All invoices are recorded in the purchase day book.		
C2 Invoices are matched to orders from the fulfilled orders file.		
C3 Invoices that match with an fulfilled order that has been signed by TI or RC are approved for payment by Adrian Walker (AW) .		Y (19)

C4	The cost per unit for each component for this delivery is updated in the factory stock records (maintained in Access – see below) from the invoice and goods received note.	
C5	The invoices are then placed on a payment pending file with the purchase order and GRN attached.	
C6	Invoices not fully supported by an approved order are sent to RC for approval.	Y (7)
C7	Authorised invoices returned by RC are added to the payment pending file.	

Payments

D1	There is a weekly purchase ledger payment run.	
D2	Invoices in the payment pending file are reviewed by AW to identify those due for payment based on the credit terms agreed with the supplier.	
D3	A list of proposed payments is produced and presented to Adele Long (AL), together with the supporting invoices, orders and GRNs, for approval.	Y (20)
D4	All payments are made by bank transfer where possible.	
D5	Once paid, invoices (with orders and GRNs attached) are filed in numerical order of the payment reference (electronic or cheque).	
D6	All payments are recorded in the cash book by the accounts department.	

Purchase ledger

E1	The purchase ledger is posted weekly from the purchase day book and cash book.	
E2	All supplier statements are reconciled as received by AW.	Y (11)
E3	Any differences are investigated by AW.	
E4	All completed supplier statement reconciliations are reviewed by AL.	Y (12)
E5	Any adjustments to a purchase ledger account as a result of a reconciliation must be approved by AL.	

Factory production

F1	Each batch of cards is given a job number. All card types use the same number sequence. A suffix is added to denote the card type.	Y (5)
	S = Sound card	
	G = Graphics card	
	N = Network card	
	T = TV tuner card	
F2	When a job is created, the production manger starts a job card and records the components to be issued.	
F3	The stores manager checks that the components issued match those recorded on the job card.	
F4	Factory inventory records are updated from the job card and the job card is initialled to indicate that this has occurred.	

F5   As the job moves through the factory, labour hours are added by each section.

F6   The completed number of cards is recorded on the job card.

F7   Factory stock records are updated from the job card before the job cards are sent to factory manager.

F8   TI reviews the job cards for all completed jobs to ensure that the materials and labour booked to each job appear reasonable.   Y (6)

F9   TI prices the job cards based on the hourly rates for each section and the cost of components booked to the job.

F10   The factory stock records are updated for the costs of new production batches by TI.

Factory stock records

G1   Records are maintained in an Access database.

G2   A despatch note is generated for all transfers to the warehouse in Taunton.

G3   The stock records are updated from the despatch notes by the stores manager, who retains a copy in date order.

G4   The component cost for each delivery is updated by the accounts department.   Y (8)

G5   All components are valued at latest invoice price although the database keeps a record of the quantity and cost of each delivery.   Y (9)

G6   A sample of stock lines is counted each week to confirm the accuracy of the stock records. The number of lines counted each week is such that every line is counted at least once a year in addition to the year-end count

G7   Any discrepancies in the counts are investigated by the stores manager   Y (7)

G8   Any damaged or apparently old stock is also reported to the stores manager.

Goods received – warehouse

H1   Stock records are updated from the factory despatch note.

H2   The goods received are not checked against the despatch note.   Y (4)

Sales

I1   All customer orders are approved by AL in terms of creditworthiness, ability to satisfy order, etc.   Y (13)

I2   Accounts check the order against the stock records to confirm that the items required are in stock.   Y (14)

This control may not work effectively as the warehouse stock records are not up to date. (AW)

I3   Where there is insufficient stock to meet an order, the order is passed back to AL, who liaises with RC to determine whether further cards should be manufactured.

I4   Where there is sufficient stock. AW generates a sales invoice from the customer order.

I5	This is a five-part pre-numbered document:	Y (15)
	1. Sales invoice to customer	
	2. Accounts copy – numerical	
	3. Accounts copy – alphabetical	
	4. Despatch note to customer	
	5. Picking list for stores.	
I6	The sales invoice is sent to the customer	
I7	The despatch note and picking list are sent to the warehouse.	
I8	Warehouse staff use the picking list to collate the order.	
I9	The picking list is initialled as fulfilled and filed in numerical order.	
I10	Goods are sent to the customer with the despatch note.	
I11	Sales are recorded on a daily basis in the sales day book	

Warehouse stock records

J1	Warehouse stock records are kept on an Access database. This is separate from the factory database but is structured in an identical way.		
J2	There is a backlog of despatch notes to be entered on the system	Y (3)	
J3	There should be weekly counts of stock lines, as in the factory stores. However, these are not undertaken, as backlogs in processing factory despatch notes and picking lists mean that the stock records are frequently wrong.	Y (3)	

Sales ledger

K1	Sales are posted daily from the sales day book.		
K2	Receipts from customers are allocated to the sales ledger in accordance with remittance advice notes on a daily basis.		
K3	Customer remittance advice notes are filed in date order.		
K4	An aged analysis of debtors is produced every month and is reviewed by AL.		Y (8)
K5	Any late payment on larger accounts is dealt with directly by AL. Smaller accounts are passed to AW to chase.		Y (9)

Payroll

L1	Payroll for the warehouse and the factory are maintained on A+Payroll package by the accounts department.		
L2	For weekly paid staff the respective payrolls (factory and warehouse) are approved by TI and TW prior to payment.		Y (22)
L3	Overtime is notified on a weekly basis and is paid a week in arrears.		
L4	Overtime is approved by the warehouse and factory managers.		Y (23)
L5	Monthly staff (directors and managers) are not paid overtime.		
L6	The monthly payroll is approved by AL.		
L7	All payments are by bank transfer.		

Other expenditure

M1	All expenditure outside the normal production process must be approved by one of the directors.

	Y (21)

Cash book

N1	The cash book is posted daily.
N2	All bank accounts are reconciled monthly by AW.
N3	All reconciliations are reviewed by AL.

	Y (10)
	Y (10)

Accounting system

O1	This is maintained on A+Accounts package.
O2	Exceptions reports are run each week by AW and reviewed by AL to confirm the integrity of data posting.
O3	There is a network across the warehouse and the factory.
O4	A back-up is run overnight at the end of each working day and stored off-site.
	There are five back-up tapes (one for each day of the week), so at any time there is five days' worth of back-ups. In addition, the month-end tapes are retained.

	Y (24)
	Y (25)

Fixed assets

P1	The fixed asset register is maintained in Excel by AW.
P2	All assets have a label with a unique number that corresponds to the entry in the fixed asset register.
P3	The register includes the cost, location and date of purchase of each asset.
P4	AW periodically checks a sample of assets from the register to the physical assets. However, this is not done on a regular basis and the records are not always retained.

	Y (1)
	Y (2)

4.8.2 Flowcharts

Flowcharts can be a useful cost-effective approach to documenting a system, particularly for larger or more complicated clients. The same points will need to be considered as for narrative notes, as follows:

- the chart should be clear and concise;
- a key should be provided to explain the symbols, especially if the standard symbols are not used;
- controls should be identified and commented upon; and
- the chart needs to be easy to review.

Flowcharts can give a good overview of how the system works, particularly for the person performing the review, and a combination of narrative notes and flowcharts for more complicated areas can be very effective. However, flowcharts can be time-consuming to produce manually and are difficult to update. For these reasons, the use of software is strongly recommended. Whilst there are specific flowcharting software packages, spreadsheet packages such as Excel have good flowcharting capabilities that are easy to use and quick to update. Excel also provides a key to each of the commonly used symbols, a plus for those not too familiar with them.

4.8.3 Questionnaires

Some firms may use questionnaires, which can be useful in helping the auditor gain an understanding of the overall system. However, where questionnaires are used, the auditor should ensure that sufficient thought is put into their completion and that they are not merely completed by rote. Furthermore, the questionnaires may not cover all the aspects of every client's key business processes and controls, so care should be taken not to omit any important areas.

An example of a completed questionnaire is shown below.

Client: Example Company Limited	Prepared by: *aw*	Date	*11/3*	Ref:
Year end: 31 Dec 2007	Reviewed by:	Date:		**S4**
File no: M0001				

INTERNAL CONTROL QUESTIONNAIRE

*This questionnaire is intended as an aid memoire to assist in the identification of systems and controls for inclusion on the Review of Design & Implementation of Controls schedule (**C5.1**). Completion of this questionnaire in isolation will not provide the evidence concerning the design and implementation of controls required by ISA 315.*

		Relevant to audit (Y/N)	Ref to C5.1	Ref to: A6 / C6.2 C6.3
	Property, plant and equipment			
1	Are minutes maintained of all board meetings and management meetings, authorising capital expenditure and disposals?	*y*		*a6.1*
2	Does the company maintain fixed asset purchase order requisitions, which are pre-numbered, authorised and controlled?	*y*	*C5.1.1*	
3	Is there evidence to show that the addition invoices have been checked for accuracy and that the posting code has been checked before the items are posted to the nominal ledger?	*n*		
4	Is the fixed asset register regularly reconciled to the nominal ledger account, and also to actual physical assets?	*n*	*C5.1.2*	*a6.2*
5	Is there independent checking of calculations of profits and losses on disposal?	*n*		
6	Is there evidence to show that there have been regular inspections of the condition and use of assets?	*n*		
7	Other:	*n/a*		
	Inventories			
8	Is there restricted access to inventories, and physical security over inventories?	*y*	*C5.1.4*	
9	Is there an independent check on all despatches, including any made by persons other than those responsible for inventories?	*n*		
10	Are regular reconciliations of actual inventory to inventory records undertaken?	*y*	*C5.1.7*	*a6.3*
11	Is there independent matching of goods in and out with purchase and sales documentation?	*y*		*a6.4*
12	Is there a system for the reporting of slow, obsolete or damaged inventory to relevant levels of management?	*y*		
13	Does the client maintain pre-numbered goods received notes (GRN) and stock requisition notes (SRN), and carry out regular checking for missing numbers?	*y*		*a6.4*
14	Is there a record of an authorisation of scrapped and damaged goods?	*n*		
15	Other:	*n/a*		

Sales cycle

16	Does the business have some form of control over whom they sell goods to on credit?	*y*	*C5.1.13*	
17	Is there prior approval by the credit department of all sales before the goods are actually despatched?	*y*	*C5.1.13*	
18	Is there prompt billing of all sales?	*y*		
19	Is effective credit control exercised over outstanding balances?	*y*	*C5.1.9*	
20	Are sales ledger control account reconciliations carried out?	*y*		
21	Does the client use pre-printed and controlled sequentially numbered invoices?	*y*		
22	Are invoices only raised when the invoicing department is given a valid order or despatch note?	*y*		
23	Is there a periodic separate check of the goods that have been despatched to ensure that they agree with the order details and the invoice details?	*n*		
24	Are despatch notes independently checked to invoices?	*na*		
25	Is invoice pricing independently checked and reviewed?	*n*		
26	Other:	*n/a*		

Bank

27	Are the duties of the person writing or posting the cash book separated from the person responsible for the nominal ledger, making payments or handling receipts and checking the bank reconciliations?	*y*		
28	Is there adequate security over blank cheques and procedures to ensure that under no circumstances should pre-signed cheques be maintained?	*y*		
29	Are cash book balances regularly reconciled to the nominal ledger control account?	*y*		
30	Are cheques despatched immediately after signature and not returned to the person who has prepared them?	*y*		
31	Does a senior member of the client's staff independently check bank reconciliations?	*y*	*C5.1.10*	
32	Are cash counts undertaken on a regular basis, without the person in charge of petty cash being aware that they are going to be undertaken?	*y*		
33	Other:	*n/a*		

Purchases

34	Are all invoices approved prior to payment?	*y*		
35	Are there controls to ensure that discounts are taken wherever possible?	*y*		
36	Are supplier statement reconciliations carried out where available?	*y*	*C5.1.11*	
37	Are purchase ledger control account reconciliations carried out?	*y*		
38	Are purchase invoices checked to pre-numbered goods received notes, which in turn are checked to authorised orders?	*y*		

39	Are invoices marked when they are being paid to prevent them being entered into the system again?	*y*		
40	Other:	*n/a*		

Payroll

41	Is the payroll independently approved for accuracy?	*y*	*C5.1.22*	
42	Does an independent department keep proper personnel records?	*y*		
43	Does the payroll department maintain a formal record of notification of changes in rates of pay, etc.?	*y*		
44	Are payroll control account reconciliations carried out?	*y*		
45	Other:	*n/a*		

General

46	Is the culture of the organisation conducive to the effective operation of internal controls?	*y*		
47	Does management use its influence in the business to promote the effective operation of internal controls?	*y*		
48	Are reliable management accounts produced at least quarterly and reviewed by management so that significant errors would be identified and corrected?	*n*		*a6.6*
49	Other:	*n/a*		

4.9 Assessing the design and implementation of controls

Once the client's key business processes and controls have been documented, the auditor should asses the design and implementation of those controls. It is important to clearly distinguish between this, and the testing of the operational effectiveness of controls. Evaluating the design of a control involves considering whether the control, individually or in combination with other controls, is theoretically capable of effectively preventing, or detecting and correcting, material misstatements. Implementation of a control means that the control exists and that the client is actually using it. This will not provide sufficient evidence that the actual operation of the control is effective throughout the period.

The auditor should consider the design of a control before checking whether it has been implemented, as there is little point in checking the implementation of a control that is known to be inherently weak or ineffectual by design.

Suitable procedures to test the design and implementation of controls may include:

- inquiring of entity personnel;
- observing the application of specific controls;
- inspecting documents and reports; and
- tracing transactions through the information system.

Paragraph 55 of ISA 315 is explicit in stating that inquiry alone is not sufficient to evaluate the design of a control relevant to an audit and to determine whether it has been implemented. Therefore wherever inquiries are made in connection with the design and implementation of controls, additional procedures should be undertaken as well.

One way to approach the testing of the design and implementation of controls is to summarise a list of key controls and test them individually. The following worked example illustrates how this approach might be documented.

Client: Example Company Limited			Ref:
	Prepared by:	*aw*	Date: *11/3*	**C5.1**
Year end: 31 Dec 2007	Reviewed by:	*BL*	Date: *12/3*	
File no: M0001			

REVIEW OF DESIGN AND IMPLEMENTATION OF INTERNAL CONTROLS

ISA 315 requires the auditor to obtain an understanding of the client's system of internal control relevant to the audit. It is compulsory to review the design and implementation of all controls relevant to the audit for all audits irrespective of any decision to place reliance on the effective operation of those controls. Completion of this schedule does not constitute tests on the effective operation of controls.

Inquiry alone is not sufficient to evaluate the design of a control relevant to the audit and to determine whether it has been implemented. Further work, such as inspecting documents or tracing transactions through the system, is required.

Ref to PAF 3.4

	Business area	Outline of information system and controls	Comment on design and effectiveness of controls	Comment on implementation of controls	Ref to letter of weakness	Further testing required? Y/N	Ref to ICE (S3) where tested
1	**Fixed assets**	All assets have a label with a unique number that corresponds to the entry in the fixed asset register. (PAF 3.4-P2)	This is an effective means of identifying specific assets.	From assets seen when touring the factory and offices, the system is being used.	N/A	N	N/A
2		Adrian Walker periodically checks a sample of assets from the register to the physical assets. However, this is not done on a regular basis and the records are not always retained. (PAF 3.4-P4)	The control would be effective if carried out on a regular basis.	Adrian Walker was unable to state when checks were last performed and he did not have any notes of checks undertaken.	A6.2	N	N/A
3	**Stocks – factory**	Goods received are checked against the GRN and this is noted on the GRN and signed by the stores manager. (PAF 3.4-B2-B4)	This is an effective control.	A review of the GRN file for June 2007 indicated that the control appeared to be operating.	N/A	Y	S3.1

4	There is a separate lockable store for the more valuable components to which only the directors, the store manager and the factory manager have a key. (PAF 3.4-B10)	The store is secure and access to the key is sufficiently restricted.	The more valuable components were found in the store during the inventory count.	N/A	N	
5	Each batch of cards is given a job number. All card types use the same number sequence. A suffix is added to denote the card type. (PAF 3.4-F1)	This is an effective control.	The job listing shows that all jobs have a sequential number.	N/A	N	
6	Terry Ipplepen reviews the job cards for all completed jobs to ensure that the materials and labour booked to each job appear reasonable. (PAF 3.4-F8)	The scope of this review is not clear. In particular, it is not clear whether the pricing of components is checked.	Job cards are priced at the same time, so some element of review must occur.	A6.8	N	
7	Any discrepancies in the weekly inventory counts are investigated by the stores manager. (PAF 3.4G7)	This is an effective control.	The file of weekly counts was reviewed and there was evidence of items being queried and followed up.	N/A	Y	S3.3
Stocks – warehouse	No controls that work!					
8	*Debtors* — The sales ledger aged debt analysis is reviewed every month by Adele Long. (PAF 3.4-K4)	This is an effective control as Adele Long knows all the major customers.	The review often takes place on screen, so there is no direct evidence as such. However, correspondence with customers about overdue accounts suggests they are reviewed and identified.	A6.3 A6.4	N	

#	Category	Control	Assessment	Findings			Ref
9		Any late payment on larger accounts is dealt with directly by Adele Long. Smaller accounts are passed to Adrian Walker to chase. (PAF 3.4-K5)	This is an effective control.	Correspondence with customers concerning overdue accounts is kept in a separate file. A review of the file during the planning visit showed that letters and emails were sent throughout 2007.	N/A	N	
10	**Bank and cash**	All bank accounts are reconciled monthly by Adrian Walker and the reconciliations reviewed by Adele Long. (PAF 3.4-N2, N3)	This is an effective control.	The year end reconciliation was signed by Adele Long and did not have any old reconciling items.	N/A	N	
11	**Creditors**	All supplier statements are reconciled by Adrian Walker. (PAF 3.4-E2)	This is an effective control.	Files of supplier statement reconciliations exist for each month.	N/A	Y	S3.4
12		All supplier reconciliations reviewed by Adele Long and any adjustments to a purchase ledger account as a result of a reconciliation must be approved by Adele Long. (PAF 3.4-E4, E5)	This is an effective control.	Some reconciliations showed evidence of review by Adele Long.	N/A	Y	S3.5
	Provisions	No controls			N/A	N/A	
	Taxation	No controls			N/A	N/A	
	Capital and reserves	No controls			N/A	N/A	
	Directors' loan accounts and transactions	No controls			N/A	N/A	
13	**Sales**	All customer orders are approved by Adele Long in terms of creditworthiness, ability to satisfy order, etc. (PAF 3.4-I1)	This is an effective control.		N/A	Y	S3.6

14		Accounts check the order against the stock records to confirm that the items required are in stock. (PAF 3.4-I2)	This would be an effective control if the inventory records were up to date. Since they are unreliable, so is the control.	There was no indication from the order that this check had taken place.	A6.5	N	
15		The picking list, despatch note and sales invoice are part of the same five-part document. Therefore, goods cannot be despatched without an invoice being raised. (PAF 3.4-I5)	This is an effective control.	This is a multi-part set.	N/A	N	
16	Purchases and other expenses	Terry Ipplepen authorises purchase orders. Those above £10,000 are authorised by Raymond Chard. (PAF 3.4-A2)	This is an effective control.	Orders are signed by Terry Ipplepen or Raymond Chard.	N/A	Y	S3.7
17		Orders with new suppliers are authorised by Raymond Chard. (PAF 3.4-A3)	This is an effective control.	Orders are signed by Raymond Chard.	N/A	N	
18		The outstanding orders file is periodically reviewed by Raymond Chard. (PAF 3.4-A7)	This would be an effective control if the review happened on a regular basis.	There is no evidence that the review occurs.	A6.10		
19		Invoices that match an approved fulfilled order that has been signed by Terry Ipplepen or Raymon Chard are approved for payment by Adrian Walker. (PAF 3.4-C3)	This is an effective control.	Invoices are signed as evidence of approval.	N/A	Y	S3.2
20		A list of proposed payments is produced and presented to Adele Long, together with the supporting invoices, orders and GRNs, for approval. (PAF 3.4-D3)	This is an effective control.	There is no evidence of the control operating; however, Adele Long was seen to be doing this on the afternoon of the planning visit.	N/A	N	

21		All expenditure outside the normal production process must be approved by one of the directors. (PAF 3.4-M1)	This is an effective control.	Invoices are signed as evidence of approval.	N/A	Y	S3.8
22	*Payroll*	Payrolls for weekly staff at the factory, weekly staff at the warehouse and for all monthly staff are authorised by the factory manager, warehouse manager and finance director respectively. (PAF 3.4-L2)	This is an effective control.	Approval was seen to be evidenced on the payrolls for the previous month.	N/A	Y	S3.9
23		Overtime is approved by the warehouse and factory managers. (PAF 3.4-L4)	This is an effective control.	Approval was seen to be evidenced on the payrolls for the previous month.	N/A	N	
24	*Accounting system*	Exceptions reports are run each week by Adrian Walker and reviewed by Adele Long to confirm the integrity of data posting. (PAF 3.4-O2)	The control is effective in terms of the integrity of data.	The reports are run on screen and so the review is not evidenced.	N/A	N	
25	*Other relevant IT systems*	A back-up is run overnight at the end of each working day and stored off-site. (O4)	This is an effective control.	A member of the accounts staff was seen to load a new cartridge each morning and pass the back-up to Adrian Walker.	N/A	N	
	Production of management accounts	No controls.			N/A	N/A	
	Production of forecasts and business plans	No controls.			N/A	N/A	

Many firms use walk-through tests to check the design and implementation of controls, and there are two common mistakes when taking this approach:

● the test focuses on following documents through the system, and does not examine whether the document controls are actually operating at each stage; and

● multiple walk-through tests are undertaken. This can be one way to test the operational effectiveness of controls (see section 4.10 below), but if the auditor is only looking at design and implementation, then one walk-through test per business process is normally sufficient.

4.10 Testing the operational effectiveness of controls

Under certain circumstances, the auditor may try to rely on the controls operating over the client's systems. Paragraph 22 of ISA 315 notes that this is required when:

a) the auditor's risk assessment includes an expectation of the operating effectiveness of controls; or

b) substantive procedures alone do not provide sufficient appropriate audit evidence at the assertion level (for example, completeness of cash sales).

In order to place reliance on them, the relevant controls of the client must be tested to ensure that they have operated effectively throughout the period under audit. This is **not** the same as checking that controls have been implemented (though it may be more efficient to undertake both types of testing at the same time). This is a common misapprehension among many auditors, and usually results in insufficient evidence to justify the reliance on controls and the reduction of substantive sample sizes, and hence insufficient audit evidence to support the audit opinion.

Many firms choose to undertake compliance testing at the same time as the main audit fieldwork. However, if the results of the compliance testing are not successful, the audit approach will almost certainly have to be changed, impacting on the substantive testing. If this has already been started, it might result in staff wasting time by having to extend substantive samples, and the staff may even run out of time to complete the work. It is generally much better to undertake any planned controls testing at the planning stage, which will allow the planning of the audit approach with a greater degree of confidence.

4.10.1 Types of controls test

The main techniques used to test controls are:

● observation;

● inquiry;

● inspection; and

● computation.

Observation and inquiry require the checking of information obtained against other sources. The auditor may want to consider performing these tests at different times during the period being audited, as the test only ensures that the test is working when the control is actually observed. This could be considered at the planning stage, during an interim visit or at the stocktake. Alternatively, where a control is computerised, the use of CAATs may provide excellent audit evidence throughout the period.

It should be noted that – as set out in paragraph 29 of ISA 315 – tests of inquiry alone are not sufficient to test the operational effectiveness of controls, and therefore additional procedures should always be carried out.

4.10.2 Sampling

Controls will vary in their frequency of performance – for example, daily reconciliation of the cash sheets to the cash in the till, or monthly bank reconciliations. The number of computations or inspections that the auditor should perform will depend on the frequency of the control and the auditor's judgment, as the types of sampling methodology used for substantive testing of a monetary population (see Chapter 14) are not suitable when testing controls. However, the following table has some rough guidelines.

Frequency of control activity	Sample size
Quarterly	2
Monthly	3
Weekly	5
More frequently than weekly	20

It is also important to carefully consider how to apply the sample size to the population. This can be done in a random way – to give every instance of the control operating an equal chance of being selected. However, it may also be beneficial to bias the sample. For example, if testing an authorisation control, it might be worth deliberately testing some items during the relevant director's or staff member's holidays or sick leave, as often this is when controls lapse.

Where the client has a computerised accounting system, as is the case with the vast majority of clients, the auditor should also consider whether there are adequate provisions in place in case of a breakdown, and whether the back-up procedures are acceptable.

4.10.3 Impact of testing results

The main advantage of the controls testing or compliance approach is that when the testing is successful, the amount of additional substantive testing can usually be reduced, a benefit that is considered further in Chapter 14. An additional benefit is that such controls need only be tested every three years, provided the auditor has checked that the area is not high risk and that there have been no changes to those controls in those years (if there have been changes, the auditor could not rely on the testing that was performed in previous years and would have to test those controls for the period under audit).

If, however, any instances of a control not operating properly are identified, the auditor should consider:

- the reason for the error, and whether it is possible to conclude if it was systematic, recurring or isolated;
- any impact on the system itself;
- the implications for the audit, particularly the risk assessment (see Chapter 6) and resulting audit approach (see Chapter 8);
- whether further testing is required; and
- the need to report to management.

Reports to management are considered further in Chapter 42. However, these are typically only thought about at the very end of the audit, often as more of an after-thought or 'box-ticking' procedure. However, compliance testing is usually done early in the audit process. If the auditor discovers significant weaknesses in controls, the sooner that management is informed, the sooner that any changes required can be actioned. This may necessitate sending an interim report to management at the planning stage.

4.11 Conclusion

In many instances the auditor will conclude that there are no controls that can be relied upon for audit purposes. In such cases, the auditor should still consider whether any controls could be introduced which could provide additional audit comfort and/or enable the client to maintain more effective control over the business.

However, where such controls exist, it is worth considering whether it would be more efficient and cost effective to go that additional step beyond the mandatory assessment of design and implementation to actually test and rely upon those controls. Even the smallest entity is likely to have some controls operating, and the compliance approach can be very effective.

Note that the auditor still needs to conclude whether or not the controls are sufficient to enable the company to prepare accounts that show a true and fair view as required by the Companies Act.

Chapter 5 Preliminary analytical procedures

5.1 Introduction

Paragraph 8 of ISA 520 *Analytical procedures* states: 'The auditor should apply analytical procedures as risk assessment procedures to obtain an understanding of the entity and its environment.'

A common reaction on first reading this is to say that this is not possible, as full draft accounts are available in advance in only a small proportion of audits of unlisted entities. This response incorrectly assumes that a preliminary analytical procedure scan only be performed on the draft statutory accounts.

This Chapter looks at the procedures the auditor can consider in order to carry out analytical review at the planning stage, particularly when draft accounts are not available. There is no doubt that the application of analytical procedures at the planning stage leads to a more effective audit plan. Such procedures enable the auditor to pinpoint, through reviewing the information available, particular areas within the accounts that have changed significantly since the previous year and those areas that are not meeting expectations. This could mean that these become potentially higher risk areas and, if not higher risk areas, then certainly areas of the audit to which the auditor will want to pay particular attention.

5.2 Analytical procedures to be used when the client produces its own accounts

Analytical procedures at the planning stage are more straightforward when the client produces draft accounts or a reasonably accurate trial balance to audit. This scenario is becoming more frequent as the audit threshold increases, as use of accounting software by larger clients is more common. The quality of information produced is also improving as clients become more familiar with that software.

The main procedure adopted when conducting analytical procedures at the planning stage will primarily be the calculation of ratios that are relevant to the particular client. Many standard accounts preparation packages are able to present such figures, ratios and variance analysis, comparing them to prior periods and/ or budget at the touch of a button.

The following table shows a list of ratios that could usefully be calculated.

Ratio	How calculated
Gross profit percentage	(Gross profit/turnover) $\times$ 100
Operating profit percentage	(Operating profit/turnover) $\times$ 100
Return on capital employed	(Profit after tax/shareholders' funds) $\times$ 100
Interest cover	Operating profit/interest payable
Debtor days*	(Trade debtors/credit sales) $\times$ 365†
Creditor days*	(Trade creditors/credit purchases) $\times$ 365†
Stock turnover	Trade purchases/closing stock
Current ratio	Current assets/current liabilities
Quick ratio	(Current assets − stock)/current liabilities
Gearing	Total borrowings/shareholders' funds
* Both figures should either include or exclude VAT.	
† This should be adjusted accordingly where the accounting period is not a year.	

It is important that only those ratios that are relevant to the particular business are calculated. Relevant ratios for other entities – such as charities, for example – may be somewhat different, such as the ratio of fundraising or administrative expenses as a proportion of income.

It should also be remembered that useful information can be obtained from comparing the results to industry statistics and other sources external to the business, as well as to internally prepared figures. Other procedures can involve the reconciliation of non-financial to financial data. For example, look at the average number of employees to assess whether or not the wages charge is reasonable.

The main reason for conducting analytical procedures at the planning stage is to identify the figures and ratios that have changed significantly since the previous accounting period. Situations where the auditor would have expected certain figures and ratios to have changed, but where in fact they have not, should also be identified. Therefore, the starting point for an auditor is to ascertain, through personal knowledge of and discussion with the client, what the expectations are for the period in question. Actual performance in key areas can then be compared with these expectations.

A typical example would be a company where the auditor knows that an additional site is being used to sell its goods, but where there has been no corresponding increase in the stock figure. This would be an area that should be specifically targeted for investigation during the main audit fieldwork.

As already noted, the benefit from preliminary analytical review derives from interpretation of the information available, so that problems and higher risk areas are identified and audit work directed to these more effectively. It is therefore important that some meaningful comments are made on the ratios calculated. It is all too common to see a schedule of standard ratios from an accounts package placed on file without comment, or only with an explanation of why the ratios are meaningless for that particular client!

Note that the conduct of the preliminary analytical review does not constitute extensive substantive analytical review procedures (which are discussed in more detail in Chapter 16) and, therefore, sample sizes on substantive tests cannot be reduced. The main objective is to help direct audit work to the key areas.

It is important to discuss the results of the planning analytical review with the client and to obtain any explanations for significant changes that were unexpected. The auditor should substantiate these explanations as part of the audit process. The results obtained and explanations given should also be borne in mind when assessing risk.

If the planning analytical review work indicates a decline in the financial health of the entity, then this should be highlighted as a potential risk and discussed further with the client at the earliest possible opportunity. The auditor should then build into the audit plan more time for considering the applicability of the going concern basis.

5.3 Budgets

The auditor can use procedures similar to those described in section 5.2 above when comparing any management accounts or trial balance produced by the client to budgets, rather than to the accounts of earlier years.

The budgets do not need to have been prepared by the client; any form of financial forecasting can be used – for example, any cash-flow or profit forecasts produced by the firm on behalf of the client.

If the accounts that are available at the planning stage show significant departures from the forecast figures, this could potentially lead to those areas being identified as having a higher risk of being materially misstated.

Any significant departures from budgets or forecasts in the figures or the ratios produced in any draft accounts presented to the auditor must be examined and explanations sought. Again, the auditor should substantiate any explanations as part of the audit process.

5.4 A common scenario – no draft statutory accounts

As long as draft accounts are available at the planning stage, conducting analytical procedures at the planning stage really only involves the application of common sense. However, ISA 520 recognises that draft statutory accounts will not always be available at the planning stage of all audits.

In such circumstances, the first response should probably be to look at the client's management accounts. With the increases in the audit threshold in recent years, the vast majority of audit clients should prepare some sort of management accounts, probably monthly or quarterly.

However, many management accounts are not prepared on the same basis as the statutory accounts – for example:

- some entities only calculate depreciation charges for year-end statutory purposes;
- no account may have been taken of any corporation tax due in respect of the current period;
- accruals and prepayments may not be calculated, or may be rough estimates only; and
- stock, debtor and warranty provisions may not always be fully updated.

The auditor should therefore determine the basis on which any management accounts have been drawn up, so as to take into account any limitations such as those noted above when analysing the financial performance and position of the entity.

Paragraph 9-1 of ISA 520 states: '...for those entities with less formal means of controlling and monitoring performance, it may be possible to extract relevant financial information from the accounting system, VAT returns and bank statements. Discussions with management, focused on identifying significant changes in the business since the prior financial period may also be useful.'

The Standard is saying that, in these circumstances, the auditor should look at whatever records the client has available in order to assess if there are any particular changes that may impact on the audit and assessment of risk. For example, if by reviewing the bank statements, the auditor determines that the company appears to be trading at or around its overdraft limit, then this could indicate a potential going-concern problem.

Many clients (for example, very small entities having a voluntary audit), although not able to prepare proper draft statutory accounts or even management accounts, may well prepare specific schedules from which the firm can prepare the accounts – for example, a listing of sales invoices issued or a sales day book. In this instance, the auditor could assess whether or not the sales were on a seasonal basis, consistent with expectations and previous years.

The auditor should aim to calculate key ratios, such as stock turnover and debtors days, as soon as the relevant information becomes available when the accounts are prepared. If the figures and ratios vary significantly from previous periods and this cannot be adequately explained, the risk assessments relating to that particular area need to be revisited and revised wherever necessary.

Analytical review at the planning stage may also take the form of a discussion with the directors of the business regarding how they feel the business has performed since the previous accounting period. Most clients will have a reasonable idea about how their business has performed in the previous 12 months. It is important, however, that the discussion is undertaken close to the year end so that any relevant events are still fresh in the minds of the entity's directors and management.

When conducting this discussion with the directors, the auditor should ensure that as much information as possible is collected in respect of any significant changes to the business. This will enable the auditor to identify any changes or fluctuations they would expect to see in the current year's accounts. It may be sufficient for the auditor to include narrative notes of the discussions with the directors regarding their expectations and what the accounts will show for the year in question.

Such a discussion has two benefits – not only does it help the efficiency and effectiveness of the audit, but it also helps client relations if the auditor shows willingness to discuss the client's business before work starts.

Chapter 6 Assessing risk

6.1 Introduction

Chapters 3, 4 and 5 looked at the gathering of information relevant to the audit. So, now we are ready to bring all that information together as we consider risk. The auditor's assessment of, and response to, risk arguably represent the most important stages of the audit. Chapters 6, 7 and 8 look at this process in more detail.

6.2 General principles

Before looking in detail at how the auditor assesses risk on a particular audit, it is useful to take a step back and look at why there is risk.

Risk derives from the expression of opinion in the audit report, and there are three key elements to consider:

1) **The auditor states that the audit has been conducted in accordance with ISAs.**

   This may not be the case if the auditor does not have the necessary procedures in place. If the omission is something mandatory, then the auditor will have issued an incorrect report.

2) **The opinion that the financial statements give a true and fair view.**

   This is obviously the key judgment, and much of this chapter deals with how the auditor addresses the risk of giving an incorrect opinion.

3) **The opinion that the financial statements have been properly prepared in accordance with the relevant statute, and for companies, that the directors' report is consistent with the financial statements.**

   The use of accounts preparation packages has in some ways made accounts preparation easier. However, some auditors have become over-reliant on such packages, and this increases the risk of incorrect or missing disclosure. Thoughtful completion of a disclosure checklist is still the best approach to ensuring correct disclosure.

The first and third risks described above are under the auditors' control. Proper use of an appropriate, up-to-date audit system and disclosure checklist should almost eliminate these risks. The second risk is less straightforward.

6.3 Audit Risk

Paragraph 15 of ISA 200 *Objectives and general principles governing and audit of financial statements* requires the auditor to '...plan and perform the audit to reduce audit risk to an acceptably low level that is consistent with the objective of an audit.' Audit risk is defined by ISA 200 as follows:

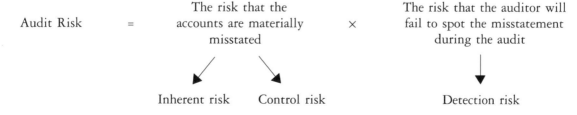

Audit Risk   =   The risk that the accounts are materially misstated   ×   The risk that the auditor will fail to spot the misstatement during the audit

Inherent risk   Control risk   Detection risk

Each element is considered in turn.

6.4 Inherent risk

Paragraph 20 of ISA 200 defines inherent risk as being 'the susceptibility of an assertion to a misstatement that could be material ... assuming that there are no related controls.'

The first point to note is that this is a risk of misstatement that is 'inherent' to an assertion, regardless of any controls that are in place. Factors affecting inherent risk can be internal or external, and are usually documented in the permanent file (as described in Chapter 3). Secondly, in order to understand the susceptibility of an assertion to misstatement, we need to understand what an assertion is.

6.4.1 Assertions

ISA 500 *Audit evidence* identifies a number of assertions made in financial statements, and categorises them by their affect on transactions, balances and disclosures within the financial statements. The auditor must obtain audit evidence to support the assertions made so they can also be considered as audit objectives.

Assertion	Definition	Category affected		
		Transactions and events	Account balances	Presentation and disclosure
Completeness	All transactions and events, assets, liabilities and equity interests that should have been recorded have been recorded, and all disclosures that should have been included in the financial statements have been included.	✓	✓	
Existence	Assets, liabilities, and equity interests exist.		✓	
Occurrence	Transactions and events that have been recorded and disclosed have occurred and pertain to the entity.	✓		✓
Accuracy	Amounts and other data relating to recorded transactions and events have been recorded appropriately, and financial and other information is disclosed fairly.	✓		✓
Valuation and allocation	Assets, liabilities, and equity interests are included in the financial statements at appropriate amounts, and any resulting valuation or allocation adjustments are appropriately recorded, and financial and other information is disclosed at appropriate amounts.		✓	✓
Rights and obligations	The entity holds or controls the rights to assets; liabilities are the obligations of the entity; and events, transactions and other matters pertain to the entity.		✓	✓
Cut off	Transactions and events have been recorded in the correct accounting period.	✓		

Classification and understandability	Financial information is appropriately presented and described, and disclosures are clearly expressed.			✓

Inherent risk is therefore the susceptibility of these assertions to misstatement before we consider any controls over these assertions.

Some assertions are generally considered to be more important than others in relation to particular types of asset, liability or transaction – for example:

- complex calculations are more likely to be misstated than simple calculations. Thus the inherent risk in a complex calculation (such as absorption of overheads into work in progress) will be higher; and

- the use of accounting estimates that are subject to significant measurement uncertainty have a higher inherent risk than financial statements consisting of relatively routine, factual data.

6.5 Assessing inherent risk

Since inherent risk factors can affect the approach to the audit generally, as well as impacting on individual assertions, the approach of most audit systems in assessing inherent risk can be illustrated in the following diagram.

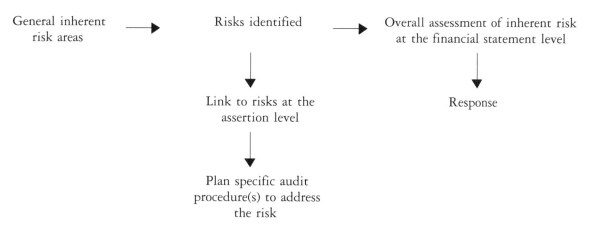

Many audit systems make use of detailed questionnaires to help the auditor identify relevant inherent risk factors. An example of such a questionnaire is given below.

Client: Example Company Limited	Prepared by:	AW	Date:	11/3	Ref:
Year end: 31 Dec 2007	Reviewed by:	BL	Date:	12/3	**C6.4**
File no: M0001					

DETAILED RISK ASSESSMENT

	General risk area	*Specific risk affecting client*	*Risk (high (H), medium (M) or low (L) or not applicable (N/A))*	*How will the audit risk be managed?*
1. General factors				
1.1	Do we have any concerns as to the integrity of the directors or management?	No particular concerns.	L	
1.2	Are there any untrained or inexperienced staff in key accounting roles?	No.	L	
1.3	Does the entity have a weak control environment?	Controls at warehouse are poor.	M	Specific assertion level risks identified on C6.3.
1.4	Is the appropriateness of the going-concern basis an issue?	No.	L	
1.5	Would you describe the relationship with the client as either 'abrasive' or 'deteriorating'?	Good relationship.	L	
1.6	Is there any significant external interest in the company's financial statements?	Only the bank and tax authorities.	L	
1.7	Are there any other risk factors that may affect the client at the financial statement level?	No.	L	
2. Industry conditions				
2.1	Is there a risk of technological obsolescence of products or services?	Products are continually renewed and updated.	L	
2.2	Is the company in a highly competitive or volatile sector of the economy?	The company has been around for some time and has regularly developed new products to keep up with the market.	M	C6.3

2.3	Is the company's business affected by fashion, demographic trends or public opinion?	No.	L	
2.4	Is the company affected by cyclical or seasonal factors?	Slight peak towards Christmas.	L	
3. Regulatory environment				
3.1	Is the client authorised by an external regulator?	No external regulator.	N/A	
3.2	Does the regulator require any special reports?	No.	N/A	
3.3	Are year-end returns or a copy of the accounts required to be filed with a trade association or regulator?	No.	N/A	
3.4	Does the client rely on membership of an association or similar body for a substantial part of its business?	No.	N/A	
3.5	Does the client operate in a business sector where there are likely to be additional regulations?	No.	N/A	
3.6	Are there any issues concerning eligibility for government grants or other aid programmes?	No.	N/A	
4. Other external factors				
4.1	Will the accounts be sent to a third party?	Bank and tax authorities.	L	
4.2	Are there any individually material third-party creditors?	Normal trade suppliers.	L	
4.3	Is there any expectation that the business (or part of it) may be sold in the near future?	Longer-term plan is to float company, but nothing in the short term.	L	
4.4	Are there any external factors (for example, a potential listing or bank financing) which could influence expected results?	None.	L	
5. Business operations				
5.1	Is the company reliant on only a few customers or suppliers?	Most components available from a number of suppliers, one exception is the nVidia graphics chip.	L	

5.2	Is the company heavily reliant on particular products or services?	Developing new products.	L	
5.3	Are there any significant related parties to the business?	No.	L	
5.4	Are there a large number of business locations and/or a wide geographical spread of its activities?	No.	L	
5.5	Are there any complex situations which might require the use of the work of an expert?	No.	L	
5.6	Is the company involved in electronic commerce, including internet sales?	Not yet, although it is planning to do this.	L	
5.7	Does the company carry out any research or development activities?	Yes, the company regularly develops new products.	L	
6. Investments				
6.1	Were there any acquisitions, mergers or disposals of business activities in the period or after the year end?	No subsidiaries, associates or joint ventures.	N/A	
6.2	Does the company have any investments in securities or loans?	None.	N/A	
6.3	Does the company have any investments in non-consolidated entities, including partnerships, joint ventures and special-purpose entities?	No.	N/A	
7. Financing				
7.1	Does the company have a complex capital structure?	Equity and loans.	L	
7.2	Are there any issues arising from the company's debt structure, including covenants, restrictions, guarantees, or off-balance-sheet financing arrangements?	No.	L	
7.3	Does the company use derivative financial instruments?	No.	L	

7.4	Are there any risks of material misstatement at the assertion level related to the fair value measurements and disclosures in the financial statements?	No.	L	
8. Financial reporting				
8.1	Have generally accepted accounting principles been complied with in the past years?	Yes.	L	
8.2	Are the accounting policies for significant matters appropriate to the circumstances of the entity? Consider: • valuation of fixed assets; • Income recognition; • depreciation; and • long-term contracts.	No.	L	
8.3	Could the treatment of any areas in the accounts be disputed by the tax authorities?	No.	L	
8.4	Is there usually a large number of related party transactions?	No	L	
8.5	In terms of related party transactions:			
	a) Is the company a member of a group that does not prepare group accounts?	No.	N/A	
	b) Are any payments made to the directors or shareholders other than remuneration or dividends?	No.	L	
	c) Were there balances due to or from the directors at any time during the year?	No.	L	
8.6	Is there any indication of risk of misstatement at the assertion level for classes of transactions, account balances or disclosures?	Poor controls over sales and warehouse inventories.	H	See C6.3
9. Objectives, strategies and related business risks				
9.1	Have we reviewed a copy of the company's long-term strategy or business plan?	There are no formal plans, although the directors do have a strategy.	N/A	

9.2	Are there any risks arising from the company attempting to achieve the objectives set out in the plan?	No.	L	
9.3	Is there a risk of failure to meet stock market (or other shareholder) expectations (which management may have encouraged), whether or not the expectations were reasonable?	No.	L	
9.4	Are the incomes of the directors and/ or management highly geared to results – either directly, through share options, or through other possibilities for large capital gains?	No.	L	
9.5	Is there pressure to meet targets to ensure protection of the jobs of directors, management or other employees?	No.	L	
9.6	Is there a desire to understate profits to reduce tax liabilities?	No.	L	
9.7	Are there legal or regulatory requirements to meet specific financial thresholds or ratios?	None.	N/A	
9.8	Is there a need to ensure compliance with loan covenants or a need to pacify bankers?	No.	L	
9.9	Are future plans for selling the company dependent upon achieving specified results?	No.	N/A	
9.10	Are the amounts for provisions set by management at the time of finalising the profit and loss account rather than being determined by others as part of the routine accounting system?	Management involved in setting the provisions in the first instance.	L	
9.11	Is there a pattern whereby accounting judgements and estimates made when finalising the accounts are all biased in the direction management desires?	Has not been in the past.	L	

9.12	Are the final figures for the company subject to significant change as a result of journal adjustments generated at head office?	No. Major adjustments in the past have been at our request.	L	
9.13	Were there any contracts or transactions undertaken, particularly close to the year end, where the commercial rationale is unclear?	No.	L	
9.14	Do the accounting policies applied by the company fall comfortably within GAAP or do they push the boundaries of acceptability in some areas?	No.	L	
9.15	Have the directors brought forward the reporting date without good reason, making it difficult to obtain the quantity and quality of audit evidence required?	No.	L	
9.16	Are the results of the company out of step with industry trends with no discernable explanation available?	No.	L	
9.17	Is management keen to manipulate profits (for example, to reduce tax or increase bonuses)?	No.	L	

10. Measurement and review of the entity's financial performance

10.1	Have accounting records been reliable in the past?	Yes.	L	
10.2	Are meaningful management accounts prepared during the year?	Yes, but they are not used properly.	L	
10.3	Has the audit report contained a qualification in either of the last two years?	No.	L	
10.4	Have there been problems with making adjustments in the past?	No.	L	
10.5	Is the engagement 'stable' (that is, long standing)?	Yes.	L	

11. Control environment

11.1	Is the extent of management knowledge and experience sufficient for operating the business?	Yes.	L	

No.	Question	Response	Risk	Ref
11.2	Do management and administrative controls appear strong?	On the whole yes, but problems at the warehouse.	L	
11.3	Are there good management information systems, and are they used?	Yes but ...	L	
11.4	Is management in a position to override any controls in existence?	Yes, but as a rule they do not.	L	
11.5	Does management promote an operating style where competence and integrity are valued?	Yes.	L	
12. The entity's risk assessment process				
12.1	Will the company's risk assessment process be used in identifying relevant risks and the actions taken in response to them?	There is no formal risk assessment process. However, the directors do know the business they are in.	L	
13. Information systems				
13.1	Are the accounting records kept up to date?	Except warehouse inventory records.	L	
13.2	Has there been any change to the accounting system?	No.	L	
13.3	Are there any particular issues arising from the use of IT that give cause for concern?	No.	L	
14. Control activities and monitoring controls				
14.1	Are there any indications that control activities, such as performance reviews or segregation of duties, have broken down or otherwise failed to operate?	Controls over inventory in the warehouse are poor and the weekly counts are not taking place.	M	C6.3
14.2	Is there an effective system of monitoring controls in place?	Other than above.	L	
14.3	Are there any indications that the monitoring controls have broken down or otherwise failed to operate?	No.	L	
15. Fraud and error				
15.1	Have there been any previous experiences or incidents which call into question the integrity or competence of management?	No.	L	

15.2	Are there any unusual financial or reporting pressures within the business?	No.	L	
15.3	Are there any significant weaknesses in the design or implementation of internal controls?	Warehouse sales and inventories.	M	C6.3
15.4	Is there a history of unusual and/or complex transactions?	No.	L	
15.5	Is there a history of problems in obtaining sufficient appropriate audit evidence?	No.	L	
15.6	Are there inadequate controls over data in the information system?	Yes.	L	
15.7	Is there a high degree of judgement involved in determining account balances?	No.	L	
15.8	Are there large numbers of assets that may be susceptible to loss or misappropriation?	Warehouse inventories, but any theft unlikely to be material.	L	
15.9	Do the results of analytical procedures undertaken to obtain an understanding of the entity and its environment show unusual or unexpected relationships that may indicate risks of material misstatement due to fraud?	One or two specific issues identified for further investigation.	L	
15.10	Are there usually large numbers of transactions not subjected to ordinary processing?	No.	L	
15.11	Are the accounting staff well trained and capable of performing the tasks allocated to them?	Yes.	L	
15.12	Are there any attitude or morale problems in the accounting department?	No.	L	
15.13	Is there a high level of turnover of accounting staff?		L	
15.14	Does any other information obtained indicate any risk of material misstatement due to fraud?	No.	L	

15.15	Is there a business rational for any transactions that appear out of the ordinary?	N/A.	L	

Conclusion

(Identify any major risks and mitigating factors to arrive at an overall assessment of risk at the financial statement level. Note, assertion level risks that will be addressed on C6.3 should not affect the assessment of risk at the financial statement level.)

> There are some higher risk factors. However, these are essentially due to specific weaknesses in some controls at the warehouse. These will be addressed at the assertion level on C6.3.
>
> The overall risk assessment is therefore low.

The assessment of risk at the financial statement level is:

Low* ~~**Medium***~~ ~~**High***~~
(*Delete as appropriate)

_____ _BL_ _____

Audit engagement partner

_____ 12/3 _____

Date

Having identified relevant risk factors, the auditor needs to consider their impact in two ways. Firstly, some risks may relate pervasively to the financial statements as a whole and potentially affect many assertions. This is **financial statement level risk**, and is often referred to as **general risk**. Secondly, some of the risk factors may have a particular impact on specific assertions of specific balances or transactions within the financial statements. This is **assertion level risk**.

We will now consider some of the issues arising under each of the questionnaire topic areas, using the same order as in the questionnaire. Much of the information needed for each question should have already been obtained and documented in the permanent file, the auditor's review of the correspondence file and through the preliminary analytical review work already performed, as discussed earlier in Chapters 3, 4 and 5. The questionnaire should therefore be used as an aide in reviewing such information with a view to identifying specific risk factors affecting the particular client.

6.5.1 General factors

When considering whether the relationship with the client is either abrasive or deteriorating, the auditor should consider not only the relationship with senior management within the company, but also the people that the audit team deal with on a day-to-day basis. In some instances, while there may be a very good relationship between the principal and the owners of the company, the same cannot necessarily be said of the relationship between the accounts department and the audit team.

The auditor should also consider the effect of any changes in the senior staff within the accounts department on the relationship with the client – for example, a newly appointed finance director may wish to exert a greater influence on the choice of audit practice.

6.5.2 Industry conditions

Where factors such as technology, fashion, demographics or seasonal variations are relevant to a client, they often result in a risk of overvaluation of products or services. They can also have a significant impact on the going concern of the entity, which should always be considered at the planning stage.

6.5.3 Regulatory environment

Having ascertained the details of any significant laws or regulations that are applicable to the entity and recorded these on the permanent audit file (see section 3.4), the auditor should consider whether there is a risk of material misstatement within the accounts as a result of breaches of any of these laws and regulations. This is likely to be an issue for entities where failure to comply with the relevant laws and regulations could have a significant impact on going concern and/or contingent liabilities.

When considering the issue of breaches of significant laws and regulations, the auditor should also consider the risk of money laundering. Where the business is in the financial sector, laws relating to money laundering will be central to the entity's business. For all other audits, although they are not central to the entity's activities, the auditor still needs to be alert for any breaches. It should be noted that identifying a business as one where there is an increased risk of money laundering activities does not mean that the auditor suspects that these activities are taking place; it simply alerts the auditor to the fact that it is possible.

Practice Note 12 (Revised) gives some guidance on considering money laundering issues in connection with auditing, although much of the Standard refers back to the general requirements of ISA 250 in respect of laws and regulations. It is, however, a useful document to refer to should the auditor identify any specific money laundering issues.

6.5.4 Other external factors

If the auditor is aware that there are people other than the shareholders who have an interest in, or will be placing any reliance on, the financial statements, this will increase the risk. When addressing this issue, the auditor should consider the ownership of the entity, whether anybody has requested sight of the accounts and whether there is a potential going concern problem. This will be particularly relevant in the case of a takeover, sale or retirement. In particular, when considering the issue of going concern, issues in addition to the financial viability of the company need to be addressed. This has been dealt with in more detail in Chapter 35.

6.5.5 Business operations

Entities that are reliant on only a few customers, suppliers, products or services can be particularly vulnerable. One recent example of this is the music, games and DVD retailer Zavvi. Its main supplier went into administration and, being unable to find an alternative supplier, Zavvi also went into administration.

Where there is a large number of business locations and/or a wide geographical spread of the entity's activities, this can pose control difficulties for management. It can also make auditing difficult where there are a number of sites to visit.

Complex situations which might involve the use of an expert should also be considered. This issue is looked at in more detail in Chapter 10.

6.5.6 Investments

Complicated group structures and acquisitions, disposals and mergers all carry the potential for risk, particularly of errors being made in the accounting for such transactions. With the recent removal of the consolidation exemption for medium-sized groups in the Companies Act 2006, this is an issue that is likely to affect many more companies than ever before.

6.5.7 Financing

Following the 'credit crunch', the accounting for complex financial instruments is a hot topic. These might arise very rarely for most auditors, and so extra care needs to be taken to ensure the auditor fully understands the nature of the transactions before trying to assess the risk arising from them. If not, consideration should be given as to whether the auditor has sufficient technical expertise in this area to continue with the audit engagement.

6.5.8 Financial reporting

Where there have been instances of failure to comply with generally accepted accounting principles in previous years, details of these should be recorded, along with the reasons and the effect that this had on the audit opinion. The updated review of accounting policies on the permanent file should also be reviewed at this point.

Areas of the accounts which could be disputed by HMRC might include items such as stock and debtor provisions, the capitalisation of assets and deduction of certain expenses.

The auditor should consider at the planning stage whether there is any likelihood of there being undisclosed related party transactions within the financial statements. This should include reviewing the register of related parties, the updating of which is discussed in Chapter 3.

It should also be remembered that paragraph 60 of ISA 240 presumes there are risks of fraud in revenue recognition. Therefore, the auditor should ordinarily expect to identify this when completing the risk assessment. If the auditor concludes that this presumption is not applicable to the client, the reasons for arriving at this conclusion must be documented.

6.5.9 Objectives, strategies and related business risks

This section looks at management's plans for the business, which the auditor should have already documented or updated on the permanent file. One issue with smaller businesses, especially those without a formal business plan, is that they may not have any specific strategies or plans for the future. This does not mean there are no risks in this area. In many sectors, particularly those with fierce competition or risk of obsolescence for technological or other reasons (see section 6.5.2 above), a business with no plan and which is treading water and not moving forward can be as at much or even greater risk than one which is.

The auditor should also consider any ongoing pressures or influences on management, such as remuneration policies, the expectations of external parties and more senior management.

6.5.10 Measurement and review of the entity's financial performance

The auditor should consider how reliable the accounting records have been in the past. If there have always been problems, then whatever promises are made by the client, it is unlikely that this is going to change during the current audit.

If meaningful management accounts are prepared and are properly reviewed during the course of the year, particularly if the practice had an involvement in their preparation and/or review, then it is less likely that problems will arise.

The impact of the auditor's prior experience of the client should also be considered, particularly:

- whether this is a new or longstanding client; and
- whether there have been any audit qualifications in recent years.

6.5.11 Control environment

Where the entity is controlled by people who have a reasonable level of experience and competence in managing such a business, the risks are likely to be lower. However, many owner-managers have expertise in the area that their business trades in, but none in business administration. This lack of competence in managing a business may result in increased risk of error. The auditor should consider the past history and any earlier problems experienced with the client.

In many owner-managed companies, even where there is a separate accounting department, the directors will be in a position to override any controls and exert influence over the transactions that occur. The auditor must therefore assess at the planning stage the impact this will have on risk.

6.5.12 The entity's risk assessment process

In many clients, it is unlikely that there will be many, if any, risk assessment procedures that the auditor can use in identifying relevant risks. However, in this respect most charities are a step ahead of their commercial equivalents, due to the Charity SORP's requirement for trustees to review the risks facing the charity and to take steps to mitigate them where possible. Auditors of clients with charitable status should always ask if the trustees have a risk register which they can review.

6.5.13 Information systems

The auditor should consider whether the accounting records are kept up to date. If they are actually written up at the time a transaction takes place, there is less likelihood of there being errors within the records. This can be a problem at smaller clients where, for example, a bookkeeper writes up all the month's transactions at the end of the month.

Any change in the accounting system should already have been identified, documented and tested for design and implementation. Nevertheless, however well-planned any change in the system, it will inevitably cause problems and potential errors may arise as a result, especially in respect of major IT upgrades.

6.5.14 Control activities and monitoring controls

Here, the auditor is looking to identify whether and how management monitors the controls over the systems and key business processes, and whether there may have been any breaches or failures during the period. These could give rise to misstatements due to error and/or fraud.

6.5.15 Fraud and error

Fraud is one area that has gained far greater prominence under ISAs than under SASs. ISA 240 *The auditor's responsibility to consider fraud in an audit of financial statements* makes clear that, due to the nature of fraud, there will always be a risk, even in an audit properly planned and performed under ISAs, that a material fraud may not be identified. Nevertheless, the auditor should obtain reasonable assurance that the financial statements taken as a whole are free from material misstatement, whether caused by fraud or error. In doing so, the auditor should maintain an attitude of professional scepticism throughout the audit.

During periods of change, the accounts become far more susceptible to error. When a member of staff leaves or joins, there is far greater likelihood of an error occurring. If this is the case, the impact on the general risk of the entity must be assessed. There may also be a specific risk to a certain class of assets or transactions, depending on the area in which the member of staff works.

- If there has been any previous experience or incidents that could call into question the integrity or competence of the management, there may be a risk of fraud or error respectively. Such instances should be recorded on the permanent file but, in practice, this type of information may only be known by the partner, who will often have known the client longer than the rest of the audit team.

- Any unusual financial reporting pressures can lead to a higher risk of misstatement – as a result of either fraud or error. If those pressures are in respect of time, it is far more likely that mistakes will be made. If there are significant budgetary pressures, particularly where these lead to bonuses either being paid or withheld, then the auditor should consider the likelihood that the figures may be manipulated to reflect a different position.

- The existence of any major weaknesses in the design and operation of the accounting and internal control system will be assessed as a result of the work undertaken on the client's systems, which is detailed in Chapter 4.

The auditor should consider the competence and conditions of the staff working in the accounting department. Are the staff are happy in their jobs? Has there been a high degree of change in the past? Is there likely to be a significant amount of change in the future? All these issues can have an impact on the likelihood of there being error and/or fraud within the accounting records.

6.5.16 Relative importance of different risk factors

One way that the relative importance of different risk factors can be assessed is by considering the likelihood of the risk occurring, and the significance for the accounts if the risk does occur. In this way, risk issues identified in these areas can be graded.

This can be illustrated by attributing a value to the event. If the likelihood of the event is remote, we may call this 1, and if the likelihood of the event is probable, we may call this 5. If the significance is low, we may call this 1 and if the significance is high, we may call this 5. By doing this, we can then grade the risk issues.

High 5	5	10	15	20	25
4	4	8	12	16	20
Significance 3	3	6	9	12	15
2	2	4	6	8	10
Low 1	1	2	3	4	5
	1	2	3	4	5
	Remote				Probable

Likelihood

As an example, if the likelihood of the client's office being flooded is low, then this could have 1 allocated to it. But if it did flood, the significance to the accounts being materially misstated would also be low as the building is insured and the accounting records backed up off-site, so the significance of the event to the accounts may be, say, a 2. The weighting of the risk is therefore 2 (that is, 1 × 2).

Compare that to the likelihood of stock being incorrectly valued, which is considered medium (say 3) but the significance to the accounts being materially misstated is also considered medium, again a 3. The weighting of the risk is 9 (that is, 3 × 3).

Hence, we are more likely to concern ourselves with stock, as the risk weighting is much higher. This is of vital importance in planning an efficient, cost-effective audit. The auditor needs to focus the work on the areas of highest risk to minimise the likelihood of not detecting a material misstatement, whilst justifying why other areas are less risky, and therefore do not need to have as much time spent on them.

6.5.17 Concluding on financial statement level risk

Having considered all of the above areas, the auditor must come to a conclusion on the overall assessment of financial statement level risk – that is, the risk of there being material misstatements in the financial statements as a result of fraud or error.

The auditor should consider all of the answers that have been given and their relative impact on the risk of this particular audit. It is not simply a case of counting the number of low, medium and high answers and taking the average or most frequent answer as the risk assessment. It may well be that there is one answer that the auditor feels has such a significant impact on the risk of the client, that even though everything else is recorded as low risk, the auditor still treats the audit as being high risk. This may be the case, for example, where the auditor has identified that a third party that is interested in purchasing the entity will be looking at the accounts. This would normally be construed as being significant enough, in itself, to require the auditor to identify the client as being a high risk audit.

6.5.18 Concluding on assertion level risk

Those risk factors identified during the risk assessment that have a particular impact on specific assertions should now be considered together and a conclusion drawn as to the level of risk for each assertion in the financial statements, even if no specific risk factors affecting that assertion have been identified. This might at first appear somewhat time-consuming, but it is actually a key process in planning an efficient audit, by ensuring that an appropriate level of work is performed for each assertion.

For example, simply concluding that stock is high risk will lead to overauditing if the main risk lies within the valuation of stock and not the other stock assertions.

6.5.19 Significant risks

ISA 315 requires auditors to determine which of the risks identified are, in the auditor's judgment, risks that require special audit consideration ('significant risks'). As we will see in Chapter 8, identifying a risk as being 'significant' has particular implications under ISAs. It is worth noting that ISA 240 states that risks of material misstatement due to fraud related to revenue recognition are significant risks.

The ISA provides the following guidance in deciding whether a risk is significant.

a) Significant risks arise on most audits. It can be deduced from this that if the risk assessment has not identified any significant risks, the auditor should probably review the risk assessment again to ensure that none have been missed.

b) The effect of any identified controls related to the risk should be excluded when making the decision.

c) Routine, non-complex transactions that are subject to systematic processing are less likely to give rise to significant risks because they have lower inherent risks.

d) Significant risks often relate to significant non-routine transactions that are unusual, either due to their size or nature, and occur infrequently, and to judgmental matters (for example, accounting estimates).

e)   Significant risks are often derived from business risks that may result in a material misstatement.

When considering the nature of the risks, the auditor should consider:

- whether the risk is a risk of fraud;
- whether the risk is related to recent significant economic, accounting or other developments;
- the complexity of transactions;
- whether the risk involves significant transactions with related parties;
- the degree of subjectivity in the measurement of financial information related to the risk; and
- whether the risk involves significant transactions that are outside the entity's normal course of business, or which otherwise appear unusual.

6.6 Control risk

Control risk is the risk that the client's systems and procedures will not prevent or detect a material error from affecting the final accounts. The documentation, review of design, checking of implementation and testing of the operational effectiveness (often optional) of systems and controls were all considered in detail in Chapter 4. Having completed these tasks, the auditor should now consider the impact of this work on the risk of material misstatement.

Control risk over a particular assertion can only be confirmed as being other than high if the relevant controls have been tested for operational effectiveness. More generally, the auditor's assessment of the general control environment and high level controls may influence the assessment of general risk.

6.7 Detection risk

This is the risk that the auditor will fail to spot that the accounts are materially misstated. It is dealt with by the audit tests and approach that is adopted by the audit team, aspects looked at in detail in Part II. This includes the auditor's judgment on how to test an area and the conclusions drawn from the test results obtained. It should be remembered that detection risk is ultimately influenced by the judgment exercised by the auditor during the audit.

6.8 Conclusion

Many audit systems use checklists or questionnaires to help the auditor determine risk. Whilst these can be useful, they should not be applied without thought, especially when auditing entities in niche sectors. The auditor should consider all of the answers that have been given and ensure they have been adequately addressed by the audit planning.

Within most audit systems, the risk assessment will affect the amount of audit work to be undertaken, so it is vital to complete the risk assessment stage properly. An overly prudent assessment will lead to over-auditing, inefficiency and added expense. On the other hand, an unduly lenient assessment may result in insufficient audit work being undertaken and material misstatements going undetected.

The auditor's response to risk is considered in Chapter 8.

Chapter 7 Audit team planning meeting

7.1 Introduction

Both ISA 240 and ISA 315 require an audit team meeting at the planning stage, principally for matters such as sharing knowledge, discussing audit issues and risks, determining the overall audit approach and communicating relevant matters within the audit team. Even if such a meeting were not mandatory under ISAs, it would still be highly recommended.

7.2 Attendance

Paragraph 28 of ISA 240 states that 'the discussion includes the engagement partner...', and both this and paragraph 17 of ISA 315 note that, ordinarily, the discussion involves the key members of the engagement team. Whilst the phrase 'key members of the engagement team' is not defined, common sense would take this to mean, as a minimum, the audit engagement partner and audit manager (or senior, if reporting direct to partner).

However, there can be benefits in all members of the audit team attending, despite this appearing at first glance to be a time-consuming option. The benefits include:

a) communication is more effective as everyone is at the original discussion and does not need to be subsequently briefed on the matters discussed (see below);

b) all team members have an opportunity to share knowledge and information about the client. Where junior staff have worked on the engagement in an earlier year, they often have detailed knowledge about the client's staff and accounting records that can be valuable to the audit planning process; and

c) it can be a good opportunity for more junior staff to develop their professional judgment and audit skills by listening to the input of the partner and manager.

Paragraph 29 of ISA 240 also states: 'The engagement partner should consider which matters are to be communicated to members of the engagement team not involved in the discussion.' This might comprise the more junior members of staff who were unable to attend the meeting.

Many small audits are carried out entirely by the engagement partner, who may be a sole practitioner. In such situations, paragraph 31 of ISA 240 notes that, having personally conducted the planning of the audit, the engagement partner should consider the susceptibility of the entity's financial statements to material misstatement due to fraud.

7.3 Matters to be discussed

This discussion is aimed at the following:

- understanding and considering the susceptibility of the company's financial statements to material misstatement due to fraud or error;

- reviewing the audit approach to these risk areas (see Chapter 8);

- emphasising the need for professional scepticism when carrying out the audit and reviewing the test results; and

- sharing the insights of team members based on their knowledge of the entity, and exchanging information about business risks.

However, other relevant matters can also be discussed as the auditor sees fit.

It is important that the audit team members approach the discussion with a questioning mind, setting aside any beliefs they may have that management and the directors are honest and have integrity. The meeting should be a 'brainstorm' or wide-ranging, open exchange of ideas between team members, and should not be limited by any preconceived ideas about the client.

In the course of the meeting new risks may be identified, and these should be added to the risk documentation.

7.4 Timing of the discussions

Beyond the fact that the initial discussion should take place at the planning stage of the audit, neither ISA 315 nor ISA 240 gives any specific guidance as to when during the planning process the discussions should take place. The timing of the discussions is therefore at the discretion of the auditor, given the particular circumstances of the practice and client, the availability of the partner and other members of the audit team, and the audit timetable as agreed with the client. The timing of the team meeting as shown in the planning flowchart in Chapter 1 is therefore a suggestion only.

Some partners prefer a first draft of the risk assessment and response thereto (see Chapter 8) to have already been prepared as a basis for the team discussion. Others favour a 'blank canvas' approach to team meetings, which can therefore be held earlier in the planning process and form the basis of the risk assessment and response process.

Either way, given that the discussions should yield a productive assessment of the risk of fraud and error, the meeting should take place before the risk assessments are finalised. Many firms are in the habit of holding the team planning meeting once the planning has been completed and approved, just before the team goes out to the client to start the detailed audit fieldwork. This is more of a team briefing, and while such meetings can be useful, this is not what is envisioned when ISAs refer to team discussions.

7.5 Documentation

Although some proprietary audit systems may provide a standard form to record the results of such a meeting, it is not essential to use such forms; such matters can easily be recorded in the detailed planning memorandum or in separate meeting minutes. Note that documentation of the discussion among the engagement team regarding the susceptibility of the entity's financial statements to material misstatement due to error or fraud, and the significant decisions reached is mandatory under paragraph 122 of ISA 315.

Chapter 8 Determining the audit approach

8.1 Introduction

As discussed in Chapter 6 most audit systems approach the assessment of risk at the financial statement level and assertion level as illustrated in the following diagram.

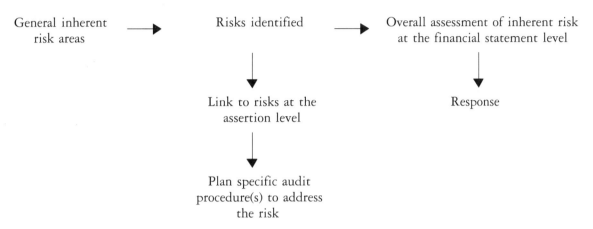

The auditor's response to those assessed risks is guided by ISA 330 *The auditor's procedures in response to assessed risks.*

8.2 Response to financial statement level risk

Paragraph 4 of ISA 330 requires the auditor to determine overall responses to address the risks of material misstatement at the financial statement level. Such responses may include:

- emphasising to the audit team the need to maintain professional scepticism in gathering and evaluating audit evidence;

- assigning more experienced staff or those with special skills or using experts;

- providing more supervision, or incorporating additional elements of unpredictability in the selection of further audit procedures to be performed; and

- making general changes to the nature, timing, or extent of audit procedures as an overall response.

The assessment of financial statement risk may also have a significant bearing on the choice of approach – that is, the relative emphases on substantive procedures (see Part II) and tests of controls (see section 4.9). In most audit systems, financial statement risk has a direct impact on the sample sizes for all substantive testing – the higher the risk, the larger the samples. This is looked at in more detail in Chapter 14.

8.2.1 Interim audits

An interim audit is often used where the reporting timetable is particularly tight, as it enables the auditor to bring forward much of the detailed audit work to an earlier date, usually before the year end. This approach can be very efficient and cost effective – for example, by assisting the auditor in identifying significant matters at an early stage of the audit, and consequently resolving them with the assistance of management or developing an effective audit approach to address such matters.

However, ISA 330 also notes that the higher the risk of material misstatement, the more likely it is that the auditor may decide it is more effective to perform substantive procedures nearer, or at, the period end rather than at an earlier date, and so the timing of the audit work should be carefully considered at the planning stage.

If use is made of an interim audit, the auditor must consider what audit evidence is required for the remaining period. Paragraph 56 of ISA 330 requires the auditor to carry out further substantive procedures (and, where relevant, tests of control) to cover this period to provide sufficient audit evidence to support a conclusion on the whole accounting period.

8.3 Response to assertion level risk

Paragraph 7 of ISA 330 states: 'The auditor should design and perform further audit procedures whose nature, timing, and extent are responsive to the assessed risks of material misstatement at the assertion level.' The key purpose here is to provide a clear linkage between the risk assessment and the nature, timing, and extent of the auditor's further audit procedures.

8.3.1 Specifically identified risks

Many audit systems will contain a standard schedule to record in more detail the significant risks identified by the risk assessment process and the auditor's proposed responses to them. An example of such a form is shown below.

Client: Manufacturing Company Limited		Prepared by:	*aw*	Date:	*11/3*
Year end: 31 Dec 2007		Reviewed by:	*BL*	Date:	*12/3*
File no: M0001				Ref: **C6.3**	

SPECIFIC RISK ACTION PLAN

	Specific risk affecting client	High (H), medium (M) or low (L)	Management response	Financial reporting areas and assertions affected	Audit approach and reference to programme	Outcome
1	The company is reliant on a relatively small number of products. Technological advances could render the companies existing products obsolete very quickly.	M	No specific systems in this area.	All	Discuss with directors as part of subsequent events review. (T2 Test13)	The directors are happy that they are in touch with technological developments and trends in the market. There is no reason to doubt that this will continue.
2	In the past, the directors have been very good at spotting opportunities in the market, and have also moved out of older technologies at the right time. There is no guarantee that this will continue in the future.	M	No specific systems in this area.	All	Discuss with directors as part of subsequent events review. (T2 Test 13)	The directors see no reason for this to change and, to date, there are no indications that it has.
3	The directors are managing the business mainly by reference to the key performance indicators and are not using the management accounts to the full. This may lead to focusing on too narrow a range of indicators.	M	No specific systems in this area.	All	Preliminary (C7) and final (B9) analytical reviews should identify any problem areas.	No particular problems identified, but matter referred to in letter of comment (A6).

4	The company's expansion plans are ambitious and, notwithstanding the company's good relationship with its bankers, could lead to financing problems.	M	No specific systems in this area.	All	Discuss with directors as part of subsequent events review. (T2 Test 13)	The directors have a good relationship with the bankers and the company is currently growing in a manageable way.
5	What would happen if directors or key staff became ill or resigned?	M	Key man insurance for the three directors.	All	Discuss with directors as part of subsequent events review. (T2)	Key person insurance is in place, but the loss of one of the directors would have very serious implications for the company. However, there are no indications that this will occur.
6	The results of the Floppy division must be disclosed as a discontinued operation.	M	No controls over accounts disclosure.	Presentation of accounts for all areas.	Test addressing this point added to test 45 on R2.	Appropriate disclosures made.
7	Company may incur R&D expenditure that is not identified and capitalised as such.	M	Reliant on Adrian Walker being informed that a job is R&D.	Understatement of intangible assets. Overstatement of cost of sales.	Addressed by EA2 T11(a).	No R&D jobs undertaken in year.
8	Non-compliance with health and safety legislation.	M	Warehouse and factory managers monitor on an informal basis.	All	1. Discussion with directors. (N2 T16) 2. Review of accident book for material or systematic problems. (N2 T29)	No apparent breaches of health and safety legislation.
9	Sales invoices may be processed as a sale this year, but the goods will not be delivered until next year.	H	Goods are delivered eventually or a credit note is issued.	Cut-off problem; overstatement of sales and receivables.	1. Review credit notes issued in 2008 for any that relate to 2007. (R2 T15(a)) 2. Follow-up unprocessed picking lists and despatch notes recorded at the inventory count. (R2 T15(b))	Cut-off errors identified and corrected.

Response to assertion level risk

10	Why the increase in pension contributions?	M	No specific systems in this area.	Expense for pension contributions may be overstated.	Analyse pension contributions added to test 36 R2.	Deliberate decision by directors.
11	What is the increase in miscellaneous expenditure?	M	No specific systems in this area.	Miscellaneous expenses may be overstated.	Analyse miscellaneous expenses added to test 36 R2.	OS
12	The overall gross profit margin has fallen, but the fall is bigger than expected.	M	No specific systems in this area.	Closing inventory or sales may be understated or purchases overstated.	Discuss with directors as part of final analytical review. (B9)	
13	Why the large increase in receivables?	M	No specific systems in this area.	Receivables may be overstated.	Addressed by J2 T4.	
14	Cut-off between the factory and the warehouse appears to be wrong.	H	Processing in the warehouse is not up to date, so the controls are ineffective.	Closing inventory may be understated.	Test to check the sequence of job numbers despatched from the factory and ensure that all were received at the warehouse added to I2. (I2 T26)	Errors found and adjusted. Recommendations on systems added to A6.

The advantage of this approach is that the auditor can draft bespoke audit procedures in response to specific risks, such that the schedule effectively becomes an additional audit programme. This also clearly demonstrates the linkage referred to above that ISA 330 speaks of. However, it is not uncommon for these planned procedures to get forgotten during the fieldwork visit, as the schedule is buried on the planning section of the file.

One solution is to move or copy the schedule to either a fieldwork section or the completion section of the file. An alternative is to cross-reference the 'audit approach' column to the detailed audit programmes. This could be to a 'standard' test, or a bespoke test may need to be added to the programme. Detailed guidance on audit programmes and procedures is given in Part II.

When auditing smaller and owner-managed businesses, the issue of management override of controls often arises. Where this is identified as a risk, paragraph 76 of ISA 240 requires the auditor to perform three specific procedures in response, as follows:

- test the appropriateness of journal entries recorded in the general ledger and other adjustments made in the preparation of financial statements;

- review accounting estimates for biases that could result in material misstatement due to fraud; and

- obtain an understanding of the business rationale of significant transactions that the auditor becomes aware of that are either outside the normal course of business for the entity or otherwise appear unusual, given the auditor's understanding of the entity and its environment.

8.3.2 Significant risks

As noted in Chapter 6, some of the specific risks identified may be determined by the auditor as significant. ISAs require such risks to receive special audit attention, as described in ISA 330:

Firstly, the auditor should perform substantive procedures specifically in response to each significant risk. In other words, a wholly controls-based approach is not acceptable in response to a significant risk.

Secondly, where the auditor plans to rely on the operational effectiveness of controls intended to mitigate a significant risk, the auditor should obtain the audit evidence about the operating effectiveness of those controls from tests of controls performed in the current period. This rules out reliance on controls testing performed in previous years under the 'three-year cycle' principle described in section 4.9.4, and requires the auditor to test such controls in the current period.

8.3.3 Other risks

There are likely to be many assertions for which no specific risk factors were identified during the risk assessment process. Nevertheless, these assertions still need to be audited, and so a conclusion of assessed risk for each of these assertions will also have been drawn, and which will therefore require a response. Again, many audit systems will contain a standard schedule to assist the auditor in this, and an example of one such schedule is given below.

Client: Manufacturing Company Limited	Ref:
Year end: 31 Dec 2007	**C6.2**
File no: M0001	

RISK RESPONSE SUMMARY

To ensure that the nature and extent of testing undertaken is responsive to the risks assessed.

Issues and risks identified (H, M) (See C6.3 & S4)	Assertions other than issues and risks identified (See ISA 500.17)		Audit approach and reference to programme
	Risks (H, M, L)	Justification of risks	
E Intangible assets	*L*	*Straightforward area with no concerns about impairment.*	*Standard programme*
F Tangible fixed assets	*L*	*Disposal of Floppy division assets addressed by standard programme.*	*Standard programme*
G Investments in group and associated undertakings	*N/a*		
H Other investments	*N/a*		
I Stock and WIP *High risk for existence of warehouse stock.*	*L*	*Factory stocks are routine and well controlled.* *There are no major concerns about determining cost and NRV.*	*Tailored programme*
J Debtors and prepayments	*L*		*Tailored programme.* *No circularisation, results of after date cash work historically good.*

99

K	Bank and cash	ℒ		Standard programme
L	Creditors and accruals	ℒ		Tailored programme. No circularisation, results of work on supplier statements historically good.
M	Long-term loans and deferred income	ℒ		Standard programme
N	Provisions and contingencies	ℒ		Standard programme
O	Capital and reserves	ℒ		Standard programme
P	Taxation	ℒ		Standard programme
R	Profit and loss — Income	ℒ	Cut-off testing is high risk.	Tailored programme, directional testing used to eliminate duplicate tests. No major concerns over completeness of sales.
	Expenditure	ℒ		Tailored programme, directional testing used to eliminate duplicate tests.
	Wages	ℒ		Analytical procedures and reliance on controls.
	Related-party transactions	ℒ		No specific programme required.
	Other	ℒ		

			Tailored programme
T	Post balance sheet events	ℒ	
U	VAT	N/a	
V	Consolidation	ℒ	
	Opening balances and comparatives – checklist	ℒ	*No particular issues arising*
	Other	ℒ	

Note

Where the risk assessment at the assertion level is low for a major transaction cycle, you should consider whether this includes an expectation that controls in that area will be operating effectively. Where this is the case, ISA 330.23 requires that tests on the effectiveness of those controls be performed.

Planning conclusion

I am satisfied that the planned audit will produce sufficient appropriate audit evidence.

Prepared by: *aw*   Date: *11/3*

Reviewed by: *BL*   Date: *12 Mar*

Final conclusion

I have reconsidered specific risks and: no changes are needed*/the following changes have been implemented* (specify):

Prepared by: *aw*   Date: *2/4*

Reviewed by: *BL*   Date: *3/4*

* Delete as appropriate

101

Again, the linkage between the risk assessment and the planned audit work is key. One of the commonest reasons for overauditing is that risk is assessed at the level of each financial statement area, and not down to the assertion level. For example, stock is designated as high risk, resulting in large sample sizes for all stock tests, whereas the real risk relates only to the *value* of stock.

This schedule provides the auditor with an overview of all the financial statement areas, and allows the audit approach to be planned for each area, as well as down to the assertion level. It also provides the opportunity to determine and document whether a section is not material at all, or whether a standard audit programme or a bespoke approach is needed.

This is vital in planning an efficient and effective audit, yet it is one area where many auditors don't take enough time. Time spent here can mean that a significant amount of unnecessary audit fieldwork is avoided later on.

8.3.4 External confirmations

The practicalities of obtaining external confirmations are considered in more detail in Part II. However, they are worth a mention at this stage, as the timing of confirmation requests is often crucial. If the auditor anticipates that external confirmations will be required, then these should be considered either at the planning stage or at the year end, whichever is sooner.

8.3.5 Stocktakes

Where stock is material, the auditor's risk response will usually include attendance at the stocktake. Audit procedures at stocktakes are covered in Chapter 20. However, some thought should go into the planning of the auditor's attendance, as the timing is critical. The auditor should liaise closely with the client before the year end to determine the likely quantities of stock that will be held at the year end and their location(s), and the timing of the stocktakes in order to be able to schedule attendance by a member of the audit team.

8.3.6 Other general points

Paragraph 49 of ISA 330 states: 'Irrespective of the assessed risk of material misstatement, the auditor should design and perform substantive procedures for each material class of transactions, account balance, and disclosure.' This reflects the fact that:

a)   the auditor's assessment of risk is judgmental, and so not all risks of material misstatement may have been identified; and

b)   there are inherent limitations to internal control, including the risk of management override. Accordingly, even if the auditor determines that the risk of material misstatement may be reduced to an acceptably low level by performing only tests of controls for a particular assertion, additional substantive procedures must still be performed.

Paragraph 50 of ISA 330 also requires the auditor specifically to:

*   agree or reconcile the financial statements with the underlying accounting records; and

*   examine material journal entries and other adjustments made during the course of preparing the financial statements.

8.4 Conclusion

The linkage between the auditor's risk assessment and planned audit procedures is vital in planning an effective and efficient audit, and yet is often missing. Too many auditors undertake a comprehensive risk assessment and then completely ignore it when planning the detailed audit procedures. The planned audit work should reflect the risk to ensure that sufficient work is undertaken to obtain sufficient appropriate audit evidence to be able to draw reasonable conclusions on which to base an audit opinion. Reasonable assurance is obtained when the auditor has reduced audit risk to an acceptably low level.

Chapter 9 Assessing materiality

9.1 Introduction

Paragraph 3 of ISA 320 *Materiality* states:

> 'Information is material if its omission or misstatement could influence the economic decisions of users taken on the basis of the financial statements. Materiality depends on the size of the item or error judged in the particular circumstances of its omission or misstatement. Thus, materiality provides a threshold or cut-off point rather than being a primary qualitative characteristic which information must have if it is to be useful.'

This definition refers to users of the financial statements. It is therefore usually appropriate when assessing materiality to consider who (other than the addressees of the audit report) will use the financial statements – that is, the members or shareholders.

The Standard goes on to confirm that the auditor should determine an acceptable materiality level so as to detect quantitatively material misstatements. This provides a guideline figure to assess the potential impact of any misstatements or errors that are found. The level of materiality is also used in most sampling techniques to help determine sample sizes.

In the planning flowchart in Chapter 1, the assessment of materiality is shown after the completion of the auditor's response to risk in the risk action plan. However, it may be beneficial to assess materiality earlier in the planning process, in order to help judge the materiality of misstatements which may arise from the risks identified at the risk assessment stage, and hence the relative importance of those risks.

9.2 Determining materiality

The auditor should firstly ascertain some base figures to provide initial guidance on the level of materiality. Obviously, some work will have been done when undertaking the preliminary analytical review to ascertain the current year's figures (see Chapter 5). Even where the auditor does not have draft accounts or management accounts available at the start of the audit, it is important that an initial materiality level is set on the basis of what the expected figures are going to be, and not just on last year's figures. Information can be gleaned from such things as the VAT returns, etc to enable the auditor to set an appropriate level.

In most cases, a number of parameters will be identified to help the auditor determine the ultimate materiality level. An example is given below.

Turnover and gross assets	Percentage of turnover and gross assets	Materiality ranges
£0 to £500,000	3%	£1 to £15,000
£500,001 to £2,000,000	2.5%	£15,001 to £50,000
£2,000,001 to £3,500,000	2%	£50,001 to £70,000
£3,500,001 to £6,000,000	1.5%	£70,001 to £90,000
over £6,000,000	1%	over £90,000

Materiality will normally be set either close to the level of the turnover or the gross asset parameter. In most systems the auditor also calculates a parameter based on the basis of the adjusted profit parameter, normally at 10 per cent thereof. When calculating this figure, the profit should be adjusted for any unusual transactions, such as directors' bonuses, which can be used to distort the profit of the entity.

The guidance figures should be calculated for each of these individual parameters and recorded on a schedule within the audit file. The auditor should then determine which is the most appropriate measure and set an ultimate level of materiality. In the vast majority of trading businesses the most relevant parameter is going to be that of turnover. In businesses such as investment businesses or the like, it may well be that the gross asset parameter is the most appropriate.

It must be emphasised that determining the materiality level is a matter of judgment. Whist various parameters are calculated to provide guidance, they are only guidance. Simply taking an average or some other predetermined calculation is unlikely to give an acceptable result.

Whatever the final level that is set, it is important that the auditor documents why this particular level has been chosen. It is also important that the level chosen is reviewed at the end of the audit to ensure it is still appropriate (see Chapter 41).

9.3 Conclusion

It is very important that the auditor remembers the purpose of materiality when determining what the level should be. When signing an audit report, the auditor is attesting that the audit work undertaken has been structured so as to identify any material misstatement within the accounts.

Chapter 10 Other planning issues

10.1 Introduction

The purpose of this Chapter is to deal with the other planning issues that ought to be considered when completing the planning for an entity.

10.2 Audit approach to individual sections

This issue will be dealt with in much more detail in Part II. However, an important part of audit planning is to consider the approach to be taken for each individual section of the file. In particular, the planner should identify those sections that need an audit programme and those sections for which an alternative approach could be adopted. It is common for an auditor to follow all of the previously described steps, but then fail to give any guidance to the individuals involved in the audit work on the specific tests required. This may result in undertaking much more work than necessary or in misdirecting the audit work that is undertaken. The planning process cannot be seen as just the completion of the planning documentation; it must involve a detailed look at the approach to be taken to each of the individual sections of the audit that are relevant to that particular client. The example schedule at section **8.3.3** can also be used to help determine the audit approach by section.

10.3 Staffing and budgets

The first step in considering the staffing should really be undertaken at the same stage as the assessment of independence (see section 2.13). This involves considering whether there are adequate staff with the necessary knowledge to enable the practice to undertake the audit of this particular client. This is especially important where the auditor is dealing with a non-standard audit, where it is necessary to determine that the staff involved have the skills to enable them to identify particular problems.

The auditor should then consider the level of staff required for the job. This can be done by reviewing the types of skills considered necessary for each individual level within a practice – for example, the attributes that are necessary for an audit manager or an audit senior and then comparing the results to an assessment of the complexity of the client's operations. This should enable the auditor to determine which levels of staff should be used for which areas of the audit.

Having gone through this process, the auditor should decide which staff within the practice should be used on the audit. It is not appropriate to simply use the staff members who are available at the time that the audit is undertaken. The auditor must ensure that the audit is undertaken by members of staff who have suitable qualifications and experience.

Note that paragraph 19 of ISA 220 *Quality control for audits of historical financial information* states;

> 'The engagement partner should be satisfied that the engagement team collectively has the appropriate capabilities, competence and time to perform the audit engagement in accordance with professional standards and regulatory and legal requirements, and to enable an auditor's report that is appropriate in the circumstances to be issued.'

A budget should also be prepared to ensure that sufficient time has been allocated for the audit staff to complete the engagement. Budgets are normally analysed by how long is needed to complete each of the individual sections. Not only should the budget include an allocation of time for each individual section, but the auditor should also ensure that sufficient time is allowed for answering review points and for a second principal review if necessary. The budgeting process should be undertaken at the same time as the overall timetable for the audit is agreed with the client and senior members of the audit team.

Very often firms fall down when completing an audit simply because the timetabling is inadequate – for example, a second principal review was planned but not undertaken because at the time that the file was ready to review, the partner was not available to do it. If the second principal review was required under paragraphs 60 and 61 of ISQC1 *Quality control for firms that perform audits and reviews of historical financial information, and other assurance and related services engagements*, such a situation might be non-compliant with Auditing Standards and therefore a breach of the audit regulations (see section 10.6.1). Such a situation should not arise if there is an adequate timetable.

Many firms shy away from preparing detailed budgets because they have insufficient information to complete them accurately. Where this is the case, an estimate should be made and the staff required to complete a detailed record of the time taken on each aspect of the audit in the current year. This record can then be used to prepare the budget for the subsequent year.

10.4 Other planning issues

10.4.1 ISQC1 *Quality control for firms that perform audits and reviews of historical financial information, and other assurance and related services engagements*

As well as ISA 220 *Quality control for audits of historical financial information*, which addresses quality control from the perspective of an individual audit, ISQC1 looks at quality control from the perspective of the firm as a whole. ISQC1 requires that:

> 'The firm should establish policies and procedures requiring, for appropriate engagements, an engagement quality control review that provides an objective evaluation of the significant judgments made by the engagement team and the conclusions reached in formulating the report. Such policies and procedures should:
>
> (a) Require an engagement quality control review for all audits of financial statements of listed entities;
>
> (b) Set out criteria against which all other audits and reviews of historical financial information, and other assurance and related services engagements should be evaluated to determine whether an engagement quality control review should be performed; and
>
> (c) Require an engagement quality control review for all engagements meeting the criteria established in compliance with subparagraph (b).' (ISQC1.60)

Additionally, ISQCI stipulates:

> 'The firm's policies and procedures should require the completion of the engagement quality control review before the report is issued.' (ISQC1.61)

Relatively few firms will have listed clients requiring a hot review (that is, an engagement quality control review performed before the audit is completed and signed off). However, many more firms will need to perform hot reviews on high risk or public interest clients. Firms should therefore:

● identify and document the criteria for determining which audits are public interest or high risk;

● review all clients against these criteria to determine whether any will require a hot review; and

● ensure that planning on the relevant audits recognises that a hot review will be required.

This will involve allocating time at the end of the audit to carry out the hot review and to deal with any points that arise. This is true particularly if the review is to be carried out externally. The extent of the review will depend on the complexity and risk of the audit and the experience of the audit team. Generally, it will involve consideration of:

- the objectivity and independence of the audit team and the firm;
- the rigour of the planning, particularly the identification of, and planned response to, risk;
- key judgments in high risk areas;
- the significance of any potential changes to the accounts that the client has refused to make;
- whether all relevant matters identified during the audit have been considered for reporting to the directors or the audit committee; and
- the appropriateness of the draft audit report.

The scope and conclusions of the review must be properly documented.

10.4.2 ISA 402 *Audit considerations relating to entities using service organisations*

The auditor should consider how an entity's use of a service organisation affects the entity's internal control, so as to identify and assess the risk of material misstatement and to design and perform further audit procedures necessary to obtain sufficient appropriate audit evidence to determine, with reasonable assurance, whether the user entity's financial statements are free from material misstatement. (ISA 402.2)

A 'service organisation' is any entity that provides services to another, for example.:

- information processing;
- maintenance of accounting records;
- facilities management;
- maintenance of safe custody of assets, such as investments; and
- initiation or execution of transactions on behalf of the other entity.

The auditor should document any involvement by service organisations in the planning section, paying particular attention to:

- the significance of the activities to the client;
- the contractual terms that apply to relevant activities undertaken, and the way the entity monitors those activities to ensure that it meets its fiduciary and other legal responsibilities; and
- their relevance of the activities to the audit – that is, the effect on risk, audit testing and any effect on how evidence will be obtained.

Note that it is not appropriate to simply rely on reports and information provided by the service organisation. In the absence of any records kept by the company itself, such reports should be treated as information produced by the company and which therefore requires auditing.

Pension scheme investment managers are probably the most common example of a service organisation. When auditing the accounts for a pension scheme, the report produced by the investment manager cannot be accepted unchallenged. This is a particular problem where the investments consist of a unitised fund. The planning section should detail the audit work required – for example:

- reconciling contributions received by the investment manager to those paid by the company;
- checking the price of units to those published in the financial press; and
- reconciling the movement in the number of units by re-performing calculations for purchases and sales.

10.4.3 ISA 600 *Using the work of another auditor*

This is discussed in more detail in Chapter 37, when considering the audit of groups and consolidations. However, it is worth mentioning here for this reason: if the involvement of another auditor is anticipated, the 'principal auditor' should consider how the work of the other auditor will affect the audit at the planning stage. By 'principal auditor', the Standard means the auditor with responsibility for reporting on financial statements which include financial information of one or more components audited by another auditor. This usually equates to the auditor of the parent entity producing consolidated accounts.

The first consideration is whether or not the auditor's own participation is sufficient to be able to act as principal auditor. In most situations, the other auditor will be auditing, for example, one overseas subsidiary, with the rest of the group audited by the auditor, in which case there should usually be no difficulty. However, care needs to be taken when the parent is merely a holding company and the majority of the trading activity is undertaken through other members of the group that are **not** audited by the parent's auditor.

When planning to use the work of another auditor, the principal auditor should consider the professional competence of the other auditor by:

- considering the professional qualifications, experience and resources of the other auditor in the context of the specific assignment;

- considering the standing of any firm with which the other auditor is affiliated, and by making reference to the other auditor's professional organisation; and

- reviewing the previous work of the other auditor.

At the planning stage, the principal auditor should advise the other auditor of:

- the independence requirements regarding both the parent and the component being audited by the other auditor, and obtain written representation as to compliance with them; and

- the use that is to be made of the other auditor's work and report, and to make sufficient arrangements for the coordination of their efforts, including provision of the timetable for completion of the audit.

Normally, a consolidation questionnaire or checklist should accompany the above. This should:

- request details of the audit procedures undertaken;

- inform the other auditor of areas requiring special consideration; and

- request information regarding the other auditor's findings from the audit.

This questionnaire or checklist should be sent out well before the year end to allow the other auditor to plan its work accordingly. Any request by the principal auditor to review the detailed working papers of the other auditor should also be made on a timely basis.

10.4.4 ISA 610 *Considering the work of internal audit*

The majority of audit clients will not have any sort of internal audit function. However, very large private companies and charities and listed companies are likely to have an internal audit department. Paragraph 2 of ISA 610 makes clear that where internal audit exists, the external auditor should consider the activities of the internal audit department and their effects, if any, on external audit procedures.

The scope and objectives of internal auditing vary widely and depend on the size and structure of the entity and the requirements of its management. Ordinarily, internal auditing activities include one or more of the following:

- monitoring of internal control;

- examination of financial and operating information;

- review of the economy, efficiency and effectiveness of operations;

- review of compliance with laws and regulations and with internal management policies, etc., and

- special investigations into particular areas (for example, suspected fraud).

The effectiveness of internal audit may be an important factor in the external auditor's evaluation of the control environment and assessment of audit risk. Where the external auditor's risk assessment is reliant on internal audit work, the external auditor should perform an assessment of the internal audit function. In particular, paragraph 13 of the ISA notes that in performing such an assessment, particular attention should be paid to the following areas.

Organisational status

The specific status of the internal audit department within the entity, and the effect this has on its ability to be objective. Ideally, the internal auditors will report to the highest level of management and be free of any other operating responsibility. Any constraints or restrictions placed on them by management would need to be carefully considered. In particular, they will need to be free to communicate fully with the external auditor.

Scope of function

Appraise the nature and extent of the internal audit work performed. The external auditor would also need to consider whether management acts on internal audit recommendations and how this is evidenced.

Technical competence

Do the internal auditors have adequate technical training and proficiency? The external auditor may, for example, review the policies for hiring and training internal audit staff and their experience and professional qualifications.

Due professional care

Examine whether internal audit work is properly planned, supervised, reviewed and documented. The existence of adequate audit manuals, work programs and working papers would be considered.

If it is intended to make use of specific work of the internal auditors, the external auditor should evaluate and perform audit procedures on that work – to confirm its adequacy for the external auditor's purposes.

10.4.5 ISA 620 *Using the work of an expert*

In the course of an audit, the auditor may need to obtain audit evidence from an expert. This might be in the form of a report, opinion or valuation. Examples are:

- asset valuations, (for example, of land and buildings);
- determination of quantities or physical condition of assets (for example, minerals stored in stockpiles);
- determination of amounts using specialised techniques or methods (for example, an actuarial valuation of a defined benefit pension scheme);
- the measurement of work completed and to be completed on contracts in progress; and
- legal opinions concerning interpretations of agreements, statutes and regulations.

When determining the need to use the work of an expert, the auditor needs to consider:

- the engagement team's knowledge and previous experience of the matter being considered;
- the risk of material misstatement based on the nature, complexity and materiality of the matter being considered; and
- the quantity and quality of other audit evidence expected to be obtained.

Once a decision has been made to use the work of an expert, the auditor should evaluate the expert's professional competence. This will involve considering:

- the expert's professional certification or licensing by, or membership of, an appropriate professional body;
- the expert's experience and reputation in the area of expertise in question, and
- the resources available to the expert.

The objectivity of the expert should also be considered. Clearly, there is a risk that an expert's objectivity may be impaired when the expert is employed by or related to the client. Such factors may impinge on the evidence which can be obtained by the expert, and an alternative approach may need to be considered – for example, alternative audit procedures or consultation of another expert.

As noted above regarding the work of internal audit, the auditor should ensure that the scope of the expert's work is adequate for the purposes of the audit. In particular, the auditor should review any terms of reference or instructions from the client to the expert.

The auditor should then evaluate the appropriateness of the expert's work as audit evidence towards the assertion being considered. This will include consideration of the following matters.

Source data used

This is particularly important when, for example, reviewing an actuarial report on a defined benefit pension scheme. Small errors in the source data can have a very material effect on the final figures produced, so it is vital to check the accuracy of the source data.

Assumptions and methods used and their consistency with prior periods

This is particularly important with the assumptions used in actuarial valuations.

When the expert carried out the work

With certain types of work, such as property valuations or stocktakes, dates are critical.

Results of the expert's work in the light of the auditor's overall knowledge of the business and of the results of other audit procedures

The work of the expert should make sense to the auditor. For example, when evaluating a property valuation, the auditor should have a rough idea about movements in the property market during the period.

10.4.6 Bulletin 1997/3 *The FRSSE: Guidance for auditors*

The audit of an entity that accounts under the FRSSE is essentially no different to that of an entity accounting under full UK GAAP. However, there are a few specific points to note from Bulletin 1997/3, set out below.

a)   Entities applying the FRSSE are exempt from complying with other accounting standards. However, in rare cases there may be a complex matter that is not dealt with in the FRSSE. The FRSSE states:

> 'Financial statements will generally be prepared using accepted practice and, accordingly, for transactions or events not dealt with in the FRSSE, smaller entities should have regard to other Accounting Standards and UITF Abstracts, not as mandatory documents, but as a means of establishing current practice.'

The auditor should therefore bear this in mind during the risk assessment, the review of disclosure and the detailed audit procedures on any complex areas.

b)   Some entities, whilst adopting the FRSSE, will nevertheless make additional voluntary disclosures in the accounts, such as a cash flow statement. The Bulletin makes clear that the auditor's responsibilities extend to all other information included within the financial statements.

c)   Care should be taken when checking the disclosure in the financial statements, particularly references to the GAAP used and the wording of the audit report (see section 44.4.1).

Chapter 11 Bringing it all together

11.1 Introduction

Many firms find the use of standard forms beneficial when undertaking the planning of an audit. They serve as a checklist to help ensure that nothing is missed. However, they are not usually sufficient by themselves, and a planning memorandum is strongly recommended to gather the planning work into a concise summary. In particular, ISA 300 distinguishes between the overall audit strategy and the audit plan. Many auditors struggle with the distinction between the two, and so this is considered further.

11.2 Audit strategy

The audit strategy sets out the scope, timing and direction of the audit in broad terms, and guides the development of the more detailed audit plan. The audit strategy therefore includes:

- determining the audit scope, including the financial reporting framework used, any industry-specific reporting requirements and the locations of any subsidiaries, associates, etc;

- ascertaining the reporting objectives in order to plan the audit timetable and agree the nature and timing of any additional reports required;

- considering the key factors that will determine the focus of the engagement team's efforts; and

- reviewing the experience gained from previous audits of the entity.

The appendix to ISA 300 contains a very useful list of matters the auditor may consider in establishing the overall audit strategy, which could be used as a checklist as part of the audit planning process (although not all matters will be applicable to every audit). These matters have been summarised below.

11.2.1 Audit scope

- Financial reporting framework and any need to reconcile to another framework.

- Industry-specific reporting requirements, such as reports mandated by industry regulators.

- Expected audit coverage, including the number and locations of subsidiaries, associates, etc.

- Group structure and control relationships for the purposes of consolidation.

- Extent to which subsidiaries, associates, etc. are audited by other auditors.

- Nature of the business and any need for specialised knowledge.

- Reporting currency to be used and any need for currency translation for the financial information audited.

- Need for a statutory audit of standalone financial statements in addition to an audit for consolidation purposes.

- Availability of the work of internal auditors and the extent of any potential reliance on such work.

- Entity's use of service organisations and how the auditor may obtain evidence concerning the design or operation of controls performed by them.

- Expected use of audit evidence obtained in prior audits (for example, tests of controls).

- Effect of information technology on the audit procedures, including the availability of data and the expected use of computer-assisted audit techniques.

- Use of interim audit procedures.

- The need to discuss matters that may affect the audit with firm staff who undertake non-audit services for the entity.

- Availability of client staff and information.

11.2.2 Reporting objectives, audit timetable and communications required

- Timetable for reporting including interim and final stages.

- Organisation of meetings and communication with management and the directors to discuss the audit work, expected type and timing of reports to be issued, etc. (for example, the audit report and letter of comment).

- Communication with other auditors.

- Communication within the audit team, including the nature and timing of team meetings and the review of audit work performed.

- Whether there are any other expected communications with third parties, including any statutory or contractual reporting responsibilities arising from the audit.

11.2.3 Direction of the audit

- Level of planning materiality.

- High risk audit areas.

- Impact of the risk assessment at the overall financial statement level on direction, supervision and review.

- Selection of the engagement team and the assignment of its audit work.

- Engagement budgeting, including consideration of the time needed for high risk areas.

- Results of previous audits that involved controls testing, including identified weaknesses and action taken to address them.

- Evidence of management's commitment to the design and operation of sound internal control and its importance in the business.

- Volume of transactions.

- Significant business developments affecting the entity – for example, changes in information technology and business processes, changes in key management, and acquisitions, mergers and divestments.

- Significant industry developments, such as changes in industry regulations and new reporting requirements.

- Significant changes in the financial reporting framework (for example, changes in Accounting Standards).

- Any other significant relevant developments, such as changes in the legal environment affecting the entity.

11.3 Audit plan

Once the audit strategy has been established, the auditor is able to start the development of a more detailed audit plan to address the various matters identified in the overall audit strategy. Although the overall audit strategy is normally established before developing the detailed audit plan, the two activities are not necessarily discrete or sequential processes but are closely interrelated, since changes in one may result in consequential changes to the other.

The audit plan is more detailed than the audit strategy, and includes the nature, timing and extent of audit procedures to be performed by the audit team members in order to obtain sufficient appropriate audit evidence. The audit plan includes:

- a description of the nature, timing and extent of planned risk assessment procedures; and

- a description of the nature, timing and extent of planned further audit procedures at the assertion level, reflecting the auditor's decision whether or not to test the operating effectiveness of controls, and the nature, timing and extent of planned substantive procedures.

Much of this information will be documented within the standard forms of the audit system being used, but it is nevertheless useful to include key matters relating to these issues within the planning memorandum as well as the audit strategy. In this way, the planning memorandum can also be used as a briefing document for the more-junior members of the audit team.

11.4 Non-use of standard forms

The majority of firms will use a proprietary audit system, which will contain a number of standard forms to assist in undertaking and documenting an audit. There can be a risk that less-experienced staff might think that it is compulsory to comply with all elements of the system without tailoring the approach to the needs of the client, and so prepare excessive and often irrelevant and costly audit documentation. Proper training and supervision of junior staff and communication within the audit team can help to overcome this risk.

However, even where a proprietary system is used, a free-form planning memorandum can be a good way of documenting the auditor's understanding of the business and the basis for the risk assessments made. Such a memorandum can easily be updated from year to year. This approach is recommended when auditing very small clients below the audit threshold, and an example of a planning memorandum taking this approach is given in Practice Note 26 *Guidance on smaller entity audit documentation*. If standard forms are not being used because the areas are being addressed through a planning memorandum, then the auditor must ensure that all the points addressed in Part I have been considered within that memorandum.

11.5 Authorisation

Once all of the planning forms have been completed, it is essential that the planning is reviewed and approved by the audit partner before the assignment commences. Allow time to do this properly; a cursory review is not sufficient. Time taken at this stage to ensure that the suggested approach is what the partner wants is time well spent. The review process is much simpler if the auditor actually thought through at the beginning of the job how the audit should be approached. Then, when undertaking the review, the auditor has merely to consider whether or not the work has been performed as set out in the planning and what the results have been.

It is also important to remember that if a second or independent partner review is needed, this may involve the partner in a review of the planning, which should be undertaken before the audit fieldwork is started.

11.6 Ongoing review

Many firms fall into the trap of preparing a very good plan and then not following it through to the audit. It is essential that planning be considered as an ongoing process during the audit. ISA 300 *Planning an audit of financial statements* states:

> 'Planning an audit is a continual and iterative process throughout the audit engagement. As a result of unexpected events, changes in conditions, or the audit evidence obtained from the results of audit procedures, the auditor may need to modify the overall audit strategy and audit plan...'

Audit planning evolves and changes throughout the audit whenever something arises that would impact on the original plan. The staff should consider at the beginning and end of any individual section if anything has occurred to affect their original assessment of risk and identification of the appropriate audit procedures to be undertaken. The two examples that follow have been selected to illustrate this point.

a) A potential fraud is identified during the audit fieldwork in an area originally assessed as low risk. This may lead the auditor to consider this a higher risk area, which would either influence the level of work to be undertaken or would lead to some specific additional procedures being undertaken to ensure that the full impact of such fraud has been identified and reflected within the financial statements.

b) The results of the substantive procedures performed during the audit fieldwork contradict the audit evidence obtained from testing the operating effectiveness of controls. The auditor would need to re-evaluate some or all of the planned audit procedures based on his or her revised consideration of assessed risks at the assertion level.

11.7 Conclusion

Having completed the audit planning, we can now move on to Part II of the book, which considers the implementation of the audit plan.

Part II   Implementation

Chapter 12 Introduction

12.1 Contents

Part II of the book considers implementation of the audit plan. There is a separate chapter for each of the individual sections that will be found within most audit files, namely:

- substantive (extensive) analytical review;
- intangible assets;
- tangible fixed assets;
- investments in group and associated undertakings and other investments;
- stock (including work in progress);
- long-term contracts;
- debtors and prepayments;
- bank and cash;
- creditors and accruals;
- long-term loans and deferred income;
- provisions for liabilities and charges, contingent liabilities and financial commitments;
- defined benefit pension schemes;
- capital, reserves and statutory records;
- taxation;
- profit and loss account – income;
- profit and loss account – expenditure;
- profit and loss account – wages and salaries;
- profit and loss account – other;
- related party transactions;
- subsequent events and going concern;
- value added tax;
- consolidation and groups; and
- cash flow statements.

Chapter 39 considers the particular issues arising when auditing financial statements prepared under IFRS, principally the audit of fair values.

12.2 Aims

The aims of Part II are to look at the specific objectives relating to each of these sections and to discuss how best these can be achieved in various circumstances.

In Chapter 6 we identified a number of assertions made in financial statements, namely:

- existence;
- rights and obligations;

- occurrence;
- completeness;
- valuation;
- measurement; and
- presentation and disclosure.

It is important that the audit work on each section is designed to ensure that each of the relevant objectives or assertions is covered and sufficient audit evidence obtained. Good audit evidence in relation to one objective does not compensate for failure to obtain audit evidence in respect of another objective. However, the auditor may in some circumstances be able to design tests that provide audit evidence in respect of more than one objective. For example, testing after-date cash on debtors may provide audit evidence in respect of both existence and valuation.

Chapter 13 Audit evidence

13.1 Introduction

The programmes of detailed audit procedures drawn up by the auditor are designed to achieve the audit objectives and ultimately enable an opinion to be formed on the truth and fairness of the financial statements. ISA 500 *Audit evidence* states that: 'The auditor should obtain sufficient appropriate audit evidence to be able to draw reasonable conclusions on which to base the audit opinion' (ISA 500.2). This evidence can be obtained in a number of different ways, but will normally result from a mix of tests of control (compliance testing) and substantive procedures, including analytical review. In many cases, particularly with small companies, where there are unlikely to be significant controls, audit evidence may be obtained entirely by substantive testing.

The tests should be designed to enable the auditor to confirm that sufficient and appropriate audit evidence has been obtained. Paragraph 7 of ISA 500 states that sufficiency is a measure of the quantity of the audit evidence, whereas appropriateness is a measure of the quality or reliability of the audit evidence obtained. Paragraph 14 adds that audit evidence is often persuasive rather than conclusive. It is therefore frequently appropriate to design more than one test relating to the same audit objective in order to allow the auditor to form a conclusion on the sufficiency and appropriateness of the audit evidence that has been obtained.

It is essential that, when designing tests, the auditor is aware of and understands the difference between compliance testing or tests of control and substantive procedures. These two types of test are described below.

13.2 Tests of control

Tests of control or compliance tests are tests that have been designed to ensure that key controls identified within an accounting system are working correctly. Further details of the types of controls can be found in Part I Chapter 4. In addition, specific controls that can be applied in individual sections have been separately identified.

13.3 Substantive testing

Substantive tests are the more usual tests to be undertaken and are tests of detail within the system. Where tests of control can be undertaken, they may enable the auditor to reduce the number of substantive audit tests that need to be carried out. However, it may be appropriate to undertake purely substantive testing both where there are no key controls that can be relied upon and where tests of such controls are time consuming and sufficient audit evidence can be obtained easily through substantive testing only. It should be remembered that analytical review is a substantive audit procedure.

13.4 Methods of obtaining audit evidence

ISA 500 identifies a number of different procedures that can be used to obtain audit evidence, and these are described below.

13.4.1 Inspection

This involves examining records, documents or assets, whether internal or external, paper or electronic.

When examining either records or documents, the audit evidence obtained will give a varying degree of comfort – depending on the nature and source of the evidence and on the effectiveness of the controls over their production.

13.4.2 Observation

This involves watching a process or procedure being performed by the entity – for example, attendance at a stocktake. Such audit evidence is usually obtained where a procedure leaves no audit trail. Using the stocktake example: except in a minority of cases where continuous stock records are maintained, if the auditor does not attend the stocktake, then it is virtually impossible to be satisfied that stock is fairly stated, as the existence objective will not have been met.

13.4.3 Inquiry

This involves obtaining information from individuals either inside or outside of the audit client. This is an audit procedure that is used extensively throughout the audit and often is complementary to performing other audit procedures. Inquiries may range from formal written inquiries to informal oral inquiries. Evaluating responses to inquiries is an integral part of the inquiry process.

The evidence obtained may provide the auditor with information that he or she had not previously obtained or it may provide corroborative evidence on a particular objective.

It should be noted that the auditor performs audit procedures in addition to the use of inquiry to obtain sufficient appropriate audit evidence. Ordinarily, inquiry alone does not provide sufficient audit evidence to detect a material misstatement at the assertion level. Moreover, inquiry alone is not sufficient to test the operating effectiveness of controls.

Care may need to be taken where sensitive information is disclosed to the auditor by an employee of the client. Issues of confidentiality may arise with respect both to the employee and to the information itself, which may pose difficulties in undertaking further audit procedures. The auditor should consider the responses to audit inquiries with due professional scepticism, and bear in mind the reporting and tipping-off requirements of the money laundering regulations.

13.4.4 Confirmation

Confirmation, which is a specific type of inquiry, is the process of obtaining a representation of information or of an existing condition directly from a third party – for example, a circularisation of customers of the entity to confirm trade debtor balances.

13.4.5 Recalculation

This involves checking the mathematical accuracy of documents or records.

13.4.6 Re-performance

This is the auditor's independent execution of procedures or controls that were originally performed as part of the entity's internal control. An example of this is re-performing the ageing of the sales ledger, either manually or through the use of Computer Assisted Audit Techniques or CAATs.

13.4.7 Analytical procedures

These procedures consist of the analysis of relationships between items of either financial or non-financial data and corroborating explanations for any fluctuations and relationships that are inconsistent with other relevant information or deviate significantly from predicted or expected amounts.

13.5 Directional testing

Most auditing systems nowadays apply a method of testing called directional testing. The objective of directional testing is to ensure that all aspects of the audit are covered as simply and cost-effectively as possible by eliminating duplication of testing.

Directional testing takes advantage of the double entry principle to reduce the number of tests. For example, the double entry to post a sales invoice to the sales ledger is debit sales ledger and credit sales. When testing the sales ledger, the issue of overstatement of the balance – which is the debit balance – is considered within the debtors' section; the issue of understatement of the balance – that is, testing the credit side of the entry – is dealt with in the testing of sales for understatement. As can be seen from this example, the method of applying directional testing is to test debit balances for overstatement and credit balances for understatement.

This method of testing minimises the amount of duplication and over-auditing and the tests suggested within the remainder of this book follow this principle. One important point to note is that directional testing must go from the cradle to the grave, and back again – that is, from the very start of a transaction cycle to the end. A directional test will not be effective if the sample for testing is selected from the wrong population. For example, when testing sales for completeness of income, it is essential that the starting point is outside of the accounting system. Thus orders, goods despatched notes or a job number could be used. Selecting a sample of sales invoices from those already recorded may be easier but does not help to achieve the objective of ensuring that all sales are fully recorded.

There are two basic rules that should be remembered when applying directional testing; these are:

- when testing for overstatement, the samples should be taken from the nominal ledger (that is, the grave); and

- when testing for understatement, the sample should be taken from the source document or, alternatively, from a reciprocal population (that is, the cradle). For example, where sales are actually directly related to purchases, then the sample for completeness of income can be taken from cost of sales. That is, the auditor could select a sample of purchases and ensure that a corresponding sale has occurred.

When undertaking the testing for overstatement, it is frequently easier to leave testing until a trial balance is available, particularly where the entity does not maintain a nominal ledger.

In addition, it must be remembered that when dealing with an area such as stock, where the balance affects the profit and loss account as a credit and the balance sheet as a debit, the testing should be designed to cover both understatement and overstatement.

Finally, and fairly obviously, where the directional testing approach is applied, it is absolutely essential that the auditor ensures both understatement and overstatement are tested. For example, when considering the sales cycle, testing for understatement of sales is undertaken in the profit and loss account section, but the tests on overstatement of sales will be in the debtors section. The auditor must check that both tests have been performed, and not simply reference the objective to another section of the file.

13.6 External confirmations

As noted in section 8.3.4, external confirmations are an important source of audit evidence, as they are generally considered to be more reliable, coming from an independent source. Examples of external confirmations are:

- bank letters;
- trade debtors' circularisations;
- confirmation of stocks held by third parties;
- confirmation of title to property from Land Registry; and
- trade creditors' circularisations.

The specific practicalities of obtaining these confirmations are discussed later in Part II in the relevant chapters.

ISA 505 *External confirmations* notes that where management requests the auditor not to seek an external confirmation, the auditor should consider whether there are valid grounds for such a request and obtain audit evidence to support the validity of management's requests. If the auditor agrees to management's request, alternative audit procedures should be applied to obtain sufficient appropriate audit evidence.

If the auditor does not accept the validity of management's request and is prevented from carrying out the confirmations, there has been a limitation on the scope of the auditor's work, and the auditor should consider the possible impact on the audit report.

Chapter 14 Sampling and error evaluation

14.1 Sampling

ISA 530 *Audit sampling and other means of testing* applies in all circumstances where a sample is taken from the population for testing in order to form an audit opinion. In certain circumstances, 100 per cent of the population will be tested; this does not constitute audit sampling. Audit sampling is a method of identifying a number of items within the population that can be tested in order to provide sufficient assurance that any material error in the population will be identified. Crucially, paragraph 3 of the ISA requires all items in the sample to have a chance of selection. However, this need not be an equal chance of selection.

Consistency is a crucial aspect when considering sampling. The auditor must ensure that the sampling method adopted by the practice is applied in every case where sampling is appropriate.

All audit systems will have their own methodology to determine sample sizes. An example methodology is detailed below. It is important to remember that sampling should be utilised wherever possible. A common pitfall that many practices fall into is to test the entire population in too many cases. This can frequently result in overauditing, but can also result in a more serious problem. For example, when testing for receipt of cash after date for debtors, the whole population is considered – that is, all cash received from the period end to the date of the test. A conclusion is then drawn along the lines that say 60 per cent of the debtors have been paid after the period end and, therefore, the results are reasonable. However, this ignores the fact that the sample represented 100 per cent of the population and, therefore, if only 60 per cent have been paid, the potential error is 40 per cent: an issue that must be addressed.

14.2 Determining sample sizes

The basis of determining sample sizes in this example uses the following parameters:

- the monetary value of the population;
- the overall level of materiality set for the audit;
- a calculated risk factor (inherent risk); and
- the identification of high value and key items.

By selecting the sample size using the combination of the first three items above, the auditor is using the assessments made at the planning stage of the audit to determine the size of the audit sample. The lower the figure of materiality and the higher the inherent risk, the larger the sample will be.

This sampling method expects the auditor to identify high value and key items separately for testing. These items are considered sufficiently important to justify selecting all of them. High value items will be identified as transactions that are higher than an identified factor, which is the level of materiality divided by the inherent risk factor: the tolerable error. Key items are other balances or transactions that are identified as significant in the particular circumstance of the test being carried out. The judgment of the auditor is required in assessing whether or not an item is a 'key' item for these purposes. No absolute definition of key items is possible.

The value of the population being tested will relate specifically to the test being carried out. For example, when undertaking existence testing on fixed assets, the population would be the net book value of the assets. However, when undertaking tests on additions, the value of the population will be the value of the additions in the period.

This sampling method requires the auditor to identify high value and key items, but also requires testing of 'the residual population'. The residual population is the value of the population after deducting the value of the high value and key items.

When determining the number of items from a residual population that need to be tested, the auditor should consider the materiality and risk. In addition, consideration needs to be given to the method of obtaining audit evidence. If a test is purely substantive, then a higher sample size will be required than if the testing also includes extensive analytical review and/or tests of control, in which case the number of substantive tests that need to be undertaken will be reduced.

Having identified a method that can be used to determine sample sizes, it must then be applied consistently. The audit working papers must incorporate details of how the sample size was selected. In addition, they must also contain details of how the ultimate sample was selected from the population.

Various means are available for selecting the chosen sample from a population. High value and key items will already have been identified. The sample selected from the residual population should be selected so as to cover fairly the whole of the population being tested.

This will involve the use of random, systematic or judgmental means of selection. The auditor should try to avoid the selection of a block of items as this is prone to bias and fails to consider the whole population adequately. The working papers should reflect where the sample was selected from and how the items were selected for testing.

Although sample sizes should feel right judgmentally, it is not sufficient to determine the size of a sample without recording the logic. Furthermore, once the sample size has been selected, it is essential that it is not changed. The only exception one would expect to see is where errors have been identified, and so the sample size has been increased to reduce these. In too many cases where the auditor is under time pressure, the sample size is reduced for no other reason than lack of time. This is dangerous. Where the time pressure results from the test that has been designed being difficult to carry out, then – instead of reducing the sample size – the auditor should consider whether there is an alternative test that can be applied to satisfy the required objective.

14.3 The evaluation of errors

The investigation and evaluation of errors encountered during audit testing is a vital part of the audit. Errors should always be followed up. In no circumstances should they simply be ignored.

When an error occurs, there are two specific questions that need to be addressed, namely:

- Could other errors exist elsewhere within the population?
- Is it possible that the errors could be material to the accounts?

If the answer to both of these questions is yes, then additional audit work must be carried out. It is important to remember that the second question is asking whether it is possible, not whether it is likely. In normal circumstances, therefore, some additional work must be carried out whenever an error is encountered. The work can be directed specifically to help the auditor answer both of those questions. Alternatively, it may be appropriate to extend the sample size in order to determine whether the level of error encountered is typical of the population as a whole.

If the method of sampling identified above has been utilised, then the level of error in the population of high value and key items will already have been fully evaluated. Therefore, any increased audit work will be within the 'residual population'.

Where the increased work identifies a certain level of error within the population, it would usually be appropriate to extrapolate that level of error over the residual population. This, combined with the errors found in the high value and key items tested, will give the most likely level of error in the entire population. Consideration must be given to whether this level of error is likely to produce material misstatement within the accounts. The actual and the extrapolated error should be recorded on the summary of unadjusted errors on the audit file (see Part III Chapter 41).

14.4 Projecting the value of errors

There are two main statistical methods of projecting the value of total errors in a population – the ratio method and the difference method. The ratio method may be more appropriate where the amount of error in a transaction is related closely to its size – that is, the bigger the transaction, the bigger the error. The difference method may be more appropriate where the size of the transaction would make no difference to the amount of the error – that is, the error is of a constant amount. The basis of each calculation has been set out below.

14.4.1 The ratio method

This method takes the value of the error found and multiplies it by the population value divided by the value of the sample to obtain the projected error in a population.

$$\text{Error in population} \quad \times \quad \frac{\text{Population value}}{\text{Total value of sample}} \quad = \quad \text{Projected error in population}$$

14.4.2 The difference method

This method takes the error found in the sample and multiplies it by the number of items in the population divided by the number of items in the sample to give the projected error in the population.

$$\text{Error in population} \quad \times \quad \frac{\text{Population mumber}}{\text{Number in sample}} \quad = \quad \text{Projected error in population}$$

Where information about the nature of errors is not known, the ratio method is normally the most appropriate method to use.

Because the projected error is unlikely to be the same as the actual error in a population, it will be necessary to consider judgmentally whether or not a material error in the accounts is likely. If it is considered that it might be material, the following options are available to the auditor:

● to request the client to investigate the errors and the potential for further errors;

● to extend the audit test again and gain a more precise conclusion;

● to perform alternative procedures (if possible); or

● to qualify the audit opinion on the grounds of uncertainty.

Action (d) should be the last option, which should only be taken after establishing that it was not possible to form a conclusion from any of the other methods. However, it is essential that the effects of any errors found in the audit tests are resolved. It is not acceptable to leave an error position 'open'; a conclusion about its impact on the individual area being tested and on the accounts as a whole must be drawn. If errors are left unresolved and their effect on the accounts not properly assessed, it is not possible to assess whether the audit opinion given is in fact reasonable.

Alternatively, an error is described as 'isolated' as a justification for not extending testing, but the reason for the error being considered isolated and not symptomatic of a wider problem is not explained. This again casts doubt on the reasonableness of the audit opinion.

Chapter 15 Procedures affecting all audit sections

15.1 Introduction

The purpose of this Chapter is to review some of the common procedures that will impact on every section of the audit file. The key point is to ensure that effort is concentrated on those tests that are crucial to forming the audit opinion. This point is reiterated several times in the following chapters.

The suggested tests in each of the individual chapters have been linked directly to audit objectives. Where any of the tests satisfy more than one objective, the test is listed under the objective that is satisfied most completely. The test is then cross-referenced to any other specific objectives it helps to satisfy.

The auditor must ensure that all of the objectives for each section are considered, ascertain where the risks are likely to occur for this particular business and select the tests accordingly. The most important tests should be completed first. Concentrating the audit approach on the risky areas first means that if time runs out, there are no critical tests still outstanding. It may well be that further audit work needs to be undertaken, but the auditor may have gained enough assurance from the satisfaction of the other objectives that sufficient comfort can be gained from analytical procedures in respect of the outstanding work.

15.2 Files and working papers

The purpose of working papers on an assignment is to provide a clear trail of the figures from the basic input to the final financial statements. Furthermore, the file should show the sources of information the auditor has received and any confirmation work the auditor has carried out. The objective is to produce meaningful financial statements with sufficient relevant and reliable evidence on file to support them.

Working papers should be **neat**, **tidy** and **logical** and should fully explain their purpose. Every working paper, regardless of whether it is prepared on paper or on computer, should contain:

- the **name** of the client;
- the **purpose** of the schedule;
- the **initials** of the person preparing the schedule and the person reviewing it;
- the **dates** on which the schedule was prepared and reviewed;
- the **accounting period** for which the schedule was prepared;
- the precise **details** of the work performed; and
- the **conclusions** drawn from that work.

It should be noted that ISA 230 (Revised) *Audit documentation* specifically requires the recording of who performed the audit work and the date such work was completed, and of who reviewed the audit work performed and the date and extent of such review. However, the requirement to document who reviewed the audit work does not imply a need for each specific working paper to include evidence of review. The audit documentation should, however, evidence who reviewed specified elements of the audit work performed and when.

ISA 230 (Revised) also requires that the identifying characteristics of the specific items or matters being tested should be documented. The Standards gives several illustrative examples, including those in the table below.

Procedure or type of sample	Information to be documented
Selection of purchase orders	Date and unique purchase order number
Systematic sampling	Source of items being selected, starting point and sampling interval
Inquiry of client staff	Date(s) of inquiry plus the name and role of the member(s) of staff
Observational test	Process/control/matter being observed, the name and role of the member(s) of staff, and where and when the observation was carried out

ISA 230 (Revised) goes on to state that when an auditor is deciding on whether the working papers of an audit file are sufficient, he or she should decide if they enable an experienced auditor, having no previous connection with the audit, to understand:

- the nature, timing and extent of audit procedures performed to comply with ISAs and applicable legal and regulatory requirements;
- the results of the audit procedures and the audit evidence obtained; and
- significant matters arising during the audit and the conclusions reached.

This has significantly raised the bar in terms of the extent of the audit documentation required compared to the old SAS 230, which noted that an experienced auditor may only be able to obtain a comprehensive understanding of all aspects of the audit by discussing them with the auditors who prepared them. Under ISAs, however, the audit file needs to be able to 'stand on its own'.

Where the auditor has used his or her professional judgment in arriving at an audit opinion, it is important that the auditor can demonstrate the relevant facts that were known at the time, and show how these were used to reach the conclusion. It must be remembered that, when the auditor's judgment is subsequently questioned, months or years may have passed and the third party will have the benefit of hindsight.

The auditor should ensure that every schedule on file has a purpose. By insisting that staff complete the items detailed above on each of the working papers, this may force them to actually think about what they are doing. Frequently, within the file there is a lot of superfluous information (copy invoices, etc.) that adds nothing to the audit evidence but which makes the file much more difficult to review. Where certain information is being included for purposes other than audit comfort, the auditor may wish to consider placing this in a separate section at the back of the file to avoid 'cluttering' the main body of the audit file.

The auditor must ensure that any work undertaken on working papers provided by the client is clearly recorded. It is not necessary to rewrite a schedule just because the client prepared it. Similarly, where there are items relevant to the current year on the previous year's file, it is perfectly acceptable to leave a copy on the previous file and bring the original forward, as long as it is marked to show that it has been reviewed for any necessary amendment.

Where the auditor is using a computerised system it is still important to ensure that the audit 'file' contains all of the above, even though some, if not all, of the schedules may be in electronic form. Where data is maintained in electronic format, it must be properly backed up and also protected from future amendment.

15.3 Initial procedures to be undertaken on each audit section

There are a number of audit procedures that should be considered at the beginning of each audit section. Although these have not been separately identified within each of the individual chapters, to avoid repetition, they are nonetheless crucial to ensuring that the objectives are all fully met. These procedures are listed below.

- Opening balances should be agreed to the previous year's accounts where appropriate.

- A lead schedule should be prepared, or checked, containing the current year's figures. The auditor should inquire into any major variations from expectations, and make notes of the reasons for them.

- Any material journal entries or other adjustments made during the course of preparing the financial statements should be examined.

- ISAs require the auditor to review and consider whether any amendment is needed to the initial materiality and/or the original assessment of risk throughout the audit. It is therefore worthwhile having a prompt at the beginning of each section to remind the audit staff that they should consider whether anything has happened in the audit so far that would revise these assessments. The auditor should then follow this through to ensure that any necessary revisions are made to the audit plan and the audit approach. Also, where an adjustment is made to either materiality or risk and audit work has already been undertaken, the auditor must consider if any further work needs to be undertaken on the basis of this revised assessment. This consideration must be documented.

- Similarly, the extent of any planned reliance on internal controls should be reviewed, and a decision made as to whether this remains appropriate.

- Analytical review procedures should be applied throughout the audit. This should be the case even though the auditor has not identified any suitable analytical review procedures that provide sufficient comfort to enable a reduction in the sample size. It should be standard procedure to review for any large and unusual items and to obtain an explanation for anything that looks 'odd'. There is a lot to be said for the auditor's 'nose', and the auditor should investigate anything that does not feel right rather than focusing entirely on the samples that the papers require.

15.4 Opening balances and comparatives

For continuing engagements where the auditor also audited the comparatives and opening balances, few procedures are required. For first year engagements, however, and situations where the comparatives are unaudited, things are a little more complicated. These issues are specifically addressed by ISA 510 *Initial engagements and continuing engagements – opening balances* and ISA 710 *Comparatives* and are considered further below.

15.4.1 Continuing engagements

For continuing engagements where the auditor also audited the comparatives and opening balances, the auditor should ensure:

a) that opening balances do not contain misstatements that materially affect the current year's financial statements;

b) that the previous year's closing balances have been correctly brought forward to the current year (or restated where necessary). This would normally comprise ensuring that the comparatives in the draft financial statements and the opening balances in the current year's trial balance both agree with last year's signed audited accounts; and

c) that accounting policies have been consistently applied, or that any changes have been made properly and disclosed in accordance with FRS 18. This would require comparing the accounting policies in the draft accounts with those in the previous year's signed accounts.

15.4.2 Initial engagements

An initial engagement is one where the client is new to the firm, and the auditor is auditing a set of financial statements of that client for the first time, and the financial statements of previous years will have been audited by another firm of auditors. In these circumstances, the auditor should follow the same approach as outlined above for continuing engagements.

Due to new provisions in the Companies Act 2006 and subsequent amendments to the Audit Regulations (such that they apply to all audited entities and not just companies), for accounting periods beginning on or after 6 April 2008 it is possible for the new auditor to request (in writing) access to the previous auditor's audit working papers. This alone may enable the new auditor to gain sufficient audit evidence over opening balances, but if such reliance is to be placed on these papers, the new auditor must assess the professional competence and independence of the previous auditor.

Where a review of the previous auditor's working papers is unsatisfactory, the auditor should perform the additional procedures described below for unaudited comparatives.

15.4.3 Unaudited comparatives

This situation can arise either when the client grows and exceeds the audit threshold for the first time, or where a client requests a voluntary audit for the first time. In both cases, the prior year comparatives will not have been audited. In these circumstances, further procedure will be required, for which guidance is given in paragraphs 9 and 10 of ISA 510, as follows:

- For current assets and liabilities, some audit evidence can usually be obtained as part of the current year's audit procedures. For example, cash received in the current year in respect of opening trade debtors gives evidence towards existence, completeness and valuation of those balances. Stock is usually more difficult and may require additional procedures, such as observing a stocktake and reconciling it with the opening position, testing valuation and cut-off of opening stock and reviewing gross profit margins.

- For non-current assets and liabilities, it will usually be possible to examine the accounting records supporting the opening balances, or to obtain third-party confirmation (for example, a bank letter for long-term bank loans), but additional procedures may still be required.

15.4.4 Qualified audit opinions in previous years

Irrespective of whether the audit is a continuing or an initial engagement, extra consideration is needed if the prior year's accounts were qualified. In such circumstances, the auditor should consider whether there is any effect on the current year's accounts. Extra care is needed if a qualification has been made in respect of stock as there is a further two-year knock-on effect.

15.4.5 Insufficient evidence

If, having followed the above procedures, the auditor is nevertheless unable to obtain sufficient appropriate audit evidence in respect of opening balances and comparatives, the audit opinion should be qualified due to a limitation on scope. Depending on the extent of the problem and materiality of the areas in question, this could either be an 'except for' qualification or, in more serious circumstances, a disclaimer of opinion may need to be given. Refer to Chapter 44 for more discussion of qualified audit opinions.

15.5 Auditing accounting estimates

An accounting estimate is defined in ISA 540 *Audit of accounting estimates* as 'an approximation of the amount of an item in the absence of a precise means of measurement.' Examples of accounting estimates would therefore include items such as:

- stock and trade debtor provisions;
- depreciation;
- deferred tax; and
- warranty provisions.

Accounting estimates are often of a non-routine nature and may be determined only at a period end, a common approach with items such as deferred tax. In other instances, they may be a routine procedure performed by the accounting system – for example, a formulaic slow-moving stock provision or fixed asset depreciation.

Estimates are often made where there is some level of uncertainty as to the outcome of future events and involve the use of judgment. As a result, there is a higher risk of material misstatement when accounting estimates are involved. Audit evidence may be less conclusive, and auditor judgment is likely to be needed, frequently making such areas more difficult to audit.

ISA 540 gives the following three procedures, which should be used either individually or in combination to audit an accounting estimate:

- review and test the procedure used by management to develop the estimate;

- use an independent estimate for comparison with that prepared by management; and

- conduct a review of subsequent events which provide audit evidence of the reasonableness of the estimate made.

15.5.1 Reviewing and testing the process used by management

This ordinarily involves a four-step procedure, as described below.

a) **Evaluate the data and consider the assumptions on which the estimate is based.**

The auditor should ensure that the data being used is accurate, complete and relevant. For example, if testing a warranty provision, the data of products sold should not include all products that were sold under warranty, but only those still under warranty.

b) **Test the calculations involved.**

Accounting estimates are often made using spreadsheets, especially at the smaller client. These are notorious for containing mistakes in formulae, such as not including the last line in a list of data when adding up at the bottom. A further risk can arise with clients who are very proficient in the use of spreadsheets, and use very complicated formulae, pivot tables, etc. It is not uncommon for such spreadsheets to contain fundamental errors, so that the calculation of the key provision is not done on the desired basis. These types of errors can be difficult to identify, especially if the members of the audit team do not have a high level of expertise in using spreadsheets.

c) **Compare (where possible) estimates made in prior periods with actual results of those periods.**

A typical example might be to compare the previous year's warranty provision with the actual costs of repairs and replacements under warranty in the following year.

d) **Consider management's approval procedures.**

Management should ideally review and approve the final estimated figure. This can be a strong high-level control when the review process is undertaken properly and evidenced.

15.5.2 Use of an independent estimate

It may be possible to obtain an independent estimate to compare with that prepared by management. In such circumstances, the way the independent estimate has been drawn up should be assessed, considering the data and any assumptions used.

15.5.3 Review of subsequent events

Review of transactions and events after the balance sheet date may provide useful audit evidence when evaluating accounting estimates. Such work may reduce, or in some circumstances remove, the need for audit procedures on the process used by management to develop the estimate or to use an independent estimate.

For example, consider a stock provision against stock which is perishable with a sell-by date. Post-year-end sales information may conclusively show which items in stock at the year end were not sold after the year end before the expiration of their sell-by date, thus giving the auditor high-quality audit evidence to support the level of the stock provision.

15.6 Common procedures to be applied in the finalisation process on each section

In the same way as there are common procedures that have to be applied at the beginning of each audit section, there are also common procedures that need to be applied at the end. These are detailed in paragraphs (a) to (c) below.

a) When forming a conclusion on the section, consideration should be given as to whether there are any items that ought either to be brought to the client's attention within the letter of comment or confirmed within the letter of representation. These items should be collated on a separate schedule, which can be put within the completion section of the file to avoid its being overlooked. It is relatively common to find specific issues being addressed within the main body of the audit file that have not been brought forward. It is therefore important to be disciplined about ensuring that these are recorded on an ongoing basis rather than collated at the end of the audit.

b) A conclusion must be formed on each section of the file. The auditor should consider the specific objectives, along with the tests which have been undertaken to satisfy those objectives, and then determine whether they have been satisfied. Where there have been problems within a particular test but the auditor is still happy that the objective has ultimately been satisfied, then this fact must be adequately recorded so that the audit evidence on the individual section actually supports the conclusion that is being drawn. It should be remembered that forming a conclusion on the individual sections for the senior is as important as deciding on the audit opinion within the financial statements for the partner and should be taken just as seriously. Where a non-standard programme is being utilised, this should be cross-referenced to the objectives so that it is clear which tests have been undertaken to satisfy each objective.

c) The auditor should then consider whether the results of testing in each section have any impact on the overall audit plan and/or risk assessment and/or materiality. Where this is the case, the auditor should ensure that any necessary amendments have been made and that these are fed through to the audit work on the remaining sections. The auditor should also consider whether any further work is required on the sections which have already been completed. The auditor should take an objective view of the work that has been undertaken and confirm:

   - that it has been performed in accordance with the audit programme;

   - that the results obtained have been adequately documented;

   - that all necessary information has been collected for the preparation of the statutory accounts; and

   - that in the opinion of the auditor, the particular area is fairly stated, subject to any matters that have been carried forward for the partner's attention.

This final conclusion is very often missing or not dealt with adequately on individual sections of the file. It appears that some audit staff are wary of putting their own names to something as significant as the conclusion on a section of a file. However, the individual who completed the work is in the best position to do this. It is essential that the person who has completed most of the work actually signs off the audit programme and the conclusion on the audit section.

Chapter 16 Substantive analytical procedures

16.1 Introduction

'Substantive analytical procedures' refers to those procedures that are applied during the course of the audit on specific areas of the accounts, or on the accounts as a whole, as a means of providing formal audit assurance. These procedures, when effective and the results are satisfactory, can, in most audit systems, enable the auditor to significantly reduce the amount of detailed audit testing.

16.2 When should they be used?

The simple answer to this question is as often as possible. Analytical procedures may be performed wherever the auditor considers that they are necessary or will be effective. Carrying out substantive analytical review procedures can lead to excellent audit assurance in certain areas and, as noted above, should reduce the extent of the detailed transaction or balance testing.

ISA 520 *Analytical procedures* suggests that auditors should use their judgment to assess 'the expected effectiveness and efficiency of the available audit procedures in reducing the assessed risk of material misstatement at the assertion level to an acceptably low level' (ISA 520.10). Therefore, at the planning stage, the auditor should make an assessment as to whether or not analytical review will be used as a substantive test on particular audit sections.

The auditor should be aware of the types of information available from the client on which analytical review can be based. This can include financial information prepared by the entity but, where this occurs, it is important that the reasons for accepting the data as 'properly prepared' are fully documented by the auditor.

In addition, substantive analytical review procedures may bridge a gap in the audit trail where, for example, detailed stock records are not maintained. This could arise in the retail trade, where detailed stock movements tend not to be recorded. If audit tests are based on copy sales invoices, it can never be certain that these contain details of all sales. What about the sale that was not recorded on a sales invoice? Transaction testing will never pick up such an error; no such transaction test can.

However, substantive analytical review procedures may provide alternative audit procedures enabling appropriate reliable audit evidence to be derived from a combination of transaction testing and analytical review, and from which it can be concluded that sales have not been materially misstated.

16.3 How substantive analytical review procedures should be used

A typical example of how substantive analytical review should be used would be a review of the purchase ledger – comparing the list of balances this year with last year's and obtaining explanations for significant differences. This work could then be used to justify cutting down on the supplier statement reconciliation work.

Paragraph 13 of ISA 520 states that when intending to use analytical review as a substantive procedure on individual audit sections, the auditor should consider a number of factors, namely:

- the suitability of using substantive analytical procedures, given the assertions;

- the reliability of the data, whether internal or external, from which expectations are developed;

- whether expectations are sufficiently precise to be able to identify a material misstatement at the desired level of assurance; and

- the size of any difference between expectation and the actual amount recorded which is acceptable.

16.3.1 The suitability of using substantive analytical procedures

Substantive analytical procedures are generally more applicable to large volumes of transactions that tend to be predictable over time. The entire premise is based on the expectation that there are relationships among data which continue in the absence of known conditions to the contrary. However, reliance on the results will depend on the auditor's assessment of the risk that even when the analytical procedures may identify relationships as expected, in fact a material misstatement exists.

In determining the suitability of substantive analytical procedures, given the assertions, the auditor should consider the following key points.

- The assessment of the risk of material misstatement.

- The auditor considers the understanding of the entity and its internal control, the materiality and likelihood of misstatement of the items involved, and the nature of the assertion in determining whether substantive analytical procedures are suitable. For example, if the controls over sales order processing are weak, the auditor may place more reliance on tests of detail rather than on substantive analytical procedures for assertions related to trade debtors.

- Any tests of detail directed toward the same assertion.

- Substantive analytical procedures may also be considered appropriate when tests of details are performed on the same assertion. For example, when auditing the collectability of trade debtors, the auditor may apply substantive analytical procedures to an ageing of customers' accounts in addition to after-date cash testing.

16.3.2 The reliability of the data from which expectations are developed

The reliability of data is influenced by its source and nature, and is dependent on the circumstances under which it is obtained. In determining whether data is reliable for purposes of designing substantive analytical procedures, the auditor should consider the following points.

- The source of the information. Information is ordinarily more reliable, for example, when it is obtained from independent sources outside the entity.

- The comparability of the information. For example, broad industry data may not be comparable to that of an entity that produces and sells specialised products.

- The nature and relevance of the information available. Budgets, for example, can be drawn up in many ways – some as an expectation of actual results, whereas others are more like a target or goal to be achieved.

- Controls over the preparation of the information – for example, controls over the preparation, review and maintenance of budgets.

- Prior knowledge and understanding – for example, the knowledge gained during previous audits, together with the auditor's understanding of the effectiveness of the accounting and internal control systems, and the types of problems that in the past have given rise to accounting adjustments.

- Whether or not the information is produced internally. The reliability of internal information is enhanced if it is produced independently of the accounting system or where there are adequate controls over its preparation.

ISA 520 also notes that the auditor should consider testing the controls, if any, over the entity's preparation of information that will be used in substantive analytical procedures. When such controls are effective, the auditor has greater confidence in the reliability of the information and, therefore, in the results of substantive analytical procedures. See Chapter 4.

16.3.3 The preciseness of the expectations set

In assessing whether the expectation can be developed sufficiently precisely to identify a material mis-statement at the desired level of assurance, the auditor should consider:

- The accuracy with which the expected results can be predicted. For example, the auditor will ordinarily expect greater consistency in comparing gross profit margins from one period to another than in comparing discretionary expenses such as advertising.

- The degree to which information can be disaggregated. For example, substantive analytical procedures may be more effective when applied to financial information on a divisional basis than when applied to the financial statements of the entity as a whole.

- The availability of the information, both financial and non-financial.

- The frequency with which a relationship is observed – for example, a pattern repeated monthly as opposed to annually.

16.3.4 The level of acceptable difference

In designing and performing substantive analytical procedures, the auditor must consider the degree of variance from expectation that can be accepted without the need for further investigation. This consideration is influenced primarily by materiality and the consistency with the desired level of assurance.

16.4 Practicalities

If there are differences between the auditor's expectation of the results of analytical review and what the figures actually show, then the auditor should perform further analysis and make inquiries of the client to obtain explanations for the differences. Such explanations often relate to unusual transactions or accounting or business changes.

The explanations obtained from the client must be substantiated. This can usually be achieved in one of two ways. The auditor would either apply his or her understanding of the business (including knowledge gained when performing audit work both in the present and in the past) and/or carry out further checking of other evidence supporting the explanations given.

When conducting substantive analytical review procedures, it is important to ensure that the amounts tested, the results (including any explanations and corroborative evidence for any unexplained fluctuations) and a conclusion are all properly documented.

16.5 Audit Programme

Suggested audit tests for performing substantive analytical procedures are included within each section of Part II.

16.6 Sampling

Many sampling systems enable the auditor to cut sample sizes (often by as much as a third) as a result of substantive analytical review. It is important, however, to note that sample sizes should only be reduced where this is justified by the extent and results of the work undertaken. Where this is the case, the analytical review is usually described as extensive.

For example, calculating debtor days on trade debtors would not constitute extensive analytical review and, therefore, merely calculating this figure and obtaining explanations for a significant change would not enable the auditor to reduce sample sizes. The detailed chapters within Part II include a number of suggested analytical review procedures that can be applied in order to reduce the extent of substantive testing and perhaps, depending on the materiality of the amounts involved, eliminate the need for detailed substantive testing.

Care must be taken when analysing the results of substantive analytical review procedures; they do not result in automatic reduction in the extent of detailed testing. Only if the results of the procedures are satisfactory can the extent of substantive testing be reduced.

Where substantive analytical review indicates unexpected variations that cannot be explained, further investigation will be required. In such circumstances, it may be inappropriate to reduce the level of substantive testing.

In some circumstances, substantive analytical review could enable the auditor to eliminate detailed substantive testing altogether on certain sections of the audit. There are several scenarios where substantive analytical review could, if successful, result in no detailed testing being performed; and three examples are given below. However, such situations are a matter of judgment and will vary from one audit to another.

If stock is around the materiality level set at the planning stage, then extensive analytical review could be wholly relied upon to assess whether or not stock is fairly stated. The types of analytical review procedures that could be used are described in Chapter 20 but, generally, the auditor would look at changes in value on individual stock lines or stock types.

This principle could be extended further to situations where the auditor has restricted the detailed substantive testing to items above the tolerable error level and other key items. The residual population may then be such that the random sample size is around or below one. In this situation, it may be more effective to apply substantive analytical procedures to the residual population.

Substantive analytical review procedures can also be used to eliminate detailed testing where a significant level of accounts preparation work is undertaken. A good example is testing wages and salaries. It may be possible to conclude that, due to the level of checking carried out at the accounts preparation stage, a certain amount of comfort can be drawn. Therefore, the auditor need only evidence a comparison of this year's expense with the previous year's expense (and possibly budgets) as additional audit evidence.

16.7 Conclusion

Substantive analytical review is an under-utilised tool within many practices. Further examples of tests that can be applied can be found in the following chapters in Part II.

Chapter 17 Intangible fixed assets

17.1 Introduction and definition

Intangible fixed assets are those assets that are, by their nature, intangible. That is to say they are assets that cannot be physically verified. FRS 10 *Goodwill and intangible assets* defines intangible assets as 'non-financial fixed assets that do not have physical substance but are identified and controlled by the entity through custody or legal rights.' It should be noted that intangible assets will not exist in many companies; and frequently where they do, they are not material. Where this is the case, it may be appropriate to undertake a test of the entire population. Intangible assets include the items referred to in sections 17.1.1 to 17.1.4.

17.1.1 Goodwill

FRS 10 defines purchased goodwill as 'the difference between the cost of an acquired entity and the aggregate of the fair values of that entity's identifiable assets and liabilities.' Goodwill may also be non-purchased. Purchased goodwill is obviously established through a purchase of a business; non-purchased goodwill is any form of goodwill other than purchased goodwill.

At present, neither the Companies Act nor FRS 10 allow the recognition of internally generated goodwill, and so the audit procedures for goodwill will only consider purchased goodwill.

17.1.2 Development costs

SSAP 13 (revised) *Accounting for Research and Development* defines development costs as 'the use of scientific or technical knowledge in order to produce new or substantially improved materials, devices, products or services, to install new processes or systems prior to the commencement of commercial production or commercial applications, or to improving substantially those already produced or installed.'

Part 2 of Schedule 1 of both SI 2008/409 (small companies) and SI 2008/410 (medium and large companies) stipulate that development costs may only be included in the entity's balance sheet in special circumstances. Neither Statutory Instrument provides a definition of those circumstances, but SSAP 13 only allows development costs to be deferred to future periods in certain specific circumstances. Under no circumstances can expenses relating to pure or applied research be carried forward. SSAP 13 states that if specific criteria are satisfied, taking a prudent view of available evidence, then the development costs may be carried forward to future periods. These criteria, contained in paragraph 25 of SSAP 13, are as follows:

a) there must be a clearly defined project;

b) related expenditure must be separately identifiable;

c) the outcome of the project must be examined for:

- its technical feasibility, and
- its ultimate commercial viability;

d) if further development costs are to be incurred on the same project, then those costs, taken together with related production, selling and administrative costs, need to be covered by future expected revenues; and

e) adequate resources must exist or must reasonably be expected to be available, to enable the project to be completed and to provide any consequential increases in working capital.

17.1.3 Brands

Internally developed intangible assets may only be capitalised if there is a readily ascertainable market value. Brands are, by their nature, unique and will therefore not meet this test. However, if a brand were sold on an arms-length basis to a third party, then it could be capitalised by the acquirer. This will not usually be relevant for private companies.

17.1.4 Other intangible assets

Other intangible assets may include franchises, concessions, patents, licences, trademarks and similar rights. SI 2008/409, SI 2008/410 and FRS 10 all allow such assets to be capitalised and included within intangible assets where:

- either the assets were acquired for valuable consideration and are not required to be shown under goodwill; or
- there is a readily ascertainable market value as noted above.

17.2 Objectives of the audit

Intangible assets are debit balances and, consequently, applying the directional approach, the audit tests will primarily be for overstatement. However, the audit work undertaken on the accumulated amortisation brought forward will be for understatement.

The specific objectives relating to the audit of intangible assets are as follows:

a) to ensure that the entity has a good title to all intangible assets;

b) to ensure that the assets exist and are owned by the entity at the balance sheet date;

c) to ensure that the assets have been correctly recorded at cost;

d) to ensure that amortisation is correctly calculated and is adequate;

e) to ensure that all intangible assets are recorded;

f) to ensure that all disposals are correctly accounted for; and

g) to ensure that adequate provision is made for impairment and any permanent diminution in value.

These objectives are considered in more detail in the next section.

17.3 Audit procedures

The individual objectives are repeated below (see sections 17.3.1 to 17.3.6), and specific tests that can be applied to satisfy each are listed. When undertaking the planning, the auditor should identify the types of assets the entity has and select relevant tests to ensure that all objectives are fully covered.

17.3.1 To ensure that the entity has a good title to all intangible assets, and to ensure that the assets exist and are owned by the entity at the balance sheet date

Tests (a) to (d), which follow, are appropriate in the case of patents and trademarks.

a) Request the UK Intellectual Property Office (known, prior to April 2007, as the Patent Office) to send a certified copy of the register entry. This will include details of the owner of the patent, along with specific details of any licences or mortgages that have been notified to the office. If the entity has a large number of material patents or licences, a sample should be selected.

b) Inspect the assignment or other agreement transferring the ownership from the previous registered owner, if the ownership is not recorded at the UK Intellectual Property Office. Where this is the case, ascertain why the registration has not been made.

c) Ensure that the trademark's registration period has not elapsed by referring to the original documentation (a copy of which can be maintained on the permanent file). Where appropriate, ensure that the trademark or patent has been renewed by tracing payment of a renewal fee in the year.

d) Where the sums involved are not material, it will usually suffice to use analytical review procedures to make comparisons with the previous year, and to ascertain details of any additions and disposals.

Tests (e) to (h), which follow, are appropriate where there are no formal documents of title – for example, in the case of royalties.

e) Review to ensure the receipt of related income, such as royalties. Also ensure that payments have been received at regular intervals.

f) Review the evidence of expenditure by the client (for example, development expenditure) and determine whether it is reasonable.

g) Obtain confirmation that a business on which purchased goodwill has arisen has not been sold or closed down. This may be done easily through a review of the management accounts and/or accounting records of the entity.

h) Review for payment of renewal fees during the year, as this provides good evidence that the item exists and is in use.

17.3.2 To ensure that the assets have been correctly recorded at cost

Assets at cost usually include a brought-forward balance, plus additions less disposals. Costs brought forward do not normally need re-auditing where they have been subject to audit in the previous year. However, opening balance tests are required.

Tests (a) to (c), which follow, are appropriate for additions to intangible assets.

a) Select a sample and agree details, including the nature of the asset and amounts, to the supporting documentation. This will vary depending on the type of intangible asset involved. Examples of the type of documentation that can be examined are as follows:

- for goodwill – the purchase agreement for the business acquired;
- for deferred development expenditure – the time sheets, invoices and schedules of overheads; and
- for licences, franchises, etc., – the purchase invoice or purchase agreement.

b) Ensure that the expenditure is correctly capitalised in accordance with:

- the entity's accounting policies; and
- Accounting Standards (for example, FRS 10, SSAP 13).

This test can be undertaken at the same time as test (a).

c) Ensure that the capitalisation is appropriately authorised.

17.3.3 To ensure that amortisation is correctly calculated and is adequate

The accumulated amortisation (a credit balance) should be tested for understatement, whilst the annual charge to the profit and loss (a debit balance) should be tested for overstatement. This can be achieved by testing the same items as used above and a sample of items taken from the charge for the year. In both cases, the tests would be similar. The auditor should:

a) determine the rates and methods of amortisation used by the client for the different types of intangible asset. These rates should be agreed to the accounting policies note in the accounts.

b) review the amortisation rates used to confirm that they give a reasonable approximation of the useful economic lives of the assets concerned. Where necessary, the auditor should ensure that amortisation is applied from an appropriate date (for example, development expenditure from the date of commercial sales or production).

c) undertake tests for understatement of the provision in respect of a sample of the assets, and include tests to ensure the following:

- that the correct rate of amortisation has been used for the type of asset concerned;

- that the calculations have been properly performed; and

- that no amortisation has been charged on fully amortised assets.

This will also partially satisfy the objective of overstatement of the provision.

17.3.4 To ensure that all intangible assets are recorded

Testing creditors for understatement will usually satisfy this objective. However, in the infrequent case where it is considered to be a particular risk, the following procedures should be considered:

a) requesting a full list of patents in the client's name from the UK Intellectual Property Office;

b) ascertaining whether any procedures or products are likely to require a patent; and

c) reviewing research and development expenditure to determine if any development costs should have been capitalised.

17.3.5 To ensure that all disposals are correctly accounted for

It is probably most efficient to test all disposals, as there are not likely to be many in a period. However, in many cases the amounts will not be material, so no work may be needed. Where there are numerous disposals and the amounts are material, sampling should be applied.

For the items selected for testing, the auditor should ensure that:

a) items have been deleted from the fixed asset register;

b) any profit or loss on disposal is correctly calculated and accounted for;

c) the disposal is properly authorised (which can be ascertained by reviewing supporting documentation, if any, or board minutes); and

d) proper consideration was given to the reasons for the disposal (for example, why patents have been allowed to lapse).

If there is a risk of unrecorded disposals, the following tests can be applied:

e) consider whether additions result in, or are associated with, disposals;

f) review minutes, correspondence, etc., for evidence of unrecorded transactions; and

g) obtain management representations that all disposals are recorded.

17.3.6 To ensure that adequate provision is made for impairment and any permanent diminution in value

Consider via discussion and the auditor's knowledge of the entity whether any intangible asset has suffered a permanent fall in value that should be provided for in the accounts.

Tests (a) to (d), which follow, will be appropriate for development costs.

- Consider whether a permanent fall in value has occurred by:
  a) reviewing the commercial viability of the project, comparing estimated future expenditure with the estimated revenue to be generated;
  b) ensuring that the client has sufficient funds to complete the project;
  c) considering how reliable the client's predictions have been in the past for other projects; and

d) considering whether it is technically feasible to complete the project. (The auditor should consider using an appropriately qualified expert in this situation.)

Tests (e) to (h), which follow, will be appropriate for other assets:

- Consider whether any of the following has occurred:

    e) the term of a patent, royalty or franchise has expired or the item has been terminated;

    f) the sale or closure of a business where purchased goodwill existed, continued losses or lack of profits by such a business;

    g) the entity has ceased to use a patent, or patented products; or

    h) there are disputes over the use of a patent or trademark.

Where any of the above has been identified, the auditor should ensure that all appropriate action has been taken and any necessary adjustments have been made.

17.4 Analytical review

Substantive analytical review may be appropriate in certain circumstances to help to reduce the amount of detailed audit work that needs to be undertaken. However, the scope with intangible assets is limited.

Where there have been no movements in respect of additions or disposals during the period, an analytical review on the amortisation charge for the year may be sufficient to partially satisfy the value-related objectives. However, the auditor should still consider whether the amortisation rate applied is adequate.

Where there have been additions during the year, then an estimation of the charge for each major category – applying appropriate rates to the current year's additions, plus the net book value brought forward – may be adequate for auditing the amortisation calculation.

17.5 Tests of control

The amount of substantive testing of additions may also be reduced if the controls within the purchase system are such that reliance can be placed on them. Further details of these controls can be found in Part II Chapter 31.

In addition, the auditor may derive comfort from the regular comparison of actual results in respect of development projects with the budgets and forecasts for such projects. This comparison should include investigation of all variances. This will give comfort that the development costs and related projects are controlled.

17.6 Common problems

17.6.1 Completeness

There is no requirement to capitalise development expenditure. It is therefore important to ensure that any accounting policy in respect of development expenditure is consistently and properly applied. It is not unusual to find companies that are only really interested in capitalising development costs when they are suffering financial difficulties or preparing to sell the company. The auditor should ensure that this has not been the case. Such a scenario is difficult to prove, but where either circumstance exists, the auditor should be aware of the risk.

17.6.2 Reviewing useful economic lives

The valuation of intangible assets is often very difficult. Determining whether or not adequate provision has been made is essential. The auditor should apply common sense to ensure that the accounting policy has been complied with and that the rates appear reasonable. The auditor should also review the success of a project where development costs have been capitalised.

With capitalised purchased goodwill, it is not unusual for clients to automatically select a useful economic life of 20 years, typically because this is the longest possible period (and hence the lowest annual amortisation) that can be chosen before an annual impairment review is required by FRS 10. In addition, it should also be noted that the FRSSE contains an absolute limit of 20 years. The client may not have given any proper consideration of the actual useful economic life of the goodwill. In such cases, it is vital that the auditor considers whether 20 years really is appropriate, by reviewing the success of a subsidiary or branch and looking at the type of industry.

This is certainly an area where the auditor may wish to seek management representations.

17.6.3 Renewals

Not all patent costs should be carried forward. Some amounts payable on patents relate to annual fees and should be taken to the profit and loss account immediately.

17.6.4 Disclosure problems

Many of the disclosure requirements for intangible fixed assets are complex, and it is essential that the auditor has sufficient knowledge of the relevant Accounting Standards and legislative requirements to ensure that full and adequate disclosure is made within the financial statements.

17.6.5 Books and records: development expenditure

Smaller clients, with unsophisticated accounting systems, may not be able to identify costs specifically related to items that the client wants to carry forward as deferred development expenditure. Under such circumstances, in the absence of other evidence, a disagreement audit qualification may be necessary if the amounts involved are material.

Chapter 18 Tangible fixed assets

18.1 Introduction and definition

A tangible fixed asset is an asset having physical substance that is intended for continuing use within the business – for example, a car, plant and machinery or a building.

The audit of fixed assets is generally fairly straightforward, although it is also an area that is frequently done badly. In fact, the most likely problem is that of overauditing, presumably because it is a relatively simple area to audit and thus 'nice' to do!

18.2 Audit objectives

As the auditor is dealing with debit balances, the majority of the testing being undertaken will be for overstatement. That is, there is a concern that the value of the assets incorporated within the balance sheet will be overstated. Understatement of fixed assets is tested in the creditors section.

The specific objectives that should be addressed when auditing fixed assets are:

a) to ensure that the assets exist at the balance sheet date;

b) to ensure that the assets are beneficially owned by the entity;

c) to ensure (where appropriate) that assets are completely and accurately recorded at cost;

d) to ensure that all revalued assets are supported by proper valuations and that the basis is acceptable;

e) to ensure that disposals are accounted for correctly;

g) to ensure that depreciation is correctly calculated and that the rates applied are adequate to write off the cost of the assets less their estimated residual value over their estimated useful life; and

h) to ensure that there is adequate consideration of impairment.

These objectives are covered in detail in sections 18.3.1 to 18.3.7.

18.3 Audit procedures

Detailed below are some individual tests that can be applied in order to help satisfy the objectives noted in section 18.2. It is not appropriate to undertake all of the tests; in each case, the auditor should review this bank of tests and determine which are most appropriate for the circumstances of the particular client being dealt with. The auditor should, however, ensure that each objective is satisfied.

18.3.1 To ensure that assets exist at the balance sheet date

To satisfy this objective, the sample must be selected from opening balances plus additions, or from closing balances. The auditor should use the closing net book value rather than original cost. If the sample is selected from closing balances, the testing of disposals will have to be tested separately.

Physical verification is best carried out when attending the stocktake. The auditor should select a sample from the fixed asset register or the record of assets maintained on the current or permanent file, including additions during the year, and seek to identify those assets at the client's premises. If the auditor selects the sample by simply noting assets seen at the stocktake, the specific objective will not have been satisfied, as selecting a sample of assets and checking these to the nominal ledger tests for understatement rather than for overstatement.

Where physical verification is not possible because, for example, an asset is not available or is inaccessible, the auditor should consider whether the objective can be satisfied through one or more of the following procedures:

a)   reviewing valuations by a third party (usually only applicable on buildings);

b)   reviewing vehicle registration documents, although these are not proof of ownership as such (if the auditor has verified existence, there is no need to perform this test);

c)   identifying appropriate expenditure – for example, insurance, repairs, maintenance;

d)   identifying income generated by the asset (it may be possible to reconcile a sample of fixed assets to income in respect of those fixed assets around the year end); and

e)   reviewing insurance policies (if an asset is insured, it probably exists).

18.3.2 To ensure that the assets are beneficially owned by the entity

Property

Since the tests on property are relatively quick and easy to do, and since property usually forms a very material part of the balance sheet, these tests would usually be done every year. For companies (such as property investment companies) with large numbers of properties, consideration should be given to using sampling, or testing properties on a rotational basis. A management representation should also be obtained if all properties are not checked each year.

- Search the Land Registry website for proof of title, ensuring that:
  a)   the client's name is shown on the title;
  b)   the description agrees with that shown in the accounts (a title map can also be requested from Land Registry at a small additional cost); and
  c)   there are no restrictions on dealing or use of the land which have been broken.

Some older properties may not yet appear on the Land Registry electronic database, especially if they have not changed hands in recent years. This is because the Land Registry is still in the process of adding such properties to the database. Should a search of the Land Registry database draw a blank, then some negative assurance that the client has not sold the property can still be gained, as a recent sale would be included on the database.

However, care must be taken to ensure that the correct search details have been used, and that the reason for an unsuccessful search is not the use of incorrect information.

- For mortgaged property, third-party confirmation of any legal charges over the property should be sought from the lender (usually the bank) and Companies House, where the register of mortgages and charges may be searched for a nominal fee.

- For leasehold property, the auditor should review the lease and consider whether any property has been mortgaged. The auditor should then ensure that the property in the lease and the mortgage are the same and that any necessary permission has been obtained from the landlord. The auditor should also ensure that the lease is in the name of the entity.

Other assets

- Beneficial ownership of assets is tested during the work on additions. However, this does not give concrete evidence that the assets owned at the beginning of the accounting period are still owned by the client at the balance sheet date. The fact that an asset exists and is being used by the client is usually sufficient evidence of continuing ownership.

- The auditor should review loan agreements or contracts to determine if any assets have been pledged as security.

18.3.3 To ensure (where appropriate) that assets are completely and accurately recorded at cost

Costs brought forward from earlier years will have been tested in the year of purchase. Therefore, the audit work should concentrate on testing additions, using sampling if appropriate. However, the auditor should ensure that tests are only performed where additions are material.

Select a sample of invoices or supporting documentation and test the following matters:

a) casts and extensions;

b) agree details to the fixed assets register;

c) ensure that the item was delivered during the period (this can be combined with physical existence work) and review of any proof of receipt;

d) (if applicable) ensure that the asset has been capitalised in accordance with the entity's policy;

e) consider whether any items should be reclassified as repairs or maintenance, and so be eligible for full tax relief;

f) consider whether VAT on cars has been incorrectly capitalised;

g) consider whether the client sets a reasonable minimum amount below which items are written off to revenue; and

h) review board minutes to confirm that the purchase was authorised (this will only happen for major items and only in larger companies that are more likely to have board minutes).

The auditor should ensure that leased assets are properly capitalised in accordance with SSAP 21 and FRS 5. The auditor should review the terms of any material leases of items that are not capitalised to ensure that they are operating leases. Further details of testing in this area can be found in Chapter 24,

Where an entity has assets in the course of construction, the auditor should review the following to ensure that costs are correctly allocated to the right asset:

- for labour – timesheets, clock cards, or any other summaries of time spent;

- for materials – invoices, internal requisition notes or any other record of the materials used; and

- for overheads – management accounts, standard costs.

The auditor should ensure that the client has obtained any grants that may be relevant. Where grants have been received, the auditor should ensure that they have been credited to a deferred income account and are being released to the profit and loss account over the useful economic life of the asset. Note that SSAP 4 does allow the grant to be offset against the cost of the asset, thereby charging a lower rate of depreciation. However, this is considered to be contrary to the fundamental principle in both SI 2008/409 and SI 2008/410 that companies should not offset assets and liabilities against one another. If the client does offset the grant in this way, the auditor should ensure that the true and fair override is applied and give appropriate disclosures in the accounts. This might occur where a client has received a grant for an asset where no depreciation is actually charged to the profit and loss account. An alternative method in these circumstances would be to take the grant to deferred income when received, and release it to the profit and loss account as and when the grant ceases to be repayable.

It should be noted that the accounting treatment for grants in the Charities SORP is somewhat different. Capital grants should be recognised as income in the SOFA when they meet the normal income recognition criteria set out in the SORP. The detailed accounting then depends on any restrictions placed on the use of the grant, as set out below.

- If the use of the related asset is restricted, the grant should be accounted for as restricted income, and the depreciation on that asset charged against the restricted fund.

- If any restriction is fully discharged by using the grant to purchase the asset, then the grant would initially be accounted for as restricted income. On purchasing the asset, a reserve transfer would be needed to move it into unrestricted funds.

- If there are no restrictions on the use of the grant, it should be accounted for as unrestricted income.

18.3.4 To ensure that all revalued assets are supported by proper valuations and that the basis is acceptable

Obtain a copy of the valuation where it has been performed by a third party and consider:

a) whether the valuer is professionally or suitably qualified as required by FRS 15 or SSAP 19;

b) whether the valuer is independent of the client;

c) the scope of the valuation – in particular, whether any assets were excluded;

d) whether the basis of the valuation will comply with the requirements of the Companies Act to show fixed assets at market value at the date of the last valuation or at their current cost;

e) whether the useful economic life of the asset should be revised;

f) which items have been included in the scope of the valuation (for example, fixed plant and machinery should not be included both in the valuation of property and under the heading 'plant and machinery');

g) whether the valuation of property separates land and buildings to identify the amount to be depreciated;

h) whether the valuer was given all relevant facts;

i) whether the disclosures are adequate;

j) whether the valuer has given permission for the valuation to be included within the financial statements of the entity;

k) whether the valuation is reasonable, compared to the auditor's knowledge of the client, the premises and the locality (for property); and

l) whether all assets of the same class have been revalued as required by FRS 15.

If the valuation has been carried out internally, the following procedures should be applied:

- consider whether the valuer has the necessary experience and qualifications;

- consider the possibility that the client would want to manipulate asset values by artificially inflating (more likely) or reducing the valuation; and

- review the valuation to see if it is reasonable. The auditor may need to compare the client's valuation with other evidence (for example in the case of property, prices of similar properties in the local area), if available.

Where a revaluation has occurred, ensure that any revaluation surplus or deficit is correctly treated. In most instances, the increase or decrease in value should be reflected in the revaluation reserve. However, if this pushes the reserve into deficit, the balance may have to be charged to the profit and loss account. As neither SI 2008/409 nor SI 2008/410 requires provision to be made for a temporary fall in value, no provision is made in the profit and loss account where the fall in value is temporary. Hence, a deficit on the revaluation reserve may be carried on the balance sheet in these circumstances. If the fall in value is permanent, full provision must be made in the profit and loss account for the deficit not covered by the revaluation reserve.

The auditor should consider whether any events have occurred since the date of the last valuation that are likely to affect the value of revalued assets, and hence whether any adjustment is required.

- The auditor should ensure that revaluations are carried out at the frequencies required by FRS 15 and SSAP 19.

- The auditor should ensure that historical cost information is kept to allow disclosure of the historical cost equivalent of revalued assets.

18.3.5 To ensure that disposals are accounted for correctly

Items can be selected from opening balances and additions in the year and combined with valuation tests (see above). If any of these items have been disposed of in the period, the auditor should consider carrying out some of the following tests, to ensure:

a) that the items have been removed from the fixed assets register;

b) that sale proceeds appear reasonable, considering the type and condition of assets sold;

c) that the profit or loss on disposal is correct and accounted for properly, and that any finance lease terms are complied with;

d) that the disposal was properly authorised and that proper consideration was received; and

e) where assets were sold or transferred to a related party, that prices were reasonable and that suitable disclosure is given.

If there is a risk that material disposals may not be recorded, the auditor should perform the following procedures:

(i) review minutes and correspondence for evidence of unrecorded disposals;

(ii) obtain management representations regarding the completeness of recorded disposals;

(iii) discuss the disposal of assets with factory managers and other client staff. This should be done when the actual work on physical existence is being carried out; and

(iv) consider if there are any changes in the business which would lead to disposals – for example, rationalisation, discontinued product lines, closure of a particular site or production line;

The addition of certain assets may lead the auditor to think that some assets have been disposed of.

The auditor should consider whether a disposal may require a provision in other areas (for example, obsolete machinery parts or grant repayment) or may affect VAT or tax liabilities.

18.3.6 To ensure that depreciation is correctly calculated and that the rates applied are adequate to write off the cost of assets less their estimated residual value over their estimated useful economic lives

Calculate the depreciation charge across the categories of fixed assets, or check a sample of the client's calculations.

Review the client's accounting policies and consider whether:

a) the policies have been consistently applied from one year to the next and between different types of assets;

b) the rates of depreciation are reasonable given the types of asset (see below);

c) any special circumstances exist which could shorten the period over which depreciation is charged (for example, franchise, licence, lease term – leasehold improvements should not be written off over a term longer than the lease); and

d) rates are consistent across similar clients or across a group.

When reviewing depreciation rates for reasonableness, the auditor should consider the following:

e) the useful economic life and net realisable value of the assets (The useful economic life is the period over which the client expects to use the asset, rather than the actual life of the asset);

f) whether the client consistently makes gains or losses on disposals. This could indicate the use of inappropriate rates of depreciation;

g) whether any changes in rates can be justified in terms of a revised useful economic life;

h) whether there is a significant number of fully depreciated assets still in use (which suggests that assets have been written off too quickly);

i) whether the client tends to replace assets after a certain period (The replacement period should then be used as the useful economic life);

j) whether the residual values (where used), are reasonable; and

k) whether any of the assets could be obsolete due to technological changes.

The auditor should consider calculating expected values for depreciation based on the previous year's charge and the current year's fixed asset amount. The depreciation charge could also be estimated for each major category of fixed asset by applying the previous year's ratio of depreciation to cost or valuation to the current year's cost or valuation.

18.3.7 To ensure that there is adequate consideration of impairment

Under SI 2008/409 or SI 2008/410, as well as FRS 11, provision is required for a permanent diminution in value or impairment of a fixed asset. The auditor could identify such assets by:

a) considering whether there has been any significant change in the level of production or the range of products, which may indicate that certain assets are no longer being used;

b) reviewing levels of repairs and renewals, as a high level of expenditure might indicate that fixed assets are approaching the end of their useful economic life and so ought to be written down; and

c) considering underuse of assets during physical inspection.

Consider whether any assets written down in earlier years have recovered in value to such a degree that the provision for diminution in value should be decreased.

Where assets have been, or are being, built by the client, consider whether the carrying value is in excess of likely open market value.

Consider the valuation of assets in the light of other available information, such as valuers' reports, trade publications, subsequent sale proceeds or the auditor's knowledge of the client.

If there are any concerns, consider obtaining directors' representations on the matter.

18.4 Extensive analytical review

It is actually quite difficult to apply extensive analytical review procedures to fixed assets. However, outlined below are some procedures that can be used to give additional audit comfort regarding whether or not fixed assets are fairly stated.

18.4.1 Additions

The auditor can compare the level of additions to fixed assets during the year with other relevant information. It should be borne in mind, however, that on accounts preparation audits this may not be that useful, as the vast majority of additions may already have been vouched to invoices as part of the accounts preparation work.

Although there is usually only a weak correlation, the auditor may compare this year's level of fixed asset additions with levels in previous years. The larger the business, the more relevant this particular procedure will be.

Very often, even small companies will have budgets for capital expenditure. The auditor may be able to compare the actual fixed asset additions to the budgeted levels. It is likely in such scenarios that the client may document any departure from capital expenditure budgets and, therefore, this can be used to corroborate any explanations for differences given to the auditor by the client. The auditor may also be able to compare actual additions made with forecasts obtained from the client in previous years.

The auditor should also consider expected increases in capital expenditure – for example, expansion of the business into new premises or outlets. Obviously, when such expansion occurs, it would be usual for a certain level of additions to fixed assets to be made. The auditor's understanding of the client's business should enable a rough estimate to be made of the types of fixed assets that would be required in the new premises. The actual level of fixed asset additions shown in the accounts can then be compared with this estimate and any variances explained.

Depending on the replacement policy of the client, the auditor may also be able to deduce that if certain assets are disposed of, then additions should be made to replace them. For example, if a director's car is disposed of, another one would usually take its place.

Finally, there will be a correlation between the level of capital expenditure and the repair policy of the client. If the client decides to repair more of the fixed assets rather than replace them, the auditor may well expect to see a downturn in the level of capital expenditure.

18.4.2 Disposals

By their very nature, disposals of fixed assets are one of the more erratic figures in a set of accounts.

However, the auditor may still be able to correlate disposals with other information. If the entity has a formal, or informal, replacement policy, then this may be compared to the actual level of disposals in a year. Also, for the reasons described above, the auditor may be able to relate disposals to particular additions. For example, when a motor vehicle is purchased, there is often a corresponding disposal.

Also, in direct contrast to one of the points above, if the entity undertakes any form of downsizing in its operations, the auditor would expect some disposal of fixed assets.

18.4.3 Utilisation

There is a standard ratio of fixed asset utilisation that can be calculated. This is:

actual sales : fixed assets

This can be compared to previous accounting periods for the same entity, or it can be compared to industry standards. However, in small companies this particular ratio may not necessarily be that useful.

As the fixed asset utilisation increases, so the entity becomes more efficient in using its fixed assets. If the ratio decreases, there is an increased chance of under-depreciation of the fixed assets, or of assets that do not exist being reported in the balance sheet. There may be other, more relevant reasons for the changes, such as poor asset utilisation or obsolescence of the fixed asset in use. Another reason for an apparent worsening in this ratio could be a decision to source assets on operating leases rather than hire purchase agreements or other sources of financing for the purchase of fixed assets.

18.4.4 Depreciation

There are very few analytical review procedures that can applied to depreciation. The auditor can assess the reasonableness of depreciation charges for categories of fixed assets when compared with the accounting policy notes and previous experience of that client. This is noted in the above tests on depreciation.

Potentially, the auditor can look at depreciation as a percentage of gross cost of the fixed assets (**(depreciation/gross cost) x 100%**). This can then be analysed through fixed asset categories.

Possible explanations for changes in this percentage from year to year, other than errors in calculation, could include the age of the assets, the different depreciation methods used, the level of fully depreciated assets included in the figures and any change in the depreciation rates used. Any of these explanations could easily be corroborated with reference to the auditor's knowledge of the client.

Another ratio that can be used to assess the reasonableness of the depreciation charge, and also the reasonableness of any additions or disposals, is the ratio of fixed assets at net book value (NBV) to fixed assets at original cost (**fixed asset at NBV : cost**). This effectively gives the unexpired life of the fixed assets. Again, this can be split into different fixed asset categories. Possible explanations for any changes to this ratio could include:

- a change in the repair and maintenance policy of the entity;
- a change in the depreciation rates and/or depreciation methods used; and
- expansion or downsizing of the business.

Again, any of these explanations could easily be corroborated with reference to the auditor's knowledge of the client.

18.5 Controls

The following are controls that are relevant to fixed assets and could, if working properly, enable the auditor to reduce the sample sizes in these areas. Even where such controls cannot be relied on to reduce sample sizes, they may provide additional audit comfort.

a) Minutes are kept for all board meetings and management meetings, recording capital expenditure and also disposals. To test this area, the auditor could select a sample of additions and disposals and ensure that they have been approved or authorised in the relevant board minutes.

b) The entity uses pre-numbered fixed asset purchase order requisitions. Again, the auditor would select a sample of fixed asset additions and ensure that there is an order for them.

c) Invoices are grid stamped to evidence that they have been checked for accuracy, and that the posting code has been checked before the items are posted to the nominal ledger.

d) A fixed asset register is maintained and regularly reconciled to the nominal ledger account, and also to actual physical assets.

e) All calculations of profits or losses on disposal are checked by the client.

f) The client undertakes and records regular inspections on the condition and use of assets. In some organisations this may be undertaken in order for them to comply with health and safety regulations.

g) The client reconciles the fixed asset registers to the results of physical inspection.

18.6 Common problems

Described in sections 18.6.1 to 18.6.8 are some problems that are regularly encountered in the audit of fixed assets.

18.6.1 Physical verification

Frequently, particularly where the client has no significant stocks, audit staff do not visit the client's premises. Consequently, physical verification of the assets has to be undertaken by alternative means. Many programmes do not give details of these alternative means, so this objective is very often missed out entirely. Details of alternative procedures that can be applied in these circumstances are given in section 18.3.1 above. However, it is necessary to consider the possibility in these circumstances that the auditor may be able to undertake sufficient work to be satisfied that the assets exist, yet not obtain adequate assurance on the condition of that asset.

Tests for physical verification are often not carried out properly. It is still common to see audit files where the physical inspection test has been carried out by touring the client's premises and ticking on the fixed asset register, say, the first dozen assets seen. This is incorrect in two ways:

● the items tested have been selected from the physical assets themselves and not the asset register. The test has therefore been performed in the wrong direction, thus testing completeness and not existence; and

● the auditor is effectively trying to verify all the assets, and if only twelve are checked, what about the other fifty that are not?

The auditor should select the appropriate sample size from the fixed asset register and ask to see those specific assets. Working papers should be clear that this is how the issue has been addressed. The sample should give an appropriate spread across all fixed asset categories, opening balances and additions, and should concentrate on higher value assets.

18.6.2 Depreciation on freehold property

It is not unusual to find a situation where freehold property has not been depreciated, but often the reason given for non-depreciation is not valid. The only reason allowed by FRS 15 for non-depreciation is where any depreciation charge and the accumulated depreciation would not be material. For this to occur, there must be a high residual value, a long economic life or both. If this treatment is to be adopted, it is essential that the auditor undertakes testing to consider the following questions.

- Is the property is being maintained to a high standard? If there has been no expenditure at all on repairs and renewals for the past five to ten years, then it may be difficult to justify a high residual value and long economic life.

- Is the assertion that the estimated residual value equates to cost, without incorporating any inflationary measure, reasonable? If this is not the case, then the difference should be depreciated.

- Would the accumulated depreciation be material? It might be easy to successfully claim that the annual depreciation charge would be immaterial, but the accumulated depreciation is often ignored, and it can become material in time.

FRS 15 also requires an annual impairment review, in accordance with FRS 11, where depreciation is not charged on the grounds of materiality due a long economic life and/or high residual value.

18.6.3 Inadequate depreciation policies

Depreciation is often charged at 25 per cent on a reducing balance basis, so as to be consistent with the rate of capital allowances. Note that such policies may not be consistent in future, as a result of changes in the capital allowances regime. This may be inadequate for assets such as computers, where the technology may become obsolete very quickly. It is essential to ensure that the adequacy of depreciation rates is considered and documented during each audit. The auditor should also consider the useful economic life of assets in terms of their use within the entity. So, in the above example, if the computers, although obsolete, will continue being used by the entity, no revision to the accounting policy may be necessary.

18.6.4 Over-depreciation of assets

Over-depreciation of assets can also be a problem. Regular material profits made on the disposal of assets, or assets written down to nil or £1 that are still in use, are both indicators of an overly prudent depreciation policy. The auditor should review the rates used in these circumstances and recommend a more appropriate policy to the client.

18.6.5 Obsolete assets and assets no longer in use

Obsolete assets and assets no longer in use may be included in the fixed assets register. While undertaking existence testing, it is essential that the auditor checks that the assets are actually *in use*, not only whether they still exist. It is also essential that the auditor looks at their condition and, even as a non-expert, considers the probability of their being worth amount at which they are included in the accounts.

18.6.6 Ownership

The key issue of property ownership is often not addressed in sufficient depth. Specific confirmation should be sought that the property is in the name of the entity. The fact that the bank may hold a charge over a property against the entity's borrowings does not prove conclusively that the property is in the name of the entity rather than, say, in the name of one of the directors.

If it becomes clear that certain assets (typically cars and property) are in the name of one or more of the directors, then the auditor should obtain specific confirmation from the directors involved to the effect that they are holding the asset(s) in trust on behalf of the entity, ideally via a formal nominee agreement.

18.6.7 Investment properties

An investment property is defined by SSAP 19 as an interest in land and/or buildings:

- in respect of which construction work and development have been completed; and
- which is held for its investment potential, any rental income being negotiated at arm's length.

It excludes the following:

- a property that is owned and occupied by an entity for its own purposes; and
- a property let to and occupied by another member of the group.

In terms of accounting treatment, investment properties:

- should not be depreciated, unless held on a short lease – that is, a lease with 20 years or less to run; and
- should be included in the balance sheet at open market value (that is, revalued annually).

From an audit point of view, an issue that is often not addressed is the reasonableness of a directors' valuation (as it will often be in a private company). It is likely in an investment property company that the amounts involved will be extremely material, yet the audit file is often silent regarding any consideration of the valuation placed on the properties. Procedures such as looking at similar properties in the area should be conducted.

18.6.8 Too much photocopying or scanning

From an audit point of view, it is not necessary to copy or scan the invoice for every fixed asset addition. Together with copies or scans of the client's fixed asset register, this constitutes a lot of clutter on the file, which impedes the audit work. Since ISA 230 requires each schedule to be signed and dated by the person who created it and also by the reviewer, there is a time cost as well. In most cases, copies of invoices are not needed, even for tax purposes; where they are required, they should be placed on a separate file and not included as part of the audit work.

Chapter 19 Investments in group and associated undertakings and other investments

19.1 Introduction and definition

It is unlikely, unless looking at a fixed asset investment company, that investments will be particularly material in the balance sheet. In many cases the investments will be managed by third-party stockbrokers who produce good third-party evidence as to the existence, valuation and ownership of the investments.

There are two main types of investments that will be considered within this Chapter – namely, fixed asset investments and current asset investments.

19.1.1 Fixed asset investments

Non-current or fixed asset investments are those investments that are held for the medium or long term. This may well include investments in group or associated companies.

Such investments should be included in the balance sheet at cost, less any provision for permanent diminution in value, or at valuation. Valuation can either be at market value or the directors' own valuation.

19.1.2 Current asset investments

Current asset investments include those investments that are a temporary investment of surplus funds. These investments should be included in the balance sheet either at the lower of cost and net realisable value, or at a valuation.

The auditor may also find within current asset investments items that were previously included as fixed asset investments and which the company is proposing to sell within the next accounting period.

Some entities may account for investments at fair value under FRS 26. Refer to Chapter 39 for details of how to audit fair valued assets.

19.2 Audit objectives

As with any other debit balance, the primary audit tests will be in respect of overstatement. The detailed objectives are as follows:

a)   to ensure that investments exist at the balance sheet date and are owned by the client;

b)   to ensure that investments are correctly stated at cost or valuation;

c)   to ensure that any profits or losses on disposal are correctly accounted for;

d)   to ensure that investment income is accounted for in full;

e)   to ensure that investments are properly classified as either fixed or current assets and that the treatment is consistent; and

f)   to ensure that there is adequate provision for any permanent diminutions in value (fixed asset investments).

19.3 Audit procedures

The auditor should select the procedures from below that will most effectively satisfy the objectives. It is intended that most of the procedures below will be undertaken on a sample basis. However, where the number of items is small, it may be easier to test them all.

19.3.1 To ensure that investments exist at the balance sheet date and are owned by the client

The auditor should inspect documents of title where these are held by the client, or obtain confirmation from third parties that they are holding such documents on the client's behalf. In particular, the auditor should ensure that:

(i)   details of the investment agree with the client's records and that the client is clearly shown as the beneficial owner;

(ii)   the client has both a signed blank transfer form and a declaration of trust in its favour where the shares are held by a nominee;

(iii) any scrip issues, rights issues or conversions have been correctly accounted for and are reflected in the share certificates. Details about listed investments may be obtained from *Extel* or other similar publications; and

(iv)   details have been obtained of any investments that have been pledged as security via discussions with the management, review of the bank letter or similar correspondence.

An alternative method of obtaining comfort on ownership is to examine dividend vouchers received. The auditor should ensure that the correct number of dividends has been received, as well as matching the details on the dividend vouchers to the share certificates and the client's records. Publications such as *Extel* give details of all dividends that should have been received.

Samples for testing may be taken from the opening balances and additions during the period, or from the closing balance. As with tangible fixed assets, additional samples will have to be taken to test the profit or loss on disposals and investment income if the closing balances are used.

The auditor should ensure that any holdings are correctly accounted for as associates or subsidiaries, where appropriate. If the entity is a parent undertaking at the year end, the auditor should ensure that consolidated accounts are prepared, unless the group is able to take advantage of an exemption from the preparation of group accounts. The auditor must ensure that full relevant disclosures are given.

If long-term loans to other parties are included as investments, the following procedures should be undertaken:

a)   obtain direct confirmation from the borrower;

b)   ensure that any differences between the client's balance and that confirmed by the borrower are valid reconciling items;

c)   review any loan agreement to confirm rates of interest and repayment terms;

d)   obtain confirmation of the loan terms from the directors, if there is no formal agreement in place; and

e)   check details of any security given.

19.3.2 To ensure that investments are correctly stated at cost or valuation

The auditor should test additions by:

a)   reviewing contract notes or purchase agreements; and

b)   ensuring that the transaction was authorised, where appropriate.

Where investments are carried at valuation, the following tests will be appropriate:

- **for listed investments** – agree their details to the *Stock Exchange Daily Official List* or *Financial Times* (this should also be extended so that the auditor also considers the post-balance sheet valuations);
- **for unlisted investments** – review the methods adopted by the directors to value the investment and consider whether they are reasonable. The auditor should also review the available accounts (net assets, profitability and likely going concern problems) and any reports used by the directors in reaching their valuation.

Where the client has a subsidiary, the auditor should review the valuation by considering whether any of the following conditions exist:

- post-acquisition losses – such future losses could indicate that the value of the investment is decreasing;
- apparently insolvent subsidiaries where provisions may be required, including against loans due to the holding company; and/or
- the holding company's share of net assets is less than the book value of the investment.

For loans treated as investments, the following procedures may be applied:

- ensure that repayments are being made on time and in accordance with any terms in the loan agreement;
- ensure that interest is being paid promptly, and in accordance with the terms of the loan;
- consider whether there are any other factors that might cast doubt on the recoverability of the loan;
- check that the security for the loan is effective (for example, charges are properly registered with Companies House) and is adequate to cover the loan; and
- discuss recoverability with the directors and management. The auditor may wish to obtain specific representations on this issue.

19.3.3 To ensure that any profits or losses on disposals are correctly accounted for

The auditor should:

a) agree details of any disposal to the contract note, correspondence or other documentary evidence;

b) ensure that the disposal has been properly authorised by reviewing board minutes or other supporting documentation;

c) ensure that disposals to related parties are properly identified and disclosed;

d) check the calculation of the profit or loss on disposal. If only part of the investment has been sold, the calculation of the unsold balance should also be checked;

e) ensure that the item sold has been deleted from any register of investments and from the nominal ledger in the correct period;

f) consider – where there are doubts regarding the independence of the broker, or where the investment is not listed – if the selling price is reasonable (for example, by reviewing the audited accounts or price/earnings ratios of similar businesses); and

g) consider – where sales are being made within the group – whether realised profits have been generated, particularly if a company is also paying a dividend.

19.3.4 To ensure that investment income is accounted for in full

The auditor should ensure that all related income has been included for a sample of investments. This can be achieved by referring to *Extel* or a similar publication (for listed companies) or the latest financial statements (for unlisted companies).

The auditor should compare expected income on fixed-rate investments (for example, loans, debentures, government securities and fixed-rate preference shares) by computing total income expected using the principal outstanding and the known interest rate.

19.3.5 To ensure that investments are properly classified as either fixed or current assets and that the treatment is consistent

The auditor should consider the nature of the assets held and discuss their treatment with management.

The auditor should decide whether the assets have been correctly classified and whether the treatment is consistent.

19.4 Analytical review

There are very few extensive analytical review procedures that can be applied to this area. However, in some circumstances ratios can be used to ascertain whether or not the return received on investment is reasonable. The following ratios can be used:

> **return on investment : cost**

> and

> **return on investment : market value.**

Both ratios should be reasonably consistent. The ratios can also be used on fixed asset investment properties to give comfort on completeness of income. However, are legitimate reasons for these ratios moving: the values of investments on the stock exchange and non-quoted companies can be fairly volatile.

The ratios are potentially more useful for companies that have investments in properties. The rent received for investment properties should be reasonably consistent. Explanations for dips or increases in the returns could include:

- properties being empty for any time during the year;
- properties acquired part way through the year; and
- rent reviews taking place in the year.

The auditor can compare values of investments with previous periods, taking into consideration general changes in the market conditions during the period, to help provide audit comfort in respect of valuation of the investments.

The auditor can compare the level of income recorded from the investments with their book value to see whether this seems reasonable in view of the past history and market conditions.

19.5 Controls

Several controls may be operating in respect of the ownership of investments that may enable the auditor to reduce the level of substantive audit work undertaken. Even where the auditor does not wish to rely on these, the existence of such controls can give additional audit comfort. Relevant controls are:

a) the maintenance of a register of investments which is regularly updated and reviewed and reconciled to the nominal ledger;

b) receipt of confirmation of investments held by third parties on a regular basis, and reconciliation of the confirmation to a register of investments;

c) use of separate investment custodians and investment managers, and regular reconciliation of the reports received from each;

d) authorisation of any acquisition or disposal of an investment by a senior officer; and

e) review by a senior officer of investment certificates on delivery.

19.6 Common problems

19.6.1 Valuation

A major problem area is the valuation of investments in group and associated companies. Any investments in unlisted entities will be more difficult to audit, particularly in respect of their ultimate valuation. It is very common for investments and inter-company balances to be agreed but for their valuation to be ignored.

The auditor should ensure that copies of the latest financial statements are obtained and, where these were prepared in the past, that information on the current situation is also obtained, so that the carrying value of the investments can be assessed. It is vital that any potential write-downs are adequately considered and documented. If a subsidiary has net liabilities, it would be very difficult to justify no write-downs. Where net assets are between nil and the carrying value of the investment, then the future growth and profitability of the subsidiary should be considered. The same issues are also relevant when considering inter-company balances.

19.6.2 Current versus fixed asset investments

At times, it can be very difficult to distinguish between current and fixed asset investments for disclosure purposes. The introduction to this Chapter stated that investment assets held on a temporary basis are current investments, with other investments being non-current or fixed asset investments. An alternative method of distinguishing between the two is to consider the reasons why an investment is held. Fixed asset investments will be held with a view to the entity deriving benefit over a long period of time. Current asset investments will be held with a view to short-term (that is, less than one year) gains. Justification for the treatment of investments as current or fixed must be documented on file.

19.6.3 Completion

FRS 2 *Accounting for subsidiary undertakings* was amended in 2004 to extend the definition of a subsidiary to include entities over which the parent company '...has the power to exercise, or actually exercises, dominant influence or control over...' As a result, some entities previously accounted for as 'quasi-subsidiaries' in accordance with FRS 5 *Reporting the substance of transactions* may now meet the definition of a subsidiary undertaking. The auditor should take care to ensure that all entities meeting the definition of a subsidiary are accounted for as such.

Chapter 20 Stock

20.1 Introduction and definition

Stock can take a number of different forms, including:

- raw materials and consumables;
- work in progress;
- long-term contracts;
- finished goods and goods for resale; and
- consignment stock and stock held by third parties.

Long-term contracts are considered separately, in Chapter 21.

The audit of stock can be one of the most difficult areas of the audit. It is certainly one of the easiest figures for management to manipulate. By altering their judgment on the valuation of stock, management can:

- decrease the value of stock, depressing profit and possibly reducing tax bills; or
- increase the value of stock, inflating profit and net assets, perhaps in anticipation of a potential sale.

It is therefore absolutely essential that where stock is material, significant time be invested in reducing the risk of material misstatement within the financial statements as a result of manipulation of, or an error in, the stock figures.

20.2 Audit objectives

Stock is a debit balance in the balance sheet, but a credit balance in the profit and loss account. The testing undertaken on stock must therefore be for both understatement and overstatement. Both the valuation and existence of stock should be tested for overstatement and understatement, hence the necessity during the stocktake attendance to check items both from the floor to the stock sheets and from the stock sheets to the floor, and also at the final stage – to test items from the test counts to the final sheets and from the final sheets back to the stocktaking records. It is essential that tests are performed in both directions to ensure that both the understatement and the overstatement objectives are fully satisfied.

The specific objectives in respect of the audit of stock are as follows:

a) to ensure that the entity has title to the stock, that it exists and that the quantities are neither understated nor overstated;

b) to ensure that correct cut-off is applied;

c) to ensure that cost is accurately determined (valued) according to one of the recognised methods (refer to SSAP 9 and either SI 2008/409 or SI 2008/410); and

d) to ensure that adequate provision has been made for all damaged, obsolete or slow-moving stock.

20.3 Audit procedures

The procedures listed below can be applied in order to satisfy each of objectives (a) to (d) in section 20.2 above. The auditor should determine which combinations of tests are most effective in the particular circumstances. However, the auditor must satisfy both the understatement and the overstatement objectives.

20.3.1 To ensure that the entity has good title to the stock, that it exists and that the quantities are neither understated nor overstated

Most evidence to satisfy this objective will come from the audit of the client's stocktake and associated procedures. ISA 501 *Audit evidence – additional considerations for specific items* notes that, ordinarily, stock is physically counted at least once a year to serve as a basis for the preparation of the financial statements or to ascertain the reliability of the perpetual inventory system.

Practice Note 25 *Attendance at stocktaking* also confirms that normally it will be necessary for the auditor to attend the stocktake where stock is material. However, the ISA goes on to state that the auditor should attend the stocktake 'unless it is impracticable to do so'.

There are therefore serious implications if the auditor is unable to attend the stocktake. If alternative procedures do not provide sufficient appropriate audit evidence, then the auditor must consider whether there has been a limitation on scope requiring modification to the audit report (see section 20.6.2 and Chapter 44).

Adequacy of the stocktaking procedures

The auditor should review the client's stocktaking instructions to ensure that they are likely to lead to an accurate count, including:

a) use, whenever possible, of independent counters not involved with day-to-day stock control;

b) checks to ensure that all items are counted and are correct;

c) cut-off procedures before and during the counts (and in relation to the year end, if different);

d) separation of stocks held for customers or third parties, so that these are excluded;

e) investigation of differences highlighted by the stock counts where the client has a continuous stock-recording system;

f) identification of obsolete, slow-moving and damaged stocks;

g) procedures to ensure that the stock records are up to date;

h) controls over movements between areas and locations during the count;

i) a logical layout of the stock to make the count easier;

j) controls to ensure no double counting of stock held at a single location, such as the marking of items once they have been counted on the floor;

k) controls to ensure no double counting of stock held at different locations (there is a potential problem if counts are held at different locations at different times – stock can be moved from one location to another, and be counted more than once); and

l) controls over the issue and completion of stock sheets.

The auditor should ensure that the stocktaking procedures as set out by the management are actually followed in practice. The auditor should therefore attend the count while it is in progress.

Attendance at stocktaking: annual

Where the client counts most or all of the stock at one time, the auditor must attend the stocktake in order to obtain adequate evidence of existence (assuming the stock figure is material). The auditor should perform following actions:

a) confirm that procedures are being followed;

b) review cut-off controls to segregate stock received during the count;

c) ensure that non-client stock is identified and excluded from the count;

d) consider checking that any measuring or weighing machine to be used in the count gives accurate results;

e) consider whether the count is orderly, well controlled and methodical from the outset;

f)   note details and serial numbers of the last goods in and out, together with goods despatched note (GDN) and goods received note (GRN) references. The information is required for cut-off testing, though precisely what the auditor requires will vary from system to system.

g)   check that stock sheets issued to counters are adequately controlled;

h)   check that slow-moving, obsolete or damaged stock is clearly identified;

i)   obtain details of a sample of selling prices of the stock lines, particularly if the client values stock at selling price less the gross profit percentage; and

j)   consider whether other audit tests for different areas need to be performed at this time – for example, petty-cash counts, fixed asset verification and trade debtor and creditor circularisations.

The auditor should obtain the rough stock sheets at the end of the count to ensure that records have not been manipulated, suppressed, added to or substituted after the count. If it is not practical to keep a full copy of the stock sheets, the auditor should extract details for a sample of items that can be checked later.

It may not be practical to attend all the stocktakes if the client has several locations. When deciding which locations to visit, the auditor should consider:

●   the relative materiality of stocks held at each location;

●   unusual stock levels, gross margins or operating results at a particular location;

●   results of the client's counts in previous years and the current period;

●   any internal audit reports; and

●   management expectations.

As a general rule, the auditor should not warn the client which locations will be visited, and should aim to cover all locations on a cyclical basis.

Where there are logistical problems in attending a stocktake, the auditor may use the services of the client's internal auditors or a local firm of auditors. In these circumstances, the auditor would have to be satisfied as to the independence and competence of the staff to be used and the scope of work to be performed.

The auditor should carry out test counts (sample sizes should be determined using estimated materiality and risk, based on the previous year's figures and known fluctuations and changes for the current year, as well as on key and material items) as follows:

a)   from the stock sheets to the physical stock, verifying the existence and quantity (that is, test for overstatement); and

b)   from the physical stock to the count records to ensure that all items are correctly included (ithat is, test for understatement).

The auditor should review any errors found and determine the potential for further errors and quantify the effect of any such errors.

Follow-up of stocktake

The auditor should:

a)   agree the balance on the nominal ledger to the final stock sheets;

b)   trace copies of rough stock sheets and test counts to the final stock records, ensuring that all items have been included in the final valuation. Usually, this test can be restricted to the stock lines counted at the stocktake;

c)   check casts and extensions on a sample of the final stock sheets; and

d)   review stock sheets and ensure that any amendments are properly authorised and valid. It may be necessary to actually review any movements by reference to the goods despatched and received records.

Perpetual stocktaking

Although the client will not count all the stock at any one time, the auditor should still attend one of the counts, preferably as near as possible to the balance sheet date. The stocktaking instructions should still be reviewed to ensure they are effective as noted above.

Alternatively, the auditor can conduct test counts at the fieldwork stage of the audit, or at the year end, checking a sample of counts from the stock floor to perpetual stock records, and vice versa.

Work in progress

The auditor should ensure that the nature and stage of completion of work in progress is consistent with the records. Where work in progress consists of a small number of high value items or projects, it may be worth the auditor taking photographs of the actual state of completion when attending the stocktake. The auditor should ensure that any important or contentious issues are included in the letter of representation.

Third-party expert stocktakers should be used where the auditor does not have the necessary expertise in relation to the stock to be counted. In such cases, the auditor would have to consider the competence and reliability of the experts' work.

Stock held by third parties

Where a third party holds stock on behalf of a client, the auditor should:

a) establish the reasons why a client's stock is held by a third party, and determine whether this is reasonable in the circumstances;

b) be particularly wary of cases where this is not in the normal course of business or is unusual in the particular industry sector;

c) ensure that the client exerts control over such stock and keeps adequate records;

d) confirm in writing with the third party that the client retains title to the goods. This should be done even if the records suggest that the third party is holding immaterial amounts of stock or none at all at the year end;

e) as an alternative to confirmation, obtain evidence that the client bought the goods and that they were delivered to the third party on condition that title remained with the client (There should be some form of confirmation to this effect – for example, the delivery address is usually specified on an invoice, which may indicate where such stock is held); and

f) consider physical inspection where the amounts held are material. This should obviously be agreed with the client and the third party. Depending on the materiality of the amounts involved, such counts could be performed on a cyclical basis.

Interim stocktakes

In some cases, it may be necessary to count stock before the year end in order to meet a short reporting deadline. If this is the case, the auditor needs to ensure that:

a) the system will produce a reliable stock figure at the year end; and

b) stock movements are tested for the period between the count and the year end. The movements may be audited by analytical review or detailed testing of a sample of individual transactions, to ensure that they are valid stock movements.

In other cases, it may be necessary to count stock at a time very close to the year end, but not actually at the year end (for example, on a day of the week when the premises are closed). The procedures will be the same in (b) above. Remember, though, that a company's actual year-end day can fluctuate by seven days either side of the accounting reference date specified to the Registrar of Companies. This is common for retail businesses and those who supply retailers.

Confirmation of title

The auditor is usually able to assume that stock held at a client's premises is the property of that client, but this is not always the case. Possible risk areas include:

a) stock purchased by the client may be subject to a Romalpa (reservation of title) clause that may need to be disclosed;

b) the client may hold stock on behalf of third parties;

c) the stock may represent items returned by customers for repair or upgrade; and

d) the client may be holding consignment stock – in which case the auditor must ensure that this has been properly accounted for under FRS 5.

Note that it is unlikely that a client would illustrate **all** the risks identified above.

Professional valuation

The auditor should consider whether attending the stocktake is the most effective method of valuing stock, as it can be cheaper and more effective to use an external valuer. If the client does not wish to pay for this service, there is no reason why the auditor should not pay and include the costs within disbursements. This is common practice when conducting audits for clubs, pubs, chemists and newsagents.

However, where a professional valuation has been used it is important that the following procedures are followed:

a) the auditor should ensure that the valuer is both independent of the entity and competent to undertake the assignment;

b) when the valuation has been undertaken, the auditor should obtain a detailed report from the valuer providing details of:

    a) how the count was undertaken;

    b) the method of valuation used;

    c) cut-off procedures; and

    d) how obsolete stock was identified.

The report should incorporate a full list of all individual stock items. If this is unavailable for any reason, the auditor should consider the impact that this will have on the audit report due to the requirements of either SI 2008/409 or SI 2008/410 to keep full details of all stocks held at the year end, and of the Companies Act 2006 to maintain adequate accounting records.

The auditor should perform a limited amount of work to confirm that the third party stock report is adequate for the purposes of the audit. In addition to reviewing the scope, competence and objectivity of the stocktaker, the auditor should also consider attending the stocktake, even if only irregularly. Also, some verification work should be performed on the valuations made by the stocktaker on a sample of stock lines. At the very least, some analytical review should be conducted on the third-party stocktaker's results.

20.3.2 To ensure that correct cut-off is applied

There is usually a higher risk of error with cut-off testing, as year-end procedures happen infrequently and such procedures can usually be easily manipulated. Also, in most instances, cut-off errors do not arise from a breakdown in the client's systems. Errors arise because different parts of the system record elements of a transaction at different times that happen to be either side of the year-end. At other times of the year, the transaction would not result in an error from an audit point of view. Cut-off tests on stock should be coordinated with cut-off tests for sales, purchases, debtors and creditors. Tests should ensure that despatches and receipts of goods are recorded in the correct accounting period and that corresponding sales or purchases are also recorded in the same period.

If stock was not counted at the year end, the auditor should test cut-off at the year end and at the stocktaking date. The following procedures should be applied:

a) using the details collected at the stocktake, the auditor should select items from the goods inwards and goods outwards records either side of the year end, and agree these to the relevant stock records, and hence to the sales and purchase records; and

b) where stock moves between internal departments or locations, the auditor should ensure that cut-off also operates correctly so that items are neither omitted nor double counted.

20.3.3 To ensure that cost is accurately determined (valued) according to one of the recognised methods

The auditor should review the method of valuing stock and ensure that it is permitted under SI 2008/409 or SI 2008/410 and SSAP 9. The following matters should be considered:

a) inclusion of import duties, transport and handling costs in the stock valuation;

b) inclusion of direct labour, direct expenses and an appropriate proportion of production and other overheads in a manufacturing company in the stock valuation; and

c) exclusion of selling and distribution overheads and inter-branch profits from the stock valuation.

The auditor should check, on a sample basis, that the unit costs recorded on the stock sheets are valid by reviewing such supporting evidence as:

- suppliers' invoices (if stock is valued on the 'first in first out' basis): the auditor should ensure that sufficient invoices have been examined to cover the amounts in stock;

- labour costs (timesheets, clock cards etc.);

- overhead allocation calculations; and

- standard costing calculations (review for reasonableness by reviewing variance analysis).

The auditor should check the casts and extensions of the final stock sheets.

Where the client has goods in transit, the auditor should ensure that the items were genuinely in transit by reviewing goods received notes shortly after the balance sheet date. FRS 5 contains some guidance on when goods in transit should be accounted as stock.

Consignment stock

The auditor should consider whether any stock held on consignment should be included in the client's balance sheet. Consignment stock is stock held by one party (the 'dealer') but legally owned by another (usually the 'manufacturer'), on terms that give the dealer the right to sell the stock in the normal course of its business or, at its option, to return it unsold to the legal owner. Such stock is commonly seen in new car main dealerships. However, the terms of individual agreements can differ widely, and the following is a summary of the circumstances that might indicate whether or not the stock should be recognised in the client's balance sheet.

Indications that the stock is not an asset of the dealer at delivery	Indications that the stock is an asset of the dealer at delivery
Manufacturer can require dealer to return stock, or transfer it to another dealer, without compensation.	Manufacturer cannot require dealer to return or transfer stock.
Penalty paid by dealer to prevent returns or transfers of stock requested by the manufacturer.	Financial incentives to persuade dealer to transfer stock at manufacturer's request.
Dealer able to return stock without penalty and does so in practice.	Dealer has no right to return stock or is not compelled commercially to exercise any right of return.

Manufacturer bears risk of obsolescence, for example:	Dealer bears obsolescence risk, for example:

Manufacturer bears risk of obsolescence, for example:

- obsolete stock is returned without penalty; or
- financial incentives given to prevent return of such stock.

Dealer bears obsolescence risk, for example:

- penalty charged by manufacturer for returns of any such stock; or
- obsolete stock cannot be returned and no compensation is paid for losses due to obsolescence.

Transfer price based on list price at date of transfer of legal title.

Transfer price based on list price at date of delivery.

Manufacturer bears risk of slow movement, for example:

- transfer price does not depend on the length of time that the dealer holds stock and there is no deposit.

Dealer bears slow movement risk, for example:

- transfer price varied depending on time for which dealer holds stock; or
- substantial interest-free deposit that varies with the level of stock held.

20.3.4 To ensure that full provision has been made for all damaged, obsolete or slow-moving stock

The auditor must confirm that stocks are valued at the lower of cost and net realisable value. This can usually be achieved by further testing of the sample used to check unit costs in section 20.3.3 above. The auditor should note that testing net realisable value is not simply checking the selling price at which one unit was sold after the year end. Any related selling costs should also be taken into account and consideration given to the number of units sold at this price. The auditor should consider the following questions when assessing the risk of net realisable value being less than cost.

a) If production levels are high and stock turnover is low, does this indicate that stock levels are excessive?

b) Will the introduction of new products make existing products obsolete?

c) Have any stock lines been discontinued?

d) What is the shelf life of goods, particularly perishables and those with expiry dates?

e) Has all inter-branch or departmental profit been eliminated?

f) Are actual stock levels high compared to expected stock levels from budgets and previous years?

g) Have the costs of completing items and any selling and distribution costs been considered?

h) Were any items identified as old, obsolete or slow moving at the stocktake?

i) Have the contract price, after-date orders and sales and other relevant information been reviewed in relation to work in progress?

20.4 Analytical review

The following procedures can be applied in respect of analytical review on stock.

20.4.1 Stock turnover ratio

This is the most basic of the analytical review procedures that can be performed on stock. This is usually calculated as part of the final review of the accounts. However, in accordance with ISA 520 *Analytical procedures*, it should also be calculated at the planning stage if the figures are available. Certainly, the ratio should be examined as soon as practicable.

The ratio may be expressed in two ways:

a) cost of sales / stock

b) (stock / cost of sales) × 365

Ratio (a) measures the number of times during the year that stock flows through the business.

Ratio (b) gives the average number of days taken for the stock to flow through the business.

On the assumption that a client would like as little money as possible tied up in stock, any increase in the figure for stock turnover days is described as 'worsening'. Similarly, if the stock turnover ratio decreases, this is also a worsening.

A worsening stock turnover ratio may indicate that stock is overstated. However, there are many legitimate reasons why the ratio would 'worsen', and it is important for the auditor to corroborate these reasons. For example, there may be a change in the stock holding policy. This could be for reasons such as potential future expansion, bulk buying to take advantage of discounts or seasonal factors (especially if the entity has changed year ends).

Conversely, an improving stock turnover ratio may indicate a potential understatement of stock. Again there may be legitimate reasons for the improvement – for example, a concerted effort by the entity to reduce stock levels to reduce financing costs. Seasonal factors or a change in the year end could also affect the ratio. It is important that the auditor fully corroborates any explanations received.

It may also be useful, if applicable, to split the ratio between the various different types of stock, such as raw materials, work-in-progress and finished goods.

If allowed by the accounting records, it may be possible to further split the stock turn ratios into stock categories. This will allow a very detailed analytical review to be performed. This is an application of the principle that the more disaggregation that you can achieve when conducting analytical review, the more reliable the evidence is.

20.4.2 Stock analysis

The main form of substantive analytical review procedure that will enable a reduction in detailed stock testing is to examine any significant changes in the value of individual stock lines or stock groups. The auditor should ensure that explanations are obtained and corroborated for all significant variances.

The auditor should also follow up any changes in the level of stock that that were expected from discussions with the client at the planning stage.

Where applicable, the auditor should also consider importing stock transaction details or balances into a spreadsheet. The stock turnover ratio for each individual stock line or group could then be calculated and compared with previous years. This would provide very strong analytical review evidence indeed.

20.4.3 Locations

Where applicable, the auditor should also carry out an analytical review on stock held at different locations, and the stock levels should be compared – in as much detail as possible – with those of previous years and also reviewed in relation to any management information available for the location.

If a client has a number of different locations and stock is checked at different times, it may be possible for the client to transfer the stock from one location to another between the two stocktakes, and effectively double-count it. Realistically, this would be very difficult to detect from a substantive stock-counting test. Therefore, the best way of actually identifying this problem is through detailed analytical review.

20.4.4 Work in progress

The audit of production work in progress is a very difficult and judgmental area. Analytical review can provide an effective tool for assessing the reasonableness of specific judgments and also of the overall work in progress figure. As noted above, the components of work in progress should be examined in as much detail as possible.

20.4.5 Seasonal fluctuations

The auditor should also consider the level of stock held by the client in relation to the cycle of activity within the business. For example, if considering a toy shop, then obviously the year end of the client would be critical when determining what a reasonable level of stock should be: stock at the end of November should be significantly higher than stock at the end of December.

There are numerous examples of situations where the level of stock held by the client will vary significantly due to seasonal fluctuations. It is important that the auditor considers whether or not the level of stock held is reasonable in relation to the cycle of activity.

20.4.6 Expansion and contraction

The auditor should consider the possibility of changes to the client's business that would result in a change in stock level. Expansion of the client's business usually means an increase in stock levels, while a contraction of the client's business usually results in stock reduction. Obviously, the timing of the planned expansion or downsizing will affect the expected change. The increase or reduction in stock may not be immediate and may take, for example, 18 months to two years to work through.

20.4.7 Provisions

Analytical review is also useful in determining the reasonableness of stock provisions. If there have been increases in the level of stock held without an adequate explanation, and there has been a worsening of the stock turn ratios, then this could, potentially, lead the auditor to conclude that an increase in the level of stock provision is required. When considering this issue, the auditor may be able to review the stock records (including details such as stock ageing) to determine the last time that a particular stock line was sold and bought. Such information will usually only be available on sophisticated stock-recording systems.

The auditor may also be able to conduct analytical review on the client's stock provision calculations. A key point with stock provisions is consistency; any changes to the level of stock provisions need to be properly justified. The auditor also needs to consider whether the method of arriving at the level of provision is appropriate, particularly where a fixed percentage is applied.

20.5 Control

The following is a list of controls that that may be applicable in relation to stock. Clearly, not all the controls will be relevant to all types of stocks, and the size of some companies may make some of them impractical. The auditor should consider which apply and how effectively they are operating.

a) Restricted access to stock and physical security over it.

b) The use of surveillance equipment.

e) Independent check on despatches made by persons other than those responsible for the stock. This may be on all despatches, or on a sample basis.

d) Regular reconciliations of actual stock-to-stock records.

e) Independent matching of goods in and out with purchase and sales documentation.

f) Reporting of slow-moving, obsolete or damaged stock to relevant levels of management.

g) Regular reviews of stock statistics.

h) Quality control checks of both purchases and finished goods.

i) Continuous stock records kept of both quantities and values.

j) Segregation of duties between storekeeping and goods in, despatch, production and accounts.

k) Labelling of stock.

l) Record of stock held by or for third party.

m) Single point of receipt for goods in.

n) Pre-numbered goods received notes (GRNs) and stock requisition notes (SRNs), along with the regular checking for missing numbers.

o) Authorisation of SRNs.

p) SRNs signed by recipient.

q) Record of or authorisation of scrapped and damaged goods.

r) Recording of money received for sales of scrap.

s) Clock cards or timesheets authorised.

t) Written stocktake instructions.

The errors that could occur if the necessary controls are not in place include:

- incorrect quantity recorded on receipt of goods;
- goods received not recorded (GRN lost);
- items wrongly described;
- items rejected on receipt recorded as received;
- unordered goods accepted;
- goods despatched but not invoiced;
- obsolete stock not identified;
- stock is omitted or double counted at the stocktake; and
- goods 'walking'.

The existence of any of the controls could either provide the auditor with additional audit comfort or enable a reduction in the amount of stock testing. The auditor should consider whether there are any key controls in operation that can be relied upon. If so, then suitable compliance tests on the operation of those controls should be performed. Even in owner-managed businesses, the auditor may wish to encourage implementation of some of the controls for the business's own protection.

20.6 Common problems

Detailed below, in sections 20.6.1 to 20.6.12, are some of the more common problems that may be encountered during the audit of stock, and tips on how best to deal with them.

20.6.1 Net realisable value

SSAP 9 requires the auditor to consider the net realisable value of stock on an item-by-item basis, and so it is not sufficient to look at it globally. The auditor should review individual lines to determine whether any provision is in fact necessary.

At the time the auditor is undertaking much of the audit work, it is usual for some items that were in stock at the year end to still be unsold. So it is not straightforward to confirm the adequacy of any provision. Analytical procedures to consider the reasonableness of the provision being made can be performed; the auditor can also consider what happened in the past and obtain representations from management. When assessing the net realisable value of work in progress and finished goods, the auditor should remember to deduct any costs to completion from the selling price.

20.6.2 Non-attendance at stocktake

Most practices do attend stocktakes for conventional stock; but, where the stock is work in progress, this may not be the case. Also, non-attendance at a stocktake may occur because previously it had been immaterial, though in this particular year it happens to be material.

The auditor is required to document on file how the existence of stock has been confirmed. This objective applies whether or not the auditor attended the stocktake. Where the auditor did not attend the stocktake and stock is material, it is essential that any alternative procedures to confirm existence are fully documented. For example, it may be that comfort can be gained through performing counts at the time of the audit and reconciling back via post-year end accounting records. Alternatively, analytical review may confirm that the stock figure is not materially misstated.

The above procedures may provide sufficient evidence in some cases, but it is often necessary to qualify the audit opinion on the basis of a limitation in scope.

20.6.3 Incorrect pricing

Another fairly common problem occurs where the stock is not valued in accordance with the stated accounting policy and this is not detected by the auditor. It is essential that checks are performed to ensure that the method of valuation applied is consistent with the stated accounting policy and is acceptable under SSAP 9 and either SI 2008/409 or SI 2008/410 as appropriate.

20.6.4 Sample sizes at stocktake

Wherever the auditor applies sampling techniques, it is essential that the sample size being tested be justified on file. One of the most common errors with sampling occurs during the stocktake. Invariably, the stocktake is performed before due consideration has been paid to risk and materiality. This, combined with the fact that draft accounts are usually unavailable, means that the auditor rarely applies the firm's usual sampling procedures. This can result in either under- or over-sampling, sometimes to a massive extent, especially on the test counts. The auditor should estimate risk, materiality and the stock value to arrive at a sample size in accordance with the firm's usual procedures.

Note that the full sample size should then be used for testing from sheet to floor, and vice versa, as these are two separate tests. Under no circumstances, should the sample size be split in two, with one half tested from floor to sheet and the other half from sheet to floor.

20.6.5 Stock valuation test

One of the key stock tests is to check the valuation of a sample of stock lines to purchase prices. However, the test is very often left unfinished, or the conclusion is based on the results of only part of the sample, as it can be very difficult to trace the latest purchase invoice from the stock details.

An alternative approach is to extract a sample of purchase invoices from the period it takes stock to turn over (say, the two months before the year end) and to check that the appropriate cost is recorded on the stock sheet. Performing this test from the purchase invoice still satisfies the objective of ensuring that stock is valued correctly.

20.6.6 Stocktake not at year end

Another common problem arises where the stocktake is not carried out at the year end. The count may continue over a couple of days, or may be timed so as to cause the minimum disruption to trade.

In addition to the usual tests, the auditor should:

- test cut-off at the year end and at the stocktake date;
- for a sample of stock lines (usually those counted at the stocktake), verify the movements between the stocktake and the year end to goods despatched notes and goods received notes. The auditor should also examine these records for any movement in those stock lines that has not been taken into account; and
- check the client's workings to confirm they match the goods-in and goods-out records for the period between the stocktake and the year end. If the client or the auditor has performed this calculation in another form, there should be some notes justifying why the calculation is reasonable.

20.6.7 Stock provisions

This is an extremely difficult area of the audit and is therefore prone to being poorly addressed. Assessing the adequacy of provisions is an area that requires judgment and discussion with the client. This often results in much of the discussion being principal led, and therefore the evidence of such discussions may be omitted from the file. The auditor must ensure that sufficient evidence has been noted on file to satisfy the objective that the level of any stock provision is fairly stated.

A number of detailed procedures have been suggested above to enable the auditor to determine whether the stock provision is materially misstated. The key issue is that the file must record the auditor's justification for that stock provisions being fairly stated. Unless the stockholdings have changed significantly, or there have been other changes to stock, the level of the stock provisions should be relatively consistent over time. The auditor should be aware that while the main risk is usually understatement of stock provisions, in the case of profitable clients, the main risk is that stock provisions are overstated to reduce the tax burden. In some cases therefore, it is important to critically evaluate whether any stock provision is necessary. Again, this may best be done through analytical review, assessing the provision for reasonableness compared with previous years and the auditor's knowledge of the client (including any changes to the business).

20.6.8 Property development companies

The problems posed by companies buying and developing a site are akin to those with a manufacturing company. Finished goods and work in progress can be very difficult to audit, and the amounts involved for each individual unit greatly increase the risk factors.

Existence of the development is relatively straightforward, and is best verified by a visit. Beneficial ownership is also straightforward and can be covered by the work described in Chapter 18.

Valuation of the development is the difficult part. Initially, the auditor will have to use his or her judgment to decide the level of completion of the properties. This is not straightforward, as a building may appear 80 per cent complete from the outside, but may be only 50 per cent complete due to work outstanding on the inside. The auditor should consider using the services of an expert valuer in these circumstances, especially if the auditor is having difficulty in ascertaining the net realisable values of the properties for valuation purposes. Obviously, the use of an expert should be discussed with the client, but it could be that the client is under an obligation to obtain regular valuations from experts as part of its financing arrangements. With such companies, there are also likely to be significant costs in selling the properties, such as estate agent's fees and solicitor's fees, which should be deducted from the selling price to arrive at net realisable value.

It is also not unusual for such companies to value stock at cost by taking the stage of completion, multiplied by the selling price of the properties, and then deducting gross profit. The work performed by the auditor should be the same as described in section 20.6.10 below, where clients value stock at selling price less gross profit. The stage of completion would also need to be considered.

20.6.9 Manufacturing companies: finished goods and work in progress

Finished goods and work-in-progress are two more areas of stock that are often not dealt with very well. The precise work involved will depend on the client's system for recording costs. But, importantly, the stage of completion of the stock should have already been considered at the stocktake.

Where the client values stock at selling price less gross profit, the procedures adopted should be in line with those described in section 20.6.10 below. If a standard costing approach is used, the auditor should select a sample of standard costs and verify its make-up. This could be done with reference to changes from the previous year on items such as labour rates. The auditor should be aware of any technological advances which should lead to labour-time efficiencies.

The issue of net realisable value should not be overlooked. The auditor should ensure that costs to completion are taken into account when arriving at net realisable value. These could be taken from the standard costing cards.

Where the production time is short, the amount of work in progress may not be material, and it may be sufficient to undertake some limited analytical review.

20.6.10 Client who values stock at selling price less gross profit

In such instances, the stock will be determined by valuing each item at selling price, and then deducting a global gross profit percentage – either across the board, or a specific rate on individual groups of stock – to arrive at cost. The auditor often fails to evidence any substantiation of the reasonableness of the gross profit percentage or the selling prices used to value stock.

20.6.11 Impact of Application Note G to FRS 5 and UITF 40 on work in progress

Both the above Standards make clear that they do not amend SSAP 9. However, they do require the seller, where the seller has partially performed its contractual obligations, to recognise revenue to the extent that it has obtained the right to consideration through its performance. For some businesses which were not previously using long-term contract accounting, this has had the impact of reducing work in progress, as work done to date is recognised earlier in the profit and loss account. The auditor therefore needs to carefully consider whether there is a contract for the provision for goods and/or services, and whether the accounting is in accordance with these provisions.

20.6.12 Too much photocopying or scanning

As with additions to fixed assets (see section 18.6.8), stock is an area where there is frequently too much copying. Is it really necessary to copy all the rough stock sheets and all the final stock sheets? Where copies are provided by the client, it is not obligatory to add these to the audit file: they could be kept on a separate file and then shredded or deleted once the audit was complete.

Chapter 21 Long-term contracts

21.1 Introduction and definition

SSAP 9 defines a long-term contract as one entered into for the manufacture or building of a single substantial asset or provision of a service, where the time taken to manufacture, build or provide is such that it falls into different accounting periods. Although it is likely that the contract will exceed one year in length, this is not an essential feature. A contract of less than one year can be defined as a long-term contract – if it is sufficiently material to the activity of the period to result in a distortion of the results if the turnover and profit are accounted for at the end of the contract.

The basic principle is that turnover and costs should be recorded, and profits recognised as the contract progresses, rather than merely on completion.

There are some complexities in respect of the accounting treatments of long-term work in progress, which are required in order to comply with SSAP 9, while the provisions of Application Note G to FRS 5 and UITF 40 also need to be considered. These can all impact on the audit risks and the audit approach, so some of the accounting issues have been addressed in this introduction.

21.1.1 Accounting treatment

SSAP 9 gives some guidelines on the accounting treatment of long-term contracts, but it is far from comprehensive. The usual method of recording a sales transaction is to record the turnover from the sale, match this with the related cost and recognise the resulting difference as the profit on the transaction. However, when dealing with long-term work in progress, this order is changed. If the auditor is dealing with contracts at the year end, the turnover attributable at the year end will be determined first and then the attributable profit, with the cost being the balancing figure. Each of these components is looked at in turn below.

Turnover

The theory is quite simple. Turnover on the contract should be recorded as the contract progresses. The practicalities of determining an appropriate level of turnover part way through a contract (that is, at a year end) are where problems occur.

The guidance in Application Note G requires a seller to measure turnover in respect of long-term contracts by an assessment of the fair value of the goods or services provided to its reporting date as a proportion of the total fair value of the contract, noting that the guiding principle is to consider the stage of completion of the contractual obligations, which reflects the extent to which the seller has obtained the right to consideration. In some contracts, this proportion will correspond with the proportion of expenditure incurred in comparison with total expenditure, but this will not always be the case.

Independent valuation

An independent valuer will assess the level of completeness of the contract at the year-end date. Thus, if a contract is certified as 60 per cent complete, then 60 per cent of the expected turnover of the whole contract should be recorded as turnover for the period. The level of 'turnover' is usually expressed as an amount rather than a percentage of completion on such valuations. Such valuations are also carried out by the 'customer'.

Internal valuation

If the entity has the necessary expertise in-house, management may be in a position to arrive at an assessment of the level of completeness of a contract.

Formula

A formula can be used, based on the costs incurred to date as a percentage of the total expected cost. This may be based on total costs, or perhaps on an element of the total cost, such as labour. The latter method may be more appropriate if there are a lot of costs of buying materials at the start of the contract; so, in this case, the labour costs incurred during the contract will be a fairer reflection of the progress of the contract.

Turnover to date = (costs to date x total expected value) / total expected costs

However, it should be noted that Application Note G to FRS 5 states that the amount of turnover recognised may only be derived from the proportion of costs incurred where it provides evidence of the seller's performance and hence the extent to which it has obtained the right to consideration.

Whatever method is used, it should be appropriate to the industry or sector in which the entity operates, it should be a fair reflection of the way the contract progresses in practice, and once a method is applied, it should be consistently applied to similar contracts and from year to year.

Once the turnover has been calculated, the profit attributable should be calculated – as a separate exercise.

Attributable profit

This can also be tricky, as the concept of prudence needs to be considered. Profit on a contract should only be recognised once the profitability of the contract as a whole is known with reasonable certainty. Paragraph 24 of SSAP 9 states:

> 'In determining whether the stage has been reached at which it is appropriate to recognise profit, account should be taken of the nature of the business concerned. It is necessary to define the earliest point for each particular contract before which no profit is taken, the overriding principle being that there can be no attributable profit until the outcome of a contract can be reasonably foreseen.'

It may be prudent, therefore, especially in the early stages of a contract, not to show any attributable profit. The turnover will be calculated and still be recorded, and the transfer to cost of sales will be an equal amount, resulting in a profit of nil being recognised.

Once it has been decided that it would be prudent to recognise profit, in most cases the method of calculating the attributable profit is consistent with the method used to calculate turnover, that is:

$$\frac{\text{(valuation} \times \text{expected profit)}}{\text{total expected value}}$$

or

$$\frac{\text{(costs to date} \times \text{expected profit)}}{\text{total expected costs}}$$

The above methods for working out profit are only guidelines. If profits do not accrue evenly over the period of the contract, then this needs to be taken into account.

Losses

Exercising prudence applies not only to foreseeable profits, but also when assessing foreseeable losses. Anticipated losses should be accounted for as soon as they are foreseen. Therefore, any projected losses should be accounted for in the period that they are first anticipated to occur. This is irrespective of:

- whether work has started on a contract;
- the percentage of total work that has been carried out; and
- the profits expected on other contracts.

21.1.2 Disclosure

The disclosure requirements are quite considerable and in practice can become quite complicated. The amounts that should be included can be summarised as:

a) amounts recoverable on contracts;

b) long-term contract balances;

c) invoiced amounts

d) payments on account; and

e) provision for foreseeable losses.

Amounts recoverable on contracts

This will be the excess of recorded turnover over payments on account, and should be classified as 'amounts recoverable on contracts' and disclosed separately within 'debtors'.

Long-term contract balances

This will include the costs incurred on long-term contracts, less amounts transferred to cost of sales, less foreseeable losses and payments on account not matched with turnover (that is, payments received on contracts in excess of valuations or turnover). The resulting balance (if any) should be disclosed separately as 'long-term contract balances' within the 'stocks' heading in the notes to the accounts. The breakdown in the notes to the accounts should show the net cost less foreseeable losses and applicable payments on account. There is unlikely to be a large balance, as the costs will be transferred to cost of sales as the contract progresses.

Invoiced amounts

This will be made up of invoices raised or requests for payments, including retentions, that have not been collected and will be included in the trade debtors heading.

Payments on account

The balance disclosed under this heading will be the balance of payments on account in excess of amounts offset against turnover and long-term contract balances. This will be classified as payments received on account, and should be disclosed within 'creditors'.

Provision for foreseeable losses

This balance will either be included under 'creditors' or 'provision for liabilities and charges', and will be the foreseeable losses in excess of the costs incurred (after transfer to cost of sales) to ascertain turnover and attributable profit.

An extensive accounting policy note will be required to explain how the figures in the accounts have been determined.

21.2 Objectives

The audit objectives that need to be satisfied when auditing long-term contracts are as follows:

a) to ensure that amounts accumulated in long-term contracts are correctly calculated;

b) to ensure that any contracts included exist;

c) to ensure that turnover on contracts represents amounts chargeable to date;

d) to ensure that all contracts are included; and

e) to ensure that all potential foreseeable losses have been correctly accounted for.

These objectives are considered in more detail in sections 21.3.1 to 21.3.5.

21.3 Audit procedures

The following procedures will be appropriate where the client has long-term contracts. The procedures are set out beneath the most relevant individual audit objectives. When considering long-term contracts, it is important that the auditor bears in mind the interrelationship between the work undertaken and that required in respect of completeness of income, creditors, debtors and, to a certain extent, cost of sales.

The extent of the interrelationship will depend on the client's system. It is important that the testing is performed on a contract-by-contract basis and that all issues are addressed for each of these contracts. This not only prevents duplication of audit effort, but also ensures that items are not omitted.

21.3.1 To ensure that amounts accumulated in long-term contracts are correctly calculated

As the accounting treatment for long-term contract balances will affect debtors (amounts recoverable on contracts), profit and loss (attributable turnover and profit) and creditors (progress payments in advance), as well as stock, this area is best dealt with as a separate piece of work, rather than considering the relevant balances under each separate area. The sample of contracts should be selected from a file containing details of quotes given and contracts offered, to ensure completeness. Where the auditor has selected a quote that was unsuccessful, the reason should be noted. The following procedures can be applied when testing the sample of contracts.

Contract costs

Standard purchase and expense tests should be used for raw materials, direct expenses, labour and direct overheads. Where there are a number of different contracts, the auditor should ensure that the amounts are charged to the correct contract.

The auditor should be alert to any questionable payments or 'commissions' by clients to secure contracts.

Attributable profits and turnover

The allocation of attributable profit will almost certainly be high risk, as it is very dependent on the use of judgment and the calculations are often quite complex. Therefore, a higher risk level should be used and the sample biased towards the high risk and material contracts, for example:

a) contracts with unusual profits or losses;

b) contracts with material profits, losses or cash flow requirements;

c) contracts in politically sensitive or volatile areas overseas;

d) contracts where costs to date, with costs to completion, are likely to exceed the original contract price; and

e) contracts that are late where there are significant penalties for late delivery.

The auditor should test the accuracy of the client's calculations, including:

f) checking arithmetical accuracy;

g) reviewing the reasonableness of any assumptions made;

h) considering whether all costs to completion have been included; and

i) taking into account the accuracy of forecasts and estimates made in previous years.

The auditor should consider undertaking a physical verification visit, particularly with reference to the stage of completion and the value of work to date (that is, turnover). The following procedures should then be applied:

j) discuss practical problems in carrying out the contract with site managers and consider whether any provision will be necessary;

k) discuss potential extra costs, for example, labour disputes, fines due to delays in completion; and

l)   review any correspondence with the customer.

The auditor should discuss the status of contracts selected for testing with contract managers, surveyors, engineers and site foremen, as well as management. Taking time to discuss the contracts with such non-accounting staff should provide additional information about the contracts and improve the auditor's understanding of the business. The following issues should be considered when discussing the contracts:

m)   whether there are any technical or building problems;

n)   potential labour disputes; and

o)   estimated completion dates and penalties for delay.

Valuations

Where an external valuer has been used, the auditor should consider the following:

a)   the independence and competence of the valuer (for example, professional qualifications and experience with this type of contract);

b)   whether the valuer received accurate information;

c)   whether the bases and assumptions used are reasonable and consistent with previous years; and

d)   where applicable, the accuracy of valuations carried out by the valuer in previous years.

The auditor should check the receipt of cash after date for an appropriate sample of amounts recoverable on long-term contracts. It is not uncommon to find that the customer pays only a percentage of the request for payment – especially if it is the contractor's valuation that makes up the request for payment. This is in addition to funds withheld as a retention.

Retentions

The auditor should consider whether retentions are valid and recoverable – by inspecting correspondence with the customer or by reviewing cash received after the balance sheet date. The auditor should also check that the customer has accepted liability for any additional work performed.

Other matters

- The auditor should ensure that progress payments are accounted for in the correct period. This will be covered by reviewing cash after date.

- If fixed assets have been purchased for a specific contract which is due to end, or has ended, the auditor should consider whether these assets need to be reviewed for impairment.

- The auditor should consider whether any contingent liability may arise where the client issues a guarantee or warranty in respect of stock.

- The auditor should ensure that events on specific contracts are considered in the post-balance sheet events review.

21.3.2 To ensure that any contracts included exist

The tests necessary to satisfy this objective would be the cash after date and physical verification work described above.

21.3.3 To ensure that turnover on contracts represents amounts chargeable to date

As the calculation of attributable turnover is usually linked to the calculation of attributable profit, the same considerations as noted above will apply. In many cases, the turnover is actually based on an external valuation that normally gives the value of the work done to date – that is, the total turnover to date on that contract. Therefore, tests on turnover should link with tests on valuation and attributable profit.

21.3.4 To ensure that all contracts are included

The auditor should review contracts at the start of the year and ensure that all such contracts are either in progress at the end of the year, or have been completed during the year.

The auditor should review minutes, correspondence, contract files and contract records to ensure that all contracts are included.

The auditor should review a sample of purchase invoices relating to raw materials, and ensure that the delivery addresses are accounted for as contracts.

21.3.5 To ensure that all potential foreseeable losses have been correctly accounted for

The auditor should review costs after the year end, budgets, contract costing and correspondence, to assess if any contracts in progress are likely to make an overall loss.

The auditor should review completed contracts to determine the reliability of the client's estimates.

21.4 Analytical review

Analytical review can frequently be used when looking at long-term contracts, to ensure that the relationships between the figures make sense. This means looking at typical ratios of, for example, material costs and labour costs to the total contract value, etc. In addition, comparisons between the actual figures and any original budgets, prepared when quoting for the project, also provide good analytical review evidence that the client's costings can be relied upon. The auditor should ensure that any variances are followed up with the client.

Analytical review could also be used to determine the level of any provision against retentions. Comparisons of retentions with previous years – both as an absolute amount and as a percentage of turnover – may be useful in determining the client's ongoing ability to recover such amounts.

21.5 Controls

There are a number of controls that could be implemented by an entity, in order to ensure that the figures for long-term contracts are fairly stated. These will include:

a) stocktakes being planned to include long-term work in progress;

b) the existence of a unique numbering and referencing system for each contract and quote which is controlled;

c) all matters relating to specific contracts being retained on one contract file, which is opened at the time that the quote is sent;

d) valuation of the contracts being undertaken by an experienced staff member or independent valuer during the course of the contract term;

e) adequate insurance of the contract; and

f) adequate supervision and segregation of duties between supervision of the work on the contracts, and the authority for the movement of materials and plant.

Where any of the above controls exist, the auditor may be able to perform compliance tests to determine whether or not the control is working effectively, thus facilitating less detailed work during the substantive testing. Even where sample sizes cannot be reduced, the existence of such controls can provide additional audit comfort.

21.6 Common problems

Some common problems that the auditor may encounter during the course of the audit of long-term contracts include:

a) failure to determine existence;

b) failure to consider the ultimate profitability of the contract;

c) failure to consider the ultimate recoverability of any retention on the project;

d) failure to account properly for long-term contracts;

e) the client's poor costing records;

f) failure to combine the work on this area with the work on the profit and loss account, debtors and creditors; and

g) front-loading of contracts.

21.6.1 Failure to determine existence

Frequently, the auditor does not do sufficient work to determine that the contracts actually exist. This is a particular problem where there is no independent valuation of the contracts at the year-end. If the auditor is unable to attend a stocktake, or lacks the necessary expertise, then looking at the movement of plant, material and subcontractor invoices, staff job sheet, etc. for a specific contract can help to obtain comfort as to the existence, if not the valuation, of the work in progress. Testing cash after date can verify both valuation and existence.

21.6.2 Failure to consider the ultimate profitability of the contract

Frequently, when considering the net realisable value of a contract, the auditor only looks as far as the next progress payment. However, this will not show whether the total costs for the project will exceed the total income. It is essential that the auditor considers the costs to completion, and looks at these together with the costs to date against the expected income from the project. This is particularly important in a market where many companies are quoting for contracts based on very low margins.

21.6.3 Failure to consider the ultimate recoverability of any retention on the projects

Many firms are very good at looking at the recoverability of short-term debts, but less scrupulous when considering long-term debts. Moreover, they frequently do not even disclose within the financial statements that the retention may be recoverable after more than one year. This is an area where analytical review can be applied. In this respect, it is possible to look at the history of recoverability of retentions and ensure that adequate provision is made against the current retentions to prevent the debtors being overstated.

21.6.4 Failure to account properly for long-term contracts

It is very common to see incorrect disclosure of long-term contracts within the financial statements. Many firms will include everything within 'work in progress', which is not the required treatment under SSAP 9. Audit staff working on the job should be familiar with the requirements of SSAP 9, and should ensure, that correct disclosure is made during the course of the audit.

21.6.5 The client's poor costing records

Not all construction companies, especially small, private companies, keep good records in respect of ongoing contracts. When asked to quote, the client will prepare a rough budget, but will not necessarily keep it on file. It is therefore entirely possible that the auditor will be faced with a situation where the client does not keep full costing records, and where the customer's valuations are used as a basis for their requests for payment.

In such circumstances, turnover will usually be the amount that has been requested for payment. Any such amounts unpaid will be the amounts recoverable on contracts. Any costs incurred in the year in question will be cost of sales. However, care will need to be taken to ensure that cut-off has been correctly observed for turnover, cost of sales and work in progress. Care also needs to be taken that this approach does not differ materially from that in Application Note G to FRS 5.

21.6.6 Failure to combine the work on this area with the work on the profit and loss account, debtors and creditors

Most audit systems structure the audit work to be undertaken by balance sheet heading and profit and loss account area. However, this approach does not work with long-term contracts, with so many interlinked figures. As noted above, the auditor can save time and obtain better quality evidence if he or she considers the whole cycle in respect of long-term contracts at the same time. The sample can be selected from the contracts or quotes records and then used to cover all aspects of the cycle. Where this has not been done, the auditor will often find either that he or she is repeating work on different sections or that there is a particular aspect of long-term contracts that has been missed entirely.

21.6.7 Front-loading of contracts

The auditor should be aware of the distortion that can arise where, for example, low costs are incurred at the beginning of the contract, which could result in a disproportionate amount being charged to the client.

Chapter 22 Debtors and prepayments

22.1 Introduction and definition

Debtors and prepayments are amounts included in the financial statements that are outstanding to the client. Debtors are those amounts that are actually payable to the client – for example, amounts receivable from customers. Prepayments are those amounts that have been paid in advance – for example, a subscription.

22.2 Audit objectives

Debtors and prepayments are debit balances, so the audit work performed will be mainly tests for over-statement. The following is a summary of the relevant audit objectives:

a) to ensure that debtors exist at the balance sheet date and that the client has valid title to them;

b) to ensure that correct cut-off has been applied;

c) to ensure that debtors are due at the value recorded and that adequate provision is made for bad or doubtful debts;

d) to ensure that any bad debt expenses are valid;

e) to ensure that all debtors are recorded in the balance sheet;

f) to ensure that amounts due from group and associated undertakings are properly recorded and receivable;

g) to ensure that prepayments and other debtors are properly classified, verified and disclosed; and

h) to ensure that income is not overstated (the under-recording of income is considered in the profit and loss account section).

Procedures for fulfilling these objectives are covered in the next section.

22.3 Audit procedures

When planning the audit, all the available tests should be reviewed to determine those that will most effectively satisfy each of the individual objectives for the client in question. Not all the tests relating to an individual objective need be carried out on each audit.

22.3.1 To ensure that debtors exist at the balance sheet date and that the client has valid title to them

These two objectives are normally dealt with either by a direct confirmation of balances with the debtors concerned or by alternative procedures, such as review of post-year end cash receipts. If there is a risk that the debtors might be recorded but not owned by the client, the auditor should consider the following:

a) reviewing the client's terms of sale and major agreements or contracts;

b) reviewing correspondence with any debt collectors; and

c) contacting significant customers and confirming the client's sales terms with them (use with caution and only with client agreement).

Direct confirmation

Direct confirmation of balances with debtors is a more reliable source of audit evidence because information is being generated by the auditor and provided by a third party not connected with the client. In addition, the auditor will obtain better evidence that the debt existed at the balance sheet date, particularly where a client does not keep remittance advices. For example, it would be more difficult to identify a teeming and lading fraud using after-date cash receipts, which is the most common alternative technique used by auditors.

However, it will only be worth the time involved in a circularisation where the auditor is likely to receive a high level of replies. The auditor should be able to identify the types of client where they are likely to get a reasonable response; this will frequently be clients with major customers that have formal accounting departments, although it is common for many large blue-chip companies to not respond. Where a circularisation has been undertaken in the past and the results have been disappointing, the auditor should consider if any action can be taken to improve the quality and/or quantity of the responses received in future years. The basic approach is to send letters to individual customers, asking them to confirm the balance outstanding at the balance sheet date or to provide further details if they do not agree. If the balances agree, or the reconciling items are valid, no further work on existence is generally required.

In some cases, it may be easier to ask for a more specific confirmation, either of individual invoices or to split the balance into its component invoices. This makes it easier for a customer to identify which invoices are included and so provide more accurate confirmation. This approach should be adopted where customers operate an 'open' sales ledger, and therefore cannot confirm balances at a given point in the past.

Standard sampling techniques should be used. A non-representative sample may be appropriate where the population consists of a small number of high value items, together with many low value items. In these circumstances, the auditor would normally concentrate on the high value balances. The auditor should adopt the following procedures.

a) The circularisation requests should be sent as soon as possible after the confirmation date – usually the balance sheet date, although if the auditor is working to a tight deadline it may be appropriate to carry out the circularisation the month before the year end and then reconcile the figures to the year-end balance. Where the auditor is requesting information at the year end, it may be sensible to extract the information during the course of the stocktake attendance and send the letters out before starting the field work. This should improve the chances of accurate replies and hence the effectiveness of the test.

b) The auditor should clear the sample of debtors to be circularised with a senior member of the client's staff. If the client does not wish a particular debtor to be contacted, the auditor should consider whether the grounds are reasonable. Even so, in this circumstance the auditor must perform alternative tests on any such balances and also ensure that the matter is included in the letter of representation. Refusal to allow the auditor to contact a particular client, and failure to retain remittance advices, may indicate a teeming and lading fraud.

c) The response to confirmation requests is usually better if they are sent on the client's headed notepaper and signed by a client official. So the auditor should either obtain copies of the client letterhead for producing the letters or provide the client with the relevant details to prepare the letters.

d) The auditor should personally place the letters in the envelopes and post the confirmation requests.

e) All replies must be returned directly to the auditor, not to the client. Hence the letter should include a reply paid envelope addressed to the audit firm. The postmark on returned letters should be checked to ensure it has come from the correct place.

f) The auditor should send follow-up letters to those debtors who do not reply, before performing alternative procedures. Such a follow-up can be more effective if performed via fax or telephone, particularly where the auditor has a tight reporting deadline.

g) If the replies do not agree to the balances on the entity's ledger, the auditor should investigate the differences. To keep audit costs down, the auditor should ask the client to reconcile statements if received and to explain any differences. Generally, differences will arise as a result of one or more of the following:

- invoices in the client's records which are not in the customer's balance. These are likely to be those items despatched just before the year end or those where there is some dispute. The auditor should ensure that items were sent to the customer before the balance sheet date. Where the item in question was despatched a long time before the year end, the auditor should endeavour to establish whether the customer is disputing receipt of the product or is anticipating a credit against the balance;

- cash in transit at the balance sheet date. This is also likely to relate to items around the year end, and the auditor should review post-year end receipts to ensure that the cash was received. The auditor should investigate any unusual delays in receiving and banking the cash, as this could indicate some form of teeming and lading fraud; and

- goods returned by the customer. Again, this should be a timing problem around the year end. The auditor should ensure that the goods were received just after the year end and that adequate provision has been made for sales returns.

Even where the auditor has received good responses to the circularisation some cash after date testing should be undertaken. Agreement of the balance outstanding satisfies the existence objective, but does not address recoverability.

Alternative procedures

The auditor should perform these tests only where it has been decided not to ask for direct confirmation from the customers or where the auditor has not obtained a reply to a confirmation request. In the latter case, there is no need to select a further sample. Instead, the auditor need only perform the following tests for the balances that have not been separately confirmed or reconciled. The auditor may need to ask the client to retain certain records that it does not normally keep – for example, remittance advices and GDNs signed by customers as evidence of receipt of goods.

The auditor should trace subsequent payments by the customer. The sample should be taken from the list of debtors at the year end, and the subsequent receipt traced for that sample. There is a tendency to start with the post-year end bank records and work in reverse. Ideally, the auditor should see some evidence that the debt was settled by the customer in question after the balance sheet date and that the balance existed at the year end. Therefore, the auditor should trace the receipt to remittance advices from the customer and to paying-in records, and ensure that the receipt has been correctly allocated in the sales ledger in accordance with the information contained on the remittance advice.

It is important that remittance advices are checked where these are available as this enables the auditor to:

- ensure cash is properly allocated in the sales ledger;

- check the ageing of balances; and

- check for teeming and lading.

If remittance advices are not available, the auditor may be able to take comfort from the fact that the remittance corresponds to one or more invoices. The nearer the date of receipt is to the confirmation date, the more persuasive is the evidence that the debt existed at that date.

If the auditor is not able to trace payment of a particular balance or invoice, he or she should seek evidence that the sales were made to the customer in question. The auditor should review the following where appropriate:

a) goods despatched records;

b) customer service records or contracts;

c) purchase orders or customer contracts; and

d) any relevant evidence that the customer received the goods in question.

The auditor should consider the recoverability of individual invoices if that customer has paid other, more recent invoices. The existence of these outstanding invoices could be the result of a dispute with the customer.

An alternative method of auditing for cash after date can be used where the client has an aged sales ledger. Provided that the auditor has verified the ageing of a sample of the sales ledger balances, and can verify that the client has not processed any credit notes or journal entries to manipulate the sales ledger aged listing, then a more global approach can be taken. If the audit is being performed four months after the year end, the auditor could review the aged sales ledger three months after the year end, and would be able to tell from the 'three months and over' column in the sales ledger which of the debtors that were unpaid at the year end remain unpaid. These debts can then be examined more closely for potential recoverability problems. Such a procedure also identifies potential bad debts that were recent invoices as at the balance sheet date – an area frequently overlooked.

Factored debts

Where the client factors some or all of its debts, the auditor should review the terms of the factoring agreement and consider whether the debts should be recognised on the client's balance sheet and, if so, whether a separate or a linked presentation is appropriate. The following table gives the details of the appropriate treatments in various situations.

Indicators that the debts are not an asset of the client	*Indicators that a linked presentation will be appropriate*	*Indicators that a separate presentation will be appropriate*
Transfer of debts for a single non-returnable sum.	Some non-returnable amounts received, but seller will get further sums from factor when debtors pay (factor will be able to reclaim some amounts if debtors do not pay).	Cost varies with speed of collection, for example: • adjustment to original amount paid for transfer; and • subsequent transfer amounts adjusted.
No recourse to client for losses.	Either no recourse or such recourse has fixed maximum amount.	Full recourse to client for non-payment by debtors.
Factor is paid all amounts from factored debts. Client has no right to further amounts.	Factor paid only out of amounts collected from factored debts, and seller cannot repurchase debts.	Seller required to repay amounts received from factor on or before a set date, regardless of timing or amounts collected from debtors.

The auditor should consider whether factoring expenses are valid by reviewing the factoring agreement.

Despite the fact that the client may have already received some – if not all – of the funds relating to the debt (as can be seen above), if the factor cannot collect the debt, the client may become ultimately responsible for that debt. So, the issue of recoverability of factored debts is still relevant. It will often be necessary, therefore, for the auditor to consider cash after date on factored debts, to ensure that all potential amounts payable have been accounted for. The validity and existence of the amounts sold to the factors should also be considered since the factor will try to reclaim any sums transferred to the client in respect of non-existent sales, even though there may appear to be no recourse to the client from the agreement.

The following tests should be performed where the factor has recourse to the client for unpaid amounts:

a) obtain a confirmation direct from the factor of the amount drawn down (that is, the borrowings);

b) reconcile the client's sales ledger to the balance of invoices outstanding shown on statements received from the factor; and

c) review statements received from the factor after the year end to identify any unpaid debts returned to the client for collection. These are usually separately identified on the 'borrowings' statement as a reduction in the maximum amount available for draw down.

The auditor needs to be satisfied that the debts are all valid and that cut-off has been correctly applied. Where a client is suffering cash flow problems it is not unheard of for invoices to be raised early, or even for false invoices to be raised. The auditor should be aware of this problem and consider testing the invoices for validity. If the client is found to be raising invoices early, or raising false invoices, the auditor should consider the impact that this will have on any contingent liabilities and also on the client's ability to continue to trade on a going concern basis.

22.3.2 To ensure that correct cut-off has been applied

As already discussed, cut-off should be linked with the work on stock and sales.

The auditor should review sales either side of the year end to ensure that items are included in the correct accounting period. This test should be checked and cross referenced to the details obtained at the stocktake. Ideally, the auditor should ensure that the customer acknowledges the date of delivery. The auditor's source for this test must be the event that triggers the invoice, such as the despatch note, as this is the day the actual sale is made.

If it is likely that debtors could be materially overstated by the omission of credit notes, the auditor should consider undertaking the following tests:

a) selecting details of items from the 'goods returned' records either side of the year end and ensuring that credit notes were issued in the correct period or that equivalent provision for sales returns was included;

b) comparing credit notes after the year end with the supporting evidence, and ensuring that items relating to before the year end were provided for; and

c) reviewing the past history of credit notes and recent sales levels to establish the level of provision that may be necessary.

The auditor should review customer receipts either side of the year end to ensure that they have been included in the correct period.

An analysis of sales by week either side of the year end may highlight sales that have been accounted for in the wrong period.

22.3.3 To ensure that debtors are due at the value recorded and that adequate provision is made for bad or doubtful debts

The basic approach to this area is:

- to review individual old or large debts to assess whether specific provisions are adequate, but not excessive; and
- to estimate the likely provision appropriate for other balances.

The risk of error is likely to be higher with the bad debt provision as it will almost invariably be an estimate. The auditor should consider using more experienced members of staff, or staff with relevant experience of that particular industry, to undertake the audit of this area, particularly where there have been problems in the past.

The best source of data to use for this work is the client's aged debtor analysis. The auditor therefore needs to ensure that this has been prepared properly, as follows:

a) select individual balances and check the analysis with the dates on invoices (the auditor may not need to do this if the customer confirmed specific invoices as part of the circularisation, or checked the allocation of after-date cash to remittance advices); and

b) check the casts and extensions and ensure that the total agrees with the debtors' control account in the nominal ledger.

If the client does not produce an aged analysis, the auditor should ask the client for a list of all debts over a certain age (specify by reference to the client's normal credit collection period).

The auditor should select a sample of items that are either old or significant, and:

- trace subsequent payment. In these circumstances, it would be better to use an aged debtor listing that is current at the time of the audit field work, as this would help to identify those balances that had been paid since the year end and those that had not. The tendency is to use the year-end list and select all items over a certain age (often 90 days), although this would not cover debts that were less than 90 days old at the year end but which have since gone bad; and
- where balances have not been paid, discuss recoverability with client staff.

In addition to the above, the auditor should also consider carrying out the following procedures if the balances have not been paid:

a) reviewing checks on creditworthiness;
b) reviewing customer's most recent financial statements (this could be important for a client with only a few material debtors);
c) comparing balances outstanding with credit limits; and
d) reviewing past payment history, particularly whether the number of days' credit taken appears to be increasing or the customer is making round-sum payments.

Where appropriate and where there are significant amounts outstanding, the auditor should also consider whether any guarantor is able to pay and the value and enforceability of any security held.

The auditor can consider whether the level of provision is adequate by:

a) reviewing the adequacy of any previous provisions;
b) considering the reasons for any changes to the policy for determining the level of provision;
c) inquiring whether any customer has gone into liquidation or bankruptcy since the balance sheet date (this can also be done by reviewing correspondence); and
d) reviewing movements in exchange rates for companies with foreign currency debtors.

22.3.4 To ensure that any bad debt expenses are valid

The auditor should review debts written off in the year, to ensure that these are appropriate and properly authorised.

The auditor should consider whether VAT is recoverable on such debts.

The auditor should review the sales ledger for evidence of debts previously written off and check whether these are written back, where necessary.

22.3.5 To ensure that all debtors are recorded in the balance sheet

This objective will usually be satisfied by understatement testing in sales. Where a risk of understatement has been identified, the auditor should consider direct confirmation of total sales in the period with selected customers.

22.3.6 To ensure that amounts due from group and associated undertakings are properly recorded and receivable

The standard approach to debtors should be applied, but the auditor should bear in mind the following:

a) it is usual to agree inter-company balances with the client and ensure that reconciling items have been dealt with in both companies;

b) the auditor should consider obtaining direct confirmation of balances from the auditors of other group companies (if their audits are not done by the firm);

c) where group companies have different year ends, there is a greater risk that errors may go undetected unless rigorous cut-off is applied to both companies at the same time; and

d) recoverability of debts, particularly for companies with going concern problems or dormant subsidiaries, must be fully considered and documented. This is an issue that is frequently ignored or forgotten.

22.3.7 To ensure that prepayments and other debtors are properly classified, verified and disclosed

The auditor should obtain a list of items included as prepayments and ascertain whether the figures are comparable through analytical review. If prepayments are material, a sample should be selected and the calculation of the prepayment verified.

The auditor should obtain a list of other debtors included within the financial statements. Where other debtors are material, a sample of them should be selected and vouched to supporting documentation as if they were trade debtors.

Where other debtors include amounts outstanding from staff, the auditor should ensure that repayments are being made on the loan in accordance with any agreement.

Within the work on debtors, the auditor should consider the position of the directors. Any loans made to directors should be highlighted, as they may need to be disclosed separately in the financial statements. Note that for periods commencing on or after 6 April 2008, the Companies Act 2006 applies, and the requirement included in the Companies Act 1985 to disclose any transaction or arrangement with the company in which a director had, directly or indirectly, a material interest has been repealed. What has been retained, though, is the Companies Act requirement to disclose loans and other credit transactions where there is a balance or obligation outstanding at the year end.

22.3.8 To ensure that income is not overstated

Many of the tests described above will satisfy this objective, as the majority of the tests are concerned with overstatement. However a further test to satisfy this particular objective is to review credit notes issued after the year end to ensure that sales have not been cancelled in the new period.

22.4 Analytical review

22.4.1 Debtor days

The main ratio to calculate when looking at debtors is debtor days. The formula is:

$$\frac{\text{trade debtors}}{\text{turnover}} \times 365$$

The ratio shows how many days, on average, customers take to pay their debts. Two points to bear in mind when calculating the ratio are:

- that an adjustment should be made for VAT. Otherwise, in most businesses, the auditor will not be comparing like with like. The auditor should either add VAT onto the turnover figure or deduct it from the trade debtors figure; and

- That the turnover figure used in the calculation should relate solely to credit sales – that is, any cash sales should be eliminated.

An increase in the level of debtor days may simply indicate that the customers are not paying up as promptly as previously, perhaps because credit control procedures are not being followed due to staff illness. However, a significant increase in the debtor days figure from one year to the next could also indicate insufficient provision for bad debt.

There may be other justifiable reasons for the figure having increased, so it is important that any explanations given to the auditor are substantiated. If the client has increased the level of activity towards the end of the year, the auditor would expect an increase in the debtor days figure, as sales made in the last month or two may not be due for payment until after the year end, and this would distort the figure.

In such circumstances, it may be worth calculating debtor days using the 'count back' method. This method calculates the length of time it takes for a debt to be settled, thus taking account of any changes in activity levels close to the year end which may otherwise distort the calculation when done on an annual basis. Two examples follow.

Example 1: Alpha Limited

Year end 31 December

	Current	1-30 days overdue	31-60 days overdue	61-90 days overdue	>90 days overdue	Total
Trade debtors (excluding VAT)	£803,000	£642,000	£56,000	£33,000	£19,000	£1,553,000

	December	November	October	September	August	Total annual
Turnover	£810,000	£805,000	£788,000	£802,000	£767,000	£9,600,000

Under the ratio method, debtor days are calculated as:

$(1,553/9,600) \times 365 = 59$ days

Under the count back method, debtor days would be calculated as follows (assuming invoices are raised evenly throughout each month):

$((803/810) \times 15) + ((642/805) \times 45) + ((56/788) \times 75) + ((33/802) \times 105) + ((19/767) \times 135) = 64$ days

Example 2: Beta Limited

Year end 31 December

Beta Limited is identical to Alpha Limited, except that Beta had a very large additional order that was despatched and invoiced in December.

	Current	1-30 days overdue	31-60 days overdue	61-90 days overdue	>90 days overdue	Total
Trade debtors (excluding VAT)	£1,500,000	£642,000	£56,000	£33,000	£19,000	£2,250,000

	December	November	October	September	August	Total annual
Turnover	£1,510,000	£805,000	£788,000	£802,000	£767,000	£10,300,000

Under the ratio method, debtor days are calculated as:

$(2,250/10,300) \times 365 = 80$ days

Under the count back method, debtor days would be calculated as follows (assuming invoices are raised evenly throughout each month):

$$((1,500/1,510) \times 15) + ((642/805) \times 45) + ((56/788) \times 75) + ((33/802) \times 105) + ((19/767) \times 135) = 64 \text{ days}$$

While the count back method can give a 'fairer' picture of the actual ageing of debt, it does have its weaknesses. In these examples, it does not highlight the sudden leap in turnover and debtors in December, which may indicate a cut-off error.

Alternatively, the auditor could extend use of the debtor days ratio calculation to look at debtor days at the end of each month. This could help the auditor to substantiate any explanations given by the client for the increases in the year-end ratio. It should also assist in identifying other fluctuations in sales during the year.

22.4.2 Sales ledger analysis

Undertaking a critical review of individual debtor balances for inconsistencies before detailed testing commences may enable the auditor to reduce sample sizes on the debtors' circularisation or after-date cash tests. Individual sales ledger balances should be compared to previous periods and explanations sought for significant changes.

Some sales ledger systems may enable the auditor to compare debtor balances to levels of activity for particular customers. This is normally possible on computerised systems. Indeed, just as with stock, the auditor may actually be able to calculate debtor days ratios for individual customers. Comparing this information to previous periods may provide some comfort as to the existence of debts and will also give a starting point for consideration of the level of the bad debt provision.

22.4.3 Ageing analysis

Another form of analytical review, which can be used to assess the adequacy of the bad debt provision, is to review the ageing of the debtors as a total. This assumes that the auditor has already checked that the aged analysis prepared by the client is accurate. When compared to previous years, the auditor may be able to draw some preliminary conclusions on whether or not the level of the bad debt provision needs to be increased. If there is an increase in the number of debtors in the '90 days plus' category, perhaps the question of the bad debt provision may need to be examined further.

22.5 Controls

There are specific controls that can potentially be relied upon to reduce testing or to at least provide additional assurance in respect of the validity of the debtors figure. These controls include:

a) the use of credit limits. It is essential to ensure that the business has some form of control over who they sell goods to on credit;

b) restriction on sales if debtors are above the limits. The auditor would need to ensure that sales could not be authorised in these circumstances. This control is only likely to be effective where the credit control department is separate from the sales department, which would make it more difficult for the control to be overridden;

c) the provision of reasonable credit terms, which are adhered to, and also follow-up procedures for debtors who have exceeded the credit terms;

d) the provision of pre-numbered documents and checks on those documents;

e) approval by the credit department of all sales before the goods are actually despatched;

f) prompt billing of all sales; and

g) insurance for overseas debts. This is normally dependent on the client adhering to certain credit control procedures. If debt insurance is to be relied upon when considering the level of the bad debt provision, the auditor should be satisfied that the client has not invalidated the policy by operating lax creditor control procedures.

Where some or all of the above controls exist, the auditor can check to ensure that they are operating effectively and hence may be able to reduce the level of substantive testing to be undertaken. At the very least, the existence of such controls will give the auditor additional audit comfort.

22.6 Common problems

22.6.1 Overauditing of prepayments

Frequently, excessive time is spent either preparing schedules of prepayments or auditing schedules prepared by the client when the actual balance is immaterial. Where the amounts are immaterial, the auditor should be brave enough to compare the current and previous year's figures to ensure that no potentially material balances have been omitted and undertake no further work. The audit work on the expenditure cycle, coupled with analytical review, should enable the auditor to identify any instances of omission of material prepayments that did not exist in the previous year.

22.6.2 Inadequate evidence of consideration of the bad debt provision

Frequently, particularly when dealing with smaller businesses, the auditor relies quite heavily on management representations to determine whether adequate provision has been made for bad or doubtful debts. Sometimes, the auditor will judge that some debts need to be written off, but the managing director or finance director insists that the amount will be paid. It is important to ensure that this issue is looked at objectively and that the auditor does not place too much reliance upon the assurances of the directors. For example, if a debt has been outstanding for the last two years with no movement on it and the client is not openly chasing for payment, the auditor may consider that a provision should be made. Even if this issue has been incorporated within the letter of representation, it is still appropriate to incorporate the amount on the schedule of unadjusted errors. If the item is material, the auditor should consider the impact that it might have on the audit opinion.

22.6.3 Failure to use the aged debtor analysis to its full effect

It is fairly common to see all of the audit work on trade debtors performed on the aged debtor analysis as at the year end when the audit is undertaken five or six months after the year end. If the most up-to-date aged debtor analysis is used, many of the debtors that were outstanding at the year end will have paid already, and this can reduce quite significantly the amount of work required. However, if adopting this approach, it is essential that adequate work is undertaken on the ageing to make sure that it is accurate and that no manipulation of the balances is possible.

22.6.4 Omission of consideration of a material debtor

It is not unusual to see auditors concentrating their efforts purely on trade debtors and prepayments, and ignoring 'other debtors' almost completely. This can be dangerous as 'other debtors' may not only be significant but may also contain items that should be disclosed separately within the financial statements, such as amounts outstanding from directors. The auditor should always obtain direct confirmation of amounts due to or from the company by the individual directors, even where there is a zero balance.

22.6.5 Cut-off work

Cut-off testing is rarely performed well, with reasons such as 'the client's system does not lend itself to cut-off testing' being given as a justification for not attempting the test. Invariably, this is because the auditor has to design a bespoke cut-off test that will satisfy the relevant objective for that particular client. Another frequent problem arises from sales invoices immediately before and after the year end being examined for correct cut-off purely by reference to the date shown on the invoice.

If cut-off is not correctly observed, it will usually be because the actual delivery of the service or goods will not have been invoiced in the correct period. Therefore, as is described above, the cut-off test should start at the point in the system before the invoice, such as the despatch note.

22.6.6 Audit of factored debts

There are two important issues, which are frequently ignored on files. Firstly, consideration of the presentation of the factoring agreement and the disclosure requirements of FRS 5 should be fully documented.

Secondly, for the reasons described above, it is imperative that the auditor gives due consideration to the existence and recoverability of the debts, particularly where the entity may become liable for any bad debts.

22.6.7 Error interpretation

It is not uncommon to see the results section of an after-date cash test saying that, as 70 per cent of the debtors examined have paid since the year-end, therefore the debtors are fairly stated. The other 30 per cent, which could well be material, are ignored. Such an approach should not be adopted unless the residual balance is immaterial.

There are two options. The auditor should either examine a further sample to test the existence of the unpaid debts, and go on to assess if they are recoverable; or should justify the conclusion to the test by showing that a 70 per cent collection rate since the year-end is expected, given the level of debtor days.

22.6.8 Valuation of inter-company debtors

Whilst inter-company balances are usually agreed with the other group company or their auditors, the issue of valuation is often overlooked. The recoverability of an inter-company debtor must be audited as with any other trade debtor.

22.6.9 Too much photocopying or scanning

As noted above (see section 18.6.9), too much copying can get in the way of the audit work and means that the schedules concerned must be initialled, dated and reviewed. Is it really necessary to copy the entire aged analysis of debtors? If this is more than a page long, only the final page should be copied, as this provides evidence of the totals and the version of the report used.

Chapter 23 Bank and cash

23.1 Introduction and definition

This Chapter considers the audit of all bank and cash balances, overdrafts and loans.

Care should be taken in this area because, although it is a relatively simple area to audit, cash and bank balances are the most liquid of the assets and therefore especially vulnerable to misappropriation. The auditor should ensure that the audit procedures minimise the risk of such misappropriation going undetected.

23.2 Objectives

Specific objectives relevant to the audit of bank and cash are:

a) to establish that all bank balances and overdrafts are owned, exist and have been included at the correct amount;

b) to ensure that only genuine items are included in the reconciliations;

c) to ensure that cash balances are genuine and have been included at the correct amount;

d) to ensure that cash sales are not overstated; and

e) to ensure that no window dressing has taken place.

Procedures for fulfilling these objectives are covered in the next section.

23.3 Audit approach

All the tests set out below should be considered when planning the audit to determine those that will most effectively satisfy each of the individual objectives for the client in question. Not all the tests relating to an individual objective need be carried out on each audit.

23.3.1 To establish that all bank balances and overdrafts are owned, exist and have been included at the correct amount

Points (a) to (g) below should be noted in relation to bank letters.

a) A bank letter should always be obtained from each of the banks at which accounts were open at any time during the year. It is important to follow this procedure, even if the client has changed its bank during the year and closed the old accounts. The old bank should still be circularised at the year end in which the accounts were closed.

b) Bank letters should be checked against other audit evidence to ensure that they are consistent. Where there is an inconsistency – either in respect of a balance or other information such as security – the bank should be approached again to confirm the information in the bank letter is correct. If there is an inconsistency, it is frequently the bank letter that needs correction.

c) Bank letters should be sent in accordance with and in the form agreed by the Auditing Practices Board with the British Bankers Association. Details are contained in the recently revised version of Practice Note 16 (December 2007), which also includes examples of the standard letters. Note that the main account number and sort code now need to be provided in order to assist the bank in locating the correct customer's details.

d) The new fast-track facility should only be used in exceptional circumstances where the normal time frame for receiving a response by the bank (one month after the year end) is likely to be inadequate – for example, a company reporting to the USA within one month of the year end.

e) Bank letters should be received by the banks at least one month in advance of the confirmation date.

f) The auditor should obtain or prepare bank reconciliations for all accounts and complete the following audit tests:

- checking the bank balances against the bank statement and bank letter;
- checking the cash book balance against the nominal ledger;
- sample checking on the casting of the reconciliation;
- if it is not undertaken within the profit and loss account audit work, checking a sample of transactions from the bank statements against the cash book, ensuring that all items have been dealt with correctly. This procedure will identify transactions that have passed through the bank but not been recorded in the entity's accounting records. Checking from the cash book to the bank statement for this objective provides little assurance. This test is not required if the auditor has performed the bank reconciliation;
- checking uncleared items against after-date bank statements, noting the dates items cleared. Any item that took longer than expected to clear should be followed up. This is particularly important in respect of outstanding lodgements, where any significant delay in the amounts clearing the bank may be an indication of a teeming and lading fraud. Where the client prepares its own bank reconciliation, the auditor may wish to check unpresented cheques into the new period on a sample basis;
- obtaining explanations for and substantiating all adjustments on the bank reconciliation (Obviously, where accounts preparation work is being undertaken, this will form part of the completion of the reconciliation); and
- testing cut-off by reviewing the paying-in book and cheque stubs to ensure that receipts and payments have been recorded in the correct period.

g) Both SI 2008/409 and SI 2008/410 stipulate that there should be a minimum amount of netting-off; hence, when there are bank balances in credit and debit (overdraft) with the same bank or different banks, the auditor should ensure that netting-off only occurs where there is a formal right of set-off.

23.3.2 To ensure that only genuine items are considered in the reconciliation

The procedures outlined above for auditing the bank reconciliation will normally achieve this objective.

In addition, the procedures applied to ensure that no window dressing has occurred may provide additional assurance.

23.3.3 To ensure that cash balances are genuine and have been included at the correct amount

Where a business receives cash income, the auditor should ensure that unbanked takings before and after the year end have been accounted for in the correct period.

Where a business receives cash income, the auditor should ensure that all unbanked takings at the year end have been promptly banked in the new period.

Where the business has material cash balances, a cash count should be undertaken and the following procedures applied:

a) cash should be counted in the presence of a member of the client's staff, and all cash balances should be counted at the same time. The client should be asked to sign to confirm the amount counted;

b) the auditor should ensure that all cash balances are received at the same time to avoid substitution;

c) the auditor should prepare a list of IOUs and obtain confirmation from the individuals concerned;

d) the auditor should discuss any staff IOUs with the management to ensure that they are properly authorised;

e) the cash balance should be agreed to the nominal ledger;

f) where the count takes place after the year end, the movement should be reconciled with the year-end balance; and

g) explanations should be obtained for any material differences. Often, the best time to undertake a cash count is at the year end when the stocktake is attended.

Certificates from the client should be obtained for all cash balances. This is particularly important where the cash is not counted by the auditor.

23.3.4 To ensure that cash sales are not overstated

The cut-off work and work undertaken on cash sales under the previous objective will also satisfy this audit objective.

23.3.5 To ensure that window dressing has not taken place

The most common methods of window dressing bank balances are:

a) including monies received after the balance sheet date;

b) using bank borrowing facilities immediately before the year end to place monies on deposit, thereby improving liquidity ratios (this may be combined with the transfer of money to other group companies, making it more difficult to detect);

c) sending cheques to creditors before the balance sheet date but not entering them in the cash book until the following period; and/or

d) entering cheques in the cash book before the balance sheet date, but not sending them to creditors until the following period.

The following tests can be undertaken to ensure that no window dressing has occurred:

- the auditor should review material receipts and payments in the final month of the year and for a reasonable period after the year end to assess whether any appear unusual;

- the auditor should investigate delays in banking receipts. This should be part of the bank reconciliation tests; and

- the auditor should investigate delays in the presentation of cheques. Again, this should form part of the bank reconciliation work and might indicate that cheques are being held back.

23.4 Analytical review

Analytical procedures are not usually appropriate for bank and cash balances because the balances are not necessarily predictable. However, a comparison of the balances with the previous period, and also with expectations, may give rise to information in respect of either going concern problems or window dressing.

23.5 Controls

Many of the controls relevant to this section are key to ensuring that cash balances are protected. The controls outlined below are some of the more common controls that may be operated by an entity. The existence of such controls may enable the auditor to reduce the amount of substantive audit procedures undertaken – provided that they are working properly and the auditor has been able to design tests to ensure that they are effective. Even if it is not appropriate to reduce sample sizes, the auditor may obtain additional comfort where the controls do exist.

This is an area where segregation of duties is desirable. As far as possible, the duties of the person writing up the cashbook should be separated from the person responsible for the nominal ledger, making payments or handling receipts and checking the bank reconciliations. In addition, wherever possible, the person who opens the post and logs cheque or cash receipts should not be the person who maintains the cashbook.

The opening of a new bank account should only be possible with the authorisation of the board of directors.

There should be adequate security over blank cheques and under no circumstances should pre-signed cheques be maintained.

Cashbook balances should regularly be reconciled to the nominal ledger control account.

Cheques should be despatched immediately after signature and not returned to the person who prepared them.

A senior member of the client's staff should independently check bank reconciliations.

Cash counts should be undertaken on a regular basis, and without the person in charge of petty cash being aware when they will take place.

Petty cash vouchers should be authorised.

23.6 Common problems

23.6.1 Outstanding lodgements

Frequently, the auditor fails to consider the length of time it takes for outstanding lodgements to clear after the year end. It is not unusual for it to take seven or eight days after the year end for the balance to clear. This may be because the outstanding lodgement is, in actual fact, cash in hand at the end of the year, but this is not addressed.

23.6.2 Cash cut-off

Frequently, the auditor fails to ensure the correct cut-off has been applied in cash businesses. It is not unusual to see a situation where the cash in hand at the end of the year is not merely the float, but also includes the takings from the last day of the year or the previous day. Obviously, this means that there have been cash sales that have been incorporated in the wrong period. The difference is unlikely to be material, but it still should have been considered.

23.6.3 Outstanding cheques

Because it is 'easy to do', the auditor will often check all unpresented cheques into the new period. This can be a time-consuming exercise, and is an area where sampling can be applied.

23.6.4 Bank letters

Audit staff do not always read bank letters fully. Often, details of security, contingent liabilities or directors' personal guarantees are specified, but end up not being disclosed.

23.6.5 Large cash balances

Large cash balances are often not critically examined to see if they 'make sense'. Such amounts may be outstanding lodgements, unanalysed expenditure, or they may indicate a teeming and lading fraud.

Moreover, where there are large cash balances, the auditor often fails to consider whether the balance is adequately insured against loss as a result of a burglary or misappropriation of funds (insured via fidelity insurance).

Chapter 24 Creditors and accruals

24.1 Introduction and definition

This section deals with the audit of creditors, being the amounts outstanding by the entity and accruals, being uninvoiced amounts outstanding for goods and services received.

24.2 Objectives

When considering the audit of creditors, the primary direction of testing is for understatement. By its nature, auditing for understatement is not as straightforward as testing for overstatement, as the auditor is looking for what is not there rather than concentrating their audit work on recorded items.

The specific objectives that should be addressed when considering creditors and accruals are:

a) to ensure that all liabilities exist and are supported by satisfactory independent evidence;

b) to ensure that trade creditors are fully and accurately recorded;

c) to ensure that proper cut-off has been applied;

d) to ensure that all hire purchase and finance leases have been accounted for in accordance with Accounting Standards;

e) to ensure that all material accruals, loans and other creditors have been properly accounted for;

f) to ensure that balances outstanding to group companies have been fully and accurately recorded; and

g) to ensure that expenditure has not been under-recorded.

These objectives are considered in more detail in sections 24.3.1 to 24.3.7.

24.3 Audit procedures

The auditor should select tests appropriate to the client's circumstances from the procedures outlined below. Some of the tests would satisfy more than one objective. Where this is the case, the test is listed under the major objective that it satisfies.

24.3.1 To ensure that all liabilities exist and are supported by satisfactory independent evidence

The auditor should:

a) obtain from the client a list of trade creditor balances, and check against the underlying records, and vice versa;

b) check the list for arithmetical accuracy;

c) compare the list with the previous period and make inquiries into any major variations from the past;

d) look at the major sources of supply of goods and, where appropriate, consider whether the level of the creditor balance is as expected;

e) prepare or obtain a control account, which agrees to the list of creditor balances;

f) obtain explanations for all material adjustments to the creditors' control account; and

g) examine material debit balances and obtain explanations, and ensure that these are correctly treated in the accounts, considering whether it is a simple overpayment, or whether an accrual should be made for an expected invoice.

24.3.2 To ensure that trade creditors have been fully and accurately recorded

The auditor may wish to consider carrying out a creditors' circularisation to confirm the completeness and accuracy of the main supplier balances. A better response is often obtained for this procedure than for a debtors' circularisation. When undertaking this procedure, the auditor should consider the following:

a) the sample should be selected from the activity report of purchases in the year that gives the value of purchase from each supplier in the year, and not the year-end aged purchase ledger. The auditor is interested in the accounts that are expected to have large balances – that is, the main suppliers, not just those accounts that happen to have high balances at the year end;

b) the sample should include a selection of high value and other items, including nil balances;

c) the supplier should be asked to provide details of the amount outstanding; the details incorporated in the ledger should not be given to the supplier; and

d) any differences between the balance confirmed by the supplier and the client's records should be investigated. The reasons for any differences will be the same as those outlined for supplier statement reconciliations below. As this test is more time consuming to undertake than a supplier statement reconciliation, it should usually only be carried out where statements are not available. To this end, the auditor should encourage the client to retain statements.

The principal test in this area is the verification of selected balances by inspection of supplier statements. These can be obtained directly from the suppliers or from the client. It would be sensible to ask the client to retain copies of all such statements in a letter sent before the period end.

As with a creditors' circularisation, the sample for testing should be selected from a source that is most likely to identify all suppliers with whom the client conducts a substantial amount of business. This could take the form of:

a) a list of creditors at the previous balance sheet date;

b) suppliers identified during the latter part of the accounting period as part of the purchases sample;

c) a review of the cash book in the last few months of the year for details of regular suppliers; or

d) a purchase ledger report listing total purchases by supplier.

Differences between the client's records and the supplier statements should be investigated. The auditor would normally expect to find the following items in such reconciliations:

- invoices included on a supplier's statement but not in the client's records. The auditor should check the date of receipt to ensure that the goods were delivered after the year end or that a provision has been made where goods were received before the balance sheet date;

- payments made by the client do not appear on the supplier statement. These will be payments made a week or so before the year end. The payment should therefore appear in the bank reconciliation as an unpresented cheque; and

- purchase returns that do not appear on the supplier statement. These will presumably be returns close to the year end. The auditor should check evidence that the goods have been returned such as despatch records and correspondence) and check that the goods were returned for a valid reason and that there is no dispute by the supplier that might mean that there is still an amount outstanding.

If supplier statements are not available from the client or direct confirmation is not possible, the auditor should consider performing the following alternative procedures, on the balances selected:

- agree the opening balance to last year's file and review movements for reasonableness – that is, ensuring that purchases were valid and that payments were made; and

- review of invoices received and amounts paid after the year end to see if any represent creditors that should have been included (this can be combined with the accruals testing).

24.3.3 To ensure that proper cut-off has been applied

In addition to checking the cut-off details contained within the stock attendance working papers, the auditor should consider undertaking the following procedures:

a) selecting debits to the creditors control account before the year end and reviewing evidence of payments, purchase returns or other supporting documentation;

b) selecting debits to the stock accounts either side of the balance sheet date and ensuring that items were included in the correct period;

c) reviewing post-year end invoices (see final point under section 24.3.2);

d) making management representations; and

e) reviewing payments made by the entity after the year end to identify any creditors not already recorded (but see section 24.6.6).

The auditor should also review transactions recorded in the next period to identify any material purchase returns that have been made and which should be adjusted for within the financial statements.

24.3.4 To ensure that all hire purchase and finance leases have been accounted for in accordance with Accounting Standards

The auditor should:

a) obtain details of all hire purchase contracts and finance leases;

b) examine any new agreements and agree their treatment in the accounts;

c) ensure that any capital balances are carried forward;

d) ensure that the amounts carried forward are correctly classified as due within or after one year;

e) for existing hire purchase contracts, ensure that the correct amount has been charged to the profit and loss account and that the correct balance is carried forward; and

f) include on the summary of unadjusted errors details of any finance leases or hire purchase contracts that have not been capitalised.

24.3.5 To ensure that all material accruals, loans and other creditors have been properly accounted for

Accruals

All *material* accruals (that is, **not** every single accrual) should be vouched to supporting documentation and any calculations checked.

Accruals should be reviewed for completeness by comparing with last year's list and with the auditor's expectations. Notwithstanding the above point, if this procedure identifies accruals that are included on the current year's list but which appear to be too low, they should be vouched to supporting documentation and/or the calculations checked.

The auditor should ensure that the level of any uncharged bank or loan interest is correctly stated.

Taxes

The corporation tax and VAT liability should be agreed to the appropriate sections on the file.

Control accounts should be prepared for PAYE and other deductions, to ensure that the correct provision has been made. The year-end balance should also be vouched to the payment made to HMRC after the year end.

Other creditors

Any other creditors that are material should be vouched to supporting documentation. For example, directors' balances should be confirmed directly with each director concerned.

Where material other creditors have been in existence in the past, but have not been included in the current period, the auditor should ensure that no unrecorded liability exists.

24.3.6 To ensure that balances outstanding to group companies have been fully and accurately recorded

Any inter-company balances should be agreed to the corresponding company's files. Where the firm does not audit some of the companies in a group, confirmation of the balance should be obtained directly from the auditors of those companies.

Any terms of repayment should be reviewed and the auditor should ensure that the liability has been recorded as being payable in the correct period.

24.3.7 To ensure that expenditure has not been under-recorded

The tests outlined above will all serve to help satisfy this particular objective.

24.4 Analytical review

24.4.1 Creditor days

A common ratio calculated as part of a general analysis of creditors is the creditors' settlement days, (or creditor days) ratio. This can be calculated as follows:

$$\frac{(\text{creditors for cost of sales}}{\text{cost of sales})} \times 365$$

The ratio gives the average number of days an entity takes to pay its creditors. However, as with the debtor days ratio, adjustments have to be made to ensure that the treatment of VAT is consistent.

Changes in this ratio are not as straightforward to interpret as those in the debtor days figure. A reduction in creditor days may indicate a potential understatement of creditors, or that creditors are being paid too quickly, which may result in cash flow problems. A significant increase in the ratio may indicate potential solvency problems, as creditors are not being paid as they fall due.

The auditor should discuss the creditor days ratio with the directors, taking particular note of the figure they would expect the business to have.

The client may understate creditors, either deliberately or in error, by recording creditors in a subsequent accounting period. The auditors should review, where available, monthly figures for purchases, payments to creditors and creditor balances. A significant increase in trade creditors after the year end could indicate a potential cut-off problem.

24.4.2 Purchase ledger analysis

A comparison of individual creditor balances with previous accounting periods, and activity reports for that particular client, may enable the auditor to reduce sample sizes for detailed balances. The procedure here is much the same as that described in the chapter on debtors, with any significant changes being explained by the client and then corroborated – for example, a case where the level of purchases has increased significantly for a particular supplier, but there has not been a corresponding increase in the level of the amounts owed to that supplier.

As with trade debtors, computerised purchase ledgers will have a facility for the auditor to review purchasing activity for particular suppliers. Obviously, this can also be referred to when comparing individual creditor balances on a year-on-year basis. The auditor should ensure that the client is asked to retain the necessary reports where these cannot be recreated by the system after the year end.

24.4.3 Accruals

Where the auditor has reviewed payments and invoices after the year end to identify missing accruals, the necessary audit work will already have been done. However, it is still useful to compare the accruals with those expected for the client and with the actual accruals in previous years.

24.5 Controls

Typical controls that may be in operation to ensure that liabilities are fully and accurately recorded include:

a) completion of pre-numbered goods received notes that are then matched to invoices, where unmatched goods received notes would indicate the presence of an unrecorded liability;

b) follow-up of any unmatched goods received notes by an independent individual;

c) independent reconciliation of supplier statements; and

d) retention and review of supplier statement reconciliations.

Where compliance tests indicate that the above controls are operating effectively it may be appropriate to reduce the amount of detailed substantive testing. Even where this is not the case the existence of such controls can provide additional audit comfort.

24.6 Common problems

Common problems that are encountered in the audit of creditors are detailed below in sections 24.6.1 to 24.6.6.

24.6.1 Lack of consideration of understatement

Often, the auditor will only consider the evidence that is provided by the client, rather than looking for missing items. This is most likely to occur where the audit is undertaken away from the client premises. It is absolutely essential that the auditor gives full consideration to the possibility of there being unrecorded liabilities.

24.6.2 Accounting records

Many companies fail to retain all the supplier statements they receive. When checking supplier statement reconciliations, it is quite common for the sample to be selected from the statements that are available rather than from the entire list of creditor balances. Obviously, if the client wished to suppress a liability, it could destroy any supplier statement once it realised that the auditor was going to adopt this approach. When undertaking this test, the auditor should select the sample from the full list of suppliers. If statements are not available, then alternative procedures should be applied – for example, circularising the creditors.

24.6.3 Creditors' circularisation

Many practices do not take adequate advantage of the benefits of supplier circularisation (see above). Where a client is purchasing from fairly large enterprises, they are quite likely respond to circularisation letters. This procedure is often more successful than a debtors' circularisation.

24.6.4 Consideration of differences or reconciling items

Where creditor circularisations are undertaken, the auditor often fails to follow up on differences or reconciling items that have occurred. Some reconciling items require adjustments in the client's accounts, so they should not be simply accepted without any thought as to their effect. Simply accepting that a statement reconciles may result in adjustments not being made or recorded on a schedule of unadjusted items. For example, an invoice on the supplier statement not recorded by the client is not a straightforward reconciling item: if the goods were delivered before the year-end, then the amount should be recognised in the accounts as a purchase and as a creditor.

24.6.5 Checking to see if creditors have been paid

Many auditors waste time by checking that recorded creditors have been paid after the year end, or by vouching recorded creditors to purchase invoices. Neither procedure gives any comfort as to completeness if they are both, in fact, tests for overstatement. The overstatement objective is, in most cases, satisfied by the testing undertaken on the profit and loss account section, so this is a duplication of effort.

24.6.6 Insufficient review of post-year end payments

One test often done is a review of payments made after the year end to identify any unrecorded liabilities. The effectiveness of this test is very reliant on the chosen length of period post-year end to review. Often, the chosen period is only a month, or less, long, and so such a test is unlikely to identify missing liabilities for an entity whose creditor days are significantly longer than this.

Chapter 25 Long-term loans and deferred income

25.1 Introduction and definitions

Long-term loans are those amounts outstanding from the entity which are payable over a period that exceeds one year. It should be noted that the audit procedures in respect of some long-term liabilities have been covered in the previous chapter – for example, liabilities under hire-purchase contracts and finance leases.

Deferred income is income that has been received in advance and has been deferred to a subsequent period. This may be in respect of contracts that straddle the year end or cash paid in advance for future sales. Deferred income should be distinguished from payments received in excess of the value of the work carried out in respect of work in progress. Such payments are not revenue items.

25.2 Objectives

As in the previous chapter, the auditor is considering a credit balance, and therefore the majority of the work undertaken will be checking for understatement. The specific objectives are:

a)   to ensure that all material loans are identified;

b)   to ensure that all material loans are correctly accounted for;

c)   to ensure that all deferred income is identified;

d)   to ensure that deferred income is correctly accounted for; and

e)   to ensure that amounts are shown as being payable at the earliest date that payment can be demanded by the lender. That is, amounts are not shown as due after one year when they are in fact payable within one year.

These objectives are considered in more detail in sections 25.3.1 to 25.3.4.

25.3 Audit procedures

Care should be taken when planning and undertaking the audit in this area. For some companies there will be no amounts due after one year, or the treatment of any loans will be straightforward – for example, bank loans that can be identified through the bank letter. However, the amounts involved are frequently substantial, and it is essential that adequate time is allocated to ensure that nothing is missed.

25.3.1 To ensure that all material loans are identified

The auditor should consider the amounts outstanding at the beginning of the year and whether these loans will still be in existence at the end of the year. Where this is the case, specific verification of the amount outstanding should be undertaken.

The auditor should be aware of the possibility of new financing arrangements being entered into during the period. This should be reviewed when looking at the cash flow within the business and through discussion with the directors.

The auditor should be aware of the possibility of 'off balance sheet finance'. Many of the Accounting Standards and financial reporting standards have been issued to try to ensure that all such liabilities are properly recorded. In addition, the Companies Act 2006 contains a specific provision for non-small companies requiring all off-balance sheet arrangements, where either the risks or the benefits are material, to be disclosed in the accounts. However, it is still possible that the client will fail to comply with all of the above in order to 'hide' liabilities.

25.3.2 To ensure that all material loans are correctly accounted for

The auditor should seek third-party verification for all material loans. This is by far and away the best evidence that can be obtained. The auditor should seek confirmation of the balance outstanding at the balance sheet date, repayments of principal made during the course of the period, and interest paid during the period. The auditor should also ask for confirmation of accrued interest at the balance sheet date, particulars of any security given and of the terms of repayment. It is essential to obtain all this information as it not only ensures that the correct liabilities are recorded in the financial statements but also that there is correct disclosure of such matters as security.

The auditor should review loan agreements and any specific terms, and consider the implications of any breaches of the provisions of the loan. There could be a significant impact if the client has failed to comply with any of the provisions of a loan agreement. Where this has occurred, there should be cross-referencing to the contingent liabilities section to ensure that adequate disclosure is made where necessary.

The auditor should either calculate or check the allocation between long-term and short-term loans. Where the amount is material, an incorrect allocation could have a significant impact on the view given by the financial statements.

25.3.3 To ensure that all material deferred income is identified

The auditor should firstly consider the nature of the client's business and identify whether there is a possibility of any deferred income. Comparison can then be made with the position during the previous period, together with a review of any changes that have occurred during the period. For example, a company may have income paid in advance in respect of contracts that cover a specific period that is different from the year end. A change in the year end would impact on the level of deferred income.

Material receipts during the year should be investigated to assess if there is any unidentified deferred income.

Deferred income should be compared with the previous period to assess if the amounts are comparable.

Explanations should be sought for any significant changes.

The auditor should examine the financing of fixed asset additions to identify any that were purchased using an element of grant finance. If this has occurred, the auditor should ensure that deferred income has been accounted for in accordance with SSAP 4.

25.3.4 To ensure that deferred income is correctly accounted for

The auditor should review the basis for deferring income in the accounts, and ensure that it is valid and has been correctly and consistently applied. This is especially true when auditing charities, as the accounting rules for the recognition and deferral of income are somewhat different to those of commercial companies.

25.4 Analytical review

Analytical review does not play a significant role in confirming long-term loans and deferred income. However, it is important for the auditor to compare the current year with their expectations and with the previous period, to gain additional comfort on the validity of the figures being recorded within the financial statements.

It is also important to review the long-term position of the entity, as this will impact on the auditor's opinion in respect of the going concern of the entity.

25.5 Controls

The auditor should determine which, if any, of the following controls are in place:

a) loans can only be entered into with the full agreement of the board of directors;

b) the terms of loans and significant agreements are minuted and reviewed to ensure that the entity does not breach any conditions imposed on it;

c) regular cash flow forecasts and budgets are prepared to ensure that the financing needs of the entity are known and met; or

d) sales contract terms are regularly reviewed, and income is only recorded in the profit and loss account when earned.

The existence of any or all of the above controls may provide the auditor with additional comfort in this area.

25.6 Common problems

25.6.1 Grant conditions

Many grants have certain conditions attached. If the terms of the grant are not complied with, then the amounts involved may need to be repaid.

The auditor should ensure that any conditions attached to such grants are identified by the client and that the client is complying with them. In cases of non-compliance, the auditor should ensure that the potential penalties are identified and properly accounted for. If the repayment of a grant could cause a going concern problem, then this issue should be fully considered and the results documented.

25.6.2 Terms of repayment

Many bank loans repaid over extended terms of many years are, in fact, often technically repayable on demand. The auditor should always check the terms of all agreements to identify any such loans. Paragraph 6 of Schedule 8 of SI 2008/409 (small companies) and paragraph 9 of Schedule 10 of SI 2008/410 (medium and large companies) both require that loans be treated as falling due on the earliest date that a lender could require repayment if all available options and rights were exercised.

Many auditors consider the reanalysis of credit balances between creditors due within one year and creditors due after more than one year to be insignificant, as such adjustments do not affect the profit and loss account. However, an incorrect analysis can have a material impact on certain ratios, which commonly form part of many banking covenants. If broken, such covenants can result in the withdrawal of banking facilities and the demand for immediate repayment. It is therefore important that such balances are correctly analysed in the accounts.

25.6.3 Loan covenants

Many bank loans and other financial instruments which are not repayable on demand have covenants built into the terms and conditions. Compliance with such covenants is intended to help reassure the lender of the borrower's ability to repay the capital advanced.

Covenants are usually in the form of specific financial criteria that the entity must meet periodically, often quarterly or monthly, but they may also include non-financial criteria as well. The entity will usually make its own report to the lender as to the entity's compliance. Examples of such financial criteria include a minimum current ratio, maximum number of debtor days or minimum profit level. Non-financial criteria may include a requirement to maintain debtor and/or other asset insurance, the sending of regular management accounts to the lender, or taking out 'key man' insurance. Numerous other examples are given in Appendix 6 to AUDIT 4/00 (TECH 29/00) *Firms' reports and duties to lenders*.

Entities which breach covenants are at risk of their banking facilities being withdrawn, as this would normally be viewed as a default on the loan, so compliance with them is an important part of the auditor's assessment of the repayment schedule as well as of going concern.

Problems can arise when:

a)   the auditor does not check whether covenants have been breached in either the current or post-year end periods. When reviewing forecasts or budgets, future compliance with loan covenants should always be considered.

b)   the auditor calculates financial covenants incorrectly and draws an incorrect conclusion as a result. The method for calculating covenant ratios is often defined very precisely in the banking agreement, and may differ from that used by the auditor for analytical procedures. Indeed, the prescribed method of calculating the 'same' ratio can differ both from bank to bank, and between different clients of the same bank.

Matters which can have the knock-on effect of adversely affecting an entity's ability to meet its loan covenants include:

●   a fall in the value of a property;

●   a goodwill impairment charge; and

●   unforeseen increases to stock and debtor provisions.

When covenants are tight, there may be a temptation for management to manipulate the figures in the accounts in order to meet covenants. The impact of audit adjustments, including those which do not affect the profit and loss account, should be considered in this context.

Finally, Bulletin 2008/10 *Going concern issues during the current economic conditions* notes that potential changes in financing arrangements, including critical covenants, may need to be disclosed in the directors' report of medium and large companies.

Chapter 26 Provisions for liabilities and charges, contingent liabilities and financial commitments

26.1 Introduction and definition

This is a more difficult area of the audit, and one that is frequently done badly. On many files, consideration of these matters is left to the last minute and there is often inadequate evidence on the file to show that the issues have been fully considered.

FRS 12 defines a contingent asset/liability as 'a possible asset/obligation that arises from past events and whose existence will be confirmed only by the occurrence of one or more uncertain future events not wholly within the entity's control'. The definition of a contingent liability continues to include obligations that cannot be measured with reasonable certainty or where it is not probable that a transfer of economic benefit will be required.

The requirements of FRS 12 in a simplified form are set out below.

Probability of a transfer or inflow of economic benefit	Liability arising as a result of past events	Assets arising as a result of past events
Virtually certain	Provision required	Recognise asset
Probable	Provision required	Contingent asset
Possible	Contingent liability	No disclosure
Remote	No disclosure	No disclosure

When looking at contingent assets and liabilities, the auditor is considering not only items that need to be recognised or provided for within the financial statements, but also any possible contingent assets or liabilities that have been identified during the course of the audit. Identifying actual assets and liabilities is relatively straightforward. However, ensuring that any possible asset or liability is adequately disclosed within the financial statements is less so.

Financial commitments can include a number of different potential liabilities, such as:

a) contractual obligations to acquire fixed assets;

b) an obligation to buy or sell items outside of the normal activities of the business;

c) an obligation to buy or sell currency or commodities under forward contracts;

d) an obligation under operating leases; and

e) an obligation to provide pensions (Defined benefit pension schemes are considered separately in Chapter 27).

26.2 Audit objectives

The main objective when looking at this area is to identify unrecorded or under-recorded liabilities. This is one of the reasons why provisions and contingencies is a more difficult area to audit. The objective is to identify matters that have not been incorporated within the accounting records and which may not be backed up by any formal paperwork – for example, an invoice.

The specific objectives relevant to the audit of this area are:

a) to ensure that full provision has been made for all liabilities where an entity has a present obligation as a result of a past event.

    It is probable that a transfer of economic benefits will be required to settle the obligation, and a reliable estimate can be made of the amount of the obligation.

b) to ensure that all contingent assets and liabilities have been identified and adequate disclosure made; and

c) to ensurine that capital and other commitments have been properly accounted for.

These objectives are considered in more detail in sections 26.3.1 to 26.3.3.

26.3 Audit procedures

The approach to this area requires the auditor to apply an element of common sense and to be aware of the possibility of provisions, contingencies, etc. when discussing the audit with the client's staff. A review of non-accounting documentation, such as correspondence files, should also be undertaken, and the auditor needs to consider whether this is practicable where the audit is not undertaken at the client premises. It may be that much of the work on this area has to be undertaken on those occasions when the auditor attends the stocktake or, at the final meeting with the client when the accounts are being discussed.

26.3.1 To ensure that full provision has been made for all liabilities where an entity has a present obligation as a result of a past event

The auditor should obtain details of any liabilities and charges and ensure that adequate provision has been made where necessary. This procedure can be applied through a review of correspondence and discussion with the officers and staff of the entity.

The auditor should discuss the subject with the client's staff and directors and review the correspondence files at the client's premises to ascertain details of any other unrecorded liabilities.

Warranty provisions

The auditor should review the client's procedures for determining the amount of any warranty provisions. This is usually done by reference to the client's claims experience in previous years and to the level of sales in the current year. Particular consideration should be given to new product lines and improvements to existing products, as there will be no claims history to review for such products.

The auditor should consider other evidence which might indicate that the warranty provision is either not sufficient or is excessive. This may include:

a) customer correspondence;

b) quality control reports;

c) significant increases in rectification or repair costs; and

d) any increase in the credit period taken by customers (which could be due to dissatisfaction with products).

For products not manufactured by the entity, which acts only as distributor or sales agent, the auditor should consider the extent to which warranty costs can be passed on to the manufacturers.

Deferred tax provisions

These are considered in Chapter 29.

26.3.2 To ensure that all contingent liabilities have been identified and adequate disclosure made

The auditors should obtain or prepare a list of contingent liabilities. This list should be reviewed for any obvious omissions by reviewing:

a)   the previous year's contingent liabilities;

b)   items recorded on the bank certificate;

c)   minutes of board or other management meetings;

d)   correspondence; and

e)   the terms and conditions of any major contracts and agreements.

The list should be discussed with the client to ensure that it is complete and adequate provision has been made for likely losses.

The auditor should consider whether it is appropriate to send a letter to the client's solicitor requesting details of all contingent liabilities noted. This is mandatory under ISA 501 when the auditor considers there to be a risk of material misstatement regarding litigation or claims that have been identified, or when the auditor believes they may exist. The letter, which should be prepared by management and sent by the auditor, should request the entity's solicitor to reply directly to the auditor.

Many solicitors will not respond to a general inquiry, as the Council of the Law Society has advised solicitors that it is unable to recommend them to comply with non-specific requests for information. The letter should therefore be as specific as possible, and should include:

•   a list of litigation and claims;

•   management's assessment of the outcome of the litigation or claim and its estimate of the financial implications, including costs involved; and

•   a request to confirm the reasonableness of management's assessments and provide the auditor with further information if the list is considered to be incomplete or incorrect.

Once a reply is received, it should be reviewed to ensure that adequate provision is made for all items noted.

If the solicitor does not reply, the auditor may meet with the solicitor to discuss the matters and to agree a file note which the auditor would consider as sufficient file evidence to support the treatment in the financial statements.

If the solicitor sends the response directly to the client without sending a copy to the auditor, the auditor should read and make notes of the relevant contents of the letter but generally will not be expected to photocopy it.

If permission to communicate with the solicitor is refused, this would be a limitation on scope and ordinarily lead to a qualified opinion or a disclaimer of opinion.

The auditor should obtain or prepare a schedule of the major insurance policies maintained. This schedule should state the amount insured, the premium payable, the period covered and the date of the last renewal. The schedule can then be used to assess whether the entity is adequately insured. If the auditor identifies an area that is underinsured, this should be highlighted to the client for future consideration. It would not, however, constitute a situation where either disclosure or provision is required within the financial statements, unless there is a possibility of the client suffering loss as a result of being underinsured. The auditor should review the following areas:

a)   the difference between the current replacement value of major assets and the sum insured;

b)   the maximum potential losses under third-party insurance;

c)   the level of employers' liability insurance;

d)   the level of insurance over loss of profits;

e)   the level of insurance for cash; and

f)   the level of insurance for stock holding.

Where there is underinsurance, it is frequently within categories (e) and (f).

The auditor should determine whether the entity has actually complied with all the relevant laws and regulations. The degree of emphasis placed on this test will depend to a large extent on those laws and regulations, and on the information that has been gleaned during the work at the planning stage. The following procedures should be considered:

a)   ask the directors to identify any laws and regulations that are central to the entity's ability to conduct its business. This should have been done during the planning of the audit;

b)   ask the directors whether they are on notice of any possible instances of non-compliance with such laws and regulations;

c)   update the permanent audit file for any changes identified at this stage;

d)   review the correspondence files with any relevant licensing or regulatory authority for any indications of breaches of laws and regulations;

e)   where legislation has been identified as central to an entity's ability to continue trading, the auditor should firstly determine what action, on behalf of the entity could cause a breach. Secondly, the auditor should consider what steps are being taken by the entity to ensure that it complies with all relevant laws and regulations. While it is not necessary to become an expert in the field, the auditor should be satisfied that the client has the requisite knowledge and that there are procedures in place to identify and rectify any instances of non-compliance; and

f)   draft specific representations for inclusion in the letter of representation. These are particularly important where there are specific laws and regulations that are central to the entity's ability to continue trading.

26.3.3 To ensure that capital and other commitments have been properly accounted for

The auditor should review any management minutes and after-date invoices to ensure that all material capital commitments have been identified.

The auditor should obtain details of future commitments under operating leases and ensure that they are correctly disclosed. Time should be spent identifying potential operating leases when undertaking work on the profit and loss account expenditure cycle.

26.4 Analytical review

This is an area that does not really lend itself to analytical review – except in the role of reviewing anything incorporated within the previous year's accounts to ensure that it has been accounted for appropriately in the current year.

26.5 Controls

The auditor should consider what controls are in place to ensure that the entity complies with all relevant laws and regulations. This may well involve ensuring that there is a member of senior management responsible for such compliance, who has a checklist of the relevant laws and regulations to assist in that task.

26.6 Common problems

The following sections (26.6.1 to 26.6.3) summarise some of the common problems encountered in respect of this particular area as a consequence of either underauditing or overauditing.

26.6.1 Compliance with laws and regulations

The major problem area is ensuring that there is full compliance with all relevant laws and regulations. Many auditors have found this difficult to cope with and have simply ignored it! The auditor should focus on those areas where a breach might have a material impact – both financially (such as fines) and more seriously, on going concern.

26.6.2 Operating lease commitments

Frequently, the auditor fails to identify operating leases when preparing the accounts. As a result, the disclosure within the financial statements is not adequate.

Additionally, some audit staff can get confused about the exact nature of the disclosures required. The note should show the total commitment due in the next year, analysed by when the leases to which those commitment relates are due to expire.

26.6.3 Other commitments

Many smaller companies do not maintain formal management minutes, so unless the auditor applies alternative means, such as inquiry of the directors, then this area is not adequately covered. It is essential that such inquiries are made and that they are fully evidenced on the audit file.

Chapter 27 Defined benefit pension schemes

27.1 Introduction and definition

FRS 17 *Retirement benefits* defines a defined benefit scheme as a pension or other retirement benefit scheme other than a defined contribution scheme. Usually, the scheme rules define the benefits independently of the contributions payable, and the benefits are not directly related to the investments of the scheme. The scheme may be funded or unfunded.

The accounting under the FRSSE is now broadly the same as under FRS 17, although the two Standards require different levels of disclosure. Due to the complex nature of the figures, this can be a difficult area to audit, and the numbers involved are often very material to the accounts. As the number of defined benefit schemes continues to decline, audit staff may be relatively unfamiliar with the accounting and auditing principles, and so extra supervision and review of this area may be needed. Practice Note 22 *The Auditors' Consideration of FRS 17 'Retirement Benefits' – Defined Benefit Schemes* contains specific auditing guidance in this area, and its key recommendations are included below.

27.2 Audit objectives

The auditor's objective in relation to FRS 17 is to consider the appropriateness of the steps that the client has taken to ensure the amounts and disclosures included in the financial statements are sufficiently reliable.

As with any other debit balance, the primary audit tests for the scheme assets will be in respect of overstatement, although as noted below in section 27.6.4, completeness of assets is also relevant. The detailed objectives are as follows:

a) to ensure that scheme assets exist at the balance sheet date and are owned by the scheme;

b) to ensure that investments are appropriately valued; and

c) to ensure that all other (non-investment) assets of the scheme are included.

Similarly, the primary audit tests for the scheme liabilities will be in respect of understatement. The specific objectives that should be addressed when considering the scheme liabilities are as follows:

d) to ensure that scheme liabilities are fully and accurately recorded;

e) to ensure that the assumptions underpinning the actuary's calculation of the liabilities are reasonable, and appropriate to the circumstances of the entity; and

f) to ensure correct disclosure of all pension scheme-related assets, liabilities and other information.

The auditor should also ensure the correct disclosure of all pension scheme-related assets, liabilities and transactions, as well as other information as required by either FRS 17 or the FRSSE.

These objectives are considered in more detail in sections 27.3.1 to 27.3.6.

27.3 Audit procedures

Given the source of much of the information used for FRS 17 purposes, much of the auditor's work may involve reliance on other auditors and experts, in particular the actuary. Reference should therefore be made to sections 10.4.3 and 10.4.5 respectively in Part I.

27.3.1 To ensure that scheme assets exist at the balance sheet date and are owned by the scheme

Consider the work of the scheme's investment custodian as a service organisation.

Obtain direct confirmation from the custodian of the investments, and confirm that they are held either in the name of the scheme or as nominee.

27.3.2 To ensure that investments are correctly stated at valuation

Agree the value of the scheme's investments to the investment manager's valuation report.

Agree the valuation of a sample of listed investments to the *Stock Exchange Daily Official List* or *Financial Times*.

The auditor may also consider using the work of the scheme auditor, especially where the entity and scheme have the same year end.

27.3.3 To ensure that all other (non-investment) assets of the scheme are included

Review the latest audited accounts and/or management accounts of the scheme, and identify any assets other than the scheme's investments. Perform additional audit procedures appropriate to the type of asset to ensure these are included where material – for example, for debtor balances refer to Chapter 22; for bank accounts held in the scheme's own name, refer to Chapter 23, etc.

As noted above regarding scheme investments, the auditor may also consider using the work of the scheme auditor.

27.3.4 To ensure that scheme liabilities are fully and accurately recorded

Consider the work of the actuary as an expert.

Obtain a copy of the FRS 17 actuarial report (not the same as the triennial valuation for the scheme's own purposes). In accordance with TECH 02/08 *Actuaries' and auditors' inter-professional communication - Pensions and other post retirement benefits*, this should be requested from the entity's directors or trustees. The auditor should only contact the actuary directly if absolutely necessary, and should first seek the client's permission before doing so.

Discuss with the client their procedures to establish the sufficiency, relevance and reliability of the source data used. If unsatisfactory, the auditor may decide to perform their own procedure – for example, reconciling data such as the number of employees and pensioner members as supplied to the actuary to the scheme records.

27.3.5 To ensure that the assumptions underpinning the actuary's calculation of the liabilities are reasonable and appropriate to the circumstances of the entity

Discuss with the client the main actuarial assumptions for appropriateness, and consider whether they appear reasonable given the auditor's knowledge of the client and the scheme (see also section 27.4 below).

Consider the sensitivity of the calculations to changes in the actuarial assumptions, and assess whether any discrepancies identified above may have a material impact on the surplus or deficit.

27.3.6 To ensure correct disclosure of all pension scheme-related assets, liabilities and other information

Review the completeness and accuracy of the pension scheme disclosures in accordance with the requirements of either FRS 17 or the FRSSE.

27.4 Analytical review

Due to the vagaries of the stock market and property prices, the surplus or deficit on a defined benefit pension scheme can vary dramatically from year to year. However, analytical review techniques can still be extremely useful.

27.4.1 Actuarial assumptions

The first point to note when auditing the actuarial assumptions is that they should be long-term expectations. As such, one would not normally expect them to vary dramatically from year to year, and so comparing the various assumptions against those used in previous years is a good starting point.

Part of the actuary's report will usually contain information about the sensitivity of the results to changes in the assumptions. Although the directors may take the advice of the actuary, it is their responsibility to agree the assumptions to be used for FRS 17 purposes. In order to do this, they should themselves have requested sensitivity data from the actuary, so this information should be available for the auditor to review without having to contact the actuary directly.

While Practice Note 22 makes clear that the auditor is not expected to have the same expertise as the actuary and cannot necessarily challenge the appropriateness and reasonableness of the assumptions, the following analytical procedures may provide additional evidence.

Discount rate

This can be compared to the yield at the entity's year end on an AA-rated Sterling corporate bond, whose term is equivalent to that of the scheme's liabilities. Bond prices and yields can be obtained on the internet. Bond ratings can be obtained from organisations such as Standard and Poor.

Trends and historical rates of return on assets

Many fund managers and insurance companies publish information on long-term trends and forecasts of the rate of return on various types of asset, especially shares.

Future salary increases

These can be compared to historical data of actual pay rises given by the entity, and should be considered in the light of the anticipated level of future inflation (see below) and the directors' intentions.

Future pension increases

Future pension increases are usually laid down in the scheme's trust deed and rules, and are frequently the lower of inflation (usually RPI) and a fixed capped amount (typically, five per cent). Comparison with the long-term expectation of inflation (see below) will indicate whether an inflation figure or the cap should be used.

Mortality rates

Average mortality rates are published on the internet (for example, by the Government Actuarial Department at *www.gad.gov.uk*).

Inflation

Inflation can be assessed by comparing the difference in yield between a long-dated fixed-interest bond and an index-linked gilt with the same term or redemption date. Gilt prices are published in *The Financial Times* and similar publications. Bond prices can be converted into yields using one of the many 'calculators' on the internet.

27.4.2 Assets

Whilst the assets can be vouched to the investment manager's report and may also be substantively tested to third-party price data, it can still be useful to assess whether the asset figure 'makes sense' given the movements in the year on the stock market, property markets, etc. Simple 'proof in total' calculations, taking into account starters, leavers, etc. should provide comfort that the assets are in the right ball park.

27.4.3 Liabilities

Analytical review does not lend itself as well to the scheme liabilities, and it is likely that, having assessed the assumptions, the liabilities as calculated by the actuary will then be relied upon with no further work done, unless the auditor suspects they contain a material error.

27.5 Controls

As far as the entity (usually the employer of the scheme) is concerned, the main controls operating over the FRS 17 process itself are:

- checking the accuracy of the data provided to the actuary;
- reviewing the actuarial assumptions for suitability;
- checking the scheme asset figures for accuracy; and
- performing an overall review of the final FRS 17 figures to ensure they 'make sense'.

27.6 Common problems

27.6.1 Not accounting for the scheme as a defined benefit scheme

It is common for management to claim that, as a participating entity in a multi-employer defined contribution benefit scheme, it is not possible to separately identify the entity's share of the underlying assets and liabilities in the scheme on a consistent and reasonable basis. Auditors should consider whether the directors have taken actuarial advice in coming to this conclusion, as in practice it is often possible for actuaries to be able to separately identify the entity's share of the underlying assets and liabilities in the scheme. The cost of appointing an actuary for FRS 17 purposes, and non-compliance with the requirements of FRS 17 in previous years are irrelevant.

27.6.2 Over-reliance on the work of the actuary

Many auditors seem to think that simply because an actuary has prepared the figures for the FRS 17 accounting and disclosures, this work can be wholly relied upon and so no additional audit work is required.

Nothing could be further from the truth. The use of the actuary should still be assessed in accordance with the guidance given in Chapter 10. Furthermore, while the auditor is not expected to fully understand detailed actuarial calculations, he or she should nevertheless review the appropriateness of the assumptions underpinning the actuary's calculations. Remember that while the actuary may give advice to the directors regarding the assumptions to be used, these are ultimately for the directors to decide.

27.6.3 Underauditing

Many auditors adopt the 'ostrich' approach when it comes to auditing the numbers arising from FRS 17 accounting, often because they don't fully understand the figures provided by the actuary or the principles of FRS 17 accounting. As a result, the figures often remain completely unaudited.

For the majority of clients with a defined benefit pension scheme, the figures arising from FRS 17 may be some of the largest on the balance sheet. So it is vital that the auditor has gathered sufficient appropriate audit evidence to conclude that the figures are not materially misstated.

27.6.4 Ignoring net assets other than the investments

Some schemes may have material net current assets – that is, other net assets beside the investment portfolio. These should also be included in the overall net asset value where material – for example, bank balances not held with by investment manager (and hence excluded from their investment management report).

27.6.5 Overseas schemes

The way pensions and retirement benefits are structured abroad can differ markedly from those in the UK. In particular, they can often be unfunded. This fact does not preclude them from being accounted for as defined benefit schemes if they meet the definition of such a scheme under FRS 17. Extra care should therefore be taken when dealing with overseas subsidiaries to ensure that all such schemes have been identified, accounted for and disclosed correctly.

27.6.6 Incorrect treatment of deferred tax

Deferred tax in the context of defined benefit pension scheme surpluses or deficits is often an afterthought, yet it can represent a substantial figure. For any entity with a defined benefit pension scheme, the issue of deferred tax should be considered at the planning stage, and appropriate tests added to the audit programme, if necessary, to ensure this is properly dealt with.

Chapter 28 Capital, reserves and statutory records

28.1 Introduction and definition

The statutory position of an entity does not often change and, as a result, can be straightforward to audit. The danger is that audit staff personnel expect nothing to change and consequently miss changes when they do occur. It is essential that the auditor considers whether a change has occurred at the start of the planning, which will help to determine the approach that should be taken in this particular area of the audit.

In the most straightforward of cases, a company will only have ordinary share capital and a profit and loss account reserve. However, within this section, all classes of shares should be considered, and there may also be different classifications of reserves. These may include statutory reserves, such as the share premium account or capital redemption reserve. Where such reserves are present, specific audit procedures should be applied to ensure that the statutory regulations have not been overlooked.

28.2 Audit objectives

The following are the relevant objectives when dealing with the audit of this area:

a) to ensure that the statutory records have been properly maintained and are up to date;

b) to ensure that any changes in share capital are supported by appropriate resolutions and are properly reflected in the accounts;

c) to ensure capital instruments have been correctly classified as either liabilities or equity;

d) to ensure that changes in reserves and other statutory information are properly reflected in the accounts; and

e) to ensure that capital, reserves and statutory records comply with the regulations.

These objectives are considered in more detail in sections 28.3.1 to 28.3.5.

28.3 Audit procedures

The following audit procedures should be undertaken when dealing with the audit of share capital and reserves.

28.3.1 To ensure that the statutory records have been properly maintained and are up to date

The auditor should firstly obtain copies of the statutory records for the period. In many private companies this might entail undertaking a company search, as the statutory records are often not up to date. A copy of the annual return submitted to Companies House, which contains details of the information that Companies House has on record, together with information from the directors about any changes that have occurred since the annual return was submitted, will usually suffice.

The auditor should ask whether all necessary documents have been filed, which should include the annual return, share transfer forms, previous periods' accounts, any appropriate resolutions and any details of changes in directors or trustees and secretary.

The auditor should review the minutes of the directors or trustees and ensure that all relevant changes have been correctly minuted. As already observed, assistance may be required in this area as in many small private companies the directors do not hold formal meetings; therefore, very often the statutory records do not actually reflect the information that is required. Although the auditor is not able to act officially as company secretary, he or she is able to assist the client, where needed, in complying with all the necessary requirements in respect of the statutory books and records.

The auditor should ensure that any mortgages and charges created during the year have been entered into the register of mortgages and charges. A company search should also be considered to ensure that all items are properly recorded.

The auditor should ensure that all changes in directors and secretary, and their interests in shares or debentures of the company, have been entered into the relevant register.

The auditor should agree details in the share register to:

a) the accounts;

b) the annual return; and

c) the directors' report.

A schedule for this purpose can be prepared which is carried forward to future years.

The auditor should review the terms within the articles of association and of any loan agreements, and ensure that the company has not exceeded any restrictions on borrowing powers imposed within either of these.

Where a final dividend has been proposed, the auditor should ensure that the accounting treatment is in accordance with FRS 21 (that is, usually non-recognition).

Where a dividend has been paid in the period, the auditor should consider whether the distribution is legal. Where this is not the case, the effect on the audit report should be recorded within the completion section of the file for the partner's attention (refer to Tech 01/08 for detailed guidance on determining realised profits in the context of distributions).

Any changes to the statutory position should be reflected within the permanent audit file.

The auditor should always undertake a full search for a new client, and should consider doing so for an existing client if there are any doubts about what is on file at Companies House.

28.3.2 To ensure that any changes in share capital are supported by appropriate resolutions and are properly reflected in the accounts

Where there have been any changes to the share capital, the auditor should ascertain what the changes are and undertake the following procedures:

a) review the provisions within the memorandum and articles of association and ensure that any authorised level of share capital has not been exceeded;

b) where authorisation of the company to allot shares was required, the auditor should ensure that the appropriate resolution was passed;

c) review the procedures applied when issuing the shares and ensure that these are in accordance with statute and the memorandum and articles of association; and

d) ensure that proper and adequate disclosure has been made within the financial statements.

Where the company has purchased its own shares, the auditor must consider whether this has been dealt with properly.

Where the company has sought to reduce its share capital, the auditor should consider whether the company is able to do this and whether the proper procedures have been followed. The accounting treatment should also be reviewed to determine whether the appropriate capital redemption reserve, etc. has been set up.

28.3.3. To ensure capital instruments have been correctly classified as either liabilities or equity

The auditor should review the accounting treatment and disclosure of capital instruments such as preference shares, and ensure they are appropriately classified as either equity or liabilities in accordance with either FRS 25 or the FRSSE.

28.3.4 To ensure that changes in reserves and other statutory information are properly reflected in the accounts

The auditor should schedule all movements in reserves and ensure that transfers between reserves are correctly treated, authorised and disclosed in the accounts.

Where transfers have been made between reserves, the auditor should ensure that these are allowed – particularly where there is a transfer between a capital and a revenue reserve.

Where an event has occurred during the period that would give rise to a statutory reserve – such as the issue of new capital out of premium or the purchase of a company's own shares – the auditor should consider whether this has been dealt with properly.

28.3.5 To ensure that capital, reserves and statutory records comply with the regulations

In all cases, particularly where there are changes, the auditor should ensure that the Companies Act has been complied with. Areas where this is of particular relevance have been outlined above.

28.4 Analytical review

The statutory section is another area where analytical review procedures will not usually be relevant.

28.5 Controls

There are several controls that may be operating that would minimise the risk of error within this area, including:

a) the use of an external person to deal with company administration;
b) the existence of sufficient authorised and unissued share capital;
c) knowledge of whether or not the directors have authority to allot shares; and
d) the existence of minutes of directors' meeting.

28.6 Common problems

28.6.1 Improper or inappropriate use of the standard audit programme

Frequently, the share capital audit programme is used in situations where it is not necessary. This results in the area being overaudited. As stipulated at the beginning of this section, the first thing that the auditor should do is ascertain whether any changes have occurred during the period. This helps in deciding whether the use of the full audit programme is in fact appropriate.

In addition, where an entity is not incorporated under the Companies Act, the auditor should ensure that the firm has staff with knowledge of the requirements of the relevant Act.

28.6.2 Lack of management minutes

The fact that many small companies do not have formal management meetings means that key decisions are often not recorded. This, in turn, may mean that the statutory records of the company are not kept up to date. It is important to ensure that the company has complied with all of its statutory obligations in terms of the maintenance of the statutory books and records. It should be noted that Section A of ISA 250 *Consideration of laws and regulations in an audit of financial statements* requires the effect on the audit report of any issue of non-compliance with material consequences to be considered.

28.6.3 Failure to update the permanent audit file

The auditor will often forget to ensure that the permanent file has been updated to reflect any changes that have been observed during the audit of this section.

28.6.4 Failure to consider adequately reserves other than the profit and loss account

Where the client has reserves in addition to the profit and loss account, the auditor often fails to consider the terms of the reserve and whether there are any statutory restrictions on its use. Where this is the case, the auditor should ensure that he or she is familiar with the relevant provisions within the Companies Act 2006.

28.6.5 Treatment of preference shares

Despite the fact that the accounting rules changed for accounting periods commencing 1 January 2005, this is still an area that seems to cause problems, either due to a lack of understanding of the accounting principles involved, or due to a lack of knowledge of the issue at all. The key issue in determining whether an instrument is a liability is the existence of a contractual obligation for the issuer to deliver cash or another financial asset. This is in contrast to an equity instrument where any payment is at the discretion of the issuer. Most preference shares will fall to be treated as liabilities, although some may have features of both liabilities and equity and therefore need to be accounted for as compound instruments.

Whatever the result, it is important ensure the issue has been fully considered, and the reasoning behind the treatment is fully documented on the file.

Chapter 29 Taxation

29.1 Introduction and definition

The purpose of this chapter is to deal with the audit of the taxation provision within the financial statements. It examines not only the issue of corporation tax but also that of deferred tax.

This area is very often dealt with badly simply because taxation matters are not always handled entirely by the audit staff. Even within practices that do not have a separate tax department, it is not unusual for the practice to have one person, whether a manager or a partner, who is largely responsible for the preparation and submission of computations and returns to HMRC. Many staff who are, by definition, auditors do not feel comfortable dealing with taxation and therefore tend to pay it little attention. However, it is an area which, if dealt with badly, could lead to significant errors in the financial statements.

29.2 Audit objectives

The specific objectives in respect of the audit of taxation are:

a)   to ensure that the taxation provision is adequate; and

b)   to ensure that deferred taxation is correctly accounted for.

These objectives are considered in more detail in sections 29.3.1 and 29.3.2.

29.3 Audit procedures

The following procedures should be applied when considering the audit of taxation and deferred taxation.

29.3.1 To ensure that the taxation provision is adequate

The auditor should obtain and check draft tax computations. If a member of the audit team is to prepare the computation, the audit principal should ensure that appropriate safeguards are in place to mitigate the resulting independence risks.

The computations should be prepared at a stage when there are unlikely to be further material adjustments to the financial statements.

An analysis of the corporation tax account and a proof of tax or tax reconciliation should be prepared. These serve as a good controls to ensure that the figure in the accounts makes sense.

The completion of a corporation tax computation checklist is something that many people find beneficial, particularly where the client's tax affairs are complex. The specific objective of such a checklist is to ensure that any corporation tax liabilities and/or available losses are correctly reflected in the accounts. The checklist should set out the common points to be considered when preparing corporation tax computations, but will very rarely be exhaustive. Common areas that need to be considered within such a checklist will include:

a)   complex areas;

b)   fixed assets;

c)   chargeable gains;

d) the treatment of losses;

e) identification of associated companies;

f) identification of group companies; and

g) close companies and loans to participators.

Complex areas

The computation should be reviewed to confirm the treatment of more complex areas where the accounting and taxation treatment may be different, or where HMRC will look closely at the items involved. This may include consideration of issues relating to revenue recognition, stock and work in progress, advertising, entertaining, repairs and renewals, leasing, legal and professional fees, bad debts, subscriptions and donations, sundry expenses, formation expenses, management charges, penalties, directors' emoluments, pension contributions, rents, royalties, charges, interest and royalties received, dividends received, dividends paid and interest paid.

Fixed assets

As the treatment of fixed assets often provides one of the biggest timing differences as far as corporation tax is concerned, the checklist should consider whether fixed assets have been treated correctly within the accounts and whether all necessary adjustments in the computations have been made.

Chargeable gains

Where chargeable gains exist, the checklist should identify the major issues that need to be addressed to ensure the computation is materially correct.

Treatment of losses

The checklist should go through the provisions in respect of losses to confirm that losses have been utilised in the most effective way by considering the various possibilities, including group relief where available.

This should also include consideration of repayable tax credits where the company has incurred expenditure on research and development, energy efficient plant and machinery, and land remediation.

Identification of associated companies

To ensure that the correct rate of corporation tax is applied, the checklist should consider whether sufficient audit work has been done to identify all associated companies.

Identification of group companies

To ensure that available reliefs are optimised, the checklist should consider whether sufficient audit work has been done to identify all group companies.

Close companies and loans to participators

The checklist should enable the auditor to identify whether the client is a close company and whether the balance sheet contains any loans made to participators. The adequacy of any section 419 liability and the appropriateness of the accounting treatment can then be considered.

The auditor should ensure that the profit before tax in the tax computations agrees with the draft profit and loss account. Where significant changes are made to the profit in the interim period, the auditor should ensure that the tax computation is amended accordingly.

The auditor should also:

a) agree the closing corporation tax liabilities to the latest computations and the CT600 return;

b) verify the movement on the corporation tax account to the CT600 return;

c) review the proof of tax for unusual items; and

d) check the arithmetical accuracy of the computations.

Personal and managed service companies

There is a common misconception that the personal service company legislation (IR35) only applies to individuals working in the IT sector. In fact, the legislation is not targeted at any particular business sector, and can apply to any business where:

- an individual provides services to a client; and
- the services are provided under arrangements involving an intermediary such as a limited company or partnership; and
- the services are provided in circumstances such that if the contract had been made directly with the client, then the worker would have been treated as an employee of the client.

Similarly, the managed service company (MSC) legislation can apply to a company where:

- its business consists wholly or mainly of providing (directly or indirectly) the services of an individual to other persons;
- payments are made (directly or indirectly) to the individual (or associates of the individual) of an amount equal to the greater part or all of the consideration for the provision of the services;
- the way in which those payments are made would result in the individual (or associates) receiving payments of an amount (net of tax and National Insurance contributions) exceeding that which would be received (net of tax and National Insurance contributions) if every payment in respect of the services were employment income of the individual; and
- a person who carries on a business of promoting or facilitating the use of companies to provide the services of individuals ('an MSC provider') is involved with the company – that is, the person benefits financially on an ongoing basis from the provision of the services of the individuals, influence or control the provision of those services, influence or control the way in which payments to the individuals (or associates of the individuals) are made, influence or control the company's finances or any of its activities (but not merely by virtue of providing legal or accountancy services in a professional capacity), or give or promote an undertaking to make good any tax loss.

Where there is a possibility of the IR35 or MSC legislation applying, the position of the company should be carefully reviewed to determine whether this is the case. If so, the auditor should then seek specialist advice as to how the company's taxation liabilities should be calculated.

Note that, given the audit exemption threshold is now £6.5 million, the number of companies both affected by IR 35 and requiring an audit is not likely to be large.

29.3.2 To ensure that deferred taxation has been correctly accounted for

Under both FRS 19 and the FRSSE, all companies should provide for the full potential liability arising from most types of timing differences. The exceptions are:

a) permanent timing differences;
b) revaluation gains and losses – unless, by the balance sheet date, the entity has entered into a binding agreement to sell the asset and has revalued the asset to the selling price;
c) taxable gains arising on revaluations or sales if it is more likely than not that the gain will be rolled over into a replacement asset; and
d) where the full potential liability is not material.

The auditor should ensure that the provision is calculated at the average tax rates that are expected to apply when the timing differences are expected to reverse, based on tax rates and laws that have been enacted or substantively enacted by the balance sheet date.

29.4 Analytical review

Analytical review procedures should be applied to the corporation tax section to confirm that nothing has been missed. Reviews of the computations and adjustments should give the auditor comfort that the ultimate liability is reasonable. It is essential that the auditor considers the impact on the ultimate provision of all matters identified elsewhere on the audit.

29.5 Controls

For the majority of audit clients, the firm is also likely to prepare the tax computation, so many of the controls in respect of corporation tax will actually be with the firm itself rather than the client. As this represents a potential management threat to the auditor's independence, most of the client's controls over tax and the presence of informed management should already have been considered as part of the firm's acceptance procedures.

The other major control operated by the client in such circumstances should be to ensure that all returns are completed promptly and submitted to HMRC on time. The auditor should also ensure that the company makes any necessary payments by the due date. It should be noted that those companies with profits at or above the upper limit for small companies' marginal relief (currently £1.5 million, as reduced by the number of associated companies) are now required to pay corporation tax by equal quarterly instalments.

Where the client prepares the tax computation, the controls operating may also include:

- regularly updating tax software;
- reviewing tax calculations prepared by either software or another member of staff; and
- checking that the figures used are taken from the final version of the draft accounts.

29.6 Common problems

29.6.1 Inadequate review of the liability

Many problems encountered in the taxation section result from the auditor's unfamiliarity with corporation tax. Often, this area is not completed at all, as the computations may be finalised after the audit report has been signed and the accounts merely include an estimated amount at the audit stage.

29.6.2 Inadequate consideration of deferred taxation

Frequently, there is no evidence on the file to show that the issue of deferred tax has been adequately addressed. Where deferred tax is not provided on the grounds of materiality, there should be a calculation on file demonstrating that this is the case, and the figure should be added to the list of unadjusted misstatements.

Extra care should also be taken where the entity has a defined benefit pension scheme, and deferred tax should not automatically be calculated and deducted from the surplus or deficit. Consideration should be given as to whether the entity:

- has the means to meet any increased contributions to cover a deficit and still be profitable, and hence benefit from a future reduction in corporation tax; and
- can benefit from a scheme surplus by reducing future contributions or by taking a contributions holiday.

Chapter 30 Profit and loss account: income

30.1 Introduction and definition

This section looks at the audit of income from all sources. The majority of this will be in respect of the turnover for the entity.

30.1.1 Impact of Application Note G to FRS and UITF 40

Both Application Note G to FRS and UITF 40 have had a significant impact on the accounting for turnover for certain types of entity, particularly those that provide goods or services under contract to their customers. With the exception of the very early stages of a contract, generally turnover should be recognised as contract activity progresses, resulting in little or no work in progress and earlier recognition of revenue than was previously the case.

Extra care therefore needs to be taken when auditing entities such as cleaning contractors, professional firms, manufacturers making to order (rather than for stock) to ensure that the accounting for turnover is correct.

30.2 Audit objectives

The main objective is to ensure that income from all sources has been fully recorded – that is, that the income for the entity has not been understated. As with the creditors section, this is a difficult area to audit as the auditor is trying to identify items that are not there rather than making sure that everything that is there, should be.

By and large, the issues of overstatement of income will be dealt with by the testing undertaken on the debtors' section. Hence the specific objectives being dealt with in respect of income are:

a)   to ensure that income is not understated and is correctly classified;

b)   to ensure that all income is accounted for in the correct period; and

c)   to ensure that accurate disclosure is given of income by class and/or geographical market, as required by companies legislation and SSAP 25 *Segmental reporting*.

These objectives are considered in more detail in sections 30.3.1 to 30.3.3.

30.2.1 Risk of fraud in revenue recognition

ISA 240 *Auditor's responsibility to consider fraud in an audit* notes that material misstatements due to fraudulent financial reporting often result from either overstatement or understatement of revenues – for example, through premature revenue recognition, fictitious sales or incorrect cut-off. The ISA therefore contains a rebuttable presumption that there are risks of fraud in revenue recognition.

The auditor should therefore consider which aspects of revenue and its recognition may give rise to such risks, and address them accordingly as part of the audit planning and drawing-up of the audit programme for income. Appendix 3 to ISA 240 gives a useful list of example circumstances which may indicate the possibility of fraud, and this could be used at the planning stage.

If the auditor has not identified, in a particular circumstance, revenue recognition as a risk of material misstatement due to fraud, the auditor should document the reasons supporting this conclusion.

30.3 Audit procedures

The auditor should firstly ascertain all the major sources of income, how they are recorded and their respective importance within the accounts. This information should be recorded on the permanent file. The auditor should then check that no changes have been made to the system and that there are no new sources of income.

The key issue here is that the auditor is looking to select a sample from a reciprocal population outside of the accounting system. Completeness of income testing should be undertaken by selecting a sample from the earliest point in the income cycle and ensuring that everything has been fully recorded. Sometimes this will require a little thought, as the client may not have a conventional system where order records and/or goods despatched records are used. The auditor may need to select items from, for example, diaries, time records or any other source that records the beginning of a sales transaction. In addition, in some cases there may be a very distinct linkage between purchases and the ultimate sale, and some work can be done to match these up.

When designing specific tests for this area, the auditor needs to use a little imagination. The following tests are examples of the types of procedures that could be applied.

30.3.1 To ensure that income is not understated and is correctly classified

Where detailed tests are to be used, the auditor should ensure that a sample is selected from the earliest stage in the recording process. Such records need to be complete and independent of the sales recording system. Examples of suitable populations include:

a) **for manufacturing or finished goods** – goods despatched notes, customer orders or cost of sales if the client records individual transfers from stock;

b) **for service industries** – where turnover is effectively time recharged plus overheads, the auditor should consider using time sheets. Alternatively, the auditor could review the contracts files for the client's customers. Where the client receives a commission, select from the cost of the goods being sold and check the calculation of the related commission (for example, for travel agents, calculate cost of commissions due on holidays sold);

c) **for building, civil engineering or large engineering businesses** – consider using debits to work in progress; and

d) **for short-term rental income** – select from the assets generating the income in the first place (but it is often more efficient to use substantive analytical review).

For businesses other than those referred to in (a) to (d) above, the following procedures may be possible:

e) Follow through a sample of purchases during the year to sales or stock. An example of such a business is a car dealership, as each purchase is separately identifiable. Where this can be done, this is an excellent test.

f) For businesses such as newspaper advertising, sales made can be seen by the general public. Testing a sample of such sales through to the invoice and on through the system is another excellent test.

g) For some businesses (such as a filling-station), it may be possible to ascertain the volume of sales of a product by looking at opening stock, closing stock and purchases.

The auditor should consider whether the following types of income could be material in the client's accounts, and the action to take in each case:

- **sales of scrap materials** – use expected levels to predict likely income;

- **by-products** – use production records to establish the nature and volume of by-products and hence the likely income;

- **rental income** – as already noted, use leases;

- **service charge or interest on overdue accounts** – review sale agreements or contracts to see if the client can and does charge interest on late debts. If so, the auditor should estimate the expected effect by reference to the average overdue debts during the year, the client's aged debt analysis and the interest rates used;

- **income from insurance claims** – consider whether any claims have been made or whether any events have occurred which might have resulted in a claim;

- **grants** – select a sample of grant notifications from correspondence files and vouch to actual monies received;

- **donations and Gift Aid (charities only)** – select a sample either from donation covering letters from correspondence files or from a log of post received, and vouch to actual monies received and Gift Aid claims;

- **royalties or other contractual rights** – review any legal agreements governing income;

- **investment income** – link with the testing of investments; and

- **bank interest income** – link with the testing of bank and cash.

Having established the various sources of income, the auditor should select the sample and apply the following tests:

a) vouch details from the source document through to sales invoices;

b) agree invoices through to the day book, nominal ledger, sales ledger or other system for recording debtors; and

c) ensure that the items are being accounted for in the correct period.

Where pre-numbered invoices are used, the auditor should check the sequence and investigate missing items. It is important to remember that this particular test cannot be relied upon to give satisfaction for completeness of income in most situations. There are certain circumstances where it would provide a great deal of assurance, but only where the client has pre-numbered, pre-printed invoices and there is control over the issue of such items. Where this is not the case, the auditor needs to consider if the test is, in fact, worthwhile.

Where the client deals in cash, the auditor should ensure that cash sales are banked regularly and in accordance with the entity's procedures.

Where there are material cash sales, a cash account should be prepared. The auditor should also select a sample of till rolls or sales dockets and vouch them to the supporting documentation. This will involve:

- checking the additions;

- checking the numerical sequence and investigating any missing items;

- checking the pricing;

- considering the level of no sales on till rolls and making sure that this is acceptable; and

- checking the total cash sales to the cash book.

The auditor should review sales returns and, where material, select a sample and vouch them to supporting documentation. If an entity wanted to suppress the level of sales, this could be achieved by cancelling genuine sales. Vouching to supporting documentation will include tests on the following:

a) making sure the details agree to the original invoice;

b) checking the quantity and the description on the credit note to a goods returned note or other documentary proof of receipt of the product;

c) vouching the posting to the sales ledger;

d) vouching the posting via the sales day book to the nominal ledger; and

e) ascertaining the reason for the return and considering whether this is within the entity's policy.

Where any other material source of income has been identified, it should be vouched to supporting documentation to make sure that it is correctly described and fully accounted for.

30.3.2 To ensure that all income is accounted for in the correct period

The auditor should consider whether there are any factors that could result in turnover not being recognised in the correct period, for example:

a)   the date when title to goods passes;

b)   the date that the goods leave the client's premises;

c)   the contract terms;

d)   any special arrangements regarding delivery or payment; and

e)   whether the client has applied a convenient date for cut-off (for example, the last Friday before the year end) and whether this could have a material effect in relation to the current and preceding year's accounts.

Other tests in respect of cut-off will have been undertaken during the balance sheet work on debtors, stock and creditors. The auditor should ensure that this area is adequately covered, but also take care that they do not overaudit.

30.3.3 To ensure that accurate disclosure is given of income by class and/or geographical market

For all companies, the auditor should check the accuracy of the geographical breakdown of turnover where the company supplies geographical markets outside the UK.

For medium and large companies, the auditor should check the accuracy of the market breakdown of turnover where the company supplies substantially different markets.

30.4 Analytical review

30.4.1 Computing an expected turnover

In many cases it is possible to use analytical review by developing an expected turnover figure and comparing it with the actual figures recorded. For most commercial companies, expected sales can be computed based on last year's results, adjusting for known changes such as:

* price increases;
* major customers gained and lost;
* changes in credit policy;
* production figures, adjusted for changes in stock levels;
* new products, discontinued product lines or changes in product mix;
* the number of days in the accounting period;
* customer orders; and
* seasonal variations.

30.4.2 Sales

There are many analytical procedures that can be applied to sales. The only limitations that are imposed on the auditor are the accounting records of the client and the auditor's imagination. Some analytical procedures that can help the auditor satisfy the key audit objective of completeness of income are listed as (a) to (f) below. The auditor may well find that there are other analytical procedures that can be used on a particular client, but these are likely to be variations on (a) to (f).

a)   Compute expected sales of clearly defined units using the unit price and number of units despatched.

b)   Compute expected sales of food or wine using the number of customers and the average amount spent.

c) Compute expected levels of apartment or hotel or other property rental income using the number of rooms or properties; room tariff; annual rent per lease (taking into consideration the average occupancy).

d) Compute expected sales of newspaper advertising using the space taken and prices charged (taking into account discounts for larger adverts and regular orders).

e) Compute expected levels of freight income using the number of containers lifted, geographical destination and the price list.

f) Compute expected levels of fee income in schools using the number of pupils and the fees charged.

30.4.3 Product lines

If the client has a number of different product lines or activities that the turnover figure can be split into, the starting point of the analytical review could be to split the sales into the activity categories. These categories should then be compared with those of previous periods.

Such a review could then be extended, depending on the level of information provided to the auditor by the client's records, to examining the gross profit percentage relating to each individual activity category. This is really an application of the principle that the more disaggregation that can be achieved when conducting analytical procedures, the more reliable the results will be.

Certain activities undertaken by the client may result in increases in turnover. The auditor needs to ascertain whether the reasons given by the client are reasonable and whether or not the turnover figures have changed in line with expectations, given the auditor's knowledge of the business.

30.4.4 Cash sales

With many clients, especially in the retail industry, auditing for completeness of sales can be very difficult at best and, at worst, almost impossible. The auditor may therefore decide that analytical review procedures are the only way to assess completeness of income. However, merely looking at the gross profit percentage from a reasonableness point of view is insufficient. A better test is split the sales figures into monthly or weekly figures. These can then be compared to previous accounting periods to identify where unexpected shortfalls have occurred. Explanations should then be sought and substantiated.

30.4.5 Bank interest

Where bank interest is material, the expected amount of bank interest can be calculated using the average bank balances during the year and published rates of interest.

30.4.6 Budgets and client expectations

The auditor should review the income figures to ensure they are consistent with any budgets or forecasts prepared by the client. Consistency with the auditor's own expectations should also be considered. Any variances should be discussed with the client and explanations obtained and corroborated.

30.4.7 Credit notes

Another useful ratio to examine critically (if possible) is that of the level of credit notes to actual turnover. When compared with previous periods, this will tell the auditor whether or not the client has a potential quality control problem in its goods or services or, potentially, whether or not any unjustified credit notes are being raised. This could raise a question over the client's controls over credit notes and the recoverability of debtors.

30.4.8 Cut-off

If there are concerns about cut-off, a useful test can be to analyse monthly turnover graphically and compare it with previous years. In particular, the monthly trend across the year-end point should be carefully examined.

30.5 Controls

Within the sales system, controls are very important to ensure that all sales are in fact fully recorded. Such types of control would include:

a) pre-printed and controlled sequentially numbered invoices;

b) invoices being raised in a department separate from the sales department;

c) invoices are only raised when the invoicing department is given a valid order or despatch note;

d) goods are only allowed to leave the premises with a valid despatch note;

e) access to the despatch area is restricted to those staff working within the department;

f) there are regular stocktakes to ensure that the records match up with the goods despatched and goods received;

g) periodically, there is a separate check of the goods that have been despatched, to ensure that they tally with the order details and the invoice details;

h) a copy of the despatch note is signed by the customer to confirm delivery;

i) despatch notes are checked independently of invoices;

j) invoice pricing is independently checked and reviewed;

k) customer orders are controlled, and unfulfilled items followed up;

l) any non-routine transactions are controlled and authorised; and

m) any unmatched despatch notes and invoices are followed up independently.

Similar controls may also exist for service companies – for example, review of uninvoiced time from timesheets, etc.

The existence of any of the controls listed above may provide the auditor with additional comfort in respect of completeness of income. The auditor should identify the controls in existence. and design tests to ensure that they are operating effectively before reducing the level of detailed testing.

30.6 Common problems

30.6.1 Failure to understand the client's system

The major problem that applies in the audit of income is that the auditor fails to properly establish the client's system, and so the audit work undertaken does not adequately address the issue of completeness. In many cases, particularly in smaller family-owned businesses, the systems will not be adequate in respect of completeness of income, and the auditor will have to obtain the necessary audit assurance via the specific tests undertaken, and also through obtaining comfort from analytical review procedures. It is virtually impossible to say that in all cases, or even in any case, that the auditor can fully establish that income has been completely recorded, but in most cases sufficient assurance can be found.

30.6.2 Failure to select the sample from the correct population

In many cases the auditor does not ascertain the details of the client's system and ends up performing a completeness of income test, having selected the sample from the wrong population. It is important that the sample is selected from a point outside the accounting system (see section 30.6.1). If the client is seeking to suppress sales, it is unlikely that a sales invoice will be raised. Unrecorded sales will not be found by testing a sample from invoices; which, in such a case, would be a waste of time.

A variation on this theme is where the auditor decides to select the sample from, say orders, but then discovers that the orders are attached to the invoices and filed together, so the auditor selects from the invoice file instead. The auditor is testing to ensure that the details on the order have all been included on the invoice, not whether all orders have resulted in an invoice.

Chapter 31 Profit and loss account: expenditure

31.1 Introduction and definition

This Chapter deals with the general expenses and recording in the profit and loss account. Payroll testing is covered separately in Chapter 32.

31.2 Objectives

Expenses are debit entries within the accounts and hence the main focus of testing is to establish that expenditure has not been over-recorded. The issue of under-recording of the expenses is addressed via the testing undertaken in the creditors' section. The specific objectives relating to this area are:

a) to ensure that expenditure is not overstated, is authorised and correctly classified; and

b) to ensure that all items are processed in the correct period.

These objectives are considered in more detail in sections 31.3.1 and 31.3.2.

31.3 Audit procedures

The following procedures should be applied when considering the audit of expenditure.

31.3.1 To ensure that expenditure is not overstated, is authorised and correctly classified

When testing this objective, the auditor should determine which of the following tests are appropriate for the particular client.

As the auditor is testing for overstatement rather than understatement, the sample should be selected from the last point in the system. Therefore, samples should be selected from debit entries in the nominal ledger. However, where no nominal ledger is maintained, the auditor may wish to select the sample from the purchase day book or cash book. The details should then be vouched to supporting documentation to checking the following:

a)   that payment of the invoice is properly authorised;

b)   that the invoice is correctly classified;

c)   that the invoice is properly addressed;

d)   that the casts and cross-casts on the invoice are correct;

e)   that the entity has taken any discount it is entitled to;

f)   that the details on the invoice have been agreed to goods received notes and orders, where appropriate;

g)   that the item has been paid; and

h)   that the paid cheque, on inspection, is made out to the person, company or entity specified on the invoice; has not been altered; and is signed by an authorised signatory.

The final test outlined above reviews paid cheques, although this test is not always undertaken. Where the owners are the only people who write cheques for payment, the auditor may consider that this test is not necessary. The auditor should consider undertaking the test where someone other than the owner-managers completes cheques and there is no separate control over their despatch.

It is important that the auditor considers whether this test is necessary. Many banks charge quite significant amounts for the return of paid cheques, so if the test does not add additional audit comfort, it should not be undertaken. If the testing of paid cheques is undertaken, it may be appropriate to test a different sample to the one chosen for the main expenditure test. The reason for this is because sampling should normally be undertaken on a random basis, selecting items to cover the whole of the accounting period. However, when undertaking paid cheque tests, it may be necessary for practical reasons to request the bank to provide the paid cheques for a specific period, rather than asking the bank to locate individual items, an exercise that can be very time consuming and hence costly. Before making such a request, the auditor should first ask the bank about its procedures and charges.

Many entities now make the majority of their supplier and other payments by electronic means, such as BACS, using internet or electronic banking, or authorised faxes. Where cheques are not used, test (h) above should be adapted so that the item on the electronic payments summary, on inspection, is made out to the person, company or entity specified on the invoice and is approved by the required number of authorised persons in line with the bank mandate.

For cash expenditure, the auditor should select a sample of cash purchases from the nominal ledger, cash book or petty cash book and vouch it to supporting documentation. This test should only be undertaken if it is not adequately covered within the tests above. The following specific tests need to be undertaken on the sample selected:

- ensure that the invoice is properly authorised;
- ensure that the invoice is correctly classified;
- ensure that the invoice is properly addressed;
- check the casts and cross-casts of the invoices; and
- check details to goods received notes and orders, where appropriate.

For purchase returns, the auditor should select a sample, where the returns are material, and vouch them to the supporting documentation, checking as follows:

- vouching details through to the original invoice;
- agreeing details to credit notes;
- vouching the posting to the purchase ledger; and
- vouching the posting, via the day book, to the nominal ledger.

31.3.2 To ensure that correct cut-off has been applied

This objective will be covered by the work undertaken on the creditors' section, although part of the main test on expenditure is to ensure that invoices have been accounted for in the correct accounting period.

31.4 Analytical review

31.4.1 Overhead comparison

One form of analytical review usually conducted on every audit is comparing the detailed breakdown of the overheads to the comparative figures for previous years. This is probably not just done on audit clients but for all jobs. It is important, however, that it is evidenced on the file that this work has been undertaken.

31.4.2 Ratios

The gross profit margin is probably the most useful ratio to calculate. This can be done annually or monthly, and compared with previous years, the auditor's expectations and the client's budgets or forecasts. Presenting the information graphically can help identify abnormal months or trends.

Although these ratios may not be useful, it is sometimes appropriate to take administrative expenses and distribution costs as percentages of turnover. These ratios can then be compared to previous periods, with fluctuations again being investigated. This could potentially identify incorrect analysis in the profit and loss account.

The auditor should also consider if there are any other relationships between categories of expenditure that could be expected to remain consistent. An example of this might be the relationship between fuel costs and vehicle servicing costs.

31.5 Controls

The following controls may be operating within an expenditure system:

a) purchase invoices can be checked against pre-numbered goods received notes, which in turn are checked against authorised orders;

b) invoices should be marked when they are being paid, to prevent them being re-entered into the system;

c) cheques should be sent to suppliers by the person signing the cheque and not by the person completing the cheque details;

d) invoices should be reviewed and authorised before payment; and

e) petty cash expenditure should be properly authorised.

The existence of some or all of the above controls within the system may, if the compliance tests indicate that they are working properly, encourage the auditor to reduce the amount of detailed substantive testing. In any case, the existence of these controls can provide additional audit comfort.

31.6 Common problems

31.6.1 Overauditing

The expenditure side of the audit is one that is normally done quite well, in many cases too well! The auditor should be aware of the risk of doing too much in this area.

31.6.2 Weak analytical review

Many firms rely heavily on analytical review when auditing expenditure. Analytical procedures can be highly effective in giving good quality audit evidence, but only when undertaken correctly. All too often an expense is dubbed 'reasonable' because it approximates to the value the previous year, with no thought being given as to whether it matches the expected figure. The auditor's expectations should be set before expenses are reviewed, and any significant unexpected variances should be followed up and the explanations corroborated.

31.6.3 Risk from electronic payments

Sometimes the cheque signatories will also be those authorised to approve bank transfers, but they may not be exactly the same group of persons with the same authority levels. A common scenario in many businesses is the anomalous situation where two directors must sign all cheques (often for even small amounts), and yet the financial controller or accountant can autonomously authorise substantial payments by BACS via online banking. It is also not uncommon to see banking password labels for BACS fax headers filed insecurely.

With the rise in the use of electronic banking in recent years, large sums of money may be transferred simply and quickly, yet the controls and risks over payments considered by the auditor are often limited to invoice approval and cheque signatories.

Profit and loss account: expenditure

With the rise in the use of electronic banking in recent years, large sums of money may be transferred simply and quickly, yet the controls and risks over payments considered by the auditor are often limited to invoice approval and cheque signatories.

Chapter 32 Profit and loss account: wages, salaries and other remuneration

32.1 Introduction and definition

Wages and salaries expenditure is often the second most substantial expenditure item after trade purchases, while in the case of a service organisation, it is usually the largest. It is also an area that is frequently either overaudited or underaudited, so it is important that the testing is properly planned.

A related area that has become increasingly complicated in recent years is that of share-based payment. Since the introduction of FRS 20, this has been an area with which auditors struggle. Many auditors will only rarely encounter share-based payment, and so a lack of knowledge and experience may compound the difficulties.

32.2 Audit objectives

The salaries or wages charge is a debit balance and therefore the auditor should ensure that this has not been overstated. The specific objectives in respect of wages and salaries are:

a)   to ensure that wages costs are not overstated in the financial statements;

b)   to ensure that all paid employees exist and work for the entity;

c)   to ensure that payroll costs are accurately stated;

d)   to ensure that specific regulations relating to PAYE and National Insurance have been fully complied with; and

e)   to ensure that amounts related to share-based payment are properly accounted for and disclosed appropriately.

These objectives are considered in more detail in sections 32.3.1 to 32.3.5.

32.3 Audit procedures

The auditor should select tests from the examples set out below to gain comfort that the objectives have been satisfied.

32.3.1 To ensure that wages costs are not overstated in the financial statements

If the number of employees is small, a list of employees and directors with their gross pay can be prepared from the payroll records or P11s. Where the total can be reconciled to staff costs in the accounts, this may be the only test required.

The auditor should prepare or obtain a summary of wages and salaries, giving details of the wages and salaries and the number of employees month by month or week by week, and obtain explanations for and verify any material fluctuations from expectations.

The auditor should select a sample of payrolls and undertake the following testing:

a)   check the casts and cross-casts;

b) check the posting on the nominal ledger;

c) check the total net to the cashbook;

d) ensure the payroll is authorised by a responsible individual; and

e) ensure that PAYE and National Insurance contributions (NICs) are properly accounted for.

32.3.2 To ensure that all paid employees exist and work for the entity

The auditor should select a sample of payments being made and agree the details back to the personnel records or another independent source outside of the wages department. In certain circumstances, the auditor may feel it is appropriate to physically verify the existence of a sample of the employees.

For any starters selected in the main sample, the auditor should ensure that wages have only been paid from the actual starting date.

For any leavers in the main sample, the auditor should ensure that wages were only paid up to the date of leaving.

The auditor should make inquiries in to any unclaimed wages and verify their reasonableness.

32.3.3 To ensure that the payroll costs are accurately stated

The auditor should re-perform the wages calculations for a sample of employees (including starters and leavers) by performing the following tests (the same sample can be used for this test as for the test set out above). The test should check:

a) that employee details agree to the personnel records;

b) that the rates of pay are authorised;

c) that the tax codes agree to HMRC coding notifications;

d) that proper authorisation has been obtained for any deductions other than tax and employees' NICs;

e) where applicable, hours against time records;

f) where applicable, production against piecework records;

g) that all overtime has been authorised; and

h) the calculation of gross pay, taxation, employees' NICs, employer's NICs, employer's and employees' pension contributions and net pay.

32.3.4 To ensure that specific regulations relating to PAYE and National Insurance have been fully complied with

In certain circumstances the auditor may wish to complete checklists to help ensure that there have been no PAYE/NI compliance problems. This is particularly important where there is a large number of people on the payroll and/or a high percentage of casual employees. It should be remembered that there could be substantial penalties levied if the entity is not complying properly with all the relevant rules and regulations. In particular, the auditor should carry out the following specific tasks:

a) look carefully at directors' emoluments paid and payable, including benefits in kind, to ensure that they have been accounted for correctly and full payment has been made for any liability in respect of PAYE and NICs;

b) check the system for ensuring that all relevant forms have been completed and submitted to HMRC on time;

c) review P11Ds and P9Ds to ensure that there are no apparent omissions and that any dispensations claimed are still valid;

d) consider whether there is evidence to show that the PAYE and National Insurance regulations have been correctly applied for all employees;

e) ensure that PAYE and National Insurance have been applied in all relevant cases, including payment to casual employees, part-time employees, honorariums, commissions, etc. In fact, where any of these categories are relevant, particular care needs to be taken to ensure that the client has complied with all of the requirements;

f) where the entity uses self-employed individuals on a regular basis, consider whether these people should be classified as employees of the entity; and

g) where the entity falls within the scope of the IR 35 legislation, consider the affect of this on the operation and administration of the entity. (A brief explanation of IR 35 is given in Chapter 29.)

32.3.5 To ensure that amounts related to share-based payment are properly accounted for and disclosed appropriately

The auditor should undertake the following tasks.

a) Confirm that an expense has been recognised in the profit and loss account where the entity has entered into any share based payment transactions.

b) For equity-settled share-based payment transactions, ensure the entity has measured the goods or services received and the corresponding increase in equity either:

- at the fair value of those goods or services; or

- if the fair value of the goods or services received cannot be reliably estimated, then by the corresponding increase in equity, indirectly, by reference to the fair value of the equity instruments granted.

c) Ensure that any vesting conditions (for example, length of service or performance targets) are taken into account, by adjusting the number of equity instruments included in the measurement of the transaction amount, by using the best available estimate of the number of equity instruments expected to vest.

d) For cash-settled share-based payment transactions, ensure that the entity has measured the goods or services acquired and the liability incurred at the fair value of the liability.

e) For share-based payment transactions where the terms of the arrangement provide either the entity or the counterparty with a choice of settlement method, ensure that the transaction, or the components of that transaction, have been accounted for as either:

- a cash-settled share-based payment transaction if, and to the extent that, the company has incurred a liability to settle in cash or other assets; or

- an equity-settled share-based payment transaction if, and to the extent that, no such liability has been incurred.

f) Where the accounting for share-based payment transactions that include the client's estimates of the number of equity instruments expected to vest, or other issues, ensure that these opinions are confirmed in the letter of representation.

32.4 Analytical review

32.4.1 Overall review

Analytical review can provide some very solid audit evidence regarding salaries and wages. The following procedures should be applied:

a) The auditor needs to complete a weekly or monthly wages analysis, giving the details of the gross wages, deductions, net wages and employer's National Insurance contributions. The list should also include the average number of employees and their average wage.

b) The auditor should then ascertain details of pay increases, changes in PAYE and National Insurance etc. and determine whether the wages and salaries have behaved in the way that they would expect.

c) Where there is both a weekly and a monthly payroll or the payroll is split into departments, the auditor may be able to obtain better evidence by looking at these separately.

There are limitations on adopting this approach – in particular, that in many smaller businesses, where the wages are not split by department or function, calculations such as average wages may be meaningless. However, where the figures are meaningful, the auditor – on achieving good results from this test – could cut down the amount of detailed testing to be undertaken.

An alternative approach is a wages 'proof in total' calculation, which starts with the previous year's wages and salaries, and seeks to predict this year's figure by adjusting for starters, leavers, pay rises, etc. It may be worth excluding directors' emoluments and any large one-off bonuses as these might skew the calculation.

32.4.2 Ratios

The ratio of **employer's NICs: wages and salaries** can be useful when compared with previous years. Unless the proportion of employees earning above the upper earnings limit changes significantly, or the rates of National Insurance change, this ratio should remain fairly constant year on year.

Similarly, the ratio of **employer's pension costs : wages and salaries** can also be useful for entities with defined contribution pension schemes with a steady contribution rate by the employer.

32.4.3 Relationship with other expenses

The auditor should consider whether there is a valid connection between the wages and salaries expenditure and other items in the profit and loss account, which can be reviewed. For example, in service industries there will usually be a strong correlation between wages to professional or technical staff and income, similarly there may be a strong connection between these wages and those paid to the administrative staff. Where this is the case, the auditor should calculate the relevant ratios and obtain explanations for any variances from expectations.

32.5 Controls

The following controls, if in place, will help to provide audit assurance in this area:

a) the payroll should be independently approved for accuracy;

b) proper personnel records should be kept by an independent department;

c) the payroll department should maintain a written record of notification of changes in rates of pay, etc.; and

d) calculations should be checked by an independent individual, particularly in respect of staff working within the payroll department.

The existence of the above controls, if working properly, could enable the auditor to cut down on the level of detailed substantive testing. This is most likely to be the case where the auditor has been able to undertake a successful analytical review.

32.6 Common problems

32.6.1 Failure to check wages calculations

The major problem that occurs in this area is the auditor's failure to check the calculation of individual wages and salaries when the entity undertakes the work. This is a particularly important test at a time when rates and bands of tax are changing, which could easily result in there being payroll errors (for example, if the entity does not update its software properly for changes).

32.6.2 Failure to consider compliance with the PAYE and National Insurance regulations

Another common problem is the failure to consider whether the PAYE and National Insurance procedures are being correctly applied, and, where any problems have been encountered, failure to properly notify the client and deal adequately with the problems. It is particularly important to remember that where the system is not being applied correctly, this will have an ongoing impact. Although an error may not be material in the year in question, cumulatively (and once fines and penalties are added) it could easily result in there being material error within the financial statements.

Where such errors have been identified, the auditor must ensure that any necessary provision is included within the financial statements, and that the client is informed of the action required in order to rectify the situation.

32.6.3 Share-based payment

The accounting for share based-payment can be complicated, and as it arises relatively rarely, many auditors struggle with it. However, the numbers involved can be very material, so it is important that the auditor seeks suitable technical advice if necessary.

Chapter 33 Profit and loss account: other

33.1 Introduction and definition

This Chapter deals with a number of sundry matters that have not been covered elsewhere. For example, ensuring that the entity is maintaining proper (for periods commencing before 6 April 2008) or adequate (for periods commencing on or after 6 April 2008) books and records and, in particular, making sure that certain items that have to be incorporated within the financial statements are properly identified and audited where necessary.

33.2 Audit objectives

The specific objectives for this area are:

a) to ensure that the nominal ledger is correctly maintained;

b) to ensure that foreign currency transactions are correctly dealt with; and

c) to ensure that other profit and loss-related disclosures have been made in the financial statements.

These objectives are considered in detail in the next section.

33.3 Audit procedures

33.3.1 To ensure that the nominal ledger is correctly maintained

The auditor should check the accuracy of the information contained within the accounting records by completing the following tests:

a) checking opening balances to the ledgers;

b) checking the casts and cross-casts of the cashbook, sales day book and purchase day book;

c) checking the casts of a sample of the nominal ledger accounts;

d) checking postings to the nominal ledger;

e) checking the extraction of the final trial balance;

f) checking the casts of the trial balance;

g) ensuring that all adjustments to the accounts and journals and transfers are recorded in the books of the entity; and

h) agreeing the closing balances to the accounts.

It should be noted that ISA 330 *The auditor's procedures in response to assessed risks* requires the auditor to agree or reconcile the financial statements with the underlying accounting records and to examine material journal entries and other adjustments made during the course of preparing the financial statements.

33.3.2 To ensure that foreign currency transactions are correctly dealt with

Where the entity deals in foreign currencies, the auditor should ensure that the translation has been undertaken properly. This is particularly important where the sums of money involved are substantial and any exchange differences could result in material adjustments to the figures in the financial statements. The auditor should undertake the following tests:

a) ascertain the accounting policy for foreign currency translation and ensure that the method has been applied consistently and accurately;

b) ascertain that the method used for translating foreign currency transactions is acceptable within SSAP 20 *Foreign currency translation* (or FRS 23 *The effects of changes in foreign exchange rates if the entity is applying FRS 26 Financial instruments: Recognition and measurement*); and

c) check that the rates of exchange used agree to those of a source document (for example, the financial press or the internet).

33.3.3 To ensure that other profit and loss-related disclosures have been made in the financial statements

The auditor should check that the following disclosures have been correctly made in the financial statements (where applicable) and that the figures agree with the trial balance:

a) auditor's fees for audit (all entities) and non-audit (large entities only) services, including expenses and any benefits in kind; and

b) operating lease rentals, analysed between 'hire of plant and machinery' and 'other'.

33.4 Analytical review

Analytical review can be used to ascertain whether the records, as far as possible, are complete and accurate. Comparison with expectations and the previous year's results will help with this.

33.5 Controls

The major controls that may apply here will be to ensure that:

- the ledgers are properly and regularly updated;
- all adjustments to the ledgers are properly authorised; and
- a review of the records is undertaken by a responsible official.

33.6 Common problems

33.6.1 Failure to check the accuracy of computer-generated information

There is a tendency for the auditor to believe that anything that has been calculated by a computer must be right. However, there is still a need to check the extraction of balances and arithmetical accuracy of lists to ensure that the auditor is dealing with complete information. Since many accounting packages can now export information into spreadsheet format, this check may not be the onerous task it once was.

33.6.2 Incorrect accounting for foreign currencies

Many clients find this a difficult area of accounting and, as such, the risk of errors arising can be high. This is often exacerbated by the auditor's failure to properly document and understand the client's accounting systems and procedures in respect of foreign currency transactions. As a result, systematic accounting errors may go overlooked. A walkthrough test of a foreign currency sale and/or purchase can highlight such problems.

33.6.3 Inadequate disclosure of auditor's fees

It is common to find inadequate disclosure of auditor's fees in large entity accounts, where the disclosures required are far more detailed and extensive than those for small and medium entities. Auditors of such entities should ensure the relevant section of the disclosure checklist is properly completed, and should refer directly to TECH 06/06 *Disclosure of auditor remuneration* for detailed guidance on the level of disclosures necessary.

Chapter 34 Related party transactions

34.1 Introduction and definition

This Chapter deals with related party transactions. These are defined by FRS 8 (Revised December 2008) as 'the transfer of assets or liabilities or the performance of services by, to or for a related party irrespective of whether a price is charged.' FRS 8 (Revised) gives a more specific definition of a related party than was the case under the old FRS 8, which is that a party is related to an entity if:

a) directly, or indirectly through one or more intermediaries, the party:

   • controls, is controlled by, or is under common control with, the entity (this includes parents, subsidiaries and fellow subsidiaries);

   • has an interest in the entity that gives it significant influence over the entity; or

   • has joint control over the entity;

b) the party is an associate (as defined in FRS 9 *Associates and joint ventures*) of the entity;

c) the party is a joint venture in which the entity is a venturer (as defined in FRS 9);

d) the party is a member of the key management personnel of the entity or its parent;

e) the party is a close member of the family of any individual referred to in subparagraph (a) or (d);

f) the party is an entity that is controlled, jointly controlled or significantly influenced by, or for which significant voting power in such entity resides, directly or indirectly, with any individual referred to in (d) or (e); and

g) the party is a retirement benefit scheme for the benefit of employees of the entity, or of any entity that is a related party of the entity.

All accounts require disclosure of related party transactions, in order to draw users' attention to the possibility that the reported financial position and results may have been affected by the existence of material transactions with related parties.

The level of disclosure required is the same, irrespective of whether FRS 8 or the FRSSE is being followed, but the scope of the two standards is different. Where the related party is a director, key employee, close family member or an entity controlled by such an individual, FRS 8 requires materiality to be judged in relation to the related party as well as to the reporting entity. This is not required by the FRSSE, so the relevant level of materiality is likely to be higher in respect of a small entity adopting the FRSSE.

However, regardless of whether or not the FRSSE is being adopted, for periods commencing before 6 April 2008, the Companies Act 1985 requires disclosure of any transaction or arrangement with the company in which a director had, directly or indirectly, a material interest. Although 'material interest' is not defined by the Act, GAAP suggests two tests to interpret it. The first test of materiality is whether disclosure of the transaction is likely to be of relevance to shareholders or creditors. The second test is whether the director's interest in the transaction is substantial.

For periods commencing on or after 6 April 2008, the Companies Act 2006 applies, and the requirement to disclose any transaction or arrangement with the company in which a director had, directly or indirectly, a material interest has been repealed. The Companies Act requirement to disclose loans and other credit transactions where there is a balance or obligation outstanding at the year end has been retained though. Apart from this, only transactions that are material to the company or material to the individual (if the FRSSE is not applied) will need to be disclosed and audited.

It should also be noted that the exemption from disclosure for 90 per cent owned subsidiaries has been removed from the revised FRS 8 (due to a legislative change) for accounting periods beginning on or after 6 April 2008. In future, this exemption will therefore only apply to wholly owned subsidiaries.

34.2 Audit objectives

The specific objectives for this area are:

a)   to ensure that related party transactions are all identified; and

b)   to ensure that related party transactions are adequately disclosed.

These objectives are considered in detail in the next section.

34.3 Audit procedures

34.3.1 To ensure that related party transactions are all identified

This can be a difficult and sensitive area and it is important to ensure that it has been adequately addressed. The auditor should apply the following procedures:

a)   first establish whether there are any individuals (in addition to the directors) or any other entities which should be treated as related parties. A record of these should be maintained within the permanent audit file. This information should be ascertained at the very start of the audit. The individual performing the analysis needs to be aware of specific related parties, so that any relevant transactions can be identified and recorded during the accounts preparation;

b)   inquire of the directors whether the entity has entered into any transactions in which any of those related parties has an interest;

c)   review any details provided for completeness by reviewing minutes, accounting records, correspondence and any other items of interest; and

d)   obtain written confirmation in the letter of representation that the information provided regarding related party and control disclosures is complete.

34.3.2 To ensure related party transactions are adequately disclosed

The auditor should:

●   consider whether any such transactions have been disclosed properly in the accounts; and

●   obtain written confirmation in the letter of representation that disclosures of related party transactions and control are accurate.

34.4 Analytical review

Analytical review can be used to add comfort that all related parties have been identified. Comparison of the information provided by the directors with previous years' disclosures will help with this.

34.5 Controls

For most private companies, there are unlikely to be many controls which apply in this area. One of the main sources of information for related party transactions is board minutes, which highlights the importance of maintaining minutes that are signed on behalf of the board as being an accurate record of meetings.

34.6 Common problems

34.6.1 Failure to obtain details of related party transactions

Many auditors are still failing to ensure that the staff undertaking the detailed work are fully aware of the types of issues that require disclosure. It is essential that all staff are fully briefed on the need to disclose related party transactions at the beginning of the assignment, and that they review the list of known related parties on the permanent file, so as to be able to identify such matters during the course of the rest of the audit. If the audit team is aware of this at the start of the assignment, it reduces the risk of disclosures being missed.

34.6.2 Incorrect treatment of transactions 'in the normal course of business' or 'at arm's length'

A common risk attached to related party transactions is that the directors may not wish to disclose certain transactions due to their sensitive nature, or because they were motivated by something outside ordinary business considerations. It is not relevant whether or not a transaction was in the ordinary course of business; disclosure is still required if it is judged to be material.

Chapter 35 Subsequent events and going concern

35.1 Introduction and definition

FRS 21 *Events after the balance sheet date* defines events after the balance sheet date as 'those events, both favourable and unfavourable, that occur between the balance sheet date and the date when the financial statements are approved for issue', and goes on to identify both adjusting events (that is, those that warrant an adjustment to the financial statements), and non-adjusting events (namely, those which may need disclosure within the financial statements but will not result in an actual adjustment).

Adjusting events

Adjusting events would include such items as:

a) the valuation of an asset that provides evidence of impairment;

b) the receipt of money in respect of stock or work in progress, which would suggest that the net realisable value is less than the cost incorporated within the valuation in the financial statements;

c) the insolvency of a debtor shortly after the balance sheet date;

d) the settlement of a court case that confirms that the entity had a present obligation at the balance sheet date; and

e) the discovery of fraud or errors that shows that the financial statements are incorrect.

Non-adjusting events

The following items are examples of non-adjusting events:

a) a merger or an acquisition;

b) the issue of new shares or debentures;

c) purchases and sales of fixed assets and investments (although if the plan was to make the sale prior to the year end, then the auditor needs to consider whether such assets should be fairly incorporated as fixed assets or should be moved to current assets);

d) opening a new trading activity;

e) renegotiating the repayment terms of debt or entering into a CVA;

f) losses of fixed assets as a result of a catastrophe, for example, through a fire or a flood; and

g) the decline in market value of investments.

Neither of the above lists is definitive but they provide examples of the types of issues that need to be considered.

Note that final proposed dividends declared after the year end should not be adjusted for (accrued) in the financial statements.

In addition to considering these potential subsequent events within this section, the issue of going concern is also addressed.

35.2 Audit objectives

There are two major audit objectives when considering the issue of subsequent events and going concern. They are:

a)   to ensure that all material adjusting and non-adjusting subsequent events are identified and correctly treated in the accounts; and

b)   to ensure that the going concern basis of accounting is appropriate.

●   These objectives are considered in detail in the next section.

35.3 Audit procedures

The procedures undertaken during a subsequent events review require review and inquiry in respect of events that have occurred since the balance sheet date.

The initial subsequent events review should be one of the last exercises undertaken during the audit fieldwork. If there is a delay between the fieldwork being completed, the accounts being approved and the audit report being signed, a further subsequent events review should be undertaken to ensure that nothing has occurred during the intervening period that would result in adjustments or disclosures being necessary.

35.3.1 To ensure that all material adjusting and non-adjusting subsequent events are identified and correctly treated in the accounts

The auditor should undertake following work:

●   review the management accounts, cash book, invoices and bank statements, correspondence, minutes of meetings and major contracts to ensure that nothing has occurred since the year end that should be disclosed or provided for within the financial statements;

●   discuss the situation with management to ensure that all material items have been identified. The auditor may need to prompt the management to ensure that all relevant issues are considered;

●   consider whether the management have effective procedures to ensure that all adjusting and non-adjusting subsequent events are identified;

●   read the management minutes of meetings held since the year end or final audit and inquire about matters discussed at meetings for which minutes are not yet available; and

●   review any available accounting records and identify whether anything needs to be reflected in the accounts.

Before the audit report is signed, the auditor should specifically inquire into the following:

a)   the current status of any items involving subjective judgment or items which were accounted for on the basis of preliminary data;

b)   whether any new commitments, borrowings or guarantees have been entered into;

c)   whether any sales of assets have occurred or are planned;

d)   whether an issue of new shares or debentures, or an agreement to merge or to liquidate, has been made or is planned;

e)   whether any assets have been destroyed;

f)   whether there are any developments regarding risk areas and contingencies;

g)   whether any unusual accounting adjustments have been made or are contemplated; and

h)   whether any events have occurred or are likely to occur which might bring into question the appropriateness of the accounting policies.

The auditor needs to ensure that the file contains evidence that all of the issues outlined above have been considered and discussed with the client.

35.3.2 To ensure that the going concern basis of accounting is appropriate

To ensure that the going concern basis of accounting is appropriate, there are a number of detailed procedures that should be completed. It is very important that the auditor considers the wider picture when reviewing going concern and does not concentrate solely on financial measures, which in some entities may not be a problem. An entity could still have significant going concern worries due to other indicators. The following work should be undertaken.

Where available, the auditor should obtain copies of the cash flow forecast and/or budgets and, in the light of the information contained within them, consider:

a) whether applicable bases and assumptions were used;

b) whether they provide adequate evidence of the entity's ability to continue as a going concern (from a financial point of view); and

c) where a period of less than 12 months has been considered, what other evidence is available to demonstrate the entity's ability to continue as a going concern.

Where, as will happen with many small clients, no cash flows or budgets are prepared, the auditor should consider what other evidence is available to demonstrate that the entity is a going concern. Very often, the approach comprises discussion with the directors and the completion of a checklist. The auditor should complete the checklist based on his or her own knowledge of the client and then discuss the answers with the directors. The checklist should consider financial, operational and other indicators, which could affect the entity's ability to continue as a going concern. Those indicators may be subdivided into financial, operational, and other indicators.

Financial indicators

The auditor should consider:

a) whether the entity has net liabilities or net current liabilities;

b) whether the entity has failed to negotiate finance to cover its borrowing requirements. At the date of writing, this may well be a significant risk for many entities, even those which may previously have been considered to be perfectly creditworthy, due to the general lack of availability of debt funding as a result of the 'credit crunch';

c) whether the entity has defaulted on a loan agreement or breached any covenant;

d) whether the entity has any liquidity or cash flow problems;

e) whether the entity has sustained major losses or experienced cash flow problems since the period end which could threaten the entity's continued existence;

f) whether the entity has sold a substantial number of fixed assets that will not be replaced;

g) whether the entity is seeking a major restructuring of its debts;

h) whether the entity has experienced problems in obtaining and/or retaining normal terms of trade credit from suppliers;

(i) whether the entity has major debt repayments which are due or are about to fall due where refinancing is necessary to meet the obligation;

(j) whether the entity is experiencing problems paying debts as they fall due; and

k) the general financial outlook for the economy in the UK, and that of any countries with which the entity has significant trade.

Operational indicators

The auditor should consider for all entities, including those that have prepared cash flows or budgets:

a) whether there have been any fundamental changes in the market or technology to which the entity is unable to adapt adequately;

b) whether there have been any externally forced reductions in operation;

c) whether the entity has lost any key management or staff;

d) whether the entity is experiencing any staffing difficulties;

e) whether the entity is relying on a few product lines and/or is operating within depressed markets; and

f) whether the entity has lost any key suppliers or customers, or there have been technical developments which could render a key product obsolete.

Other indicators

The auditor should also consider the following issues for all clients:

a) whether the entity is involved in any major litigation in which an adverse judgment could imperil the entity's continued existence;

b) whether there are any issues which involve a range of possible outcomes so wide that an unfavourable result could affect the appropriateness of the going concern basis; and

c) whether there are any other factors which could adversely affect the appropriateness of the going concern basis.

Undertaking such a review and discussion with the directors is actually a way of providing the client with a better quality service. For example, if on completing the review it becomes clear that the entity is relying very heavily on one major customer or supplier, then discussion with the client regarding its contingency plans should it lose the client may prompt the client to plan an alternative course of action.

Where the completion of the going concern work and discussion with the client has identified that there are significant levels of concern then the auditor should consider, whether there is adequate disclosure within the financial statements and also, the impact the situation will have on their audit report.

The auditor should ensure there is disclosure in the accounts, or mention in the audit report, where the directors have reviewed going concern for a period of less than 12 months.

35.4 Analytical review

Analytical review procedures in terms of reviewing the accounting records in the new period, (for large and unusual items and other relevant information) form a major part of the standard work to be undertaken on subsequent events and going concern reviews. The comparison of key ratios at the current date with the year end date, or the equivalent date in the previous period is also important. The auditor should ensure that explanations are obtained for any variance from expectations.

35.5 Controls

The major controls that can be introduced in respect of subsequent events and going concern are via the use of budgets, cash flows and management accounting information. If the general movements within the financial records are being recorded and updated on a day-to-day basis, the management is ensuring that the entity's financial position is protected; this is the best control.

35.6 Common problems

There are a number of common problems that can be identified when looking at the area of subsequent events and going concern.

35.6.1 Undertaking the review too early

The subsequent events review is frequently undertaken too early in the audit. As already stipulated, it should be the last task performed before the audit field work is completed. This will mean that if completion is quick, it will not be necessary to go back and do any further detailed work on the area. Undertaking the review too early often results in additional and unnecessary effort.

35.6.2 Failure to revisit subsequent events when the accounts are finalised

For many small practices, there is often a significant delay in the completion of the audit and also delay from the time that the accounts are sent to the client for approval and the final audit report is signed. Such delays should lead to a further consideration of the situation in respect of going concern and post-balance sheet events, but very often this does not happen. It is essential that one of the final things the auditor considers, before signing the audit report, is whether there is sufficient evidence to determine if there are any adjusting or non-adjusting events that should have been adjusted or disclosed within the financial statements.

The audit completion process should be speeded up as much as possible to obviate the need to undertake additional work.

35.6.3 Failure to review budgets and forecasts critically

It is not uncommon to find that the auditor has simply put a copy of the client's budget or forecast on the going concern section of the file and barely given it a second glance. It is important that budgets and forecasts are reviewed critically, and that the auditor maintains an attitude of professional scepticism when doing so. It is easy to manipulate assumptions to show a favourable picture, in which case the budget or forecast will not provide reliable audit evidence. The entity's management should be robustly challenged on the validity of assumptions and optimistic predictions.

Chapter 36 Value added tax

36.1 Introduction and definition

Value added tax is the tax added to the value created for a supply. The audit of this area needs to be undertaken with care as the penalties for serious or persistent misdeclaration can be very significant, and can have a material impact on the entity's financial statements.

36.2 Audit objectives

There are two main audit objectives that should be considered when addressing the issue of value added tax, which are:

a) to ensure that VAT has been correctly accounted for; and

b) to ensure that any potential liabilities have been identified.

These objectives are considered in detail in the next section.

36.3 Audit approach

36.3.1 To ensure that VAT has been correctly accounted for

In order to satisfy this objective the auditor should:

a) obtain and check or prepare a VAT control account confirming that the VAT creditor or repayment due has been correctly recorded in the debtors or creditors section of the file;

b) vouch the entries on the VAT control account to the VAT returns, making sure that the returns have been correctly completed; and

c) reconcile the potential VAT on the turnover per the accounts to the outputs on the VAT control account. Basically, this means computing the theoretical VAT on the basis of the turnover recorded within the financial statements and making sure that this can be reconciled to the VAT paid to HMRC.

36.3.2 To ensure any potential liabilities have been identified

As well as many of the tests outlined above, the auditor should reconcile the turnover per the accounts to the outputs recorded on the VAT returns. This is different from the last test under the previous objective, in that the auditor is now looking at the net turnover figures rather than just the VAT element, ensuring that the turnover within the accounts does actually reflect the position recorded on the VAT returns. Obviously, any variations should be investigated.

The auditor should review the client's VAT returns, including any correspondence, and ensure that adequate provision has been made for any possible penalties and interest on under-declarations.

The auditor should check that VAT on private expenses, including car fuel, has been properly accounted for.

The auditor, in order to satisfy both of the objectives, should consider the completion of a VAT compliance checklist, which will help to identify whether the client is at risk of there being material misstatements or problems within the financial statements as a result of not complying properly with the necessary requirements. The sorts of issues that should be addressed within the checklist are as follows.

Registration issues

The auditor should consider whether the registration position of the entity is appropriate, and this should be done, even where the auditor is dealing with an unregistered entity.

Sales

The auditor should consider whether sales have been subjected to the correct treatment in respect of their VAT rating. This is particularly important where the entity deals in a mixture of standard-rated, zero-rated and exempt supplies. The auditor also needs to consider whether, if there are exports, adequate evidence of EU despatches and exports is kept to ensure that difficulties do not arise.

Purchases

The auditor should consider whether input tax has only been claimed when evidence is maintained on file and that all invoices are retained and accessible. The auditor should also determine whether there is a proper system to identify non-deductible inputs and whether these items have been dealt with properly within the accounts.

Partial exemption

Where the registered entity is partially exempt, the auditor should ensure that any annual adjustment has been carried out correctly and that any special methods used have been formally agreed with HMRC.

Accounting records

The auditor should consider whether the accounting records are adequate for the purposes of HMRC, whether the records are maintained for the correct period of time and whether the invoices, etc. issued contain all the relevant details.

Groups of companies

Where the entity being audited is a member of a group, the auditor should ensure that VAT between the group companies is being accounted for correctly.

Property sales and development

Property transactions represent one of the more complex areas as far as VAT is concerned, and whenever the entity is entering into such transactions, the auditor should consider whether all aspects have been dealt with correctly and whether reference to a VAT specialist is required. Due to the amounts involved in such transactions, any error is especially likely to be extremely material. Special consideration may be needed where the client is a charity.

Second-hand, retail and other schemes and global accounting

Where the entity has adopted any scheme in respect of the computation and/or payment of VAT, the auditor should consider whether the entity still meets the criteria and, where it is required to maintain any special records to qualify, whether those conditions are being satisfied.

Deregistration

Where an entity has deregistered for VAT, the auditor should consider whether output of VAT has been properly accounted for on assets on hand such as stock.

Penalties and assessments

Where there have been any penalties or assessments in the period, the auditor should consider whether these have been correctly reflected within the accounts.

36.4 Analytical review

Many of the tests to be undertaken on VAT are analytical review based. The turnover reconciliations are analytical review substantive tests, which help to achieve the standard objectives.

36.5 Controls

The auditor should consider whether there are adequate controls in place over the accounting records and the timing of the completion and submission of returns; and whether there is an independent check on the figures being incorporated within the return by a responsible person before its submission to HMRC.

The existence of any of the above controls may provide the auditor with additional comfort in respect of value added tax.

36.6 Common problems

The major problem is the failure by the auditor to undertake the VAT turnover reconciliation, particularly when dealing with an entity that has a mixture of exempt, zero-rated and standard supplies. This is a standard procedure that should be undertaken for all VAT-registered clients.

Chapter 37 Consolidation and groups

37.1 Introduction

The purpose of this Chapter is to consider the auditing and accounting procedures that should be applied when preparing consolidated accounts. Since medium-sized groups are no longer exempt from preparing group accounts for periods commencing on or after 6 April 2008, it is likely that many firms will be auditing more group accounts in future than previously.

This may pose two particular problems. Firstly, it may be that in some smaller firms none of the partners or staff has undertaken a group audit for a long time, if ever. Adequate training and technical support should be sought at an early stage if the firm is to continue with the engagement to ensure that the audit team has an appropriate level of technical expertise.

Secondly, there are likely to be many medium-sized groups where the finance director and other accounting staff have little or no experience of consolidation. Such clients may require a certain amount of 'hand holding', especially in the first year when additional information is needed for comparatives, for example, which may pose both management and self-review threats. In addition, the client's systems and procedures may not be able to provide all the necessary information.

The Audit Faculty of the ICAEW published new guidance in November 2008. Entitled *Auditing in a group context: Practical considerations for auditors*, it gives many practical tips when undertaking a group audit. Its key recommendations have been included in this Chapter.

37.2 Objectives

The major objective of this area is to ensure that the consolidation is prepared in accordance with company law and the relevant Accounting Standards.

37.3 Audit procedures

The audit procedures necessary to enable the auditor to demonstrate that the above objective has been satisfied are set out below.

37.3.1 Planning

The individual entity audits will be performed separately and have their own planning documents. However, the group audit also needs to be carefully planned because more than one entity is involved and there is always a risk of misunderstanding or a breakdown in communication. There may be added complications if several audit firms are involved.

However, the procedures adopted and the problems considered should follow the same process as for single companies. It should also be remembered that where the group has a common accounting system, it may be appropriate to do the planning on the group as a whole, effectively treating it as a single entity with a number of different departments or divisions. Undertaking the planning and audit in this way will mean that the auditor does not waste time repeating procedures for each individual entity.

The following procedures should be applied to update the auditor's knowledge of the client:

a) reviewing the permanent file, including details of any standing journals;

b) reviewing board minutes, correspondence and results to date, and a note made of any significant issues;

c) ascertaining details of any likely future developments of the business;

d) following inquiries, recording details of any changes in group structure, including subsidiaries, joint ventures, associates and branches. Details will also be needed of actual and proposed acquisitions or disposals;

e) following inquiries, recording details of any changes in the accounting systems;

f) following inquiries, recording details of any changes in group accounting policies or GAAPs used across the group; and

g) where the group has an internal audit department, obtaining copies of the reports and making a note of any issues of interest.

Where there have been any acquisitions in the period, the auditor should:

h) agree at an early stage whether it is to be accounted for as an acquisition or a merger;

i) ensure that accounts are available for the new subsidiary as at the date of acquisition;

k) look at the basis of arriving at fair value of assets and liabilities to ensure they are appropriate (for acquisition accounting);

l) liaise with secondary auditors if necessary (see section 37.3.4);

m) review the accounting policies of the acquired company to identify and deal with differences from group policies; and

n) where there are non-coterminous year ends, discuss with the client whether these are to be changed and, if not, whether the necessary information will be produced.

For disposals, the auditor should ensure that the holding company will have adequate information covering the period to the date of disposal.

For reorganisations, the auditor should examine the reasons for the reorganisation, considering whether this may have been done to manipulate figures in some way.

The auditor should consider the group's accounting system and consider whether there are any specific areas that could cause a problem on the audit.

The auditor should ascertain details of, and consider the impact on, the accounts and audit of any changes in group accounting policies. In particular, the auditor should:

- consider whether the policies applied are the most appropriate for the group; and
- view with scepticism any change that is not a result of a new or revised Standard, unless it is bringing policies into line with existing Accounting Standards.

In some groups, particularly where some elements are based overseas, the GAAP and accounting policies used may vary across the group. The auditor needs to gain an understanding of any other GAAPs used, and agree who is responsible for any conversion needed.

The auditor should consider whether the group is exempt the requirement to prepare consolidated accounts, not only through size, but also because of its activities.

The auditor should agree a timetable within the group, covering the following issues:

a) reconciliation of intra-group balances;

b) agreement of group tax provisions;

c) provision of information for GAAP conversion;

d) deadlines for information;

e) submission of subsidiaries' accounts to the Registrar;

f) preparation of draft group financial statements; and

g) AGM arrangements. Although these are no longer necessary for private companies under the Companies Act 2006, some companies, particularly incorporated charities, may well choose to continue to hold an AGM.

When setting group materiality, the auditor should use the draft group accounts. This level can be used for the individual audit companies where common accounting systems are used. However, for this to apply, it is essential that the accounting function is controlled from one centre. The auditor must also ensure that audit risks are considered adequately within each of the individual companies. It should be remembered that the accounts of the individual subsidiaries must still give a true and fair view.

It cannot be emphasised enough that communication is vital when undertaking a group audit, and the more that relevant information is shared among the various auditors concerned, the smoother the process will probably be. It can be particularly useful to share discussions of client knowledge and risk in order to strengthen the planning and audit approach, and to foresee problems which may arise.

37.3.2 Detailed audit procedures

The main aim of the audit work on groups is to check the consolidation calculations, and ensure that the appropriate disclosures are made in the accounts. Materiality should be calculated on a group basis using the key components in the group accounts. The following detailed procedures should be undertaken.

For an entity not preparing group accounts

Obviously, consolidated accounts are not being produced, but additional disclosures are required, particularly in respect of related party transactions. In some cases, it may be easier to prepare group accounts than give the necessary disclosures regarding intra-group trading in the accounts of each group entity. The auditor should use a suitable disclosure checklist to ensure that no items are missed.

For a group entity preparing group accounts

Where the client is preparing the consolidation calculations, the auditor should perform the following work:

a) review calculations to ensure that all group members are included;

b) trace individual items from the entity accounts into the group accounts to ensure that no items have been excluded;

c) trace items from the consolidation workings back to the individual entity accounts to ensure that no items are overstated;

d) check any currency calculations, using the published rates ruling at the accounting date(these can be obtained from the financial press, major banks or internet sites);

e) check the casts and cross-costs;

f) ensure that all intra-group eliminations have been made where necessary, for example:

- inter-company accounts;
- unrealised profits on stock or fixed assets bought from other group companies;
- interest paid and received; and
- sales and cost of sales;

g) ensure that all journal adjustments are valid and posted to the correct balance sheet or profit and loss account heading;

h) ensure that the deferred tax implications of any elimination of unrealised profits are properly accounted for; and

i) ensure that bank balances and overdrafts are only offset where a legal right of set-off exists.

Where the group structure has changed, the auditor will also need to:

- check the calculation of the pre-acquisition reserves for any subsidiaries accounted for as acquisitions;

- ensure that goodwill is dealt with according to FRS 6 and FRS 10 and that the amortisation policy is reasonable in the circumstances;

- check the fair values used;

- ensure that the conditions are met and the calculations properly made where merger accounting is applied;

- confirm that the accounting policies of new subsidiaries agree with those of the group or that any necessary adjustments have been made; and

- check calculation of profit or loss on the sale of subsidiaries with the contracts for sale, also check to see if sale conditions give rise to any contingent liabilities.

Where a subsidiary's accounts are qualified, the auditor should consider whether the qualification is sufficiently material as to affect the opinion on the group as a whole; and the group tax charge may have to be audited separately from the work on individual companies within the group. Particular attention should be paid to the following:

- **group relief eligibility** – do the surrendering and receiving companies qualify as a group for tax purposes? Has any payment for group relief been treated correctly?

- **deferred tax** – trading losses carried forward in one company cannot be offset against deferred tax in another.

37.3.3 Audit completion

The completion procedures should not be very different from those for a single entity, but some additional information will be required. The auditor should carry out the following specific procedures:

a) preparing an overall reconciliation of group reserves and tax to ensure that everything has been accounted for correctly;

b) undertaking a subsequent events review for the group as a whole;

c) completing an audit highlights report for the group as well as for the individual member companies; and

d) preparing a group summary of the errors not adjusted and including it with the audit highlights memorandum.

After the audit is completed, a thorough debrief is recommended, to ensure that any lessons learned can be taken forward to next year's planning.

37.3.4 Reliance on other auditors

When auditing group accounts, the auditor has sole responsibility for the opinion, even if another firm audits some of the group members. The group auditor is not able to discharge his or her responsibility by simply accepting audited accounts from another firm. ISA 600 (Revised) *Using the work of another auditor* looks at the relationship between the principal auditor and other auditors, and deals with the issues that need to be addressed where there are other auditors involved in the group audit. Specifically, the following procedures should be considered.

The primary auditor should review the general scope of the secondary auditor's work, particularly:

a) the terms of engagement;

b) any limitation in the scope of the secondary auditor's work;

c) the nature, extent and standard of the secondary auditor's work;

d) any differences between Accounting, Auditing and other Standards; and

e) the independence of the secondary auditor.

This can usually be achieved by using a questionnaire or standard reporting form. Paragraph 14-1 of ISA 600 (Revised) requires the principal auditor to document any review it undertakes, for the purpose of the group audit, of the audit work conducted by other auditors.

A recent change to the Audit Regulations requires that where part of a group audit has been carried out by a non-EEA auditor whose regulator does not have a mutual cooperation agreement with the UK Professional Oversight Board (POB), the principal auditor:

a)   obtains the other auditor's agreement that it will provide unrestricted access to its working papers;

b)   obtains copies of that auditor's working papers; or

c)   where (a) or (b) is not possible, the group auditor documents the reasonable steps that he or she has taken in order to obtain copies or access, and why these steps were unsuccessful.

There are two practical considerations here. Firstly, the principal auditor should make the request early enough to show that it has taken reasonable steps to obtain access or copies. The easiest way to do this is to include a request in the referral instructions issued to component auditors requesting them to confirm whether or not they will provide access or copies in their confirmation letter.

Secondly, what will constitute 'reasonable steps' to obtain access or copies? Since the Audit Regulations do not provide examples, this will be a judgment for the audit partner that will need to be documented on the group audit file.

The primary auditor should review the subsidiary's financial statements and prepare a summary of significant matters arising.

The primary auditor should decide during the course of the audit whether any further evidence is needed, taking into account materiality.

If further details are required, the auditor of the group, as the primary auditor, has to decide how best to obtain this evidence – for example, simply by discussion with the secondary auditor, by a review of their working papers, or in some other way. The group auditor does not express an opinion on the subsidiary's financial statements, and it should not be necessary to redo the secondary auditor's work. The secondary auditor normally performs any additional work required.

Where both companies are incorporated in Great Britain, the Companies Act 2006 imposes a duty on the subsidiary and its auditors to give the holding company's auditors 'such information or explanations as he thinks necessary for the performance of his duties as auditor.' If the subsidiary is not a British company, the holding company's auditor may require the holding company to 'take all such steps as are reasonably open to it' to obtain such information or explanations from the subsidiary or its auditors. If the auditor is not able to obtain all the necessary information and explanations required, he or she should consider qualifying the audit report on the basis of a limitation in scope.

37.4 Analytical review

Once the consolidated accounts have been prepared, the auditor should undertake analytical review procedures as outlined in Chapter 41, to ensure that the accounts make sense in view of the auditor's knowledge of the client and the audit evidence obtained. In particular, analytical review can be applied to ensure that all intra-group trading has been fully eliminated from the consolidated accounts.

Comparisons against group management accounts, budgets and forecasts can also be useful, but the auditor needs to have a thorough understanding of the basis on which they have been drawn up. Group reporting information is no different to that of a single entity in that matters such as tax, accruals, provisions and depreciation may not be very accurate or even included at all, and there is the added risk of consolidation errors being made by the client, all of which may limit the usefulness of comparison with the draft consolidated accounts.

37.5 Controls

In a group context the auditor would expect to see evidence that the intra-group accounts are regularly reconciled and agreed. In addition, where the client prepares the consolidation and undertakes any GAAP conversion needed, the auditor should consider any controls which operate over the process, particularly those of a checking or reviewing nature. Consolidation can be a complicated procedure, which may require a number of journals, which can increase the risk of both fraud and error, and so controls in this area are important.

Of course, the principal auditor is also interested in the general accounting controls operating over both the holding entity and the subsidiaries, as described earlier in Chapter 4.

37.6 Common problems

37.6.1 Failure to meet group reporting deadlines

Group audits can be complex, and a failure to adequately plan and communicate upfront is probably the single biggest reason why deadlines are missed and things go wrong. There really is no substitute for taking the time to properly plan a group audit, and to communicate with all the relevant parties.

The ICAEW's *Auditing in a group context: Practical considerations for auditors* contains a useful eight-point plan to undertaking a group audit. Those points are:

a) understand group management's process and timetable to produce consolidated accounts;

b) design group audit process to match management's process and timetable;

c) clearly communicate expectations and information required, including timetable from end;

d) obtain information early where practicable;

e) keep track of whether reports have been received;

f) respond to any issues raised in a timely fashion;

g) conclude on the audit; and

h) consider possible improvements for the next year's process including management letter issues.

37.6.2 Inadequate disclosure where group accounts are not prepared

Where dealing with an entity that is able to take advantage of the exemptions from preparing group accounts, the auditor often fails to remember the additional disclosures necessary within the financial statements. If these disclosures are not highlighted at the planning stage, they can be missed. The use of specific checklists in these circumstances will help to prevent errors.

37.6.3 Reliance on other auditors

Where one of the subsidiary companies is audited by another practice, it is essential that the auditor ensures that a detailed audit questionnaire is sent out and that reliance can be placed on the work undertaken by the other practice. This can cause particular problems when dealing with a foreign entity where it may well be that an audit has not been undertaken or the scope of the audit is different. It is essential that the auditor undertakes adequate testing where this is the case. The auditor should fully document the considerations he or she have made and establish whether it is reasonable to place reliance upon the information that has been received.

A related issue is that of over-reliance on other auditors. This can occur where the auditor of the parent entity does not audit a sufficient proportion of the group to be able to assume the role of principal auditor – for example, where the parent entity is only a holding company, and the vast majority of the group's activities are undertaken by subsidiaries not audited by the parent auditor. The issues to consider not only include the materiality of the part of the group audited by the principal auditor, but also the risk of material misstatements in the financial statements of components audited by other auditors. The relationship of the principal auditor with other auditors should also be considered.

37.6.4 Inadequate consideration of intra-group transactions

It is essential that all intra-group transactions are adequately considered, particularly to ensure that intra-group dividends are only recognised when they are earned. The auditor should also ensure that the issue of tax is properly dealt with, especially where there are tax losses transferred between group companies. Finally, the auditor should ensure that details of any cross-guarantees are adequately disclosed and their impact on the individual entity is fully considered.

Chapter 38 Cash flow statements

38.1 Introduction

Under FRS 1 *Cash flow statements*, a cash flow statement is required to be included in the accounts of all medium and large entities unless their results are included in the consolidated accounts of a parent entity which produces a consolidated cash flow statement. It is also recommended, but not required, for inclusion by small companies.

The audit of the cash flow statement is often done badly, if at all, but its prominence as a primary statement means it is an important audit area.

38.2 Objectives

The major objective of this area is to ensure that the cash flow statement is prepared and presented correctly in accordance with the requirements of FRS 1.

38.3 Audit procedures

The main aim of the audit work on cash flow statements is to check that all the adjustments needed have been made during its preparation, and to ensure that the appropriate disclosures are made in the accounts. The following items should be checked to ensure they have been treated correctly:

a) fixed asset additions and disposals, including:

- any trade creditors for unpaid purchases and debtors for disposal proceeds; and

- additions acquired under hire purchase or finance lease arrangements;

b) corporation tax, particularly where the client has made payments on account during the period;

c) interest debtors and/or creditors;

d) exceptional items;

e) foreign exchange movements, especially on cash and/or debt;

f) movements on debt, particularly repayments of borrowings and new financing taken out during the period; and

g) the classification of cash balances, remembering that cash and cash equivalents are defined by FRS 1 as those funds which can be accessed within 24 hours.

Where accounting software has been used to prepare the cash flow statement and related notes (and hence where there are no actual workings to check), the auditor should consider whether it is more effective to completely rework the cash flow statement, especially where there are complicated items such as acquisitions or foreign exchange movements.

38.4 Analytical review

Once the cash flow statement has been prepared, the auditor should undertake analytical review procedures to ensure that it makes sense in view of the auditor's knowledge of the client and the audit evidence obtained.

38.5 Controls

There are no relevant controls for dealing with this section, beyond the general business controls that have been outlined in the previous chapters.

38.6 Common problems

38.6.1 Undue reliance on accounts production software

Given that most firms now prepare statutory accounts using accounts production software, a problem that often occurs is that the auditor relies on this being the case, and does not actually audit the cash flow statement. When an external file review visit identifies errors in a cash flow statement, the response from the auditor is often along the lines of '...but the accounts were prepared using [the name of the firm's accounts production software], so it must be right, mustn't it?'

Accounts software is only as good as the data entry, which is of course subject to human error. One firm managed to omit several million pounds of invoice discounting debt from the net debt note (with consequential impact on the cash flow statement) simply because the creditor balance had been analysed within Other Creditors, and so the software did not identify it as debt. It is vital that the cash flow statement is checked to ensure it is correct.

38.6.2 Lack of critical analytical review

It is quite possible for a cash flow statement to balance, and yet contain numerous material errors. This was the case in the example given above in section 38.6.1, and a brief analytical review of the cash flow statement should have identified that something was wrong. An overall review of the statement, to ensure that all the figures that were expected have actually been included, is valuable in ensuring that nothing major has been omitted.

38.6.3 Insufficient knowledge and experience of staff

In many smaller practices, the majority of audits can be entities below the audit threshold, which are having a voluntary audit for some reason. Audit staff may rarely come across cash flow statements in much of their day-to-day work, and this inexperience can lead to errors going unnoticed in the cash flow statement. In such circumstances, it is important that a senior member of the audit team reviews the cash flow statement in detail.

38.6.3 Incorrect classification of 'cash' balances

Care needs to be taken to ensure that only cash balances meeting the FRS 1 definition of cash and cash equivalents (see section 38.3 above) are disclosed as cash in the cash flow statements. Items such as notice accounts and amounts on treasury deposit may have to be classified as liquid investments rather than cash.

Chapter 39 Auditing financial statements prepared under IFRS

39.1 Introduction

This book has been written on the basis that the vast majority of audited entities use either full UK GAAP or the FRSSE. However, a number of entities, mainly large UK listed (and some private) companies, and some UK subsidiaries of large overseas companies, are now reporting under IFRS (note that at the date of writing, UK charities are not permitted to adopt IFRS).

In many respects, the choice of GAAP should not significantly affect the way that financial statements are audited. However, there are some accounting matters which are more prominent under IFRS which may affect the audit approach, and these need to be considered – in particular, fair value accounting.

39.2 Definitions

IFRSs are defined to include the numbered IFRSs issued by the International Accounting Standards Board (IASB), International Accounting Standards (IAS) originally issued by its predecessor body (as amended), as well as approved interpretations of these Standards. The expression is therefore used in this broad sense in this book unless clear reference is made to a specific Standard.

A problem facing the auditor is that different financial reporting frameworks have different definitions of 'fair value'. However, for the purpose of auditing under IFRS, IAS 39 *Financial instruments: Recognition and measurement* defines fair value as, 'the amount for which an asset could be exchanged, or a liability settled, between knowledgeable, willing parties in an arm's length transaction.'

ISA 545 *Auditing fair value measurements and disclosures* notes that the concept of fair value ordinarily assumes a current transaction, rather than settlement at some past or future date. Accordingly, the process of measuring fair value would be a search for the estimated price at which that transaction would occur.

39.3 Objectives

The major objective of this area is to ensure that fair value measurements and disclosures and other specific considerations under IFRS are appropriately audited.

39.4 Acceptance procedures and initial audit planning

IFRS has only made a serious impact on UK accounting relatively recently, and many audit practices will have few or no clients accounting under IFRS. Whilst recently qualified and current trainee accountants will have studied IFRS as part of their accountancy qualifications, many experienced accountants may not have encountered it before. As a result, audit principals need to consider carefully whether they have sufficient knowledge and technical expertise within the firm before accepting an audit engagement of an entity accounting under IFRS. This issue should be addressed as part of the firm's acceptance, or in the case of an existing client changing over to IFRS, reacceptance procedures.

Larger clients may have sufficient expertise in-house to prepare financial statements in accordance with IFRS. Others, especially small subsidiaries of listed or overseas parent companies, may not have such expertise, and may rely on the audit practice for advice. In the first year of adoption of IFRS in particular, some clients may need considerable 'hand holding', and the auditor needs to consider the independence implications of providing such advice and support, since Bulletin 2005/3 *Guidance for auditors on first-time application of IFRSs in the United Kingdom and the Republic of Ireland* reminds us that it is still the responsibility of management to prepare the accounts. For unlisted entities, ES5 reminds us that the auditor may provide accounting services only if:

a) such services do not involve initiating transactions or taking management decisions and are of a technical, mechanical or an informative nature; and

b) appropriate safeguards are applied to reduce the self-review threat to an acceptable level.

While it may be possible for the audit firm to apply appropriate safeguards, such as a partner or manager outside the audit team providing IFRS accounting advice, the requirement not to take management decisions could pose difficulties, and so this would need to be carefully considered before the engagement is accepted.

Entities adopting IFRS for the first time are strongly encouraged by Bulletin 2005/3 to prepare an 'impact analysis' of IFRS on the financial statements, and to draw up a formal plan to manage the changeover process. The auditor should review this information when undertaking the audit risk assessment.

The auditor should consider also the need for consultation on those matters deemed critical for an entity in its IFRS financial statements in the year of transition.

As with any other accounting policy, the auditor should obtain sufficient appropriate audit evidence that fair value measurements and disclosures are in accordance with the entity's applicable financial reporting framework. This evaluation can be very dependent on the auditor's knowledge of the nature of the business, especially where the asset or liability or the valuation method is highly complex. Particular consideration should also be given to situations where there is choice over the method used to determine fair values.

Paragraph 27 of ISA 545 requires the method used for fair value measurements to be applied consistently. The auditor should therefore consider:

●   whether the method has been applied consistently;

●   whether consistency is actually appropriate in the circumstances of the entity, and

●   whether any change of method adopted by the client provides a more appropriate basis of measurement or is required by changes to IFRS.

It should always be remembered that management is responsible for determining fair value measurements. The auditor should therefore obtain an understanding of the entity's own internal process for determining fair value measurements, and of any relevant controls over that process, to be able assess the risks of material misstatement at the assertion level. Many fair value measurements are based on estimates that are inherently imprecise, and may be derived from complex calculations, both of which factors may increase the inherent risk of material misstatement due to both fraud and error.

39.5 Determining the audit approach

●   As with any other risk, if the risk of material misstatement relating to a fair value measurement or disclosure is determined to be a significant risk that requires special audit consideration, the procedures outlined in section **8.3.2** should be followed.

●   Fair value accounting often requires input from an external independent expert or service organisation, options that were considered in sections **10.4.5** and **10.4.2** respectively.

●   As noted above, many fair value measurements are based on estimates. Accordingly, the provisions of ISA 540 Audit of accounting estimates may be relevant to the audit of fair values. Auditing accounting estimates were considered in section **15.5**.

39.6 Audit procedures

Whilst ISA 545 provides guidance on auditing fair value measurements and disclosures, audit evidence obtained from other audit procedures may also provide audit evidence relevant to the measurement and disclosure of fair values. For example, inspection procedures to verify the existence of an asset measured at fair value also may provide relevant audit evidence about its valuation – for example, the physical condition of an investment property. The audit procedures discussed in the preceding chapters in Part II may therefore still have relevance when auditing fair values.

Because of the wide range of possible fair value measurements, from relatively simple to complex, the auditor's procedures can vary significantly in nature, timing and extent. However, the following procedures should be applied when considering the audit of fair values and related disclosures.

39.6.1 To ensure fair value measurements are appropriately determined

The existence of published price quotations in an active market is ordinarily the best audit evidence of fair value – for example, share prices quoted on a recognised stock exchange.

Where a valuation model is used, the auditor should evaluate:

a) whether the assumptions used by management are reasonable, focusing on those which have the most material impact on the outcome of the valuation, including those that are sensitive to variation or uncertainty in amount or nature and those susceptible to misapplication or bias;

b) whether an appropriate model was used; and

c) whether management used relevant, accurate and complete information that was reasonably available at the time. Specific audit procedures might include verifying the source of any data used, mathematical recalculation and reviewing information for internal consistency.

Where management's intentions with respect to an asset or liability are criteria for determining fair value, the auditor should obtain audit evidence about management's intent to carry out specific courses of action, and consider its ability to do so. These might include:

● considering management's past history of carrying out its stated intentions;

● reviewing written plans, budgets, minutes, etc.;

● considering management's stated reasons for choosing a particular course of action; and

● considering management's ability to carry out a particular course of action, given the entity's economic circumstances and any contractual commitments.

Consideration should also be given to the effect of subsequent events on fair values. For example, a sale of investment property shortly after the year end may provide audit evidence relating to the fair value measurement. However, fair value information after the year end may also reflect events occurring after the year end and not the circumstances existing at the balance sheet date, and so care needs to be taken here.

The letter of representation should confirm that, in the directors' opinion, significant assumptions pertaining to fair values are reasonable, and that those assumptions reflect their intent and ability to carry out specific courses of action on behalf of the entity. Letters of representation are considered further in Chapter 43.

39.6.2 To ensure adequate disclosure is made under IFRS, particularly of fair value measurements and related disclosures

The disclosure requirements under IFRS are somewhat different to those under UK GAAP and, as such, it is essential that a specialist disclosure checklist is used. Many checklists will only cover the requirements of IFRS, and yet consideration must also be given to other disclosures required in UK accounts. *Interactive Company Accounts Disclosure Checklist*, published by Wolters Kluwer, addresses the requirements of IFRS, UK company law and any other relevant requirements.

The financial statements should be carefully reviewed to ensure that all references to the entity's applicable reporting framework refer to IFRS, including those in the audit report.

The auditor should confirm that the additional disclosures required in the transitional year to IFRS – such as a reconciliation of IFRS information to the previously used GAAP, and more extensive disclosure of estimation uncertainty – have been included.

Fair value disclosures are often very important to users of financial statements, due to the complexity of determining many fair value measurements, and their materiality to the accounts. Paragraph 57 of ISA 545 also points out that some entities disclose additional voluntary fair value information in the notes to the financial statements. Accordingly, extra care needs to be taken when checking fair value disclosures to ensure that they are complete and accurate. Particular attention should be paid to the level of disclosure where there is a high degree of measurement uncertainty.

39.7 Analytical review

The auditor may make an independent estimate of fair value to compare with management's fair value measurement. This might involve the use of an auditor-developed model and separate assumptions.

As noted in section 39.3 above, consistency of methodology is important in fair value accounting. Analytical review of fair values against prior periods can therefore be useful.

It should be noted that analytical review techniques may be of limited use in the first year that IFRS is used.

39.8 Controls

The main controls to be considered are those over the client's process of determining fair values. These may include:

a) calculations and estimates being made by an experienced member of the accounting staff;

b) review of estimates by a director or member of senior management;

c) checks as to the accuracy of spreadsheet formulae and calculations; and

d) ensuring the relevant accounting staff, management and directors have sufficient training and expertise.

Other controls over the particular area in question identified in earlier chapters in Part II may also be relevant.

39.9 Common problems

39.9.1 Insufficient knowledge of IFRS

A common scenario is where an audit practice is asked to audit a new client which accounts under IFRS. Despite having no prior experience of IFRS accounting, but not wishing to turn away new clients, the firm accepts the appointment. Similarly, some firms continue to audit existing clients that change over to IFRS when they do not have the requisite training and expertise. Invariably, panic ensues when the firm realises it does not understand the underlying accounting principles and has no idea what disclosures should be made in the accounts.

One of the most important, but often overlooked, parts of audit acceptance procedures is the consideration of whether the firm has sufficient technical knowledge and experience. This is no less relevant when auditing financial statements prepared under IFRS, and must be considered **before** accepting a new engagement or reaccepting an existing engagement.

39.9.2 Lack of understanding of the valuation model used for determining fair value

Many valuation models contain highly complex mathematical formulae. Where such models are used to determine fair values, the auditor must ensure that the model is fully understood. Otherwise, there is a risk that the auditor may fail to identify a material misstatement, either an error made by the client in the calculation or a deliberately fraudulent attempt to manipulate the result.

Part III   Completion

Chapter 40 Introduction

The purpose of this section is to run through the completion and review procedures that should be applied when finalising an audit assignment. This is an area that must be taken seriously and the auditor must ensure that time is incorporated within the budget and timetable to allow for this process to work properly.

The contents of this section are as follows:

- **Preparing the file for review** – considering the completion procedures that should be undertaken by a member of staff before the file is passed to the partner for review. The key issue is for the file to be as complete as possible before it is passed to the partner or manager for review. If any matters that can be dealt with at staff level have not been dealt with, then ideally they should be before the file is reviewed.

- **Reports to directors and management** – dealing with the need to send letters of comment to the entity. As well as being mandatory under ISAs, letters of comment provide clients with additional, valuable information.

- **Letters of representation** – considering the content and purpose of these letters. Whilst such letters are not the preferred form of audit evidence, a letter of representation can, in certain circumstances, be a useful confirmatory tool.

- **The audit report** – dealing with ISA 700, the APB Bulletin on audit reports and the matters that should be taken into account when drafting the audit opinion. There are too many occasions where the audit opinion on the file does not match the actual opinion in the report.

- **Reviewing the file** – working through the file review procedure. Guidance is given on the important issue of quality control, including the requirements of ISA 220.

- **Planning for next year** – including an examination of how the lessons learned during this year's work can be applied to plan a more effective audit in the future.

Chapter 41 Preparing the file for review

41.1 Introduction

It is important that the audit staff responsible for the detailed work ensure the audit file is as complete as possible before it is given to the partner or manager for initial review. Reviewing a file that contains incomplete information and unfinished work is much more difficult and time consuming. Where a partner is presented with such a file, there is a risk that either the job will significantly exceed budget, as the partner has to take more time both reviewing the file and completing some of the unfinished work, or there is a risk that the audit will be left incomplete and that potentially important issues will be missed.

As the most expensive, it is the partner's time that should be saved.

41.2 Completion of the individual sections

This area has been covered in more detail in Part II. The audit senior should ensure that all the individual sections of the file have been properly completed and signed off. The senior should:

a) review each section and ensure that the work has been undertaken in accordance with the audit plan, and that all of the planned work has been done;

b) check that the file is fully cross-referenced and that every test identified at the planning stage as being necessary has actually been completed. In addition, any further testing that has been identified as being necessary should also have been completed;

c) make sure that where a test requires a working paper, one has been prepared and properly cross-referenced within the programme; and

d) ensure that all points within the main body of the file that need to be brought to the reviewer's attention have been brought forward. These should be recorded either on an audit highlights schedule or on a 'Points for partner attention' schedule if the senior cannot clear them.

41.3 General points

41.3.1 Review of juniors' work

Where there is a tiered structure within the practice, the senior or the manager must ensure that all original work by junior staff has been properly reviewed. The normal procedure is for the person next on the 'ladder' to review the work of the person below.

The same review procedures as outlined within Chapter 45 should be applied.

41.3.2 Clearance of queries

The audit senior should ensure that all queries and review points have been adequately cleared before the file is presented for review. Where there are queries that the senior is unable to clear, these should be noted on a separate schedule for the partner to discuss with the client. Similarly, at this stage the senior should complete a schedule of outstanding points, detailing any outstanding work that is required prior to the audit report being signed. A file is not ready for review if this list of outstanding points includes the undertaking of a substantial amount of original work within the main file sections. In such circumstances, the file would effectively be reviewed twice, which would obviously increase the cost.

41.3.3 Outstanding points

In most circumstances the only outstanding points should be in respect of information that has not yet been provided to the audit staff, such as an outstanding bank letter. Other outstanding points might include a letter of comment being still in draft form, but they should not include an entire section of the audit file being still outstanding.

41.4 Other procedures

Other matters that should be addressed by the senior in charge of the audit before the file is presented for review are outlined in (a) to (i) below.

a) Do the working papers record all the work done and do all schedules record the source of information? This will include checking that all key tests contain a clear summary of the results and a conclusion stating what the results actually mean.

b) Has the current file has been fully cross-referenced? A file that contains either no cross-referencing or inaccurate cross-referencing takes considerably longer to review. There is nothing likely to irk a reviewer more than being referred to a particular schedule to see how a figure was arrived at, and finding that that schedule does not contain that detail, or that the schedule does not exist at all! The search for the relevant schedule will then waste even more time.

c) Have the budget and actual time summaries been completed and explanations provided for any variances? Notes with any recommended action for subsequent years should also be made. Indeed, depending on the agreement with the client regarding fees, this could be an essential tool for explaining any budget overrun to the client and in negotiating a fee increase, if the client takes responsibility for the extra time spent.

d) Has the permanent file has been updated for any changes highlighted during the course of the audit? It is important for the reviewer to check that this has been completed, as the senior involved may not be available when the audit is planned the following year.

e) Has the planning been updated for any changes highlighted during the course of the audit? If this was the case, and additional audit procedures were planned as a result, have these been performed and documented?

f) Have any commercial observations on the client's business been recorded on the file for the partner's attention? This is an important issue that is frequently missed. It is also an area that allows the auditor to add value to the service provided to the client.

g) Have all issues that require inclusion in the letter of representation been recorded on the file? This issue is addressed in more detail in Chapter 43.

h) Has a list of points for inclusion in the letter of comment been made, or preferably, has a draft letter been prepared? This issue is dealt with in more detail in Chapter 42.

i) Has the level of materiality been reassessed on the basis of the final accounts? If any adjustment is deemed necessary, the senior should consider whether the audit work is sufficient in light of the adjusted figure.

41.5 Compliance with Auditing Standards

The purpose of the audit is to ensure that the auditor is able to form an audit opinion and sign an audit report stipulating that the audit work has been undertaken in accordance with International Standards on Auditing (UK and Ireland). The audit file should therefore document this fact, including evidence of a review by the auditor at the end of the assignment to confirm that all ISAs have been complied with.

The simplest means of documenting such a review is the completion of a checklist. However, the auditor should be careful to ensure that individual questions are not simply signed off without considering whether the evidence to support a 'yes' answer to a question is actually on file.

The example checklist below indicates the specific issues that should be addressed.

Client:	Prepared by:	Date:	Ref:
Year end:	Reviewed by:	Date:	**B2**
File no:			

AUDIT STANDARDS REVIEW QUESTIONNAIRE

This questionnaire should be completed, where considered necessary, to enable the reviewer to answer question 1 on the Initial Partner Completion.

ISA		Yes/No N/A	Comments	Initials
200.4	In conducting the audit, has the firm complied with:			
200.4.1	(a) The IFAC code of ethics; and			
	(b) APB ethical standards?			
210.2.1	Do we have an up-to-date letter of engagement?			
210.18	Has the firm been asked to agree to a change to the terms of engagement where there is no reasonable justification for doing so?			
220.2	Have the firm's quality control procedures been properly applied to this audit client?			
220.18	Has any information come to light that would have caused the firm to decline the audit engagement if that information had been available earlier?			
220.21	Has the audit work been properly directed, supervised and reviewed?			
230	Has audit documentation been prepared that would enable an experienced auditor, having no previous connection with the audit, to understand:			
230.9	(a) the nature, timing, and extent of the audit procedures performed to comply with ISAs and applicable legal and regulatory requirements;			
230.9	(b) the results of the audit procedures and the audit evidence obtained; and			
230.9	(c) significant matters arising during the audit and the conclusions reached thereon;			
230.12	(d) the identifying characteristics of the specific items or matters being tested;			
230.16	(e) the content of discussions with management and others concerning any significant matters.			
230.18	(f) how any contradictions or inconsistencies between the information received and the audit conclusions reached on significant matters have been addressed;			
230.21	(g) how alternative audit procedures performed achieved the objectives of the audit where it was considered necessary to depart from a basic principle or an essential procedure;			
230.23	(h) who performed the audit work and the date such work was completed; and			

230.23	(i) who reviewed the audit work performed and the date and extent of such review.			
240.3	In planning and performing the audit to reduce audit risk to an acceptably low level, did we consider the risks of material misstatements in the financial statements due to fraud?			
240.85	Did analytical procedures undertaken when forming an overall conclusion as to whether the accounts as a whole are consistent with our knowledge of the business indicate a previously unrecognised risk of material misstatement due to fraud?			
240.86	Have we considered the implications for the audit where one or more of the potential adjustments listed on **B7** gives an indication of fraud?			
240.110	Where we have concluded that the risk of material misstatement due to fraud related to revenue recognition is not applicable in the circumstances of the engagement, have we documented the reasons for that conclusion?			
250.2	Has the audit been planned and performed having considered the risk of material misstatement arising from non-compliance with relevant laws and regulations?			
250.28 250.28.1	Have we considered the impact of any suspected or actual non-compliance with laws and regulations, subject to compliance with legislation relating to tipping off, on our reports to the management, shareholders and any external regulators?			
250.31	Have we considered the implications of any non-compliance with laws and regulations in relation to other aspects of the audit, particularly the reliability of management representations?			
250B.2	Have any matters arisen during the audit that are required to be reported to an external regulator?			
260.16.1	Have we communicated in writing all the significant findings from the audit to those charged with governance? (See **B3.1** Q18)			
260.11.16	Has the effect on the accounts of any unadjusted errors been considered?			
	Unadjusted errors:			
260.11.19	Where the client has refused to adjust for misstatements drawn to their attention (see **B7**): does the letter of representation include the reasons given for not adjusting?			
300.16	Has the audit plan been reviewed and updated, where necessary, during the course of the audit?			

315.2	Do our audit files contain information adequate to provide an understanding of the company and its environment, including its internal control, sufficient to identify and assess the risks of material misstatement of the financial statements, whether due to fraud or error, and sufficient to design and perform further audit procedures?			
315.122	Does the file document:			
	(a) the discussion among the engagement team regarding the susceptibility of the company's financial statements to material misstatement due to error or fraud, and the significant decisions reached;			
	(b) key elements of the understanding obtained of the company's environment, including the components of internal control, to assess the risks of material misstatement of the financial statements; the sources of information from which the understanding was obtained; and the risk assessment procedures;			
	(c) the identified and assessed risks of material misstatement at the financial statement level and at the assertion level; and			
	(d) the risks identified and related controls evaluated.			
320.11	Has materiality been reviewed during the course of the audit?			
	Preliminary materiality:			
	Final materiality:			
330.66	Have the risk assessments been reviewed to determine whether the assessments of the risks of material misstatement at the assertion level remain appropriate?			
330.73	The auditor should document:			
	(a) the overall responses to address the assessed risks of material misstatement at the financial statement level and the nature, timing and extent of the further audit procedures;			
	(b) the linkage of those procedures with the assessed risks at the assertion level;			
	(c) the results of the audit procedures;			
	(d) the conclusions reached with regard to relying on internal controls that were tested in a prior audit.			
402.2	Where the client uses a service organisation, has sufficient appropriate audit evidence been obtained to determine whether the accounts are free from material misstatement?			
501.42	Where applicable, have we obtained sufficient appropriate audit evidence regarding the presentation and disclosure of segment information?			

505.25	Were satisfactory alternative procedures applied in instances where management had refused permission for the use of external confirmations such as circularisation requests?			
510.2	Is there sufficient, appropriate evidence that amounts derived from the previous period are free from material misstatement and are appropriately incorporated and presented in the current period's accounts?			
520.2	Does the file contain sufficient evidence of analytical review at the planning and overall review stages of the audit?			
520.13	Has an adequate overall review of the accounts been performed?			
530.2	Has audit sampling been applied in an appropriate manner?			
540.8	Does the file contain sufficient, appropriate evidence concerning the reasonableness of accounting estimates?			
550.2	Is there sufficient, appropriate evidence that there is adequate disclosure of related-party transactions and control of the entity in the accounts?			
560.2	Has an adequate post-balance sheet events review been performed?			
570.2	Has the appropriateness of the going-concern basis been considered?			
580.2	Has a letter of representation, covering all necessary representations, been drafted?			
580.9	Have any occasions where representations received were contradicted by other evidence been fully investigated?			
600.2	When using the work of other auditors, is there sufficient appropriate evidence that the work of the other auditor is adequate for the purpose?			
610.2	Where the client has internal auditors, has adequate consideration been given to the effect this should have on the audit?			
620.2	When using the work of an expert, is there sufficient, appropriate evidence that the work is adequate for the purpose?			
700.2	Is the audit opinion consistent with the audit evidence and conclusions?			
700.41	Has any imposed limitation in scope been dealt with adequately?			
710.18	Where the prior period's financial statements were not audited, does the auditor report state that the corresponding figures are unaudited?			
720.2	Has other information to be issued with the financial statements been read so as to identify material inconsistencies?			

41.6 Audit highlights

The audit senior or manager should prepare an audit highlights memorandum. This is an essential part of the audit evidence. It is particularly important within a smaller practice, where very often the logic behind some of the decision-making has not been fully evidenced elsewhere on the file. This is usually as a result of an open-door policy applied within a practice, which means that queries are dealt with as they arise, and the issues are not always fully addressed within the audit file. The audit highlights memorandum gives the senior or manager an opportunity to review the key issues on an audit, outlining the problems that have arisen, how these have been dealt with and forming an ultimate conclusion on the audit.

When prepared well, an audit highlights report can significantly reduce the amount of time taken by a partner to review the file, as it directs the partner's attention to the higher risk or problem areas. The main purposes of such a memorandum, therefore, are:

- to assist the partner to efficiently review the audit work and assess the suitability of the conclusions drawn;
- to help to focus the partner's review on the significant areas and issues; and
- to provide a link between the audit plan and the actual work performed.

The memorandum should not record details of all the work that has been undertaken on each individual section, thus regurgitating the entire audit programme. Neither should it be a one-line response for each section, referring the reviewer to each of the individual sections of the file. Its contents should typically include all of the following elements.

a) **Update to background information** – changes to the entity's results and/or financial position after the year end, any new sector, regulatory and other external factors, changes to shareholders, directors, trustees, etc. and new accounting systems or changes in controls since the planning was completed and the permanent file updated.

b) **Audit strategy** – details of and reasons for any changes to the overall audit strategy and plan.

c) **Results of audit procedures and responses to risk** – work done in response to the key risks identified in the audit plan. How were the identified risks mitigated? This section should also include details of conclusions on the important audit and accounting matters arising. Typically, this would involve some commentary on how comfort was drawn on each individual audit section.

d) **Unadjusted errors** – any significant errors should be summarised and a conclusion given as to whether any need to be adjusted.

e) **Subsequent events** – a summary of any significant subsequent events and whether disclosure or adjustment is required.

f) **Review of financial statements** – brief comments on any significant matters arising from the final analytical review, plus any other disclosure or presentation issues.

g) **Justification of the audit report** – an overall conclusion. If the senior or manager were to sign off the report, what would he or she say?

h) **Audit administration and practicalities** – including any significant problems that occurred during the course of the audit and how these were dealt with, timetable to completion, clearance meeting arrangements, comments on the client's delivery of any requested schedules and information, etc.

The preparation of this schedule is not a waste of time. It saves expensive partner review time.

41.7 Justification of the audit report

Drafting the audit report is covered in more detail in Chapter 44. However, it is important that the auditor considers the applicability of the audit report that has been attached to the draft financial statements. This should be documented either within the audit highlights memorandum or as a separate schedule on the file.

A frequent problem is that the audit evidence does not back up the audit opinion. This is not because the opinion is incorrect, but because there is not a full record of how the opinion was formed documented on file. For example, there may be a problem highlighted on file but the resolution of the problem, which gives credence to the final audit opinion, has not been explained. This is invariably due in part to poor documentation of the discussions of such issues between the partner and the client.

Specifically, the auditor should consider the following issues:

a)	What impact will any qualified audit report from the previous period have on the current year's opinion? For example, the previous year's audit was qualified on the basis of limitation in scope due to the stocktake not being attended because the auditor had not been appointed until after the year end. In this situation, the auditor needs to consider the impact this will have on the current year's audit report, due to the opening balance on stock. This would usually lead to the profit and loss account being qualified, but not the balance sheet.

b)	Have there been any problems with books and records? In particular, the auditor should consider the issues of recording cash sales, the existence of a fixed asset register and whether adequate stock records have been maintained.

c)	Have all necessary information and explanations been obtained from the directors?

d)	Have adequate returns been received from any branches not visited during the course of the audit to enable an opinion to be formed?

e)	What is the impact of any potential going-concern problems (identified by completion of a going-concern review) on the audit opinion? Where this is the case, the reasons for the report given should be fully documented on file. The report should be in line with the requirements of ISAs 570 and 700, and the relevant APB Bulletin *Auditor's Reports on Financial Statements*.

f)	Where the entity is a holding company and exemption has been claimed from preparing group accounts, is the group entitled to this exemption? A specific report is no longer required on this issue, although consideration of the matter should still be fully documented. This issue is particularly relevant given the withdrawal of the exemption for medium-sized groups for accounting periods beginning on or after 6 April 2008.

g)	Have any other matters come to light that may affect the audit opinion?

All of the above matters should be addressed in a schedule justifying the audit opinion – even if the schedule records that they are not applicable to the entity in question. An example of such a schedule is reproduced below.

Client:		Ref:
Year end:		**B6**
File no:		

JUSTIFICATION OF AUDIT REPORT

This form should be used to schedule any problems encountered during the audit which could have an impact on the audit report.

		Yes/No N/A*	If yes, give details
1	Was the audit report qualified in the previous period?		
2	Have there been any problems with books and records?		
3	Have you encountered problems obtaining from the directors all information and explanations necessary for the audit?		
4	Have the directors refused to confirm any representations in writing?		
5	Have you confirmed that, or were you unable to conclude whether, the financial statements are materially misstated as a result of fraud?		
6	Have you had problems obtaining adequate information concerning suspected non-compliance with relevant laws or regulations?		
7	Is there evidence of non-compliance with laws or regulations that have a material effect on the accounts and which have not been properly reflected in the accounts?		
8	Has management refused to give permission for direct communication with the company's legal advisers?		
9	Has management refused to give permission for the use of external confirmation requests, such as the circularisation of debtor or creditor balances or third-party stock confirmations?		
10	Has management not amended the financial statements (adjustment or disclosure) in circumstances where it is believed that they need to be amended?		
11	Where other auditors are involved in the audit of subsidiary companies, are there any instances where their work cannot be relied upon?		
12	Are there any material inconsistencies between the financial statements and the directors' report or any other information to be issued with them?		

13 Were there problems obtaining adequate returns from branches not visited?	
14 Are there any problems with going concern? (Ref **T3**)	
15 Is there a problem with exemption from preparing group accounts where claimed by the company?	
16 Have any other problems occurred which could have an impact on the audit report?	

Conclusion

Wherever there is a 'yes' answer, detail below what effect this will have on the audit report or our ability to continue the engagement:

I am satisfied that any unqualified report is appropriate.* **Or**

In my opinion, the attached fundamental uncertainty/emphasis of matter and/or qualification is appropriate.*

Prepared by: _____   Date: _____

Reviewed by: _____   Date: _____

* Delete as appropriate.

41.8 Summary of unadjusted errors

ISA 320 *Audit materiality* requires the auditor to consider the impact of the unadjusted errors identified during the course of the audit on the audit opinion. All such errors should be highlighted on one form, which should be filed within the completion section. The auditor should then conclude on whether any adjustment is necessary. The errors should be split between extrapolated errors and actual errors, and their impact on the profit and loss account and the balance sheet should be recorded. The cumulative potential effect of the errors also needs to be noted.

A suggested format for recording unadjusted errors is given below.

Client:	Prepared by:	Date:	Ref:
Year end:	Reviewed by:	Date:	**B7**
File no:			

SUMMARY OF UNADJUSTED ERRORS

Final materiality _____

Narrative	Extrapolated errors		Actual errors		Profit and loss	Balance sheet	Considered trivial* Y/N
	DR	CR	DR	CR			
Total of potential adjustments							

Conclusion

1. The client has been asked to adjust for all misstatements noted above, other than those that are marked as clearly trivial*.

2. Where the client has not adjusted for misstatements drawn to its attention, the letter of representation explains the directors' reasons for not adjusting as required by ISA 260.11.19.

3. None of the potential adjustments listed above are considered to be indicative of fraud.

4. The effect of the unadjusted misstatements on our audit report is ...

*This is not another expression for 'immaterial'. Matters which are 'clearly trivial' will be of a wholly different (smaller) order of magnitude than the materiality thresholds used in the audit, and will be matters that are clearly inconsequential, whether taken individually or in aggregate and whether judged by any quantitative and/or qualitative criteria. Further, whenever there is any uncertainty about whether one or more items are 'clearly trivial' (in accordance with this definition), the presumption should be that the matter is not 'clearly trivial'. (ISA 260.11.16, note 6)

It is important to note that extrapolated errors are not usually adjusted. If the cumulative unadjusted errors, including extrapolated errors, are such that the auditor feels that an adjustment would be necessary, then it may be necessary to carry out further audit work to ascertain the likely level of the actual error, rather than contemplate adjusting for an extrapolated error within a particular population.

The auditor should ensure that there is proper consideration of the level of unadjusted errors. Frequently, there is simply a conclusion to say that no adjustment is necessary, yet on review of the file it becomes clear that there have been stock pricing errors, etc. that have not been recorded within the summary of unadjusted errors.

On completion of the schedule, it should be remembered that the summary should include any errors in the accounting treatment of particular items. Take, for example, the situation where an entity has bought a new computer on hire purchase but has decided not to capitalise it, as it is a relatively small item. The auditor may agree that the potential adjustment to the financial statements is not material. However, the fact that an asset that should have been capitalised has instead been written off to the profit and loss account and the hire-purchase payments have been treated incorrectly, should be recorded on the summary of unadjusted errors.

The auditor should also remember to include unadjusted errors in the previous period that would also have an impact in the current period – for example, errors relating to stock.

Having ascertained the details of the level of error within the financial statements, the auditor should consider whether any adjustment is needed. The level at which an adjustment is required will depend on the particular client – for example, adjustments may be made at a fairly low level where the entity is trading at or around the breakeven level. In other circumstances, it may be that adjustment is only made when the cumulative error is approaching the level of materiality.

ISA 320 requires the client to justify errors found that have not been adjusted for, and such justification should be included in the letter of representation. The terminology used in the ISAs refers to errors that are not material, but which are not considered to be 'clearly trivial' (as these do not have to be communicated to the client). If it cannot be decided whether an error is clearly trivial or not, then the auditor should err on the side of caution and assume that it is.

41.9 Final analytical procedures

This is the basic critical review of the accounts, which should always take place at the end of the audit. ISA 520 *Analytical procedures* requires analytical procedures to be performed when completing the audit. ISA 520.13 states:

> 'The auditor should apply analytical procedures at or near the end of the audit when forming an overall conclusion as to whether the financial statements as a whole are consistent with the auditor's understanding of the entity.'

This will generally involve the completion of a schedule highlighting key ratios and absolute figures, and comparing these to past accounting periods. However, the critical review of the accounts does not end with the simple completion of this form and the calculation of the various ratios. It is imperative that any unexpected variations and, indeed, any unexpected consistencies, are properly followed up, explained and substantiated. Remember that the conclusion the auditor is trying to arrive at in the critical review of the accounts is that the accounts 'make sense'. So it is vital that the auditor explains any such variations.

For some types of client, it will not really help the critical review of the accounts to complete a standard analytical review form, perhaps because the ratios that are calculated when completing the form are not meaningful for that particular type of business. In these situations, the auditor should develop a bespoke programme with indicators and ratios that should be calculated and critically examined every year.

The ISA also states that conclusions drawn from the results of such procedures (that is, that the accounts make sense) are intended to corroborate conclusions formed during the audit of individual components or elements of the financial statements and to assist in arriving at the overall conclusion on the reasonableness of the financial statements.

It is also stressed that this closing analytical review may identify areas requiring further audit procedures. For example, if the critical review of accounts highlights an unexpected increase in the debtor days ratio, this may cause the auditor to investigate further, whether or not there is a sufficient bad-debt provision in the accounts.

Many firms have no difficulty in calculating ratios, but interpreting the results and properly following up unexpected fluctuations is often not done well. If relevant notes were made during the preliminary analytical review and no significant changes have been put through the accounts, the auditor may cross-reference the completion section to the relevant figures and ratios on the planning section of the file. However, preliminary analytical review is aimed at identifying risk for the purpose of focusing the audit effort, whereas final analytical review is to ensure that the accounts fairly reflect the results of the business. Even where there has been no change in variances or ratios since the planning stage, a new conclusion will still need to be drawn at the completion stage, as an absolute minimum.

41.10 Disclosure checklists

The auditor should ensure that the draft accounts comply fully with all relevant FRSs, SSAPs and legislative requirements. The easiest way to do this, even where a computerised accounts preparation package is being used, is to use disclosure checklists. Not only do the checklists enable the auditor to demonstrate that disclosure has been checked, but they also provide a useful check on whether everything that should have been disclosed, actually has been.

It is obviously important to ensure that the most up-to-date version of a checklist is utilised and that it is appropriate for the year-end under audit.

Time should be allocated in the budget and timetable to ensure that the checklists are filled out properly, and not just tick-boxed without thought.

41.11 Common problems

41.11.1 Time pressure

The major problem that arises within audit completion is that the auditor does not leave sufficient time to finish things off. The completion of disclosure checklists and all the other checklists and preparation of an audit highlights report is a time-consuming exercise, and does not seem to require any less time on smaller jobs than it does on larger ones. Therefore, the auditor must allow sufficient time to tidy up the file and make it ready for review, and to clear any review points arising therefrom.

41.11.2 Failure to complete disclosure checklists

The disclosure checklist aspect of the section is particularly important, as the disclosure requirements currently remain quite complex. Many practices rely too heavily on the accounting software being used, rather than undertaking a separate procedure to ensure that there are adequate disclosures in the accounts.

Chapter 42 Reports to management

42.1 Introduction

ISA 260 *Communication of audit matters with those charged with governance* states:

> 'The auditor should consider audit matters of governance interest that arise from the audit of the financial statements and communicate them with those charged with governance.'

It should be noted that under ISA 260, the issuing of a letter of comment in writing is mandatory, even if only to explain there is nothing the auditor wishes to bring to the attention of management. Nevertheless, the letter of comment is a useful by-product of the audit as it gives the auditor an opportunity to add value to the audit process.

The ISA also states that, 'The auditor should communicate audit matters of governance interest on a timely basis'. It is important that the auditor remembers this, as it is quite common to find recorded systems and controls weaknesses within the file which have not been brought to the client's attention in writing. In addition, there is often no evidence on the file that the points have even been discussed with the directors and management. Many firms send a letter of comment to the client along with the final accounts, which may not be sufficiently prompt under ISAs. For example, if at the planning stage the auditor identifies a material weakness in the client's internal controls, an interim report should be issued at that stage.

42.2 Contents of the letter

The points that ISA 260 requires to be included within the letter are:

a) the auditor's views about the qualitative aspects of the entity's accounting practices and financial reporting;

b) the final draft of the representation letter that the auditor is requesting management and those charged with governance to sign. The communication should specifically refer to any matters where management is reluctant to make the representations requested by the auditor;

c) uncorrected (non-trivial) misstatements;

d) expected modifications to the auditor's report;

e) material weaknesses in internal control identified during the audit. This might include details of any recorded instances of the non-operation of accounting and internal control systems already in place. These points should not be limited to instances where an error has been discovered, but should also include instances where the auditor has identified that error could occur. However, the auditor should ensure that the points raised are not too contrived or pedantic, and where possible, should recommend improvements that could be made;

f) matters specifically required by other ISAs (UK and Ireland) to be communicated to those charged with governance; and

g) any other audit matters of governance interest (for example, advice on potential economies or improvements in efficiency and other commercial matters).

42.3 Style

The style of the letter is very important. The following points should be considered:

a) the fundamental rule is that the letter should be clear, constructive and concise – in particular, it should:

- use good, simple English;
- avoid accounting jargon; and
- avoid personal remarks;

b) the letter must be positive and helpful; (If it is not, the client may become defensive);

c) the auditor must ensure that the points being raised are cost-effective, and so the following matters should be borne in mind:

- the recommendations must be realistic, not contrived;
- avoid trivia which can 'cloud' the issue; and
- focus on the client (Too often, these letters focus on things that will make the auditor's life easier and not on those that will benefit the client);

d) the auditor must ensure that the points being raised are factually accurate and specific;

e) the points being raised must be put into a context that makes them relevant to the client's business;

f) the auditor must explain the points being raised, and not just provide a comprehensive statement of all the weaknesses;

g) the letter should be prepared promptly and sent at the appropriate time; and

h) at all times, the auditor must remember the client's priorities, which are:

- cost reduction and control;
- profit ('bottom line');
- future development; and
- flexibility – reacting to circumstances and opportunities.

42.4 Layout and procedure

The letter should be drafted in a standard format and should include:

a) an opening paragraph explaining the purpose of the letter;

b) the body of the letter, with details of the issues described above;

c) a closing paragraph summarising the action that should be taken by the client and making it clear that the audit is not designed to identify all matters that may be relevant to those charged with governance. The auditor should also seek to be courteous and thank the client and its staff for the assistance given during the audit;

d) the standard paragraph from ISA 260.20-1, limiting the auditors' liability to third parties in respect of the contents of the letter;

e) an appendix to the letter, setting out the following points for each of the issues being raised. These points should be drafted in such a way that either the most significant appear first or the points are graded in terms of their relative importance:

- a summary of the existing system;
- the nature of the weakness and its actual or potential impact; and
- the auditor's recommendations;

f) the auditor should discuss the draft with the client before sending the letter. This is particularly important where the letter is being sent to someone other than the person in charge of the accounts department;

g) the letter should leave space for the client's responses, confirming the action that the client is proposing; and

h) a copy of the letter should be carried forward to next year's audit file so that the action can be followed up.

42.5 Effect of the letter on the audit opinion

Sending a letter of comment to the client is not a substitute for any of the following:

- qualifying the audit opinion;
- adjusting for material errors in the accounts;
- maintaining proper books and records; or
- reporting to any regulatory body on the client's systems of internal control.

42.6 Liability arising from letters of comment

In order to avoid the risk of liability arising out of the issue of such a letter, the auditor should seek to put the following protections in place:

a) the letter should make it clear that it is a confidential report, solely for the client's internal use;

b) the letter should contain a paragraph making it clear that the audit may not have identified all weaknesses or potential weaknesses in the system; and

c) the auditor should find out from the client how the letter is to be used. The client should be informed of the need to obtain the auditor's express permission to issue the letter to any other party.

Chapter 43 Letters of representation

43.1 Introduction

ISA 580 *Management representations* states that, 'The auditor should obtain appropriate representations from management ... before the audit report is issued'. The letter of representation is a form of audit evidence that can be used to confirm both specific points and also general matters. It is important as it will also serve to reinforce the directors' responsibilities for certain items within the accounts and because it reduces the possibility of any misunderstanding.

43.2 Layout of the letter and procedure

When drafting a letter of representation, the letter should be addressed to the auditors and typed on the client's letterhead. Where the client does not have its own letterhead, the auditor must ensure that all the details that must be contained on a valid company letterhead are included in the letter. This will include:

a) the full registered name of the company;

b) the company's registration number and the part of the UK in which the company is registered; and

c) the company's full postal address, along with telephone and fax numbers.

Many firms fail to ensure that all these details are included within the letters that are drafted for the client to sign.

ISA 580 states that the auditor may write the letter to the client. For many smaller businesses, this is a favoured approach. Effectively, the auditor drafts a letter setting out the specific representations made by the client, and asks the client to sign and return a copy of the letter, thus indicating agreement with its contents.

ISA 580 goes on to state that the letter '...would ordinarily be signed by the members of management who have primary responsibility for the entity and its financial aspects', typically the Managing Director (Chief Executive for charitable entities) and Finance Director. However, it then goes on to confirm the usual UK practice of requesting that the letter be discussed by all those charged with governance (usually the board of directors) and then signed on behalf of the board by, for example, the Chairman. In these circumstances, it may be appropriate to ask the client to send a copy of the minutes of the board meeting where its contents were discussed and agreed.

Alternatively, the auditor may stipulate that all directors should sign it. For many smaller companies, where they are unlikely to have formal minutes of meetings, this approach is the most favourable.

43.2.1 Confirmation of understanding by the client

The auditor should discuss the contents with the directors prior to sending the letter for signature, in order to ensure that they understand what it is that they are being asked to confirm (ISA 580.4-1).

It was noted in the course of the hearing following the collapse of Barings that the Barings director who signed the representation letter had little knowledge or understanding of Nick Leeson's activities, despite being nominally his boss. However, the director made written statements to the effect that there had been no irregularities involving management or having a material effect on the financial systems, and that the financial statements were free of material errors and omissions.

Despite this, the director was not found to have been recklessly fraudulent, as it was not established that he signed the representation letters:

a) knowing that the statements in the letters were untrue, without an honest belief in their truth, or indifferent as to whether or not they were true; and

b) knowing that he had no reasonable grounds for making the statements, without an honest belief that he had such grounds, or indifferent as to whether he had or not.

As a result, the Audit and Assurance Faculty of the ICAEW issued AUDIT 4/02: *Management representation letters – Explanatory Note.* This advises the auditor to add a sentence to the letter of representation along the following (illustrative only) lines:

> 'We confirm that the above/following representations are made on the basis of enquiries of management and staff with relevant knowledge and experience (and, where appropriate, of inspection of supporting documentation) sufficient to satisfy ourselves that we can properly make each of the above/following representations to you.'

Whilst this Technical Release was issued some years ago, prior to the introduction of ISAs, the recommendation still forms part of best practice in connection with letters of representation.

43.3.3 Timing

The letter should be sent to the client when the financial statements are despatched for approval, and the client should date it on the day the accounts are signed. The auditor may wish to send a new letter if there is a significant delay in signing the audit report.

A draft of the letter should be sent to the client, with the letter of comment as explained in section 42.2. The draft should be sent before the final version and the directors/trustees given sufficient time to make any enquiries they feel necessary to satisfy themselves that the representations can be properly made.

43.3 Contents

The letter should be used to ask the directors to:

a) acknowledge their duty to prepare accounts showing a true and fair view;

b) acknowledge their responsibility for the design and implementation of internal control to prevent and detect fraud;

c) confirm that they have disclosed to the auditor the results of their assessment of the risk that the financial statements may be materially misstated as a result of fraud;

d) confirm that they have disclosed to the auditor their knowledge of fraud or suspected fraud affecting the entity involving management, employees who have significant roles in internal control or others where the fraud could have a material effect on the financial statements;

e) confirm that they have disclosed to the auditor their knowledge of any allegations of fraud, or suspected fraud, affecting the entity's financial statements communicated by employees, former employees, analysts, regulators or others;

f) confirm that they have made all the accounting records available to the auditor;

g) confirm that all transactions have been included in those records;

h) confirm that all other information has been provided to the auditors;

i) confirm the reasonableness of significant assumptions, including whether they appropriately reflect their intent and ability to carry out specific courses of action on behalf of the entity, where relevant to fair value measurements or disclosures;

j) confirm that, in their opinion, the entity is a going concern;

k) confirm that there are/have been no directors' loans, transactions, etc. or – where there have been – that these have been adequately disclosed within the accounts;

l) confirm that there are no adjusting or non-adjusting post-balance sheet events, contingencies, etc. or – where there are – that these have been adequately disclosed within the accounts;

m) confirm that there have been no specific instances of non-compliance with significant laws and regulations, or – where there have been any instances of actual or possible non-compliance – that details have been disclosed (where necessary) and any necessary accrual for any resultant liability has been made;

n) confirm that there are no undisclosed related parties and transactions therewith;

o) explain their reasons for not correcting misstatements brought to their attention by the auditor; and

p) confirm any specific representations made during the course of the audit. Typically, this will include such matters as the adequacy of any specific provisions.

The auditor may also include details of directors' loan accounts within the letter, but this is probably better confirmed within separate letters to the individual directors.

43.4 Other issues

Other matters that should be considered when preparing a letter of representation are set out below.

a) It is essential that a schedule is maintained during the audit, on which the auditor can and does record details of any specific representations made during the course of the audit and that these are included within the letter sent to the client for signature.

b) The letter should be used to corroborate other evidence; it is not a substitute for audit work. Nor should it be used to confirm issues that the auditor has been able to verify through the audit work undertaken. Using the letter to confirm anything and everything can lessen the impact of some of the specific representations that the auditor wishes to rely on.

c) The auditor must consider whether the representations are reasonable and whether they can be relied on. In particular, the auditor must consider whether there is anything that may indicate that the auditor cannot 'trust' what he or she has been told.

d) If the representations are the only evidence available and relate to significant matters, the auditor should consider whether specific reference is required in the audit report.

e) Any contradictory representations should be investigated.

43.5 What if a client refuses to sign a letter of representation?

In the rare event that a client does not wish to sign the letter of representation, the auditor should take the steps set out below.

a) The letter of engagement will usually contain a paragraph stipulating that the client may be asked to confirm representations made in writing, which should be pointed out to the client.

b) The auditor should explain the purpose of the letter and seek to settle the disagreement.

c) Where the client still refuses to sign a representation that the auditor considers necessary, ISA 580.15 makes clear that this is a limitation of scope that requires an audit qualification. In such circumstances, the auditor would evaluate any reliance placed on other representations made by management during the course of the audit and consider if the other implications of the refusal may have any additional effect on the audit report.

Chapter 44 Drafting the audit report

44.1 Introduction

The specific issues that should be addressed when drafting the audit report were contained within Chapter 41. The purpose of this Chapter is to look at the requirements of ISA 700 *The auditor's report on financial statements* and relevant APB Bulletins, and the specific types of report that may be drafted. The final report should normally be drafted by the senior or manager on the assignment and then agreed by the audit principal.

Because ISAs (UK and Ireland) have international origins, the guidance given on audit reports in ISA 700 is more general than was the case with SAS 600. As a result, this ISA was heavily supplemented with 'grey shaded paragraphs' (additions by the APB) when introduced into the UK. It frequently refers to the Bulletin entitled *Auditor's Reports on Financial Statements*, which gives additional detail for UK audit reports, including numerous examples of suitable wording covering many different scenarios. The Bulletin is periodically revised and reissued by the APB to take account of legislative and other changes affecting the wording of UK audit reports. At the date of writing, the most recent version is Bulletin 2006/6 although Bulletin 2008/8 deals with short accounting periods in compliance with the Companies Act 2006 (see section 44.10.2).

As with all other Auditing Standards, ISA 700 applies to the conduct of any audit of financial statements. Paragraph 2 of ISA 200 *Objective and general principles governing an audit of financial statements* states that an audit comprises any exercise whereby the auditor is to express an opinion whether the financial statements are prepared, in all material respects, in accordance with an applicable financial reporting framework. The two phrases used to express the auditor's opinion, and which are equivalent terms, are 'give a true and fair view' and 'present fairly, in all material respects'.

44.2 Definitions

The following definitions apply in interpreting the requirements of ISA 700.

Financial statements

The balance sheet, profit and loss account (or other form of income statement), statements of cash flows and total recognised gains and losses, notes and other statements and explanatory material, all of which are identified in the auditors' report as being the financial statements.

Material

A matter is material if its omission or misstatement would reasonably influence the decisions of a user of the financial statements. Materiality may be considered in the context of the financial statements as a whole, any individual primary statement within the financial statements, or individual items included in them.

Uncertainty

An uncertainty is a matter whose outcome depends on future actions or events not under the direct control of the entity, but which may affect the financial statements. Uncertainties are regarded as significant when they involve a significant level of concern about the validity of the going-concern basis or other matters whose potential effect on the financial statements is unusually great. A common example of a significant uncertainty is the outcome of major litigation.

44.3 Basic elements of the auditor's report

44.3.1 Contents of the auditor's report on financial statements

ISA 700.5 stipulates that the auditor's report should include the following matters:

a) a title identifying the person or persons to whom the report is addressed;

b) an opening or introductory paragraph identifying the financial statements audited* and giving the respective responsibilities of directors (or equivalent persons) and auditors;

c) a scope paragraph describing the nature of an audit, including a reference to the ISAs or relevant national standards or practices and a description of the work the auditor performed;

d) an opinion paragraph containing:

   ● a reference to the financial reporting framework used to prepare the financial statements (including identifying the country of origin of the financial reporting framework when the framework used is not International Accounting Standards); and

   ● an expression of opinion on the financial statements; and

e) the date of the report, the auditor's address and signature.

* APB Bulletin 2006/6 also suggests other changes to the style of the audit report where it will be published in electronic format (for example, reference to the titles of the primary statements and notes rather than to page numbers).

44.3.2 Bannerman paragraph

This now famous case (held in the Scottish Court of Session) decided that it was possible that the auditor owed a duty of care to a creditor (in this case, the bank) if the auditor knew, or ought to have known, that the creditor would be relying on the accounts. In practice, this simply clarified what had previously been inferred.

However, as a result, the ICAEW Audit and Assurance Faculty issued guidance that recommended that a suitably worded disclaimer paragraph be included in the audit report. This is Audit Technical Release 1/03 *The Audit Report and Auditors' Duty of Care to Third Parties*.

As this disclaimer was issued by the Audit and Assurance Faculty, and not by the APB, it is not included in any of the example reports given in Bulletin 2006/6. All ICAEW firms are recommended to add the disclaimer to the model reports. It should be noted that the ACCA strongly suggests that its member firms should **not** include such disclaimers in their audit reports.

44.3.3 Statements of responsibility and basis of opinion

Auditors should distinguish between their responsibilities and those of the directors by including in their report either:

a) a reference to a description of the relevant responsibilities of those charged with governance when that description is set out elsewhere in the financial statements or accompanying information; or

b) where the financial statements or accompanying information (for example, the directors' report) do not include an adequate description of directors' relevant responsibilities, the auditors' report should include a description of those responsibilities.

Appendix 5 to APB Bulletin 2006/6 sets out the following illustrative wording of the directors' responsibilities:

> 'The directors are responsible for preparing the Annual Report and the financial statements in accordance with applicable law and regulations.

Company law requires the directors to prepare financial statements for each financial year. Under that law the directors have elected to prepare the financial statements in accordance with United Kingdom Generally Accepted Accounting Practice (United Kingdom Accounting Standards and applicable law). The financial statements are required by law to give a true and fair view of the state of affairs of the company and of the profit or loss of the company for that period. In preparing these financial statements, the directors are required to:

- select suitable accounting policies and then apply them consistently;

- make judgments and estimates that are reasonable and prudent;

- state whether applicable United Kingdom Accounting Standards have been followed, subject to any material departures disclosed and explained in the financial statements;*

- prepare the financial statements on the going concern basis unless it is inappropriate to presume that the company will continue in business.†

The directors are responsible for keeping proper accounting records that disclose with reasonable accuracy at any time the financial position of the company and enable them to ensure that the financial statements comply with the Companies Act 1985. They are also responsible for safeguarding the assets of the company and hence for taking reasonable steps for the prevention and detection of fraud and other irregularities.

The directors are responsible for the maintenance and integrity of the corporate and financial information included on the company's website. Legislation in the United Kingdom governing the preparation and dissemination of financial statements may differ from legislation in other jurisdictions.' §

* Large companies only

† If no separate statement on going concern is made by the directors

§ Where the financial statements are published on the internet

44.3.4 Basis of opinion

Auditors should explain the basis of their opinion by including the following in their report:

a) a statement as to their compliance or otherwise with International Standards on Auditing (UK and Ireland), together with the reasons for any departure there from;

b) a statement that the audit process includes:

- examining, on a test basis, evidence relevant to the amounts and disclosures in the financial statements;

- assessing the significant estimates and judgments made by the reporting entity's directors in preparing the financial statements; and

- considering whether the accounting policies are appropriate to the reporting entity's circumstances, consistently applied and adequately disclosed; and

c) a statement that they planned and performed the audit so as to obtain reasonable assurance that the financial statements are free from material misstatement, whether caused by fraud or other irregularity or error, and that they have evaluated the overall presentation of the financial statements.

44.4 Expression of opinion

Paragraph 4 of ISA 700 states: 'The auditor's report should contain a clear written expression of opinion on the financial statements taken as a whole.' Paragraph 17 goes on to clarify that it should comprise:

'...the auditor's opinion as to whether the financial statements give a true and fair view (or are presented fairly, in all material respects), in accordance with that financial reporting framework and, where appropriate, whether the financial statements comply with statutory requirements.'

44.4.1 Entities adopting the FRSSE

The audit opinion for entities adopting the FRSSE needs to note this fact. This is done by amending the 'true and fair' opinion so as to read '...in accordance with United Kingdom Generally Accepted Accounting Practice *applicable to Smaller Entities*...' as shown in the first example audit report in Appendix 1 to Bulletin 2006/6.

44.4.2 Reporting on the consistency of the directors' report with the financial statements

In the UK, the auditor also reports on whether the information in the directors' report is consistent with the financial statements (although this does not apply to unincorporated charities). It is rare to see any evidence on audit files that this issue has been formally considered, and given that relatively few disclosures are required in the directors' report of small companies, it might legitimately be seen as a low risk area.

However, this is not the case with medium and large companies, who now have to produce a fairly detailed business review covering matters such as risk and financial performance including, key performance indicators (KPIs), and charities, who have extensive disclosure requirements for the trustees' report. It is therefore important to ensure that:

- figures quoted from the main body of the financial statements;
- ratios and other KPIs; and
- narrative commentary

are all carefully checked for consistency with the financial statements. Indeed, ISA 720 (Revised) *Section B - The auditor's statutory reporting responsibility in relation to directors' reports* requires the auditor to read the information in the directors' report and assess whether it is consistent with the financial statements. If it is not, the auditor should seek to resolve the inconsistency.

If the inconsistency cannot be resolved and is considered to be material, the auditor should state that opinion and describe the inconsistency in the audit report. If an amendment to the financial statements is needed and management refuses to make it, the auditor should express a 'modified' opinion – see below.

44.4.3 Modified opinions

Other than an unqualified opinion, both the ISA and Bulletin use the word 'modified' to describe any other audit report which, depending on the circumstances, may or may not affect the audit opinion. For example, the inclusion of an emphasis of matter paragraph does not, in itself, affect the audit opinion. In contrast, a qualified opinion, which does affect the audit opinion, is issued when either of the following circumstances exists:

a) there is a limitation on the scope of the auditors' examination; **or**
b) the auditors disagree with the treatment or disclosure of a matter in the financial statements;

and, in either case, in the auditors' judgment the effect of the matter is or may be material to the financial statements and, therefore, those statements may not or do not give a true and fair view of the matters on which the auditors are required to report, or do not comply with the relevant accounting or other requirements.

These scenarios are considered in more detail below.

44.5 Emphasis of matter

In certain circumstances, the audit report may be modified by adding an emphasis of matter paragraph to highlight a matter affecting the financial statements, and which is included in a note to the financial statements that discusses it more extensively. ISA 700 gives two such scenarios:

a) The auditor **should** modify the auditor's report by adding a paragraph to highlight a material matter regarding a going-concern problem; and

b) The auditor **should consider** modifying the auditor's report by adding a paragraph if there is a significant uncertainty (other than a going-concern problem), the resolution of which is dependent upon future events and which may affect the financial statements.

The addition of such a paragraph does **not** affect the auditor's opinion. The paragraph would preferably be included after the opinion paragraph and would ordinarily refer to the fact that the auditor's opinion is not qualified in this respect.

44.5.1 Significant uncertainties

Uncertainties about the outcome of future events frequently affect, to some degree, a wide range of components of the financial statements at the date they are approved. It is not possible for the directors to remove the uncertainties by obtaining more information at the date they approve the financial statements; these can reflect only the working assumptions of directors as to their financial outcome and, where material, describe the circumstances giving rise to the uncertainties and their potential financial effect.

In forming an opinion, auditors take into account the adequacy of the accounting treatment, estimates and disclosures of uncertainties in the light of evidence available at the date they express that opinion.

Forming an opinion on the adequacy of the accounting treatment of such uncertainties involves consideration of:

a) the appropriateness of accounting policies dealing with uncertain matters;

b) the reasonableness of the estimates included in the financial statements in respect of inherent uncertainties; and

c) the adequacy of disclosure.

Auditors distinguish between circumstances in which an unqualified opinion is appropriate and those in which a qualification or disclaimer of opinion is required, due to a limitation on the scope of their work. An uncertainty can be expected to be resolved at a future date, at which time sufficient evidence concerning its outcome would be expected to become available. When evidence does or did exist (or reasonably could be expected to exist) but that evidence is not available to the auditors, the scope of their work is limited and a qualification or disclaimer of opinion is appropriate.

In some circumstances, the degree of uncertainty about the outcome of a future event and its potential impact on the view given by the financial statements may be very great. Where resolution of such an uncertainty could affect the view given by the financial statements to a significant degree, they include an explanatory paragraph describing the matter giving rise to the uncertainty and its possible effects on the financial statements, including (where practicable) quantification. Where it is not possible to quantify the potential effects of the resolution of the uncertainty, the auditors include a statement to that effect. Reference may be made to notes in the financial statements, but such a reference is not a substitute for sufficient description of the fundamental uncertainty so that a reader can appreciate the principal points at issue and their implications.

Communication with the reader is enhanced by the use of an appropriate subheading differentiating the explanatory paragraph from other matters included in the section describing the basis of the auditor's opinion.

In determining whether an uncertainty is significant, auditors should consider:

a) the risk that the estimate included in financial statements may be subject to change;

b) the range of possible outcomes; and

c) the consequences of those outcomes on the view shown in the financial statements.

In addition to the use of an emphasis of matter paragraph for matters that affect the financial statements, the auditor may also similarly modify the audit report to report on other matters. For example, if an amendment to other information in a document containing audited financial statements is necessary and the directors refuse to make the amendment, the auditor would consider including in the audit report an emphasis of matter paragraph describing the material inconsistency. An emphasis of matter paragraph may also be used when there are additional statutory reporting responsibilities.

44.6 Limitation on the scope of an audit

A limitation on the scope of the auditors' work is something that prevents them from obtaining sufficient evidence to express an unqualified opinion.

A **disclaimer of opinion** is expressed when the possible effect of a limitation on scope is so material or pervasive that the auditor has not been able to obtain sufficient evidence to support, and is accordingly unable to express, an opinion on the financial statements.

A **qualified opinion** should be issued when the effect of the limitation is not so material or pervasive as to require a disclaimer. A qualified opinion should be expressed by stating that the financial statements give a true and fair view, 'except for' the effects of any adjustments that might have been found necessary had the limitation not affected the evidence available to the auditor.

The audit report should include a description of the factors leading to the limitation in the opinion section of the report. This enables the reader to understand the reasons for the limitation and to distinguish between:

a) limitations imposed on the auditors (for example, where not all the accounting records are made available to the auditors, or where the directors prevent a particular procedure considered necessary by the auditor from being carried out); and

b) limitations imposed by circumstances (for example, when the timing of the auditor's appointment is such that attendance at the entity's stocktake is not possible and there is no alternative form of evidence regarding the existence of stock).

> 'If the auditors are aware, before accepting an audit engagement, that those charged with governance of the entity, or those who appoint its auditor, will impose a limitation on the scope of the audit work which the auditor considers likely to result in the need to issue a disclaimer of opinion on the financial statements, the auditor should not accept that engagement, unless required to do so by statute' (ISA 700.41-1).

> 'If the auditor becomes aware, after accepting an audit engagement, that those charged with governance of the entity, or those who appointed them as its auditor, have imposed a limitation on the scope of the audit work which they consider likely to result in the need to issue a disclaimer of opinion on the financial statements, the auditor should request the removal of the limitation. If the limitation is not removed, the auditor should consider resigning from the audit engagement' (ISA700.41-3).

Where a limitation of scope is imposed by circumstances, auditors would normally attempt to carry out reasonable alternative procedures to obtain sufficient audit evidence to support an unqualified opinion.

44.7 Disagreement on accounting treatment or disclosure

Where the auditor disagrees with the accounting treatment or disclosure of a matter in the financial statements, and in the auditor's opinion the effect of that disagreement is material to the financial statements, the auditor should include in the opinion section of the report:

a) a description of all substantive factors giving rise to the disagreement;

b) their implications for the financial statements; and

c) whenever practicable, a quantification of the effect on the financial statements.

If the auditor concludes that the effect of the matter giving rise to disagreement is so material or pervasive that the financial statements are seriously misleading, an **adverse opinion** should be issued. An adverse opinion is expressed by stating that the financial statements do not give a true and fair view.

When the auditors conclude that the effect of a disagreement is not so significant as to require an adverse opinion, they express an opinion that is qualified by stating that the financial statements give a true and fair view 'except for' the effects of the matter giving rise to the disagreement.

44.7.1 Compliance with relevant accounting requirements

Section 396 of the Companies Act 2006 requires financial statements to give a true and fair view. Whilst neither SI 2008/409 nor SI 2008/410 specifically state that Accounting Standards should be followed, paragraph 45 to Schedule 1 of SI 2008/410 requires medium and large companies to:

a) state whether applicable Accounting Standards have been followed; and

b) disclose particulars of any material departures from applicable Accounting Standards, together with the reasons for the departure.

Furthermore, the foreword to Accounting Standards notes that they are applicable to financial statements which are intended to give a true and fair view.

Therefore, in order for financial statements to meet the requirements of these Statutory Instruments, they should follow rather than depart from Accounting Standards, and any departure will be regarded as sufficiently abnormal to require justification.

Departure from an Accounting Standard would therefore, where material, result in a qualified audit report, unless the departure can be and is justified. The disclosure requirement of paragraph 62 of FRS 18 *Accounting Policies* would also need to be included.

44.8 Date and signature of the auditor's report

44.8.1 Dating the audit report

The auditor should not date the report earlier than the date on which all other information contained in a report of which the audited financial statements form a part have been approved by the directors, and the auditor has considered all necessary available evidence.

The auditor is not in a position to form the opinion until the financial statements (and any other information contained in a report of which the audited financial statements form a part) have been approved by the directors, and the auditor has completed the assessment of all the evidence the auditor considers necessary for the opinion or opinions to be given in the auditor's report. This assessment includes events occurring up to the date the opinion is expressed. The auditor therefore plans the conduct of audits to take account of the need to ensure, before expressing an opinion on financial statements, that those charged with governance have approved the financial statements and any accompanying financial information and that the auditor has completed a sufficient review of post-balance sheet events.

The date of an auditor's report on a reporting entity's financial statements is the date on which the auditor signed the report expressing an opinion on those statements (ISA 700.23-1).

The date of the auditors' report is, therefore, the date on which, following:

a) receipt of the financial statements and accompanying documents in the form approved by the directors for release;

b) review of all documents which they are required to consider in addition to the financial statements (for example, the directors' report, chairman's statement or other review of an entity's affairs which will accompany the financial statements); and

c) completion of all procedures necessary to form an opinion on the financial statements (and any other opinions required by law or regulation), including a review of post balance sheet events,

the auditors signed (in manuscript) their report expressing an opinion on the financial statements for distribution with those statements.

If the date on which the auditors sign their report is later than that on which the directors approved the financial statements, the auditors should take such steps as are appropriate:

- to obtain assurance that the directors would have approved the financial statements on that later date (for example, by obtaining confirmation from specified individual members of the board to whom authority has been delegated for this purpose); and

- to ensure that their procedures for reviewing subsequent events cover the period up to that date.

44.8.2 Signing the audit report

For accounting periods beginning before 6 April 2008, the audit report is signed by the 'Responsible Individual', in the name of the audit firm. ISA 700 notes that this is because the firm assumes responsibility for the audit, and also confirms that the report states the auditor's status as a registered auditor.

However, for accounting periods commencing on or after 6 April 2008, the Companies Act 2006 changes the way audit reports are signed. For such periods, the audit report must be signed by the 'Senior Statutory Auditor', in the individual's own personal name rather than the firm's name. (This is also permitted by paragraph 26 of ISA 700.)

This change was incorporated into the Audit Regulations in 2008, but the scope of this requirement is not extended beyond that of the Companies Act 2006. Audit reports of entities outside the scope of the Companies Act 2006 (such as charitable trusts) will therefore continue to be signed in the name of the firm.

44.9 Other information in documents containing audited financial statements

It is sometimes the case that an entity's annual report contains information other than the audited financial statements. This is commonly found with listed companies and some charities, but can also occur with other entities – for example, the inclusion of a Chairman's Report in the annual report of a private company.

Whilst the auditor has no obligation to report on such information, the auditor should still read it to identify any material inconsistencies with the audited financial statements – in which case, the auditor should seek to resolve them. This might involve amending either the financial statements or the other information.

- If an amendment is necessary in the audited financial statements and the entity refuses to make the amendment, the auditor should express a qualified or adverse opinion.

- If an amendment is necessary in the other information and the entity refuses to make the amendment, the auditor should consider including in the auditor's report an emphasis of matter paragraph describing the material inconsistency, or taking other actions. The actions taken, such as not issuing the auditor's report or withdrawing from the engagement, will depend upon the particular circumstances and the nature and significance of the inconsistency. Legal advice regarding any further action should be sought.

If the auditor becomes aware that the other information appears to include a material misstatement of fact, the auditor should try to resolve the matter by, if necessary, requesting that the other information be amended. The auditor should also request management to seek legal advice. If the auditor concludes that there is a material misstatement of fact in the other information, which management refuses to correct, the auditor should consider:

a) notifying those charged with governance, in writing, of the auditor's concern regarding the other information;

b) obtaining legal advice; and

c) whether to include an emphasis of matter paragraph in the audit report describing the material misstatement.

44.10 Future developments

44.10.1 ISA 700 (Revised)

At date of writing, the APB is currently consulting on a revised version of ISA 700 (UK and Ireland). This revision has its roots back in 2007, when the APB issued a Discussion Paper entitled 'The Auditor's Report: A time for change?', which sought views on what steps needed to be taken to reflect the changes introduced by the Companies Act 2006, and whether other, more wide-ranging, changes should be made to the form and content of the auditor's report.

The draft ISA proposes a much more concise auditor's report, made possible by removing much of the standard language (for example, relating to the auditor's responsibilities and the basis of the auditor's opinion) from the auditor's report and instead including it within a 'Statement of the scope of an audit and the auditor's reporting responsibilities' which would be posted to the APB's website and cross-referred to from the auditor's report. The proposals also include requiring the auditor's opinion on the financial statements to be separated from other opinions required by law and regulation.

It is proposed that the revised ISA will take effect for accounting periods ending on or after 5 April 2009.

44.10.2 APB Bulletin 2008/8

APB Bulletin 2008/8 provides illustrative auditor's reports for use in the UK relating to those (short) accounting periods that commence on or after 6 April 2008 but end before 5 April 2009 and which are required to comply with the Companies Act 2006. This Bulletin effectively bridges the gap between the current guidance (ISA 700 and APB Bulletin 2006/6) and the revised ISA 700 noted above.

It is likely that a full update to Bulletin 2006/6 will be issued some time in 2009 to take account of these changes.

Chapter 45 Reviewing the file

45.1 Introduction

When referring to individual audits, ISA 220 *Quality control for audits of historical financial information*, states that, 'The engagement partner should take responsibility for the overall quality on each audit engagement to which that partner is assigned' (ISA 220.6).

In addition, it states:

> 'The engagement partner should take responsibility for the direction, supervision and performance of the audit engagement in compliance with professional standards and regulatory and legal requirements...' (ISA 220.21).

The extent of the direction, supervision and review will be decided by the audit engagement partner and those personnel with supervisory responsibility, by considering the professional competence of those members of the audit team to whom work is delegated.

A review of an audit file should ensure:

a) the work has been performed in accordance with the audit programme;

b) the work performed and the results obtained are adequately documented;

c) any significant audit matters have been resolved and are reflected in audit conclusions;

d) consultation has taken place wherever necessary and with an appropriate individual;

e) the objectives of the audit procedures have been achieved;

f) an independent review has been undertaken where required;

g) the conclusions expressed are consistent with the results of the work performed and support the audit opinion; and

h) any threats to the firm's independence or objectivity were identified and remedial action taken.

The results of the review may mean that areas are identified where further work is required.

When reviewing the file other considerations, not directly related to the audit opinion, need to be taken into account, such as 'were the correct staff used on the job?' The review can also be used to provide training for staff through positive feedback.

With the exception of the training aspects of the file review, these objectives fall into two broad categories. The first is looking at the work that the reviewer is presented with and ensuring that it is satisfactory. This is the easier of the two aspects. The second is to identify what should be on the file but is not. This is the more difficult area and the one that gives most problems.

The review of a file needs to be systematic and is best done without interruptions. This improves not only the efficiency of the review, but the effectiveness as well. Part of the skill in reviewing a file is to consider the file as a whole. When looking at one area within the file, the auditor needs to be aware of and consider whether this is consistent with other information.

The auditor should not be afraid to delve into another part of the file if he or she sees something which indicates a potential problem. However, the auditor should always make sure to return to the original place and to continue to work systematically through any file. 'Post-it' notes can prove invaluable in this process as they enable the auditor to mark his or her position in a paper file.

If using a paperless audit system such as CCH ProSystem Audit Automation, the software keeps a record of those working papers and tests signed off as having been reviewed, which ensures that it is not possible to inadvertently miss a working paper when reviewing. It may also allow several working papers to be viewed on screen simultaneously in 'tabs', allowing the reviewer to easily cross-refer to other sections in the file.

The extent of the file review that the auditor needs to carry out will depend upon the structure of the file and any previous reviews that others have carried out.

45.2 The review pyramid

When establishing the review procedures in any firm, it is essential that the firm create clearly defined levels of responsibility. A firm's structure might typically define levels such as manager, senior and junior, but more important than the job title, from a control point of view, is the fact that each assistant on an assignment understands his or her role precisely, including review responsibilities. In addition, members of staff should also appreciate the role of their peers. The task is more likely to be completed effectively if audit staff members can look at their own role from the position of the reviewer on the next level of the review pyramid.

The review procedure can be considered as a pyramid. In firms with a formal structure, the pyramid might look like this:

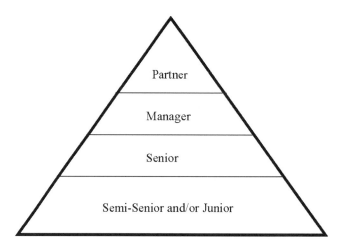

Each level in the hierarchy is responsible for reviewing the work done by the lower level. In this way, someone else reviews all work other than original partner work. One further point is that under the Audit Regulations, the partner must be a responsible individual (RI) – that is, someone authorised to sign audit reports. Any work performed by a non-RI partner would need to be reviewed by an RI. It should also be noted that under the revised audit regulations a responsible individual can be an employee of the practice, and hence his or her work would not need to be reviewed by the partner. Note that, as mentioned above, this terminology is changing to that of the 'Senior Statutory Auditor'.

If we consider the structure illustrated in the pyramid, the junior or semi-senior will do most of the basic analysis work. The senior should review this. The senior will complete the main sections on the file and present the file to the manager for a detailed review. The manager will then normally pull the job together and summarise it in the control section of the file for the partner. Provided there is an *effective* manager review, then in this situation, the partner would normally only need to look at the financial statements and the control section of the file. The partner would not need to delve into the detail of the file unless triggered to do so by the control section.

The word 'effective' is highlighted since this approach indicates that the partner is putting an extremely high level of reliance on the manager. This approach will also only operate where the manager is independent from the detailed work. If the manager produced any schedules in his or her own right, then these too would need to be reviewed by the partner.

It would not be appropriate for the partner automatically to assume that any manager review will be effective. The firm will need some form of quality control system to verify this. It can be achieved either by the partner occasionally re-performing the manager review, or by the review being examined under a system of 'cold' file review, either by other members of the firm or by an outside third party (for example, SWATuk). Many firms will operate without the manager position referred to above. A senior and a junior will work on the file and report directly to the partner. In this situation, or in a situation where the partner cannot rely on any manager review to be effective, the partner has to carry out not only the partner review, but a manager review as well. The partner will therefore be involved in looking at each of the detailed schedules on the file, other than the junior's schedules, which have been reviewed by the senior (unless referred to such a schedule by the senior following a review point).

The file review checklist for audit assignments (reproduced at the end of this Chapter) highlights some of the key problem areas that exist on audit files. The reviewer can use this to ensure that the common problem areas on the file have been properly dealt with.

This checklist can also be utilised in the situation where the partner (maybe a sole practitioner) is undertaking the whole assignment. In this case, the review process still needs to be undertaken but the sole practitioner needs to wear several different 'hats'. The use of checklists helps this. It is also useful, wherever possible, to have a 'cooling-off' period between the completion of the fieldwork and the review of the file, so that it is easier to change 'hats'.

45.2.1 Changes to the senior statutory auditor

As noted above in 44.8.2, the audit reports of companies with accounting periods commencing on or after 6 April 2008 will need to be signed in the name of the senior statutory auditor rather than in the name of the audit firm. In Bulletin 2008/6 *The "Senior Statutory Auditor" under the United Kingdom Companies Act 2006*, the phrase 'senior statutory auditor' has the same meaning as 'engagement partner' within ISAs.

ISA220 contains the following definition of engagement partner:

> 'The partner or other person in the firm who is responsible for the audit engagement and its performance, and for the auditor's report that is issued on behalf of the firm, and who, where required, has the appropriate authority from a professional, legal or regulatory body.'

The question therefore arises as to what the implications would be if the senior statutory auditor were unable to be present to sign the audit report. In response, the Bulletin says that, under section 503(3) of the Companies Act 2006, the senior statutory auditor must sign the audit report. Another partner, or responsible individual, is not able to sign for and on behalf of the senior statutory auditor.

If the senior statutory auditor is unable to continue taking responsibility for the direction, supervision and performance of the audit, the audit firm must appoint a replacement senior statutory auditor. The new senior statutory auditor must review the audit work performed to the date of the change. The review procedures must be sufficient to satisfy the new senior statutory auditor that the audit work performed to the date of the review has been planned and performed in accordance with professional standards and regulatory and legal requirements.

Where there is a change of senior statutory auditor towards the end of the audit, this will necessarily require an extensive review, which will be expensive and time consuming.

45.3 The role of planning

Three of the objectives of the review procedures, specified earlier, were to ensure that:

a) all work is carried out to an adequate standard;

b) all work is completed satisfactorily and efficiently; and

c) the correct grade of staff is used on the job.

These objectives can only be achieved if proper planning of the work precedes the review. Without such planning, the review will be essentially negative – in merely identifying problems without providing solutions.

As a minimum, if the review indicates that some or all of these objectives have not been satisfied, then it is essential that corrective action be taken in future years. In practice, this should be achieved by recording the problems and the solutions on a schedule of points forward to the following year. This should be reviewed at the planning stage of the following year's audit and the necessary amendments to the approach and the staffing of the job should be made. It is, of course, better if such potential problems are identified and corrective action taken before they are encountered.

45.4 File review checklist for use on audit assignments in practice

When reviewing an audit file, the reviewer should concentrate on those areas with the greatest materiality or audit risk, and the following are items that should be specifically addressed. These have been produced in the form of a checklist so that they can be copied and used as such. The auditor should adapt them and update them for specific issues that are relevant to the client or the practice. They are not an essential tool, but many practices find them very useful.

	Yes/No/N/A
45.4.1 Financial statements	
• Do the financial statements agree with the lead schedules (including any late adjustments)?	
• Do they present the figures in a logical manner?	
• Do they seem reasonable in the light of your knowledge of the client?	
• Has an up-to-date accounts disclosure checklist been completed satisfactorily?	
• Do the financial statements comply with all the relevant disclosure requirements?	
• Have you checked: (a) the page references on the audit report? (b) that the reference to a profit or a loss on the audit report is consistent with the results per the profit and loss account? (c) that the numbering of, and the amounts in, the notes to the financial statements agree to the balance sheet or profit and loss account where relevant?	
45.4.2 Quality control	
• Is there an up-to-date letter of engagement?	
• Has any overall conclusion on the file been completed and signed off by the partner(s)?	
• Have any completion questionnaires been **properly** completed?	
• Has an independent review been undertaken where required by the firm's procedures?	
• Have the objectives and conclusions on each section of the file been **properly** signed off?	

45.4.3 Planning

• Have all the points raised at the planning stage of the job been fully actioned?	
• Have the audit tests taken account of the materiality and degree of risk of the amounts involved?	
• Have the levels of tests been properly documented?	

45.4.4 Professional judgment

• Has the audit risk been overstated?	
• Has the materiality been understated?	
• Have the client's systems been recorded and formally assessed for their adequacy for the basis of preparing financial statements?	
• If sample sizes have been overridden during the audit, is this reasonable?	

45.4.5 Efficiency

• Is the file fully cross-referenced (that is, is it possible to see where all the figures go to and come from)?	
• Does the file contain excessive scheduling?	
• Are all analyses: (a) necessary? (b) consistent with the final analysis required on the financial statements?	

45.4.6 Analytical review

• Have the standard ratios been calculated where appropriate, that is: (a) gross profit percentage; (b) stock turnover; (c) debtor days; (d) creditor days; and (e) other relevant ratios for this business?	
• Have any explanations been provided for all major variations in these ratios and any other figures in the accounts?	
• Are there any apparent anomalies in the financial statements, for example: (a) increase in bank charges, but decrease in bank overdraft; (b) increase in turnover and debtors, but decrease in the provision for bad and doubtful debts; or (c) increase in turnover, but decrease in direct costs?	

45.4.7 Audit evidence

• Is there adequate evidence of the work performed?	
• Are the levels of testing adequate?	

• Is the audit work sufficient? In particular, does it cover: (a) existence, valuation and ownership for each asset; (b) existence, valuation and completeness for each liability; (c) validity and authorisation for expenditure; and (d) validity and completeness of income?	
• Is there sufficient audit evidence to support late adjustments?	
• Do the working papers contain adequate conclusions?	
• Have all the errors been followed up?	
• Are we happy that management representations included in the letter of representation can be relied on?	
• Has consultation occurred wherever necessary or required, and the details been adequately recorded on the file?	
• Where there are any specific requirements (for example, reporting to a separate regulatory body), has this been adequately dealt with?	

45.4.8 Common problem areas

• Has the file adequately dealt with the following areas: (a) ownership of land and buildings; (b) existence of plant and equipment, particularly amounts brought forward from previous years; (c) recoverability of inter-company investments and debts; (d) existence of stock; (e) reliance on third-party stocktakes; (f) cut-off; (g) recoverability of old debts; (h) auditing the bank reconciliation; (i) completeness of creditors and accruals; (j) adequacy of post-balance sheet events review; (k) adequacy of going-concern review; and (l) completeness of income?	

45.4.9 General

• Have all the significant differences (for example, on cash account) been investigated?	
• Have the VAT records been reconciled to the turnover per the financial statements, and the outputs on the VAT return?	
• Is the client complying with any relevant tax requirements, for example: (a) correct charge of VAT; (b) deduction of PAYE on casuals?	

45.4.10 Commercial awareness

• Are there any commercial points that can be raised to help the client improve profitability?	
• Are there any weaknesses in the client's systems or procedures that we should report?	

Chapter 46 Final completion and planning for next year

46.1 Final completion

Once the file has been fully reviewed, the partner should ensure that it goes back to the staff and that they are given sufficient time to clear all the review points. When the file is returned after this review, the partner should make sure that the points have been cleared satisfactorily, at which point the accounts can be sent to the client for signature.

When the accounts come back from the client, having been signed, the auditor needs to consider whether the following questions have been addressed:

a) Have all outstanding items have been adequately dealt with?

b) Has a signed letter of representation has been received?

c) Where the letter has been received and has only been signed by one director on behalf of the board, has a minute been seen agreeing its contents?

d) Has adequate consideration has been given to whether the directors' representations can be relied upon?

e) Is the audit opinion is reasonable?

f) Has a letter of comment has been prepared?

g) Has the subsequent events review been updated when necessary?

h) Do the accounts comply with all of the legislative requirements and have only those exemptions that are available to the entity been taken? Do the accounts agree with the file?

Once all of the above questions have been answered to the partner's satisfaction, the audit report can be signed.

46.2 Planning for the following year

Once the audit has been signed off, a debriefing should occur and consideration should be given as to whether:

a) the audit engagement can be accepted for the next period – that is, a reassessment should be made of the practice's independence, etc. and whether any issues have occurred during the course of the audit that would put doubt on the auditor's ability to be independent or to properly perform the audit in subsequent years; and

b) whether anything has occurred during the course of the audit that would impact on the approach that is going to be taken in the following year's audit. It is important that any audit inefficiencies are recorded on a 'points forward' schedule to ensure that they do not recur in subsequent years.

Chapter 47 Conclusion

The purpose of this book has been to provide the reader with some guidance on how to audit more efficiently and effectively. In order to do this, it is essential that thought is put into the audit process. Auditing is not an exact science; it is an art that is continually evolving, and it is essential that the auditor continually assesses his or her approach to ensure that it is the most appropriate for the entity being dealt with.

Having completed reading the book, you should now go back to the beginning and start again, thinking about the connections between sections and how the approach can best be utilised within your own practice to improve the efficiency and effectiveness of your audits.